The Roman Empire in Crisis, 248–260

The Roman Empire in Crisis, 248–260

When the Gods Abandoned Rome

Paul N Pearson

Pen & Sword
MILITARY

First published in Great Britain in 2022 by
Pen & Sword Military
An imprint of
Pen & Sword Books Ltd
Yorkshire – Philadelphia

Copyright © Paul N Pearson 2022

ISBN 978 1 39909 097 1

The right of Paul N Pearson to be identified as Author of this work has been asserted by him in accordance with the Copyright, Designs and Patents Act 1988.

A CIP catalogue record for this book is available from the British Library.

All rights reserved. No part of this book may be reproduced or transmitted in any form or by any means, electronic or mechanical including photocopying, recording or by any information storage and retrieval system, without permission from the Publisher in writing.

Typeset by Mac Style
Printed and bound in the UK by CPI Group (UK) Ltd, Croydon, CR0 4YY.

Pen & Sword Books Limited incorporates the imprints of Atlas, Archaeology, Aviation, Discovery, Family History, Fiction, History, Maritime, Military, Military Classics, Politics, Select, Transport, True Crime, Air World, Frontline Publishing, Leo Cooper, Remember When, Seaforth Publishing, The Praetorian Press, Wharncliffe Local History, Wharncliffe Transport, Wharncliffe True Crime and White Owl.

For a complete list of Pen & Sword titles please contact

PEN & SWORD BOOKS LIMITED
47 Church Street, Barnsley, South Yorkshire, S70 2AS, England
E-mail: enquiries@pen-and-sword.co.uk
Website: www.pen-and-sword.co.uk

Or

PEN AND SWORD BOOKS
1950 Lawrence Rd, Havertown, PA 19083, USA
E-mail: Uspen-and-sword@casematepublishers.com
Website: www.penandswordbooks.com

Contents

Acknowledgements vi
List of Plates vii
List of Maps ix
Introduction xiii
Prologue: Millennium xv

Part I: Philip to Decius, 248–251 CE — 1

Chapter 1	Empire at the Millennium	3
Chapter 2	Rebels	18
Chapter 3	The Forces of Conservatism	33
Chapter 4	Escalation of the Gothic War	43
Chapter 5	Ostrogotha Takes the Initiative	58
Chapter 6	The Road to Abritus	82

Part II: Gallus to Valerian, 251–260 CE — 107

Chapter 7	Gallus	109
Chapter 8	253: World in Flames	127
Chapter 9	Restorers of the Human Race	156
Chapter 10	Turbulence	176
Chapter 11	Nadir	194
Chapter 12	Disintegration	212

Epilogue: Rome Abandons the Gods 231
Literature Cited 237
Notes 256
Index 295

Acknowledgements

I thank Cardiff University for supporting my investigations through the provision of an Honorary Professorship. Jesper Ericsson of the Hunterian Museum in Glasgow was very helpful in arranging photography of the Sponsian coin and several other associated pieces, and discussed their significance. Aleksander Bursche provided helpful input relating to his discoveries of Roman gold in Eastern Europe and commented on the relevant text sections. I am grateful to Jana Grusková and Otto Kresten for permission to reproduce photographs of the Vienna Palimpsest with spectral imaging, as made at the Österreichische Nationalbibliothek by the Early Manuscripts Electronic Library Project FWF P24523-G19; and also Gunther Martin for discussion of the *Scythica Vindobonensia*. I am grateful to the staff of the Maltepe Open Air Museum in Plovdiv District, Bulgaria, for kindly arranging access to that fascinating site before the formal opening, and also the staff of the Regional History Museum at Razgrad for discussions regarding the topography of Roman Moesia and the battlefield of Abritus. I am very grateful to Bridget Wade for her support and discussion throughout the project and helping interpret the archaeological sites in Plovdiv. Peter Davies, Christine Dubery, Diana Frost and Trisha Humphreys of the Crewkerne Ancient History Group contributed to various convivial discussions while the work was in development. Thanks also to Phil Sidnell, Matt Jones and Chris Trim for their efficient and professional work seeing the manuscript through to publication.

List of Plates

Plate 1. All coins: cngcoins.com.

Plate 2. Vienna palimpsest from Martin and Grusková (2014), Vienna, Osterreichische Nationalbibliothek, Hist.gr. 73, fol. 195r, spectral imaging by the Early Manuscripts Electronic Library. Project FWF P24523-G19, public domain. Bust of Decius, Capitoline Museum, Rome, public domain. Libellus modified from Claytor (2015) courtesy of Luther College, Iowa, public domain. Other photographs, the author.

Plate 3. Coin: cngcoins.com. Photographs, the author.

Plate 4. The Great Ludovisi Sarcophagus. A, the lid (Landesmuseum, Mainz, public domain). B, the front panel (photograph by Jastrow, public domain). C, details of the central figure (Photograph by I, Saliko, license CC-BY-SA 3.0). D, coin of Herennius Etruscus (cngcoins.com). E, coin of Herennia Etruscilla (Roma Numismatics). F, detail of the female figure on the lid (Landesmuseum, Mainz, public domain). G, bust of Herennia Etruscilla (British Museum 1873,0820.734, public domain). H, detail of captured barbarian, possibly Ostrogotha (photograph by Jastrow, public domain).

Plate 5. The Battlefield of Abritus. Satellite image: Google Earth. Photographs: the author. Pierced coin of Decius with permission, Warszawskie Centrum Numizmatyczne 54/11.

Plate 6. Bust of Gallus, Vatican Museum, Rome. Mosaic, Zeugma Mosaic Museum, public domain. Coins of Volusian, the author. Coins of Aemilian, Gallienus and Salonina, Roma Numismatics. Coin of Valerian, cngcoins.com. Coin of Silbannacus, British Museum 1937,1203.1.

Plate 7. Photograph of Manole mound, the author. Paris cameo, Marie-Lan Nguyen, CC-BY 2.5. Coin of Shapur, cngcoins.com. Bust of Odaenathus, Lord of Tadmor (Ny Carlsberg Glyptotek (Carole Raddato, CC-Share Alike license, public domain). Naqsh-i-Rustam relief carving (Diego Delso, delso. photo License CC-BY-SA).

viii   The Roman Empire in Crisis, 248–260

Plate 8. Coin of Sponsian diameter 18 mm, with thanks to Jesper Ericsson, Hunterian Museum, Glasgow GLAHM:40333 (photographed for this work and available at http://collections.gla.ac.uk/#/details/ecatalogue/600253). Augsburg Altar, Romisches Museum Augsburg. Coin of Postumus, British Museum C_1864-1128-141. Coin of Dryantilla, Dr Huber Lanz at wildwinds.com. Other coins: cngcoins.com.

List of Maps

Map 1. The Roman Empire in the mid-third century (modified from Pearson 2016).   4

Map 2. Possible line of Ostrogotha's invasion of 248 CE based on the *Getica* of Jordanes and coin hoards.   19

Map 3. The Battle of Verona, 249 CE. Decius drew his strength from the armies of the Danube. Philip commanded the imperial forces from Rome.   30

Map 4. Reconstruction of the invasion of Argaithus and Guntheric and the sieges of Marcianopolis and Philippopolis, 250 CE. Ostrogotha may have been campaigning simultaneously in Roman Dacia. The Battle of Galtis between Goths and Gepids is based on Jordanes.   51

Map 5. Reconstruction of the opening moves on the Danube in 251 CE according to the interpretation preferred here. The Goths began operations in midwinter with a surprise attack on the key crossing point at Oescus. Ostrogotha then marched into Roman Dacia while Cniva on the south bank divided his force. He led one division toward the legionary base at Novae, leaving the other division ('Div. 3') free from interference to plunder part of Moesia. In response, Trebonianus Gallus, the *dux* (regional commander) concentrated his forces at Novae.   60

Map 6. The Battle of Novae, 251 CE. Cniva was repulsed by Gallus and moved on to besiege Nicopolis as Decius and his powerful strike force arrived in the area.   68

Map 7. The Battle of Nicopolis, 251 CE. Decius re-captured Oescus then attacked Cniva who then retreated south across the Haemus by the Shipka Pass. The third Gothic division began to besiege Priscus in Philippopolis.   70

Map 8. The Battle of Beroe, 251 CE. The Third Division of Goths under an unknown commander commenced the siege of Philippopolis. Gallus was ordered to Oescus to hold the crossing. Decius crossed the Haemus Mountains via the Shipka Pass but his vanguard was destroyed by Cniva in the vicinity of Beroe.   76

x   The Roman Empire in Crisis, 248–260

Map 9. The siege of Philippopolis, 251 CE. Decius retreated to join Gallus at Oescus while Cniva linked up with the besieging force.   77

Map 10. The assault on Philippopolis, 251 CE. Urban plan based on Mateev (2016). Arrow shows the suggested Gothic attack up Nebet Tepe hill.   80

Map 11. Suggested background to the 'hypothetical Battle of Romula', 251 CE. Ostrogotha moved south tracked by the Dacian legions while Decius blocked his approach somewhere before Romula-Malva and fought a defensive battle there. Ostrogotha's advance facilitated Cniva's flight from Philippopolis.   84

Map 12. The developing situation in Moesia prior to the Battle of Abritus in 251 CE. Decius started in pursuit of Cniva while Gallus was posted downstream to Durostorum to block the likely escape route.   95

Map 13. The final move before the Battle of Abritus in 251 CE. Cniva avoided the Roman pincer by selecting a battlefield on the road to Sexaginta Prisca.   96

Map 14. The battle of Abritus, 251 CE. According to this author's interpretation, the three divisions of the Gothic army spread out across the progressively constricting valley with their left flanks pinned against the cliffs. The Roman army arrived from the direction of Abritus and attempted to advance up the valley, destroying the enemy in the process.   98

Map 15. Barbarian raids into Thrace and Asia Minor according to Zosimus, probably 252 CE. The distances covered and the places raided imply attacks by both land and sea.   122

Map 16. The Battle of Barbalissos, 253 CE. Shapur advanced up the south bank of the Euphrates, probably besieging Dura and Circesium and destroying smaller forts. The Romans gathered their forces at Barbalissos in an attempt to block the route into Syria.   131

Map 17. Reconstruction of the Persian invasion of 253 CE after Barbalissos based on the roll call of conquered territories in the *Res Gestae Divi Saporis*. Phases 1 to 8 of the campaign discussed in the text are numbered.   133

Map 18. The Battle of Interamna Nahars, 253 CE. Aemilian marched on Rome and Gallus marched out of the city to meet him. Valerian was unable to intercept the rebel.   143

Map 19. The Confrontation at Narnia, 253 CE. Valerian continued his march and met Aemilian just a little south of the previous battle at Interamna Nahars.   0

List of Maps xi

Map 20. Siege of Thessalonica and Battle of Thermopylae, probably 253 CE. How and where the Goths entered the empire is unknown, but naval transport seems probable. The most likely route from Thrace was along the *via egnatia*. Marianus led a scratch force from several Greek cities. Reinforcements from Scupi and Crete are based on the dubious *Historia Augusta*. The siege of Amphiopolis is conjectural, based on Eusebios of Thessalonica. 154

Map 21. The attack of the Borani on the Bosporan Kingdom and Colchis, probably in 255 CE. The nominal borders of the Roman Empire, Bosporan Kingdom, Colchis, and Persian Armenia are shown but were highly fluid at the time. 168

Map 22. The Gothic raid on Bithynia probably in 257/8 CE as described by Zosimus, The map shows all the known settlements in this densely populated area and the cities which are said to have been sacked. 180

Map 23. The 'barbarian' invasion of 259/260 CE. A: Numbers indicate coin hoards catalogued by Demougeot (1962). Many other hoards in the area of the *limes* frontier and *agri decumates* are not plotted for clarity. B: Summary map based on written records and coin hoarding. It is speculated that Gallienus's main army was simultaneously involved in fighting across the frontier in Germania and so could not immediately respond. Numbers refer to phases of the invasion discussed in the text. 196

Map 24. The Battle of Edessa, probably 260 CE. Shapur advances up the Euphrates to besiege Carrhae and Edessa. Valerian moves up to Samosata and the armies clash somewhere in between. The Roman force from Cappadocia is based on Firdawsi. 203

Map 25. Persian raiding in the aftermath of the Battle of Edessa, probably 260 CE. Numbers refer to phases discussed in the text. The cross-hatched area is that previously despoiled in 253. 208

Map 26. The long Persian retreat, probably 260 CE. Persian army groups in Cilicia probably withdrew via the Amanus Mountains (1), harried by forces under Macrianus (2). Ballista's naval squadron relieved the siege of Pompeiopolis (3) and destroyed a Persian force beyond Sebaste (4). Shapur and the main force probably withdrew via Comana (5) and passed Edessa (6). Odaenathus attacked retreating Persian forces along the Euphrates (7) and deep into Persian territory, destroying the Jewish academy at Nehardea (8). 215

Map 27. The Battles of Mediolanum and Augusta Vindelicorum, probably 260 CE. Gallienus arrives in Italy by the Great St. Bernard Pass and defeats a large concentration of 'barbarians' near Mediolanum. One substantial group of raiders had already exited by the Brenner Pass only to be intercepted by a scratch force commanded by Genialis outside Augusta Vindelicorum. 220

Map 28. Approximate situation at the end of 260 CE according to this narrative. In reality there was much chaos and the position of many provincial administrations is unknown. 231

Introduction

This book is a narrative account of a dozen momentous years in the history of Rome intended for anyone interested in ancient history. The timeline stands alone, but it roughly follows on from my earlier book, *Maximinus Thrax*, which was published in 2016. As I remarked in the introduction to that book, the third century has a special appeal because it is not part of the corpus of shared learning that has become known as 'general knowledge'. Many people can name a string of famous Romans – soldiers, statesmen, emperors, and even poets – but one can safely bet that none of them would hail from the period discussed herein. That is not because it was an uninteresting or unimportant time; far from it, as I hope the reader will agree.

Although I am an academic, my intention here is to tell the story for the general reader rather than scholarly research as such. It is, therefore, mainly a work of synthesis. I have engaged with a wide range of questions that are actively being studied by many specialists. Occasionally I have made what I believe to be proposals that may be worthy of broader consideration by scholars. I have made copious use of footnotes to try to do justice to the wide range of primary and secondary literature and so that none of my suggestions or inferences stands unsupported.

The central organizing principle of the text is the passage of time. I find that describing events in sequence, without too much foresight, is a fine way of imagining what it must have been like to experience them. Decisions that people made are often best understood without the benefit of hindsight. Putting the story together was especially challenging for the final few years of my chosen period when the precise timing and sequence of events is not firmly established and subject to vigorous debate. I did not want to trouble the reader by presenting too many alternative timelines and scenarios, so I have chosen what I think is the most likely chronology, while signposting where the major uncertainties lie. My justification is that the narrative is itself what scientists call a 'model' – a framework explanation that can be confirmed or refuted when new evidence comes to light.

Telling the story of the crisis years is no easy task. Events are fast-moving and intricate and the historical sources are particularly patchy and challenging to interpret. Because of this, sweeping histories of Rome have tended to skirt over the period in just a few sentences. Fortunately, however, important new information has come to light in recent years. Significant archaeological finds have been made that are directly relevant to the period, foremost of which is the discovery of the great battlefield of Abritus, which I have studied myself. Fundamental new insights have also been gleaned regarding the nature and course of an appalling pestilence that swept the empire. Most amazing, however, is the discovery of substantial new chunks of history which were written down for posterity by Dexippus of Athens, a man who lived through the period. These priceless pages have been meticulously recovered, published and translated for the first time, the definitive edition appearing in 2020.[1] I applaud everyone in that task for the heroic effort of scholarship involved and the spirit of openness and collaboration that is evident from all the publications. Dexippus's text is still very incomplete, and more may yet be deciphered, but it invites a radical new interpretation of events that had previously defied analysis. Details of all these discoveries – scientific, archaeological and historiographical – will be provided in due course, but together they make it possible to throw new light on a neglected but important interval of history when classical civilization crumbled and a new world order began to emerge.

Prologue

Millennium

The year that we now count as 248 of the Common Era was Rome's millennium. By the standard reckoning a thousand years had passed since Romulus had used his plough to mark out the city boundaries on the Palatine Hill. The Romans even claimed to know exactly when the city was founded: 21 April, 753 BCE. Every year, that day was celebrated as Rome's birthday and also as a festival sacred to Pales, god of livestock, shepherds and drovers (or perhaps goddess; the Romans seem to have been undecided on the sex of this particular deity, or even whether there were one or two of them, so ancient was the cult).[1]

Romulus was the mortal son of Mars, the god of war, and as every Roman knew he had been abandoned at birth with his twin brother Remus on the banks of the Tiber. The babies had been discovered by a she-wolf who sustained them with her milk, then by a woodpecker who fed them morsels, and finally by a shepherd, who took them in. As adults, the twins decided to establish a settlement but they argued bitterly about the best location. The dispute became so violent that Romulus killed his brother before founding the city that bears his name.[2] The story would seem to portend a violent and warlike future for Rome with much internecine struggle. Subsequent generations usually managed to live up to that expectation, and never more so than in the period covered by this book.

Amazingly there may be some vestige of truth in the city's legendary origin. Archaeological discoveries on the Palatine Hill – rudimentary buildings, the remains of a wall, and so on – date back to around the middle of the eighth century BCE when Romulus is supposed to have lived there. An important riverbank trading centre was established around that time, with links across the Mediterranean.[3]

The first major milestone in the city's history is of deep significance for understanding the events described in this book. Around 509 BCE, the fledgling city-state had become tired of tyrannical rulers and expelled the last of its kings. An orderly Republic was instituted, headed by pairs of supreme magistrates called consuls who were elected annually. It should have been a time of celebration and optimism but a great plague struck the city, indicating the displeasure of the gods. One of the new consuls, Publius Valerius Publicola, sought to appease them by sacrificing to Proserpine, goddess of fertility. In the winter months, this goddess (who is identified with the Greek Persephone) was confined to the Underworld as the part-time enforced wife of Pluto, but she was set free in the spring, bringing new life to the fields and crops. Perhaps Proserpine could bring about spiritual renewal for Rome? The sacrifices worked. The plague ceased, heralding a new springtime and a joyous new age or *saeculum* in which Rome was set to thrive as a free Republic with endorsement from on high. At some point it was decreed that the sacrifices should be renewed every hundred years, each time ushering in a new Golden Age.

Rome survived as a Republic for almost 500 years until an effective monarchy was re-established by Octavian, who ruled from 27 BCE and is regarded as the first Roman emperor. Crucially, he did not base his claim to rule on his evident military genius and ruthless suppression of all challengers but rather on his successful intercession with the gods through his role as highest priest. Octavian was careful to style his autocratic rule as denoting another dawning Golden Age. The Senate of Rome awarded him the numinous title *augustus* (related to the word for religious augury) as a personal name, hence he is generally known simply as Augustus. The propaganda of his regime focused relentlessly on the benefits of peace and prosperity that had been brought about through his divine offices, in contrast to the catastrophe of civil war that had preceded it. Every subsequent emperor appended the name Augustus to their own so it quickly became synonymous with the office.

In 48 CE, the emperor Claudius, a descendant of the first Augustus by aristocratic adoption, celebrated the eight hundredth anniversary of the founding of the city and another new Golden Age. He held a spectacular event called the *ludi saeculares* (or 'secular games' as the phrase is usually translated). It was styled as the spectacle of a lifetime because no person then alive would live long enough to see the next such event.[4] A century later in 148 CE it was the turn of Antoninus Pius to celebrate 900 years.

In the early third century, the theme of cyclical decline and renewal continued to be ingrained in the Roman worldview, especially via the Stoic philosophy. The more gloomy intellectuals were apt to regard their world as having been in long decline and in desperate need of renewal. All manner of ills from failed harvests and diseases to earthquakes and strange portents were blamed on the fact that the world was in old age (*senectus mundi*). The foremost historian of the time, Cassius Dio, had famously declared 'our history now descends from a kingdom of gold to one of iron and rust'.[5] A new springtime was to be expected, but as usual it would require approval from the gods.

In 248 CE the emperor at the millennium was Marcus Julius Philippus, or Philip I as he is known to history. It is clear from the propaganda that he made a huge effort to celebrate the glory of Rome. Three days of public holiday were declared, running from 21 – 23 April. It was the perfect time of year for a street party with spring well underway and the dead heat of summer yet to arrive. But far from being 'secular', in the modern sense of non-religious, the whole event was steeped in the traditions and rituals of Roman religion. The focus was on averting evil by honouring, appeasing and pleasing the gods through sacred ritual, including solemn sacrifice, spells and incantation.[6]

The ceremonial heart of the city was given a splendid facelift in anticipation. Rome was probably the largest city in the world, with over a million inhabitants, and travellers and officials from every nation would have converged there as well. Of central importance for the millennium were processions and libations organized by the houses of the gods. On the Capitoline Hill, directly opposite the city's ancient nucleus, sat Rome's most sacred site, the sublime and ancient Temple of Jupiter Optimus Maximus (Jupiter Best and Greatest of the gods), a building so opulent that in comparison 'all else is like earth compared to heaven', it was remarked. Jupiter was worshipped there together with his wife Juno and daughter Minerva, goddess of wisdom. The inauguration of the millennium celebrations would have happened here with the emperor Philip officiating in his role as the highest priest of the Roman religion and the greatest builder of bridges – the *pontifex maximus* – between the mortal world and the divine.[7]

The Sacred Way (*via sacra*) emerged from the temple precinct and ran steeply down past a complex of forums, the Senate House, and other public buildings, and on to the great Flavian amphitheatre, or Colosseum. As the name suggests, this processional route was lined with many other great temples, some of which even hailed from the time when Rome had kings, although they had been rebuilt in ever more splendid style in lock step with the fortune of the city. It is now an archaeological park in the centre of Rome visited by millions each year.

Let us look at some of these establishments, which are now mostly reduced to their foundations and wall lines and instead imagine them smothered in gaudy paintwork and sparkling with gold leaf and burnished bronze statues. At the foot of the Capitoline Hill is the Temple of Concord, representing social harmony, which doubles as something of an art gallery; and that of Saturn, god of wealth and celebration, which also houses the state treasury. Next is the Temple of Vesta, goddess of the hearth, protector of the state, and home to an eternal flame tended by the revered Vestal Virgins who live in demure opulence in an adjacent palace; and that of Janus, the god of time and new beginnings. Janus has two faces, one looking back and the other forward, which is especially relevant on this occasion. Then there is the

Temple of Castor and Pollux, the youthful twin sons of Jupiter, who, it is said, were glimpsed in ancient times in the din of battle at the head of a Roman army. More recent additions along the route include the magnificent Temple of Mars the Avenger, guarantor of military victories, dedicated by the first Augustus himself, and various other houses sacred to the imperial cult. All of these were sending up fugs of incense and prayers.[8]

But the special focus for this particular occasion, and the likely culmination of the three-day event, was the combined Temple of Rome and Venus which stood on a huge gleaming marble platform between the forum and Colosseum. Most cities, towns and even villages of the empire had their home gods and shrines but there was nothing anywhere to match Rome's brash monument to itself. Rome was the Eternal City, victorious in war and mistress of the world. A giant cult statue of Roma was seated within the enormous colonnades, the general effect being somewhat like the modern Lincoln Memorial in Washington (and on which architectural tradition that monument was based). But unlike Lincoln, Roma was dressed for war, holding spear and shield, and in her right palm sat the winged figure of Victory. This building was designed by no less a person than the Emperor Hadrian, who fancied himself as a refined man of culture. (Not everyone liked it, however: a condescending architect at the time joked that the statue was so large that had she stood up she would have bumped her head, a remark that cost him his life.)[9]

As with other ancient festivals there would have been a vibrant fringe, with theatrical events and literary readings across the city, and entertainment of all levels of sophistication. Most popular would have been chariot racing at the Circus Maximus, a racecourse that could seat no fewer than three hundred thousand people and which has been claimed as the largest building ever made for entertainment purposes. Here the traditional teams (red, white, blue and green) competed for lavish prizes and glory, mostly in the four-horse rig. It was the city's sporting obsession: a visitor remarked that the populace 'wear themselves out from dawn to dusk, wet or fine, in detailed discussion of the merits and demerits of horses and their drivers'.[10]

Another focus of the millennium party was a huge concrete reservoir specially constructed on the far bank of the Tiber and designed for staging naval battles. Teams of gladiators took each other on in deadly entertainment. When the festivities came to an end, the reservoir was used to supply clean water to a large area that had previously suffered from shortages. There is something quintessentially Roman about combining the requirements of a lavish and brutal public spectacle with a pragmatic engineering solution to an everyday problem.[11]

And of course there were gladiatorial bouts at the Colosseum, the great gleaming oval amphitheatre that still dominates the city (named after a colossal statue that once stood beside it). These events were also considered sacred, with the ritual fighting dedicated to the gods. The acts in the 'arena' (the Latin word for sand, used to soak up the blood) at the millennium included, according to an admittedly dubious source,[12] no fewer than a thousand gladiatorial pairings which would equate to thirty bouts per hour of daylight throughout the festivities, if evenly spread out. The following animals are also mentioned: thirty-two elephants, ten elks, ten tigers, sixty tame lions (presumably for tricks) and ten wild ones (for fighting), thirty leopards, ten hyenas, six hippopotami, one rhinoceros, ten giraffes, twenty wild asses, forty wild horses, and 'various other animals of this nature without number'. Some of these unfortunate beasts were provoked into fighting one another in strange groupings while others were ritually hunted by highly skilled gladiators using lances or arrows. Events were carefully choreographed in the enormous venue with its many underground passages, elevator cages, trap doors, and other cunning artifices.

Anyone who has lived near a sports stadium will know the enthralling sound of a crowd when heard from the empty streets outside. Nowadays it is difficult to imagine any great city without constant traffic noise, Rome especially, but in ancient times the surging roar of sixty or seventy thousand spectators when a gladiator met a gruesome end must have reverberated back across the famous seven hills, adding to the communal sense of occasion. In the evenings one can imagine great flame-lit barbecues in the city's open spaces, all at the imperial expense, in which the crowds feasted on the exotic animals of the arena as well as the many beasts sacrificed in the temples to propitiate the gods and pray for good fortune in the dawning age.

To mark the event a beautiful and highly distinctive coinage was issued in huge quantities by the great city mint (Plate 1), bearing the legend *saeculares augg* ('epochs of the two emperors'). The second emperor was Philip's young son, known as Philip II, who was then only about 12 or 13 years old but had nevertheless been given the exalted title of *augustus* the year before. There were six departments or *officinae* in the mint, and there were six main designs. Uniquely in the whole series of Roman coinage the departments identified themselves numerically, which looks like a conscious attempt to add to the commemorative value and even collectability of these pieces. On the tails sides, five of the six designs show animals to be sacrificed in the arena: Number I is a lion, advancing menacingly to the right and evidently mid-roar; number III is a goat, in a more peaceful posture; number IIII (it was written like that, not IV) is a hippopotamus; number V is a stag, with magnificent horns and a shaggy coat; and number VI is a graceful antelope. The odd one out, design II, shows the she-wolf suckling the twins Romulus and Remus. Departments I, II, V and VI issued coins in the name of the senior emperor, Philip I. Department III was allocated to his son. Department IIII was for Philip's wife, the *augusta* (empress) whose name was Marcia Otacilia Severa. The leading lady is shown with intricately plaited hair as was fashionable in that era. It seems she did not object to being uniquely associated with the hippopotamus.

Such coins make very charming artworks, partly because the dies wore out so many variants had to be made. Modern specialists estimate that each die was used tens of thousands of times before being discarded, but even so it is uncommon to find two coins struck from the same template, indicating that millions of each type must have been minted.[13] After the event, another new coinage was issued showing the Temple of Roma with the legend *saeculum novum* ('a new age'). Another shows Roma herself holding the figure of Victory with the legend *romae aeternae* ('Eternal Rome').

The public celebrations were not limited to sports and fighting: poets, artists, writers and philosophers were also involved, competing for prizes and fame. Many of these would have used the occasion to showcase their public speaking skills by praising the emperor or elaborating on the amazing story of the city which, in a thousand years, had grown from a few huts on the Palatine to the greatest metropolis on the planet. Indeed, the span of a thousand years was of great significance to historians in particular. It so happens that the legendary foundation of Rome (753 BCE) came just a little after the first Olympiad in Greece (776 BCE) and the appointment of the first named Athenian archons (chief magistrates) with time-limited powers (764 or 753 BCE). The archives of these institutions permitted research among the scrolls and the development of a fairly sound chronology. The historian Asinius Quadratus, probably writing during the celebrations, entitled his (sadly lost) history of the civilized world *Millennium*. The span of a thousand years may also have been used by the great Dexippus of Athens for his own historical chronicle written some decades later. This historical age contrasted with the dim and distant time before a thousand years past which was considered the proper domain of poets like Homer and Virgil.[14]

And history has few more astonishing trajectories than the rise of Rome. The settlement supposedly founded by Romulus had started by subduing and dominating its Latin neighbours, town by town, and gradually its influence had expanded across much of what is now central Italy. The Greek-speaking colonies of the Italian peninsula were conquered, bringing new wealth and opportunities to what was, by that time, a nascent empire. The first 'overseas' province (*provincia*) was established on what is now the southern coast of

France (in an area still called Provence), followed by the conquest of Sicily and Carthage in a most brutal series of wars that made Rome the undisputed regional superpower. Greece and Spain, Egypt, Asia Minor and the Levant, Gaul, most of Britain, Thrace (roughly, Bulgaria), Dacia (roughly, Romania) all followed so that the entire Mediterranean became fringed by Roman territory and came to be known as *mare nostrum*, 'our sea'.

A state of peace usually prevailed over Rome's dominions where before there had been a morass of warring tribes and city states. This circumstance allowed for massive economic integration and technological development. The great city at the hub of all the infrastructure constantly reminded the world that it had brought peace – *pax romana* – to the world, albeit at sword point, and to many it must have seemed that Rome was indeed destined to endure for eternity as the propaganda claimed.

But swaggering confidence in the city and its empire was not universally held. As befits the gloom of the Stoics then in their ascendency, there were also nervous murmurings and predictions of some imminent and calamitous change in the world order.[15] We now know, with the full benefit of hindsight, that the empire was about to tumble into a period of extreme crisis, indeed the most extraordinary phase of its history. The strife would be military, but it was also political, economic, social, and even spiritual. In the great struggle that lay ahead there would be winners and losers. Few could have predicted it during the millennium celebrations, but the days of the eternal gods themselves were numbered. A hundred years on there was to be no repeat of the secular games: by that time Rome was no longer the functioning heart of the empire and a strange eastern cult called Christianity had become the favoured religion of state.[16]

The triumph of Christianity is one of history's most astonishing facts and is of course of enormous importance for the subsequent trajectory of Europe and the world. The incumbent pluralistic religion of the Greeks and Romans had existed and evolved from time immemorial. By contrast, Christianity was a foreign cult, Jewish in origin and seditious, insofar as Jesus had been sentenced to death and crucified by a Roman magistrate during the reign of the Emperor Tiberius. Against all odds, it would be Christianity that dominated western history in the new millennium that the emperor Philip was busy inaugurating in 248, and beyond that too.

The central thesis of this book is that a few years of turmoil that followed the secular games are key to appreciating this momentous historical transition. The crisis was so profound that all the old assumptions were shaken to the core. Let us, then, attempt to re-live those years when to many people it must have seemed that the gods had abandoned Rome.

Part I

Philip to Decius, 248–251 CE

Chapter 1

Empire at the Millennium

Organization and Economy

There is a saying about the third century Sassanian (Persian) Empire which might just as well apply to Rome: 'The kingdom relies on the army, and the army on money, and money on the land tax, and the land tax on farming'.[1] As in all ancient empires, wealth was generated mainly from working the land where the vast majority of the population toiled, producing enough to feed themselves and, ideally, a small surplus. Because of this, prosperity and population were correlated.

The total number of people in the Roman Empire in the 240s is hard to estimate because the rural poor leave little in the way of an archaeological footprint. Estimates suggest that it probably stood at around 65 million people, about its highest ever level. That is equivalent to the current population of countries like France or the United Kingdom, although of course distributed over a far larger area. A slightly better comparison is the population of the United States around the Year 1900, but that is also very misleading because numbers in the empire were not in the process of booming: endemic diseases, climatic fluctuations and the carrying capacity of the land put a check on further growth.[2]

The empire was, above all, a stupendous feat of organization (Map 1). Its size and longevity are astonishing when one considers the cultural and religious diversity that it encompassed, the tardiness of communications, and the limited means of law enforcement available. The great theme of the empire's decline and fall has famously captivated historians for centuries, but in some ways its capacity for survival and reinvention is just as interesting to contemplate.

One reason for the system's durability was the balance between devolved administration and central authority. Most decisions were made in the cities, towns and villages, where local dignitaries wielded great power and influence. In many cases these people were the direct descendants of the civic or tribal elites that had existed before incorporation into the empire. Settlements were grouped into a hierarchy and ultimately into provinces. Elite officials would serve fixed-term appointments in the provincial administration, moving

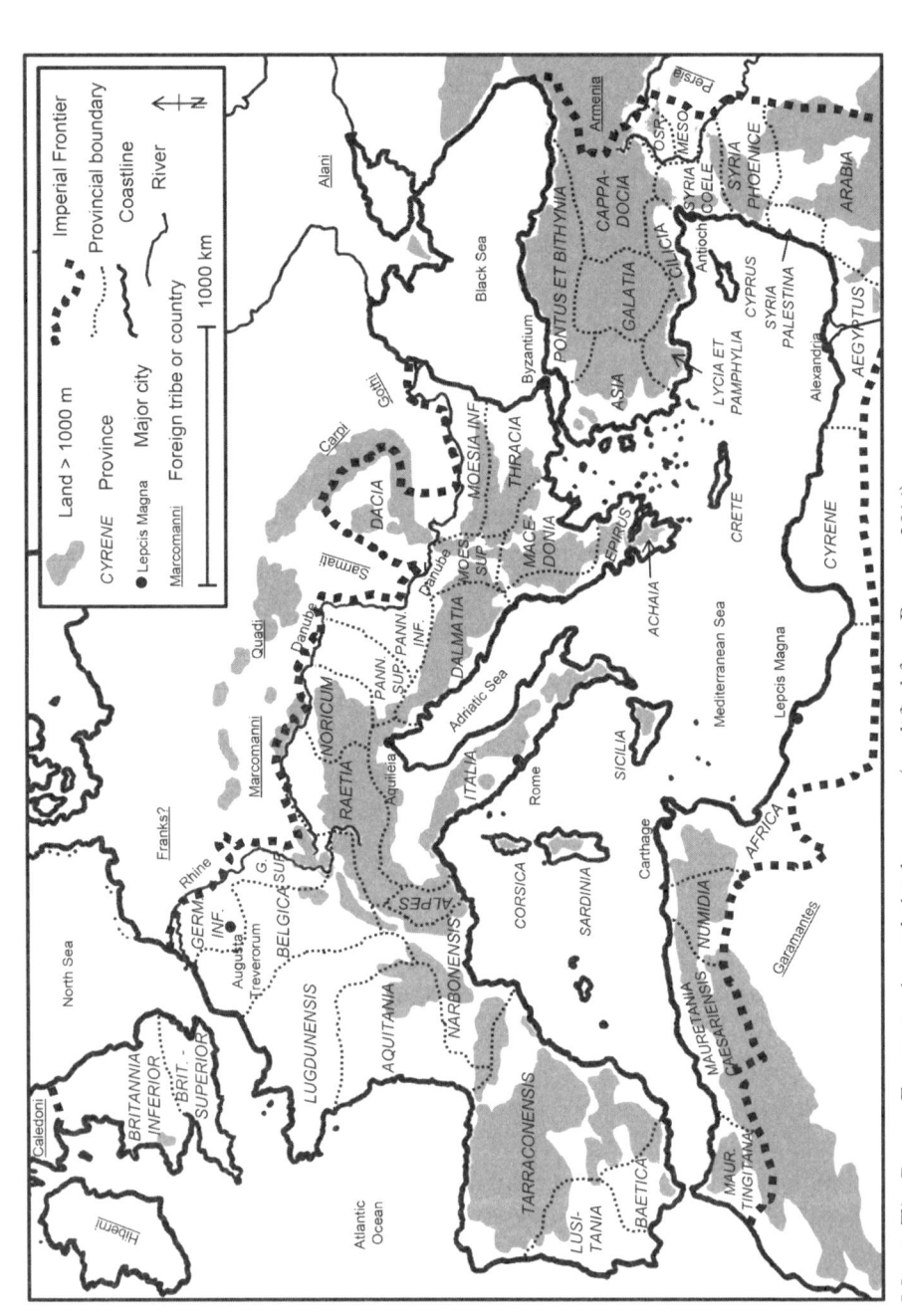

Map 1. The Roman Empire in the mid-third century (modified from Pearson 2016).

around and advancing their careers, a major factor that helped maintain cohesion as well as loyalty to the imperial centre. By the third century it was no longer the case that the leading citizens were all, or even mostly, native Romans or Italians: they were drawn from the ambitious aristocracy of the whole empire, albeit disproportionately from the wealthier parts.

The famous Roman army, which provided the security, has been a source of endless fascination to historians and the popular imagination alike. It was, as everyone knows, a well-equipped and professional military machine. Its organization and internal culture were wonderfully uniform such that senior commanders and even mere foot soldiers could be switched from one end of the empire to the other and know their job. By the mid-third century it was still divided into scores of legions (each, nominally, of about 4,000 men), plus a wide variety of smaller auxiliary units, but the segmented plate armour and curved shields treasured by modern re-enactment groups had mostly been replaced by other types of standard issue kit. Recruits were drawn from the varied peoples of the empire but were organized and paid for by the central administration. As long as the army remained loyal and united, and the flow of pay was maintained, this arrangement was quite resilient and had proved itself sufficient to protect the borders and police the internal workings of the state.[3]

The basic level of military pay (*stipendium militum*) was set by government and was the main outlet for distributing coin. Emperors could win favour with the army by increasing pay across the board, but as the monetary value of all other labour was benchmarked against it, such an act would cause general inflation. So instead of permanent increases, a scheme of one-off payments (donatives) gradually became the norm, although if repeated too often they too would have an inflationary effect. The issuing of a donative was preceded by a vow of loyalty to the emperor, something that would have made good sense to any ruler who was in a position to fund major handouts, but it did establish a direct link between money and loyalty. Woe betide the emperor who found himself unable to sustain the supply of pay to the frontiers or fund a donative when the troops expected it.

The state clawed its money back through taxation, either in coin or in kind. From early imperial times the coinage had been based on gold, silver and bronze (the aureus, denarius and sestertius, respectively) which exchanged at the ratio of 1 to 25 to 100. Critical to this system is that the coins had value as bullion, in contrast to modern paper or electronic money which is intrinsically worthless. This seems to have made the currency effective at limiting inflation so long as the weight and purity of the coins could be maintained. Losses of precious metals were made good from the imperial mines – dire pits of human misery that existed in various parts of the empire. But economic tensions could arise if the productivity of the mines failed or if large amounts of precious metal exited the empire as payment to foreign powers. The imperial administration might attempt to 'print money' by slowly debasing the weight or precious metal content of the coins or by manipulating the 'face value' and/or exchange ratio, but the economic impact of such moves could be far-reaching and unpredictable. By Philip's reign the monetary system functioned much as it had done for centuries although by that time the old single denarius had been replaced by a double which was only about fifty per cent pure. Its value seems to have slipped against gold such that one aureus was by now worth about twenty of these doubles.[4]

The idea that the empire had been in a state of stagnation during the decades running up to Rome's millennium seems to have some basis in fact, although it is very difficult to quantify. There seems to have been a general absence of innovation in science, technology, literature and art, which contrasts markedly with previous centuries and has led to the period being described as an 'age of anxiety'. The yearning for renewal and a new Golden Age seems understandable in retrospect.[5]

The gods

The intellectual poverty of the early third century does not apply to the sphere of religious thought. Perhaps it is inevitable that people turned to the gods in difficult times, hence there was much debate, discussion and innovation in matters spiritual across the empire. The formal state religion had a dual focus on the traditional gods of Rome and the imperial cult which were expected to be revered everywhere. The so-called 'Capitoline Triad' of Jupiter, Juno and Minerva were the most senior of the gods, but there were countless other deities around the empire which might rise and fall in popularity with the times.

Religious activity was as much about observance as it was belief, and was both private and public. It was very pluralistic, even tolerant, which is one reason the empire was generally acceptable across so wide a range of cultures. In a single day one could honour the memory of one's ancestors and household gods, revere the light of some woodland glade as the expression of a local sylvan deity, make communal worship involving procession, music and dance, give donations at a temple of healing, file a sacred curse to inflict hideous revenge on the person who stole one's cloak, sacrifice to a fashionable foreign deity, pray for the deified emperors and the genius of the current one, and then argue the meaning of it all with a diverse range of itinerant sages and philosophers.[6]

We have already mentioned the Stoics as being in vogue during the period. Their focus was on personal introspection, the simple life, and doing the right thing to achieve spiritual peace in accordance with nature and the will of the gods. The higher virtues such as wisdom, justice, and fortitude should dictate one's actions along with logic and reason rather than emotion and the appetites of the body. The inner strength thus gained allowed one to cope with the trials and tribulations of life, which were many. Health and wealth were appropriate goals for any person to aspire to but the Stoics taught that illness, disability and poverty are also an inevitable part of existence that had to be accepted. The Stoic focus on manly self-reliance could easily align with traditional Roman discipline so as to lead a father to expose an unwanted baby to die or a resolute commander to reluctantly order the genocidal massacre of an entire unruly tribe.[7]

Stoicism had been around in one form or another for hundreds of years, but a new philosophical movement that is today (although not then) identified as 'Neoplatonism' was emerging. The famous Egyptian philosopher Plotinus had just set up his school at Rome, attempting to merge and take the best from all the schools of philosophy, both eastern and western, using the works of Plato and Aristotle as central reference points. According to Plotinus, the entire universe and everything within was in a process of unfolding, driven from above by a divine and benevolent principle. Evil was explained as somehow external to this divine will, arising from chaos. Some strains of Neoplatonism had mystical or magical elements, straddling the boundary between philosophy and religion. An allied group were the so-called Neopythogoreans who expanded on the symbolic geometry and number theory of Pythagoras to argue that there was a natural scale from universal one-ness to the infinite, with the mortal world in between. A prominent figure among these had been the sage Apollonius of Tyana who is said to have travelled to India, interacted with Buddhist monks, and regularly worked miracles such as casting out demons, healing the sick and raising the dead.

As is well known, the Roman deities paralleled the Greek gods of Mount Olympus insofar as Jupiter was identified with Zeus, Juno with Hera, Minerva with Athena, and so on. The so-called 'syncretic' identification of the gods went much deeper, however, such that local tribal deities across the empire could readily be incorporated to the pantheon, and hence be accorded due respect. In many cases regional forms of worship continued virtually unaltered beneath a new veneer of imperial respectability. Even the ancient Egyptian gods were regarded as manifestations of the same set of deities (Horus was Mars, Anubis was Mercury, Osiris was Pluto, and so on, although the fit seems somewhat contrived).

The syncretic custom meant that foreign religions could easily spread far and wide within the empire. Examples that were popular at the millennium are the cults of Jupiter Dolichenus, which had its origin in the worship of Baal at Dolichene on the Euphrates, and Serapis, who was a Graeco-Egyptian god worshipped at Alexandria. These two movements were mystery cults wherein initiates were promised access to escalating levels of arcane power and knowledge to be imparted via once-in-a-lifetime ceremonies as they progressed through various grades of enlightenment. Other mystery cults were those of Mithras, which was of Persian origin with roots in Zoroastrianism, and Cybele, the 'Great Mother' from Asia Minor.

This whole system was famously rejected by the Jews who worshipped just one god, their own. As is well known, this had been the source of enormous tension between them and their Roman overlords, ultimately leading to the Jewish revolt of 66 CE and the destruction of the city of Jerusalem along with its great temple in 70 CE. A temple to Jupiter Capitolinus was later built on the ruins and Jews were banished from the city, contributing to the so-called 'Jewish diaspora' in which emigrant communities developed in many places across the eastern empire. Despite this, the Roman authorities conceded that the Jews were following the religion of their ancestors (however misguided it may have seemed to them) and accepted Judaism as *religio licita* (permitted religion), allowing its practitioners special exemption from public communal ceremonies and worship. They were tolerated as long as they paid special taxes and were willing to pray for the good of the empire and the imperial family.[8]

Christians

Although Judaism undoubtedly gained occasional converts, it was, on the whole, confined to one ethnic group. A much greater problem for the Roman authorities was an offshoot whose devotees worshipped a Jewish holy man and preacher called Jesus of Nazareth. This man had been executed around 30 CE and was believed to have been bodily resurrected and taken to heaven. Jesus was regarded as the 'Christ' (anointed one) foretold by the prophets and the 'son of God'. Christian thinkers increasingly came to identify him as a living manifestation of the one true God. This radical religious group features very prominently in the story of Rome's crisis so it is worth considering them in a little detail. The religion had spread rapidly through non-Jewish communities, largely due to the efforts of the Apostle Paul, an early convert, who preached Christianity as a universal religion. By the mid-third century there were over a million adherents distributed through most of the empire. Christianity was generally regarded as an innovation and a cult (*superstitio*) as opposed to a permitted religion although different emperors undoubtedly varied in their attitude towards it.

Christianity retained many aspects of Judaism including a reverence for its texts, but as a trans-cultural movement it also absorbed influences from many other religions and philosophies. The writings of the so-called 'gnostic' Christians, for instance, were strongly influenced by Neoplatonism and the mystery cults. Modern Christianity is of course extremely diverse but in the third century it was arguably more so, as communities in different places developed their own theologies, concepts, rituals and practices. Many gospels (lives and sayings of Jesus), accounts of the deeds of his apostles and visionary tracts were in circulation that were later purged as unorthodox or heretical, some of them presenting a very different concept and personality of Jesus and his followers that can be startling today. The *Infancy Gospel of Thomas*, for example, features a malevolent child Jesus who demonstrates his powers by killing a boy who punched him and then blinding the boy's parents when they complained. The *Acts of Peter* tells of how when the Apostle Peter was in Rome he struggled for supremacy with a false Christian, the levitating Simon Magus, in an escalating series of tricks. Peter trumps Simon's conversational dog by resurrecting a kippered herring from a market stall and setting it swimming in the public fountain. It is easy to laugh at such stories, of which there are many more, but they were evidently widely revered at the time along with those various other miracles attributed to Jesus and his followers that eventually made the final cut.[9]

Jesus preached love, peace, and charity, something that undoubtedly contributed to the religion's appeal during this age of anxiety. Christian communities cared for the weak and vulnerable, including unbelievers, something that is also evident in contemporaneous Judaism and various other religions. The figure of Jesus was not entirely immune to the syncretic tendency of the period, however. Many people were prepared to revere him as a holy man and discuss his teachings without necessarily regarding him as a god, let alone the one true God. An interesting example is the emperor Severus Alexander (ruled 222–235 CE) who is said to have kept statues of various holy men in his household sanctuary including Apollonius of Tyana, Jesus Christ, Abraham and Orpheus.[10]

Perhaps in reaction to this diversity of belief, the church developed an increasingly strong focus on orthodoxy and dogmatism within a rigid hierarchical structure. Its organization mirrored the imperial administration by being divided into cities and provinces with elected bishops sitting above ordained presbyters, beneath whom were deacons, sub-deacons, acolytes, and readers. The bishops communicated freely using letters, many of which survive from the period, and they also met in convocation, often attempting to suppress 'heretical' ideas. What emerged was an insistence that Jesus was divine and in some sense one and the same as the God who created the universe. It was also an apocalyptic end-time religion. The return of Jesus was imminent and fully expected in the lifetimes of his devotees. It would lead to the final judgment of mankind whereupon only the souls of the believers would be saved.[11]

These aspects of Christianity naturally made it very unpopular with other religious groups and the authorities. Like the Jews, most Christians rejected all gods but their own, but this did not necessarily mean they denied their existence or power; other gods were regarded as demons. The Christians were demonized in return. The sect was officially banned in the second century and became associated in the popular imagination with other forbidden practices like druidism and human sacrifice. And although for most of the time its devotees were not actively persecuted, there was a tendency to blame them for all manner of ills, often unfairly. According to the historian Tacitus, it was 'a most mischievous superstition' and its practitioners were 'hated for their abominations'.[12]

This hatred and suspicion seems to have boiled over at the time of Rome's millennium in Alexandria, a major city with about a quarter of a million inhabitants. The disorder may have been related to the fact that a new Golden Age required appeasement of the gods, but the Christians refused to participate in the sacrifices, thereby potentially bringing ruin on everyone. Bishop Dionysius of Alexandria says that the riot started when an old man called Metras refused to utter what he called 'impious words' and was beaten and stoned to death outside the city gates. Then a woman called Quinta was dragged to a temple in an attempt to force her to worship the gods: she refused and was also cruelly beaten and stoned to death. The mob then turned on all the city's Christians, pillaging their property and burning what was left so that the Christian quarter of Alexandria appeared as if burned by an enemy. Order was eventually restored, but the riot well illustrates the millennial tensions and anti-Christian sentiment that existed in Egypt and probably across much of the rest of the empire.[13]

Was Philip a Christian?

The emperor's public persona was entirely traditional and he undoubtedly officiated as *pontifex maximus* of the state religion in the normal way. The coinage advertised an array of deities, among them Mars, Fortuna, Salus, and others. Surprisingly, however, he was later to be numbered among the pious by the Christians of the following century. Historians have viewed the claim with suspicion and opinions differ markedly as to its veracity. It is, nevertheless, plausible on one level. Philip's birthplace at Shahba to the east of the Sea of Galilee was not far from the centre of origin of the religion which was certainly prospering in that area.

Near-contemporaneous evidence from the third century is, however, limited to a lukewarm comment by Bishop Dionysius of Alexandria that Philip was 'a ruler who had been not unfavourable to us'. The main basis for the idea is the fourth century *Ecclesiastical History* of Eusebius which recounts a curious story in which Philip 'being a Christian, desired, on the last day of the paschal vigil, to share with the multitude in the prayers of the Church'. The minister (un-named) refused to admit him until he confessed his sins 'on account of the many crimes he had committed'. This he readily did, 'manifesting in his conduct a genuine and pious fear of God'. Another account comes from John Chrysotom's late fourth century *Homily on St. Babylas*, who was Bishop of Antioch during Philip's reign. According to this version, Babylas refused entry to an un-named visiting emperor because of his sins and ordered him to join the penitents. Some modern historians have argued that these two accounts independently corroborate a real event while others have regarded the story of the abasement of a reigning emperor as utterly implausible.[14]

Following Eusebius, Philip was widely regarded as the first Christian emperor by various other ancient writers from Jerome and Jordanes down to Bede. The tradition cannot be dismissed altogether. There was no state-sponsored persecution of the Christians during Philip's reign, notwithstanding the riots in Alexandria, and there seems to be no particular reason why later Christian propagandists might have fixed upon him as an exemplary character if there had been no truth in the suggestion. Perhaps it is best to think of him as having shown respect and toleration toward the Christian religion as part of his imperial duties or even having private beliefs which did not interfere with his official role as head of state.

Peace in Our Time

It may seem a little strange to us now that the emperor at Rome's millennium (see the bold portrait coin on Plate 1) was not a blue-blood Roman patrician but an ethnic Arab from an oasis town in the province of Arabia Petraea (now part of Syria). Philip had granted his home the high status of *colonia* and ordered its wholesale reconstruction in Roman style. The works there included a theatre, bath complex, temples, palaces, and magnificent colonnades that led to a great triumphal arch. Its centrepiece was a sacred memorial to the emperor himself, the Philippeion;[15] and to leave nobody in doubt as to the significance of the place, or the emperor's level of modesty, Shahba was renamed Philippopolis.

Appended to a collection of works attributed to the second century Greek author Aelius Aristides there is an anonymous speech in praise of an unnamed emperor, delivered, it tells us, on a festival day held during a season sacred to the gods. On the basis of both style and content most modern scholars attribute it to a later, unknown, author writing for Philip, possibly for the millennium celebrations. The writer is at great pains to argue that the emperor had acceded to the throne in a correct and lawful manner unlike some of his predecessors, which is a strong hint that there were rumours to the contrary. He is painted as the ideal ruler, mild in temperament, reverent to the gods and just toward men, and wholly dedicated to his imperial duty. The empire had been in a piteous state, but he had been able to restore calm and bring about peace and even lower the tax rate (something that is most unlikely to have been claimed if it wasn't true). He had calmed rebellious troops by limiting their donatives and submitting them to military drill. And rather than defeating the enemy in costly battles he had outwitted them through prudent strategy. The people no longer lived in fear of spies and informers, the sea-lanes were open, the harbours were full of merchant ships, and joy pervaded the plains.[16]

So much for the propaganda, but it must be admitted that when the millennium year dawned, a period of stability had indeed been achieved by Philip who by that time had held supreme power for about three and a half years. The previous emperor, a young man known as Gordian III, had died in mysterious circumstances during a military campaign deep inside Persian territory. The official line was that he had succumbed to an illness and we know that he was laid to rest in a great and magnificent mausoleum at Zaitha on the Euphrates. Some said he had suffered serious injury sustained when falling from his horse. A more likely (or, perhaps, more complete) explanation is that he died of injuries sustained in battle. Philip's new administration was trying to cover up for a serious defeat and the disadvantageous and hasty peace terms that had to be agreed with the Persians as a result.[17]

The Romans had been battling the Persians on and off for over fifteen years, since a new dynasty – the so-called Sassanians – had emerged there under the first King of Kings Ardashir I (ruled 224–242 CE). Whereas the preceding regime (known as the Arsacid dynasty, or the Parthians) had been content to rule in lower Mesopotamia and further east (the areas that are now Iraq and Iran), Ardashir had claimed ancient title to all the lands of Asia Minor, Syria and much of the eastern Mediterranean which had been in Roman hands for centuries. This was, of course, a severe provocation, as well as an economic setback for both empires because war disrupted the Silk Road trade. Ardashir had fought with some success against the Romans and had earned respect as a great warrior, but after his death the Romans had decided to invade Persian lands and challenge his untested son, the new King of Kings, Shapur I.

At Naqsh-i-Rustam, near Persepolis in modern Iran, there is a magnificent necropolis with a series of huge rock carvings recording the deeds of two great royal houses from different periods of Iranian history. The first includes the burial chambers of Darius I, Xerxes I and Artaxerxes I from the Fifth Century BCE (these tombs are believed to have been despoiled on the orders of Alexander the Great). The second series are the tombs of Sassanid kings, including those of Ardashir and Shapur. A great inscription records the deeds of Shapur and includes the following lines which pertain to the death of Gordian and the accession of Philip:

> … when I first became established in the land, Gordian Caesar drew together an army from all the land of Rome, Gothia, and Germany; and to Asurestan he came against Iran and me, and at the boundary of Asurestan at Mishik there was a great face-to-face battle. Gordian Caesar was killed, and the army of the Romans was destroyed, and the Romans made Philip Caesar. And Philip Caesar came to me for supplication, and for their souls gave 500,000 dinars in blood money to me, and he was established as a tributary. And because of this I gave Mishik the name Peroz-Shapur (Victorious-is-Shapur). [*Res Gestae Divi Saporis* 6–8.]

The location of Mishik (sometimes spelled Misiche, Mesiche, or Massice) is debated but was probably north-west of the Sassanian capital Ctesiphon in the vicinity of modern Fallujah. The battle may not have been as one-sided as Shapur's inscription claims, and it omits to mention that the previous year the invading Romans had triumphed in another pitched battle at Rhesaina – modern Ra's al'-Ayn on the northern border of modern Syria. In reality both sides had suffered and were probably anxious to conclude a peace treaty.

There is no reason to doubt, however, that the Romans agreed to pay a huge indemnity in order to evacuate the remains of their forces from Persian lands. The half million dinars in Shapur's account are usually interpreted as being gold coins (aurei, or more correctly denarii aurei) equating to about 2.5 metric tons of gold which, it has been suggested, was probably about as much as the Roman treasury could realistically stretch to. The deal also seems to have involved Philip ceding some land to the Persians, but certainly not everything that had recently been re-conquered. A further term was a solemn promise to stop meddling in the affairs of Armenia, a nominally independent kingdom that had been allied to Rome and housed various Persian dissidents including the remainder of the old Arsacid royal family in exile. Philip sold the deal as a diplomatic success although it is telling that the very first coins in his name from the great mint at Antioch announce *pax fundata cum persis*, 'Peace is made with Persia', rather than *victoria persica*, 'Victory over Persia' as would originally have been hoped for.[18]

Perhaps because of the murky circumstances surrounding the death of Gordian, rumours began to spread that he had in fact been killed on the orders of Philip and his sinister brother, the praetorian prefect Gaius Julius Priscus. Various elaborations of this theme were in circulation, including the unlikely suggestion that Philip, who it was claimed was not himself with the main army at the time, had cunningly delayed the food supplies to the front, encouraging the troops to rebel. In reality, however, the evidence for such a conspiracy is thin.[19]

It is a curious fact that Philip, as opposed to his elder brother Priscus, was made emperor. The two must have agreed this amicably and the reason may be that Philip had a young son, also called Philip, who was thereby heir apparent. Everyone must have appreciated the assurance of a future dynasty. While Philip made his way straight to Rome to secure the new regime (arriving by 23 July 244 according to the evidence of official documents), Priscus stayed in the east with sweeping powers where an inscription accords him the unique title *rector orientis*, or ruler of the east. In effect this extraordinary command placed him directly over the heads of the provincial governors and military commanders, effectively a deputy emperor. Later Roman tradition states that Priscus made himself unpopular by exacting heavy taxation in an attempt to recoup some of the financial losses that had been incurred from buying off the Persians and he was described as 'of intolerably evil disposition'.[20]

Subsidy and subjugation

An intriguing aspect of the great inscription at Naqsh-i-Rustam is the mention of 'Gothia', the land of the Goths, as a distinct place from which a sizeable proportion of the invading Roman army had been drawn. Gothia was, presumably, the area north of the Roman border on the lower Danube and the northern fringes of the Black Sea but may also have included broad lands from modern Ukraine to Poland and the Baltic. From Shapur's inscription we can infer that the Romans had recruited warriors from this area as mercenaries. This accords well with the Gothic history of Jordanes which confirms that the Romans were in the habit of paying them an annual subsidy in return for allied status and service in the army, an arrangement that seems to have been going on since at least the 230s.[21] Also mentioned in the inscription are troops from Germania, that is, the lands east of the Rhine. Again it is likely that these had been enrolled as part of a deal with an independent king. The Romans had long been in the habit of selectively extending the hand of friendship beyond their imperial borders and enriching certain tribal leaders as a mark of imperial favour. It was a complex diplomatic game used as part of a divide-and-rule policy so as to prevent powerful and antagonistic confederations emerging in what the Romans called *barbaricum*.

One group who had not benefitted from Philip's largesse was a populous tribe called the Carpi who inhabited the upland areas around the Carpathians, a range of mountains named after them (see Map 1). They seem to have been angered by the unfair treatment and launched sustained raids into the Roman province of Dacia. This area had been conquered by the Emperor Trajan in the second century but remained a dangerous, highly militarized frontier province, home to two legions and a variety of auxiliary units. The mountains were rich in gold and silver, the main reason the Romans were there. The mining operation was sustained by fortified highways running across the hills and plains towards the Danube. Inevitably a series of Romanized towns and villages had developed along the road network, especially in the region known as Dacia Malvensis, that is, the flat area north of the Danube around the town of Romula-Malva. Archaeological evidence from destruction and coin hoards suggests that this was the main scene of the action in Philip's reign. The fighting seems to have escalated over several years, eventually requiring the presence of the emperor himself. Inscriptions show that he brought with him detachments from legions normally based on the Rhine. The historian Zosimus also alludes to a detachment from Mauretania, presumably light cavalry for which that province was famous. Eventually, in the summer of 247, Philip was finally able to declare *victoria carpica* – Victory over the Carpi. He then seems to have remained in the area, exacting reprisals and putting his victorious troops to work reconstructing and refortifying the key strongholds. It has been suggested that Philip was still in Dacia when the millennium year dawned, although he was soon to depart to Rome in preparation for the celebrations.[22]

Around the beginning of 248, the regime seems to have conducted what in modern parlance might be called a strategic defence review. With the shaky peace with Persia still holding and the Carpi defeated, the situation was now more settled than it had been for many years. The upshot was that Philip decided to cancel the annual subsidy paid to the Goths.[23] Perhaps the Romans now felt more secure along the Danube and equal to any threat that the Goths themselves might present should they decide to turn on their former allies. The policy of paying tribute to 'barbarians' may have been regarded as out of step with Rome's image in the dawning Golden Age: such payments were often looked down upon by the more hawkish elements of the elite as a sign of weakness, however prudent they might be in practice. Cutting the payments would also improve the public finances and so could help pay for the coming celebrations. Only time would tell if it was a wise decision.

The monster wakes

At about the same time, far beyond the limit of the empire, most likely somewhere in central Africa near the headwaters of the Nile, someone was struggling for life. Their body was under massive assault from a virulent infection with an overwhelmed immune system and a sky-high temperature. Within hours, blood began to ooze from around the eyes and every other orifice. The pain was excruciating, especially at the extremities. The people around the unfortunate individual must have been terrified at this sudden affliction and did their best to help, perhaps becoming blood-spattered in the process, but there was little that could be done for the first victim beyond making him or her as comfortable as possible.

Although nobody at the time could possibly have comprehended it, the reason for the illness was microscopic: viral particles in the bloodstream, each just a few thousandths of a millimetre across. Ordinarily, in its host (most likely a primate or bat) the viral load would have been held in check by the immune system, producing no symptoms at all. Now, finding itself unexpectedly in a human body with no natural defences, the virions (individual viral particles) began to replicate out of control, their numbers increasing geometrically, pumping around the bodily organs, destroying cells and dissolving tissue. It may have been a particularly nasty and deadly form of influenza, but the latest detailed historical and epidemiological research points the finger at something even more terrifying: a filovirus.[24]

Most viruses are tiny, just large enough to carry their cargos which are a replicating molecule, either DNA or RNA, but filoviruses are the monsters of this world, looking more like bacteria in fact, with long twisted tails. They are a unique and weird life-form that only became known to science in the later part of the twentieth century. Nevertheless, filoviruses have been around for at least tens of millions of years, establishing themselves in various animal hosts. Like all viruses they evolve very quickly – so fast, indeed, that we can be sure there is nothing exactly like the third century pathogen on Earth today, and for that we can be thankful. The closest modern relative is ebola.

Filoviruses have a very particular balancing act to perform if they are to cause an epidemic. They do not survive outside the blood stream, so they cannot be transmitted by coughs and sneezes; blood droplets must be transferred and get beneath the skin somehow, through scratches or via mucosal membranes. So if the virus causes a victim to spurt blood over everyone present in double-quick time that would seem like a good strategy for replication. But being totally and instantly lethal is no good at all to a hypothetical virus: such a pathogen might wipe out a small group of people but that would be the end of it. Far better to infect, incubate, and spread a little more slowly. This particular virus seems to have possessed, or quickly evolved, the perfect combination of infectivity and incubation period. The result was that people began to acquire the virus and flee the infected area in terror, spreading it far and wide. Soon enough some virions, circulating in the bloodstream of an unknown traveller, made it to the banks of the upper Nile. From there they hitched a ride on a boat heading north, downstream, towards the Roman Empire.

Chapter 2

Rebels

Ostrogotha invades

The Roman decision to cut the Gothic subsidy did not go down well north of the Danube. Ostrogotha, King of the Goths assembled an army more or less immediately and invaded Roman territory in reprisal. That, at least, is the gist of the account given by the Gothic historian Jordanes:

> Now when the aforesaid Philip – who, with his son Philip, was the only Christian emperor before Constantine – ruled over the Romans, in the second [actually, the fourth] year of his reign Rome completed its one thousandth year. He withheld from the Goths the tribute due them; whereupon they were naturally enraged and instead of friends became his foes. For though they dwelt apart under their own kings, yet they had been allied to the Roman state and received annual gifts. And what more? Ostrogotha and his men soon crossed the Danube and ravaged Moesia and Thrace. – Jordanes, *Getica* XVI.89–90

It is likely that the Goths invaded across the lower reaches of the Danube in the area of the delta, an area difficult to police. The great river was more easily fordable than further up as it spread out over a wide plain, becoming sluggish and dividing into multiple distributary channels separated by shifting marshy tracts. This direction of attack is supported by the presence of coin hoards that were apparently buried at this time in the coastal zone of Thrace far to the south, indicating an incursion along the Black Sea littoral (Map 2).[1]

The Danube river fleet (*classis moesica*) was responsible for policing the border, with an estimated strength of 1,600 men. The pride of this force was a ship called the 'pristis' which was a very fast and highly manoeuvrable galley with two banks of oars, a ram and mounted artillery. As a military asset it provided overpowering force on the river and could easily sink any other vessel within minutes. The fleet operated from a base on the delta at Noviodunum which, in addition to the navy, was staffed with a sizeable legionary detachment. However this base seems to have been destroyed in the mid-third century and it seems likely that it was the first action of the Gothic war. The fleet could have escaped by rowing upstream to their main

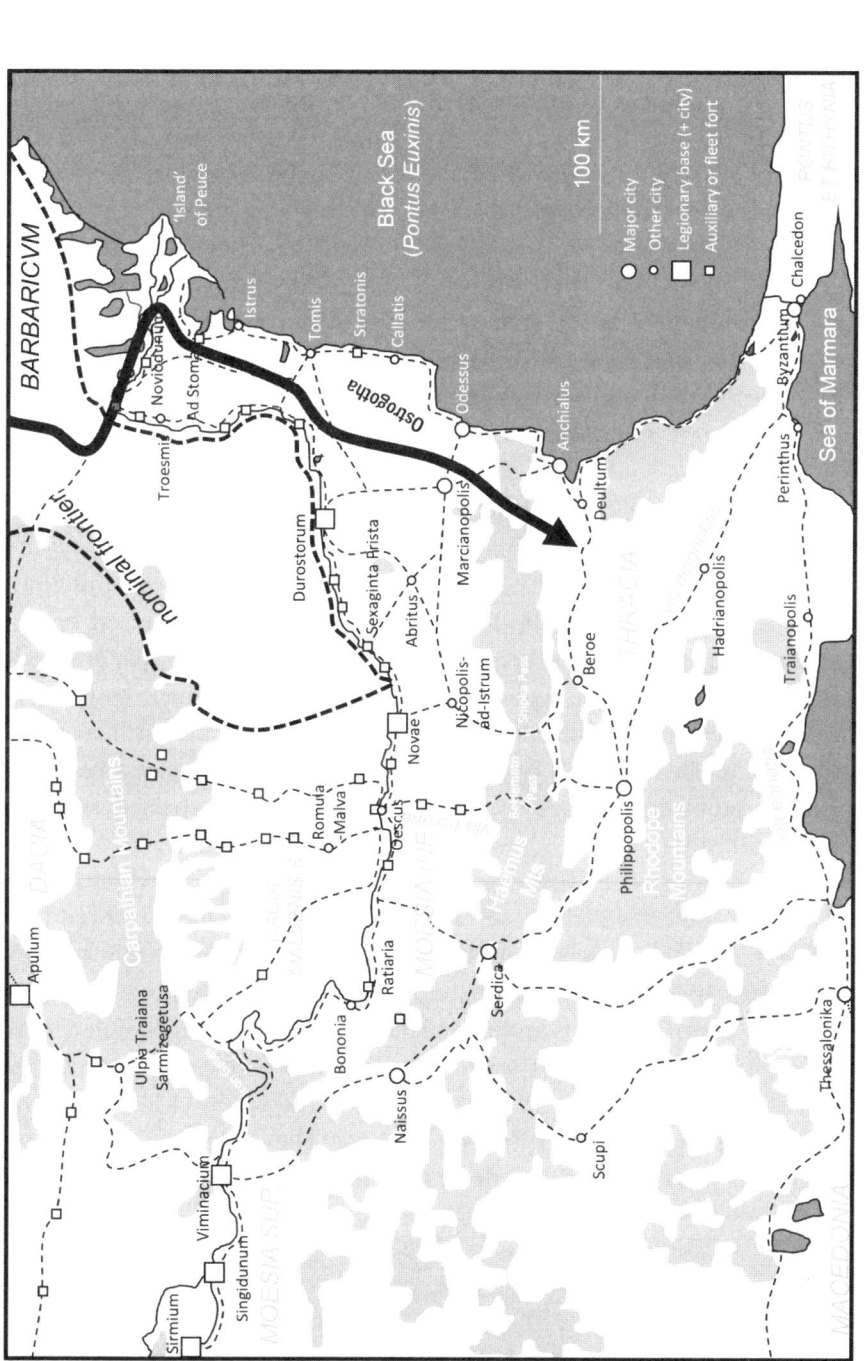

Map 2. Possible line of Ostrogotha's invasion of 248 CE based on the *Getica* of Jordanes and coin hoards.

base at Sexaginta Prista, but they were evidently powerless to prevent a full-scale invasion. Sexaginta Prista literally means sixty warships which gives a convenient indication as to the size of the facility there.[2]

The main Roman forces in Moesia Inferior were *legio* XI *claudia* at Durostorum and *legio* I *italica* at Novae. Each legion mustered about 4,000 men, but this was by no means the sum total of the manpower in the province as there were also a variety of auxiliary units dispersed across a network of smaller forts. Detailed study of military discharge documents, inscriptions and stamped tiles allows only a partial roster of these units, but in the mid-third century they included three cavalry detachments (*alae*), three mounted cohorts (*cohortes equitata*), one cohort of mounted archers (*cohors equitata sagittariorum*), six infantry cohorts and one cohort of archers (*cohors sagittariorum*). In theory each of these units could field either 500 or 1,000 men, depending on the type, so in combination the auxiliaries at least matched the legions in overall numbers. Their main duties were patrolling, policing and general security, but they could also take a place in line of battle. Many of these units have proud ethnic labels which indicate their place of origin. The naval base at Sexaginta Prista, for instance, also housed the exotic *cohors* II *flavia brittonum equitata* (the second Flavian cohort of mounted Britons) which had arrived in Moesia at the end of the first century. Whether they were still recruited from Britain or the name was just a distant memory is uncertain. These men presumably provided military security at the base and patrolled the river banks on both sides.[3]

Jordanes mentions the Goths ravaging Moesia and Thrace which, if it is to be trusted, indicates action over a substantial area including beyond the Haemus range. No cities are mentioned, however, so the invaders presumably targeted unfortified towns, villages and rural estates. The major cities in the area, such as Tomis, Odessus and Anchialus on the coast, and Marcianopolis in the interior, possessed stout walls and gates and were probably thronged with refugees from the countryside. By the most likely chronology, this Gothic incursion was getting underway just as the citizens of Rome were enjoying their great celebration a thousand miles to the west.

Pacatian

Written history gives us very little indication of what the Roman response to Ostrogotha's invasion was, but there are three pieces of information that may all somehow be connected. Philip is reported to have earlier created an extraordinary command for his father-in-law Otacilius Severianus in the Balkans (Moesia and Macedonia are specifically mentioned, but Thrace must have been included and probably Dacia, Pannonia and Dalmatia as well). Historians have concluded that this role was similar to the command created for Philip's brother Julius Priscus as *rector orientis* in the east, and it may have been established at the beginning of his reign as part of a connected policy. As close family, Priscus and Severianus could be trusted. The secret police (*frumentarii*) presumably reported directly to them as well as the emperor in Rome and one of their roles would have been to keep an eye on the loyalty of the provincial governors and military commanders within their jurisdiction. But the first piece of information is that nothing is heard of Severianus in connection with the events of 248 on the Danube. It may well be that he had joined the festivities in Rome and the Balkan high command had passed to a subordinate, possibly only temporarily. The second fact of interest is that Ostrogotha and his force must have exited the empire at some point, probably in the second half of 248. The third and most significant fact is that a serious revolt against the regime of Philip and his family erupted at this time further up the Danube.[4]

The leading figure of the insurrection was a man named Pacatianus (or Pacatian as he is generally known) who was described as a 'unit commander' by a later historian. This rebel quickly managed to gain control of the great city of Viminacium (see Map 2 for location), capital of Moesia Superior and home to *legio* VII *claudia* (near Kostolac in modern Serbia, now the site of an extensive museum). It is likely, then, that Pacatian was the commanding officer of that legion, and it has been suggested that he may have been of senatorial rank. *Legio* VII *claudia* was the long-time partner of *legio* IIII *flavia felix*, which was posted a little further up the Danube at Singidunum (modern Belgrade) which presumably also came under Pacatian's control at this time: there is no evidence of fighting between these forces which were placed sufficiently close to one another that they are likely to have acted in concert or not at all.[5]

The simplest way to reconcile these circumstances is to imagine that the Balkan forces remained under unified military command at the time of Ostrogotha's invasion. The invasion threat was deemed sufficiently large that the regular forces of Moesia Inferior were insufficient to repulse it, so instead the response was organized from upstream at Viminacium. The two legions of Moesia Superior could have advanced quickly into Thrace via Naissus and Serdica along the main highway known as the *via diagonalis*. Combining in some manner with the forces already on the lower Danube, the armies were able to confront and eject the Goths, scoring a significant victory over the invaders in the face of perceived weakness and lack of support from the imperial centre. The whole debacle may reasonably have been blamed on

Philip's decision to cut the subsidy. Perhaps it was that which prompted the troops to proclaim their own man as emperor at this time.[6]

Philip's government looked on this rebellion with apprehension because the mutinous legions were among the empire's best. They drew their strength from the Thracians and Pannonians, peoples of fearsome martial reputation albeit long since absorbed within the imperial system. They had fought a series of aggressive campaigns across the Rhine and Danube under the skilled and decisive command of the emperor Maximinus in the years 235–238, winning a string of major victories and battle honours, and some of the veterans of these campaigns would still have been in the ranks.

The city of Viminacium had a mint as well as a legionary fortress. Although it had hitherto been restricted to making low denomination regional bronze coins, it now started to issue imperial currency in silver. The coins give us the rebel's full name: Tiberius Claudius Marinus Pacatianus. The designs are quite diverse, showing Fortune, Concord of the Army, Faith of the Soldiers, Felicity, Rome, Victory and Eternal Peace – all completely normal types for the central government issues, but when taken together they spell out the ambition of Pacatian's rebel regime rather succinctly. They are mostly in good quality silver and of standard weight or even rather heavy (averaging about 4.2 g), something the men would have appreciated. Close study of these pieces has allowed a chronology of issues to be deciphered. One of the earliest types is *fortuna redux* (good fortune on the happy return of the emperor) which indicates that Pacatian had, apparently, been out of town near the start of his reign: possibly, we may speculate, fighting Goths in Lower Moesia and chasing them back across the Danube.[7]

Jotapian

A second rebellion erupted in the east at around the same time that Pacatian's men were proclaiming him emperor at Viminacium. There is no evidence that the two uprisings were co-ordinated and it may simply be that millennial murmurings, fear, and insecurity produced the same result twice over. Julius Priscus had made himself unpopular as ruler of the east, and it is not impossible that he too had been invited to the great millennium celebration in Rome, failing to appreciate that his extraordinary authority was essential for maintaining regional order. Perhaps he and Otacilius Severianus were sitting together in the royal box at the Circus Maximus while their extraordinary commands simultaneously dissolved. Perhaps the millennial games themselves produced a temporary financial crisis and an interruption in the money supply to the regional armies. In any case, both revolts produced a new emperor-on-the-spot.

The trouble in the east began in the province of Cappadocia which is in the eastern part of modern Turkey (see Map 1). The central figure was called Iotapianus (or Jotapian as he is usually known in English). His name is interesting, and it has been suggested on the basis of inscriptional evidence that he may have been related to the ruling house of the old Hellenistic kingdom of Commagene, among whose earlier princesses were two ladies named Iotape. Commagene was a smallish kingdom on the west bank of the upper Euphrates, centred on the city of Samosata, but now incorporated into Roman Cappadocia. It was said of Jotapian that he boasted descent from Alexander, which presumably means Alexander the Great of Macedon. As a member of this old royal house, Jotapian could well have been a direct descendant of the foremost warrior of the ancient world. Most provincial usurpers of the third century were military commanders like Pacatian, raised to the purple by their own rebellious troops whether they assented to the honour or not. Jotapian may have been different in this respect, being a local noble, which hints at nationalism as a motive although there is no way that his uprising could have got off the ground without strong military support. He may have been a figurehead for a mutiny led by other more shadowy figures in the army who wished to make the most of local sentiment.[8]

It may seem odd that part of the eastern empire would rise against Philip, himself from the east, who was clearly prepared to honour his home province in the most visible manner through his building programme at Syrian Philippopolis and neighbouring cities. But there is also some evidence that local rivalries may have been stirred by the uneven distribution of the emperor's munificence. The area of the rebellion was nominally under the control of *legio* XII *fulminata* ('the thunderbolts') based at Melitine, a great crossing point on the upper Euphrates (modern Malatya, Turkey) so we can infer that this legion was the source of the trouble. It may also have involved the other Cappadocian legion, *legio* XV *apollinaris*, which was based further north at Satala (modern Sadak, Turkey). These legions, just like Pacatian's, are unlikely to have acted independently of their immediate neighbours.

Initially, at least, the revolt enjoyed substantial success, with the unrest apparently spreading into parts of Syria. Jotapian managed to gain control of a mint. His surviving coins are rather crude and it has been suggested that the texture and style are consistent with the mint at Nicopolis in Seleucia, a coastal city in the far north-eastern corner of the Mediterranean. If so, Jotapian had managed to bring a relatively large tract of land under his control, stretching at least 200km from the Euphrates to the coast.[9]

The historical sources say rather little about Jotapian which makes the coins particularly valuable as historical evidence. To date, only about twenty have come to light, some struck from the same dies, and most are of the same basic type, with the obverse showing the emperor with a radiate crown and the reverse depicting the winged figure of Victory advancing to the left, holding a wreath and palm. The portrait is quite distinctive and consistent across several known dies so it can be considered a genuine attempt at a likeness (Plate 1). It seems to show a middle-aged man with a prominent forehead and aquiline nose. The coins give his full name IMP M F RV IOTAPIANVS (Imperator Marcus Fulvius Rufus Jotapianus) or similar (several apparent variants exist, most of them apparently bungled in some way by the die-cutters). One important coin includes the letters AVG which directly identifies him as *augustus* [emperor] as well as *imperator* [commander]. The reverse legend on all of them is *victoria aug*, celebrating the emperor's unspecified victory, a common design in the period. It could commemorate an initial victory by Jotapian over local forces as he consolidated his gains and expanded his dominions, or it might just be generic propaganda.[10]

These coins establish that Jotapian's rebellion was not merely an eastern enclave seeking secession from the empire under its old royal house. The double-denarii are in the style of Rome with Latin inscriptions (although the die cutters would have preferred Greek, judging from the frequent errors), and the reverse is impeccably imperial in style. This was the standard coin of military pay. It would have been a departure for the mint at Nicopolis, or wherever it was, because the eastern mints were normally geared up to issuing eastern style money with Greek legends. This confirms that Jotapian was styling himself emperor of Rome and another direct challenger to Philip.

Some of Jotapian's surviving coins were struck to the normal weight standard but others are under-weight by a quarter. Although the metal content has not been assessed systematically, the pieces being so rare, they have the appearance of being darker and more debased than the regular coinage of Philip. So much might be expected from a provincial usurper attempting to establish a regional government while eking out a precious metal supply that may have been restricted to the coffers of just one or two legions and whatever silver could be requisitioned from the dinner services of the local elite. But the slightly home-made quality of the money should not detract from the fact that senior military commanders had picked a fight with the central administration which they must have believed they could win.[11]

If the mint was indeed in Seleucian Nicopolis (the name means City of Nike, or Victory) then it was close enough to threaten Antioch itself, just a few days' march to the south. Evidently, Jotapian was not trying to hide in the desert: this was a challenge to battle. It was at Antioch, capital of the east, that Priscus normally held court as *rector orientis*, but either he was absent at the time – possibly at the millennium games, as we have speculated – or he did not feel sufficiently strong or confident enough of the loyalty of his legions to crush the insurrection immediately. It was dangerous, however, to dither in the face of rebellions which had a habit of growing fast if not checked immediately.

Eternal Rome in the Year 1001

Among Pacatian's coins from Viminacium the most interesting type by far depicts Eternal Rome with the legend *romae aeter(nae) an(nus) mil et primo* – 'To Eternal Rome in the Year 1001' (Plate 1). It was virtually unheard of for Roman coins to be dated from the city's foundation, so much so that as recently as the 1990s sceptical historians dismissed the one known example as a fake, until others turned up. This type seems to have been minted to celebrate New Year on the Danube and by implication a new order for the entire Roman Empire. Pacatian was the man to bring about the promised Golden Age. Unusually, it styles him as *invictus* – the unconquered – rather than *augustus* as was more usual. The whole message is confident and assured. Jotapian, in the east, also seems to have been active throughout the winter but he was not as imaginative in his propaganda. It all promised hard fighting ahead when the new marching season began.[12]

With these storm clouds gathering, the New Year celebrations in Rome must have been rather more muted than on the Danube. To have one rebel claiming to be *augustus* and minting coins in his own name was a severe provocation – it had not happened for generations – but to have two doing it simultaneously was humiliating. Clearly the contagion needed to be crushed. Assessing the uprisings, the strategists in Rome would have most feared the revolt on the Danube given the veteran troops involved and the potential for the rebellion to spread through the powerful legions all along the frontier up to the Rhine. If Pacatian was indeed a senator of high standing, he would have had patronage and considerable support amongst the upper classes in Rome, among whom some may have regarded the Syrian Philip with contempt. Rumours, whether true or not hardly matters, were circulating regarding Philip's treachery against Gordian. The eastern revolt was less of a threat to central government but the greater danger was that the Persians might take advantage of the disarray and smash their way into the empire from the east. Philip was so thoroughly disheartened by events that he is reported to have offered to abdicate the throne.[13]

Bad as it may have seemed, Jotapian and Pacatian controlled just a small proportion of the empire's military might. For each pretender there was little option but to seek battle and win, with final success perhaps requiring not just one but a series of escalating victories in the field and mass transfers of loyalty from among the neutrals. It had all been accomplished before. The emperor Vespasian, for instance, had been a provincial rebel before securing his dynasty back in the summer of 69. Septimius Severus had done the same in 193, starting from the very same legionary bases that Pacatian now occupied, with his opponents melting away before him as he advanced on Rome.

But losing such a rebellion would mean torture and death for everyone complicit in the plotting plus their families and dependants. The commanders also needed to rely on their own men under such circumstances, even though every single one of them had sworn a formal oath of loyalty (*sacramentum*) to Philip. It is impossible that everyone in the rebellious legions approved of what was happening, and many on the frontier may not have relished the prospect of marching against organized imperial forces as opposed to the 'barbarian' raiders that they were used to fighting.

As it turned out, Pacatian was not destined to get the battle he desired, nor to see in the Year 1002. Details are virtually nonexistent: all we know is that he was killed by his own men early in 249 by the most plausible chronology.[14] The resulting situation was suddenly chaotic: should the fractious Balkan legions plead for mercy from Rome, having disposed of their leader, or should they elect another emperor, and quickly, to continue the uprising? We know nothing of the fallout, the arguments in the high command or the mood on the parade grounds. In the event, wiser heads prevailed: the legions remained in their barracks, awaiting the return of central authority and, of course, army pay, from Rome (with Philip's head on it once again). Meanwhile Jotapian's insurrection continued.

Enter Decius

Philip, it seems, was too canny to vacate Rome and move to the Danube frontier himself under these dangerous circumstances. He had secured the capital and there he decided to stay, a spider in the centre of the web. Instead, he entrusted the mission to one of his most senior subordinates who was sent to restore order, a man who knew the region well: Caius Messius Quintus Decius Valerinus. This man hailed from a village called Budalia near Sirmium in Pannonia and was a most distinguished aristocrat of the regional type. His name, however, is Italian, so it has been suggested he came from a Roman family in the local administration. Sirmium lay beside the River Savus, a great tributary to the Danube, and sat astride the imperial highway that ran from Italy to Byzantium and beyond, the fulcrum of the empire. At about fifty-eight years old, Decius was at the height of his career, and was later described as 'a man furnished with all skills and virtues, calm and congenial in civil affairs, well prepared in military ones'. He had shown early promise by achieving senatorial rank at a young age and then by progressing through a series of senior appointments in his formal career, the *cursus honorum*, winning great respect and, no doubt, considerable wealth and influence. In the early 230s, during the enlightened reign of Severus Alexander, his talent had been rewarded with the high rank of consul.[15]

Another point that may be relevant to his mission is that at the time of the Civil War of 238 Decius had been governor of Hispania Tarraconensis (equivalent to most of modern Spain). Everyone knew that he had sided with the emperor Maximinus, steadfastly refusing to acknowledge the senatorial cause which he probably considered illegitimate and unconstitutional. He maintained this principled stance until the very end, even after Maximinus had been assassinated and the reason for fighting had evaporated. When the war ended, it seems that one of the most senior senatorial representatives, Rutilius Pudens Crispinus, a major hero from the other side, was dispatched to Spain to negotiate peace with Decius. This may have made him one of the key figures involved in the peace treaty of 238. His experience of delicate negotiations and his reputation for having upheld the honour of Maximinus and, by implication, the Balkan legions, would surely have recommended him for the task of bringing them into line once again.[16]

Decius may have been serving at that time in the high office of City Prefect of Rome, which would have been an especially great honour at the time of the millennium. According to the most likely sequence of events, he had impressed Philip by predicting that Pacatian would very likely be killed by his own men having embarked on so foolish an undertaking. When precisely that outcome had come to pass, Philip asked him to act as a special envoy to Viminacium. Decius was conferred with the title *dux moesiae et pannoniae*, putting him in command of the entire Danube frontier. He also took with him a huge amount of regular money to pay the mutinous troops once order had been restored to his satisfaction. The task was most exceedingly delicate: Decius had to root out and condemn the guilty, to be sure, but at the same time he needed to restore order and confidence among the troublesome legions which were required to be strong enough to fulfil their core duty of protecting the frontier against further Gothic invasion. Interestingly, Decius is supposed to have asked the emperor to be excused this duty which was undoubtedly dangerous and might easily backfire, but Philip insisted that he was the only man for the job.[17]

Judging from other such occasions, when Decius arrived on the Danube his mission would have begun with a great address to the troops at which they were required to renew their oath of allegiance to Philip before a sacred image of the emperor. Most of the men were probably absolved of blame, insofar as they had been following orders and because they had disposed of the rebel Pacatian in the end. Tribunals were presumably set up to consider the cases against those senior officers who had engineered the uprising and any other die-hards in the ranks. The tactful thing would have been not to investigate the plot too assiduously, but we know from later events that Decius was something of a traditionalist and disciplinarian.[18]

Disturbing evidence of the punishment that may have been meted out at the time comes from a 2011 archaeological investigation of a necropolis near Skopje in Upper Moesia (Roman Scupi, or Colonia Flavia Scupinorum). Here the diggers made an especially grisly discovery – a trench filled with over two hundred bodies, most of which had been tied up and decapitated on site. Only a section of the trench was excavated, so the number of dead is just a minimum. The skeletons are all apparently male between the ages of twenty and forty years except one man who was about sixty, and their bones attest to a hard life involving extensive physical training and frequent injury. The archaeologists concluded that they were soldiers. The dating evidence is only approximate, but the executions could have been ordered as part of the reprisals following Pacatian's revolt.[19]

Decius may also have campaigned briefly against the Goths, or at least overseen the mopping up operation following Ostrogotha's invasion the previous year. He launched an enquiry into how the Gothic army had managed to penetrate the empire, finding serious fault with some of the units whose first duty was to prevent such a disaster. Jordanes tells us that he cashiered a significant number of soldiers 'and sent them back to private life, as though it had been by neglect that the Goths had crossed the Danube'. Although we do not know how many men received dishonourable discharge, it seems the tactic backfired, for 'when the soldiers found themselves expelled from the army after so many hardships, in their anger they had recourse to the protection of Ostrogotha, King of the Goths'. In other words, some fully trained Roman soldiers crossed the Danube and joined the enemy – enough of a contingent to have been remembered hundreds of years later.[20]

The convocation on the Danube would have involved the senior officers of all the legions as well as the provincial governors and other civic dignitaries, producing an ideal opportunity for late night plotting and intrigue. No doubt many of these men impressed upon Decius the ongoing and serious threat presented by the Goths and the desperate need for additional cash and manpower to maintain security. Some share of the blame for the neglect of the frontier must surely lie with the central administration which had lavished resources on the millennium celebrations while cutting the Gothic subsidy and ignoring external threats. Now was surely the time for a massive punitive campaign against the Goths to deter any future repeat of the recent outrage.

Proceedings went little further because the high command at Viminacium rebelled again, and with ultimate irony that this time they forced Decius himself to be their champion and emperor, very much against his own will if the highly sympathetic account of the historian Zosimus is to be believed. Of course it may be that Decius orchestrated events, perhaps when he realized that he could rely on the personal support of many of the senior officers along the Danube. If all the Moesian and Pannonian armies joined the uprising, Decius might have found himself in command of between ten and twelve legions and their associates a much greater force than Pacatian had previously commanded.

Whatever the truth of the matter, Decius is supposed to have written to Philip saying he had been forced at swordpoint to become nominal emperor, begging him not to be alarmed if he marched toward Rome, and promising to relinquish imperial pretensions as soon as he was able. He did not mint a single coin in his own name which might support this story; or perhaps that was also a ruse in this unusual game of thrones. Philip was not to be fooled, however, and started to prepare an army to confront and suppress the rebels of the Danube once and for all. A new coinage proclaiming the good faith of the army was issued to remind the soldiers of the sacred oath (*sacramentum*) they had taken in Philip's name. And for all his protestations of loyalty, Decius rapidly began to assemble a strike force with the aim of marching on Italy and confronting Philip in the field.[21]

The Battle of Verona

The date of Decius's proclamation on the Danube is unknown but it must have occurred some time in the first half of 249. In estimating the date we must allow time for Pacatian to have issued his coins celebrating the New Year, for his assassination and news of it to reach Rome, for Decius and his entourage to journey up to the frontier, for the tribunals, and finally for Decius to be proclaimed emperor himself.[22]

Philip held the imperial capital and centre of communications, and most of the empire probably remained loyal (evidence is sparse but we know from dated papyri that Egypt continued to support him, for instance). His problem, however, was that the vast majority of troops were stationed around the borders

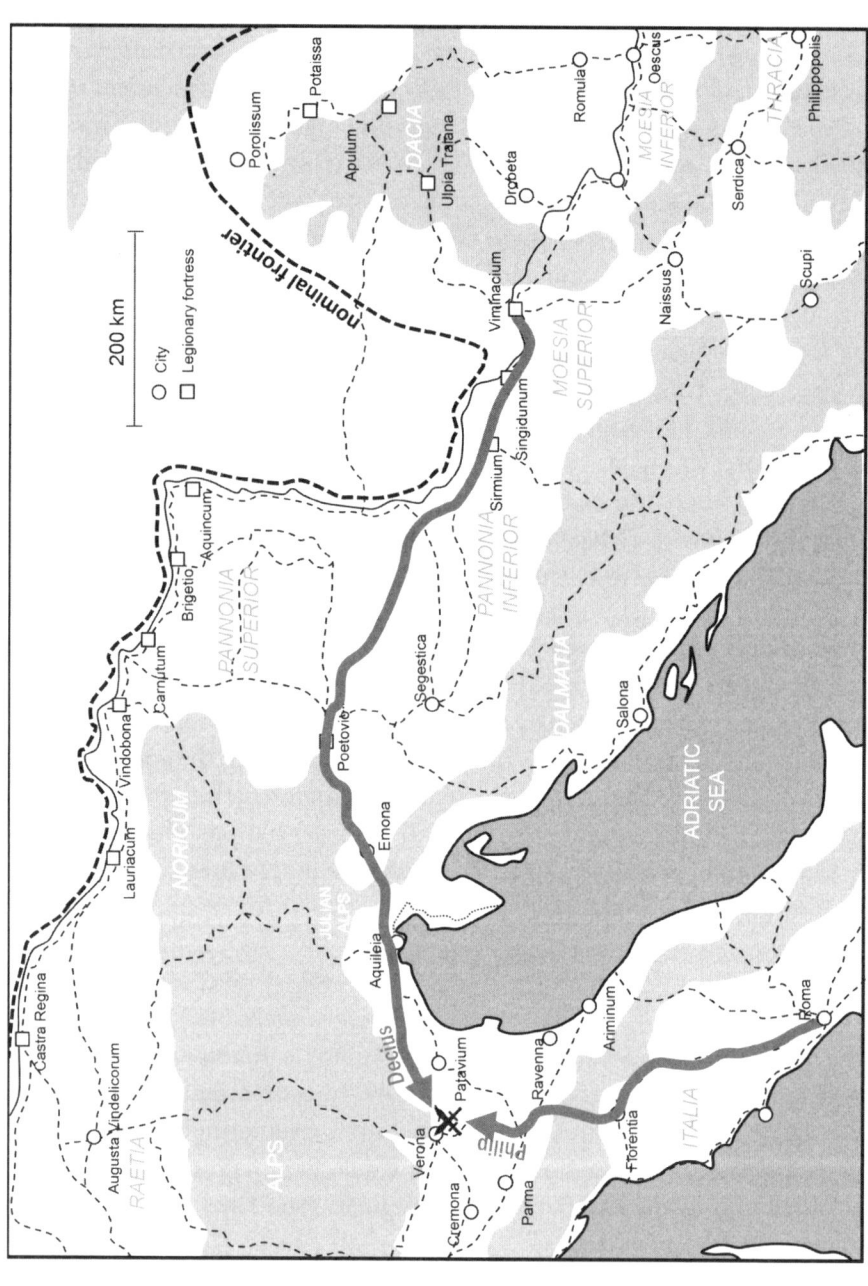

Map 3. The Battle of Verona, 249 CE. Decius drew his strength from the armies of the Danube. Philip commanded the imperial forces from Rome.

and could not be assembled quickly. The troops in Rome consisted principally of the elite Praetorian Guard and the imperial horseguard (*equites singulares augusti*) plus one special legion, *legio* II *parthica*, which was stationed south of the city. However some of these troops may have been allocated to Decius when he went up to the frontier. Philip may have been concerned about the loyalty of the horseguard which was traditionally composed of troops selected from among the most promising soldiers of the very same Danubian legions that he was about to confront.

According to Count Zosimus, a historian writing around the beginning of the sixth century, the rebel army 'though they knew the enemy had the imperial forces, still retained their confidence in Decius, trusting his great skill and prudence'. He moved fast, taking what appears to have been a relatively small force up from Viminacium and crossing the Julian Alps into northern Italy. His target was Rome and he needed to get there as quickly as he could. But Philip also moved quickly and the two armies converged on the *via postumia* near the city of Verona, a strategic place on the intersection of several major roads (Map 3).[23]

Sporadic imperial rescripts (legal opinions), as collected centuries later in the law code of Justinian (*codex iustinianus*) are an important, if rather accidental, resource for reconstructing events, because they very conveniently name the emperor, place and date of issue for each ruling. These tie the battle to between 17 June and 16 October 249. Zosimus reports that Philip had the larger army but the troops of Decius were confident in their commander, claiming that Philip was enfeebled by age. In contrast, the much later (twelfth century) historian Zonaras tells us that Philip led his army from the front. There is no dispute about the outcome. The imperial rescript from 16 October is in the name of a new emperor, Decius, who by then had been officially accepted in that capacity by the Senate. Philip had died in battle. One source gives us the grisly detail that the top of his head had been sliced off from just above the teeth. His young son and nominal co-emperor, Philip II, was slain by the praetorians in Rome once the outcome of the battle became known there. The fate of the empress Otacilia Severa (she of the hippopotamus coins) is not recorded. Nobody knows what happened to her father, Otacilius Severianus, or Philip's powerful brother, Julius Priscus, but in those violent times it is difficult to imagine them escaping with their lives.[24]

Death on the Nile

As these momentous events were unfolding in Italy, one of the empire's great provinces found itself in the grip of terror for an entirely different reason. The pestilence that had crossed the species barrier far to the south had been moving down the Nile and now, in the summer of 249, it took hold across Egypt. The result was described at the time as human suffering and catastrophe on a scale unparalleled in any previous epidemic. Our witness on the spot is Bishop Dionysius of Alexandria, some of whose letters survive. He described a kind of zombie apocalypse in which the contagion spread unchecked and people were so terrified of the sick that they were cast out by their own families to wander the streets. Dead bodies, still highly contagious, lay uncollected or were gathered by slaves and cast into mass graves.

One such locality has been discovered by archaeologists on the west bank of the Nile near Luxor. Excavations there show that bodies were heaped up in a large pit with quicklime cast over them as a disinfectant, the lime being manufactured on site in a series of hastily built kilns which burned Egypt's ubiquitous limestone. Quicklime is a very effective biocide with the triple effect of killing pathogens, slowing the rate of decomposition, and neutralizing the acids formed as bodies rot down.[25] But according to Dionysius, the Christians did not allow their infected to be disrespected as others did. His flock cared for the sick and treated the dead bodies with reverence, 'closing their eyes and shutting their mouths, bearing them on their shoulders and laying them out for burial, clinging to them, embracing them, washing them, decking them out'. Unsurprisingly, perhaps, the mourners soon became ill in their turn. 'The very pick of our brethren lost their lives in this way, both priests and deacons and highly praised ones from among the laity, so that this manner of dying does not seem far removed from martyrdom, being the outcome of much piety and stalwart faith'.[26]

Dionysius was among the survivors. Another letter he wrote explains how the population of Alexandria had been ravaged, quoting as his source the much-diminished roll-call of those entitled to free food distribution. He does not give precise numbers, but from his evidence it has been estimated that the population of the city may have declined by more than half – presumably due to both death and exodus. That kind of mortality in a great trading city was bound to have a serious economic impact. And of course once the disease had a foothold there, it seemed only a matter of time before it spread further. The only hope was that God, or the gods, might intervene to prevent further calamity.[27]

Chapter 3

The Forces of Conservatism

Trajan Decius

It must have been a delicate task for Decius to re-balance the armies after the Battle of Verona and return the troops who had fought on both sides to their bases under trustworthy commanders. The Danubian legions were badly needed back in their fortresses to discourage and protect against further 'barbarian' invasions, and so they probably did a rapid about turn and set off on the long slog back to the river frontier, albeit with a victorious spring in their step and a hefty reward. Indeed the handout of a major donative – a cash bonus – to all the troops of the empire was by now a necessary first step for any new emperor to smooth the way, and those who had fought on his side were bound to receive extra. To get their hands on this money, everyone including the vanquished were required to take a solemn vow of loyalty to the new man which, it seems, they were largely happy to do. Decius was sufficiently confident of his security to travel on to Rome protected by the praetorians and imperial horseguard, men who had so recently been his enemies.[1]

On his arrival around August 249, Decius was invested in his priestly role as *pontifex maximus*. He would have been well accustomed to officiating at religious ceremonies throughout his career, an important task for both military and civil officials. Now he was himself the most numinous individual of the empire, to be worshipped almost as a god in the temples of the imperial cult. His predecessor Philip was damned to memory.[2]

Decius appears to have been a man of great rectitude and moral certainty and yet considerable imagination, a strange mixture of traditionalism and innovation. His great role model was the emperor Trajan (ruled 98–117 CE) who was remembered as the perfect ruler (*optimo princeps*), having governed wisely and waged great wars. Trajan was the last man to have significantly extended the imperial dominions and it seemed that ever since those glory days the empire had mostly been on the back foot. So one of Decius's first acts was to assume his hero's name, becoming Trajan Decius. He was no descendant of that emperor so it was an unusual move, and it is worth wondering why he chose to do it. It may be relevant that Trajan had founded the province of Dacia on the far bank of the Danube: Trajan's column still stands in Rome as a monument to that victory which had been achieved by a series of lightning military campaigns and with an enormous amount of bloodshed, mostly that of the inhabitants. Adopting Trajan's name could have been both a special compliment to the Danubian legions that had brought him to power and an undisguised threat to King Ostrogotha of what to expect next.

No new rebellions erupted. Decius was a senior and respected senator with a strong military reputation – a congenial prospect to the Roman aristocracy and probably to broader public opinion in the provinces. Soon after arriving in the capital, Decius received an unexpected delivery: the rotting head of Jotapian, pretender of the east. It seems that this man's soldiers had realized that their rebellion had failed and took the necessary step. One can almost imagine the collective sigh of relief as the empire was once again united under a widely admired new emperor. Many would have hoped that the promised *saeculum novum* had now truly arrived after a somewhat faltering beginning.[3]

Decius made a special point of honouring the army and provinces of the Danube on his new coinage. A common type in gold, silver and bronze was dedicated to the 'Genius of the Illyrian Army' which must have greatly pleased the men there when it appeared in their pay packets. The two Pannonian provinces (Pannonia Superior and Inferior) were personified in the guise of a pair of goddesses. More common still is the personification of Dacia. She is sometimes depicted attended by a lion (symbol of *legio* XIII *gemina*) and an eagle (symbol of *legio* V *macedonica*) or is shown carrying a Dacian war staff surmounted by an ass's head (although some prefer to see a dragon rather than the supposedly ignoble ass).[4] This was a conspicuously public commitment to a troubled and exposed province surrounded by enemies on the far bank of the Danube. No doubt part of Decius's calculation was that Dacia was very rich in precious metals that underpinned the imperial economy and his policy was to hold it at all costs.[5]

An immediate order went out to restore the roads all along the frontier from Vindobona (Vienna) to the Black Sea coast. We know this because a series of milestones survive, including from the exposed north bank, with imperial titles that show they were erected before the year was out. The rest of the empire was not to be neglected either: other road improvements are recorded soon after as proved by inscriptions found in far-flung places such as Britannia, Galatia, Africa, and Palestine.[6]

Decius's wife, Herennia Etruscilla, is thought to have been an Italian noble, probably descended from an ancient Etruscan family of consular rank. She is honoured on the coins as *augusta*, with the reverse designs celebrating Juno (the wife of Jupiter), Pudicitia (sexual virtue) and Fecunditas (fecundity). All this relates to the fact that she had provided Decius with two grown-up sons, and nobody need doubt the true succession. The sons were Quintus Herennius

Etruscus Messius Decius and Caius Valens Hostilianus Messius Quintus – or Herennius Estruscus and Hostilian as they are generally known. But for now they remained esteemed citizens and were not give any formal role.[7]

We can imagine Decius sitting in the palace in Rome in the last months of 249 contemplating the deified emperors who had gone before him. The task before him was as difficult as any his predecessors had faced, with parts of the empire still in disarray and threatened by fearsome enemies: most notably as we have seen along the Danube and in the east, but also with growing trouble on the Rhine frontier and in Gaul. Incoming reports of a terrible epidemic gripping Egypt must have been viewed with great trepidation. Vast numbers of ships would ply the sea lanes between Alexandria and Rome and other great cities when the winter was over.

An interesting question is to whether any practical public health measures were enacted to limit the spread of the disease. On one level, infected individuals would have been feared and ostracized by their communities, as we have already heard from the testimony of Bishop Dionysius. Neighbourhoods, districts and even whole towns would have been considered cursed when the contagion struck. Ancient medics well understood that some diseases spread from person to person and that the sick should be isolated. There was also a dim recognition of the concept of an incubation period, that is, a period between infection and the manifestation of a disease. Unfortunately there is little direct surviving evidence of how the authorities reacted, but comparison with the later 'plague of Justinian' of the sixth century suggests that a variety of measures would have been taken including a focus on hygiene, limiting gatherings and restricting movement from infected areas. It is quite possible, for instance, that sailors arriving from Egypt in Rome's highly organized port city of Ostia and other major cities would have been banned from disembarkation.[8]

As he looked across from the splendid imperial palace through winter squalls at the temples of the *via sacra*, with the view dominated by the looming complex of Jupiter Optimus Maximus on the Capitoline Hill, Decius may have wondered at the root cause of all the recent evil. There can be little doubt that the priestly elite in Rome would have agreed with his conclusion: the gods were offended and their anger must be assuaged.

Restitutor Sacrorum

At the New Year celebrations for Rome's one thousandth and second year, or 250 CE as we know it, Decius was appointed consul as was normal for a new emperor. He chose as his partner a senior patrician called Gaius Vettius

Gratus, about whom little else is known. Also early in 250, possibly at the same time, the emperor (via a compliant senate) bestowed the rank of *caesar* (junior emperor) on his elder son Herennius Etruscus. It was a popular move: Herennius was twenty-two years old and, if the message on the coins and statues is to be believed, he was handsome and full of martial vigour and promise. The armies would have been especially pleased by this news: not only was there now a clear heir apparent, the occasion entailed a new cash handout.

According to a much disputed late text, Decius may have shown his traditionalist side by resurrecting the old Republican office of *censor*, a senior magistrate who was responsible for upholding the public morality. Then he dropped his bombshell: he issued an edict requiring all the inhabitants of the empire to sacrifice to the gods, to eat sacrificial meat, and to swear an oath to the effect that they had always sacrificed. This they were required to do in front of local magistrates. In return they would receive a certificate (*libellus*), a copy of which would be entered into the ledgers, and they would be left to get on with their lawful existence. Failure to comply would result in legal action and might be considered treasonous, leading to trial, confiscation of property, banishment or even death. It was an extraordinary measure, confirming Decius as a man of innovation, albeit of a fundamentally conservative nature. A surviving inscription from the town of Cosa in Italy describes him as *restitutor sacrorum* (Restorer of the Sacred Rites) in relation to this initiative.[9]

The people of the empire were accustomed to having to turn up and be counted for the occasional census, and this may have been another part of the reason for the edict. After the recent tumult and poor administration, the new emperor may have wanted to take stock of the realm in terms of population, wealth and resources. And as a bonus, every single person would be made aware that there was a new man at the helm. The administrative burden for the new edict may not have been too great because everyone in the empire was supposed to know his or her master (if slave, child or woman), tribe, or city, and there was a complex devolved local bureaucracy. Nevertheless, universal (or near universal) compliance in a decree to sacrifice would take many months to enact. Instructions were sent out by central government, then passed on to regional magistrates and their local subordinates, who then arranged times and dates for all the interviews at town or village level.

Remarkably, a fair number of the certificates that were issued on these occasions survive to this day (Plate 2). Conveniently, they were dated. The earliest known example is from 28 February from the province of Pamphylia in Asia Minor. The greatest crop of surviving *libelli* is forty-five from Egypt, where hot and dry conditions were sometimes conducive to the preservation of papyrus documents. Those all date to between 12 June and 14 July which indicates the huge scale of the exercise. One wonders to what extent the inevitable movement of people may have fuelled the growing epidemic there.

We learn from the *libelli* that a formulaic text was used and that individuals signed in person before the document was ratified by the presiding magistrates. If someone was illiterate they were required to have another person formally countersign for them. Interestingly, even some of the presiding magistrates seem to have struggled writing their names. For the text we may take as an example an exceptionally interesting one that was issued to Aurelia Ammonous of the city of Arsinoe:

> To the commission chosen to superintend the sacrifices. From Aurelia Ammonous, daughter of Mystus, of the Moeris quarter, priestess of Petesouchos, the great, the mighty, the immortal, and priestess of the gods in the Moeris quarter. I have sacrificed to the gods all my life and without interruption, and now again, in accordance with the decree and in your presence, I have made sacrifice, and poured a libation, and partaken of the sacred victims. I request you to certify this below. [Decian Libellus.][10]

Arsinoe is modern Fayum, south of Cairo, and Moeris was one of its districts. The mighty and immortal Petesouchos was a divine crocodile no less, and indeed the ancient Greeks had nicknamed the city Crocodilopolis for this distinctive form of religion. The highly revered cult was already *thousands* of years old, going back to the period of Egypt's Old Kingdom. Aurelia Ammonous was obviously a significant minister of this religion but she had no problem in also acknowledging the full pantheon of Rome or of sacrificing to the deified emperors, as is proved by her treasured certificate.

But the edict was not aimed at crocodile worshippers: that was *religio licita* and it was not they who were widely suspected of bringing the empire into disrepute. The real target was Christianity, adherents of which maintained that their immortal souls would be lost if they should worship any but the one true god. Against this, the prospect of torture, banishment, or death were small things to weigh (or so their bishops instructed them). It was exactly this attitude that so offended the Romans, who viewed their failure to comply as treasonous and disrespectful to the gods, potentially bringing misfortune on the whole empire. The decree of Decius seems very well designed to smoke out these malefactors, or at least the more fanatical ones, so that they could be punished or killed and their property confiscated. Not only would this please the gods, it would also help restore the stretched imperial finances.[11]

Cyprian to the Lions!

Some modern historians have wondered if the effect of Decius's edict on the Christians might have been largely accidental. Perhaps the new emperor simply enacted a crass and blundering policy, oblivious to the impact that it would have on some of his subjects.[12] But while it is certain that the primary aim was to assuage the gods and help bring about peace, stability and prosperity to the empire, it is hardly credible that the emperor and his advisors would be so ignorant of the effect that their decree would have on so large a body of the citizenry. The Christians of antiquity well understood that they were the intended target of the measure and that this was a deliberate persecution, and indeed it turned out to be a most effectual weapon against them.

The first victim of the purge was Fabian, Bishop of Rome. This man had set a firm example to his flock by refusing the imperial decree. According to church tradition, he was interrogated by Decius himself and then paid with his life by decapitation on 20 January 250. His colleagues, the priests Moyses and Maximus and the deacon Nicostratus, were imprisoned at the same time. Others soon followed Fabian to martyrdom including such notables as Alexander, Bishop of Jerusalem, and Babylas of Antioch (the man who had supposedly refused communion to the Emperor Philip). Terrified of suffering the same fate, many Christians throughout the empire hurried to their local magistrates to say and do whatever was necessary to obtain their *libelli*.

An interesting witness to the edict in Alexandria is the same Bishop Dionysius who had so recently described the coming of the plague:

> All were truly affrighted. And many of the more eminent in their fear came forward immediately; others who were in the public service were drawn on by their official duties; others were urged on by their acquaintances. And as their names were called they approached the impure and impious sacrifices. Some of them were pale and trembled as if they were not about to sacrifice… so that they were jeered at by the multitude who stood around, as was plain to everyone that they were afraid either to die or sacrifice. But some advanced to the altars more readily, declaring boldly that they had never been Christians… Of the rest… some fled and some were seized. [Letter of Dionysius to Fabian.][13]

Those who refused the imperial decree were in breach of the law and should have been imprisoned and then dealt with by due process, but passions were stirred and a new glut of mob violence accompanied the process, echoing the millennium riots of just two years earlier. Dionysius recalls a man called Julian who was unable to walk and, accordingly, was brought forward to the sacrificial altar by two helpers. This man bravely refused to deny his god as did one of those who had helped him forward and they were immediately seized by the onlookers, strapped to camels and publicly scourged across the entire city before being burned alive 'surrounded by all the populace'. A soldier named Besas tried to intervene on their behalf, but he too fell victim to the crowd and was beheaded. It is not even clear if Besas was himself a Christian or just trying to assert law and order. Others were sentenced to torture and death by fire according to the law, including various women. Some, however, escaped with their lives. A brave boy of fifteen called Dioscorus was brought before a judge who did everything he could to persuade the lad into making a sacrifice. He was taken away and tortured, but eventually let go, the judge saying that 'on account of his youth he would give him time for repentance'.[14]

Similar scenes occurred in Carthage where the incumbent bishop was an educated upper class convert called Thascus Caecilius Cyprianus (or Cyprian as he is generally known). He is one of the best historical sources for our period because many of his letters and sermons survive, and we will hear a lot more from him in the coming pages. He described a headlong rush up the hill by the frightened Christians to the civic centre where the formal sacrifice was being conducted. Some offered bribes to get their exemptions while still others were simply handed them by sympathetic officials who did not want to cause a bloodbath. Cyprian himself was targeted by the mob who demanded that he be thrown to the lions. He went into hiding along with many of his flock, and despite having enlarged at great length in his recent sermons on the joys of martyrdom, he managed to avoid that fate by keeping his head down. But even so there were a great many people who refused to run away, and having failed to turn up at the appointed time they were hunted down and dragged before zealous officials. Many of these individuals, of whatever sex or social station, were tortured in detention. Some could not withstand this and so made the required sacrifice under duress. Others died in custody or were given lesser sentences such as banishment and confiscation.[15]

Martyrdom was regarded as the highest honour by the Christian faithful. Relics of sainted men and women were assiduously collected by the remaining flock because they were thought to have magical powers. The cult of martyrdom was so strong at the time that some obdurate believers actively sought it. In this they followed the teaching of St. Paul who had said that he wanted 'to know the power of his [Christ's] resurrection and participation in his sufferings, becoming like him in his death, and so, somehow, attaining to the resurrection from the dead'.[16] Paul had eventually achieved this aim sometime around 65 CE in Rome during the reign of Nero. According to this powerful theology, to die a martyr's death was to instantly travel to paradise into the eternal presence of God and Jesus Christ, and also to be revered by those left behind in this world of suffering. So much is evident from the great Christian writers of the day including Cyprian of Carthage and his master Tertullian, and also Dionysius, bishop of Alexandria.[17]

The most influential Christian intellectual of the day, however, was now an old man, an ascetic called Origen of Alexandria who had travelled widely, taught many bishops, and written many commentaries on the scriptures which had helped define the increasingly sophisticated theology. He was known and respected across the Christian world and even beyond it, having preached to the imperial household in more sympathetic times. More enthusiastic than most, he is reported to have castrated himself as a youth according to an instruction in the gospel of St. Matthew. Origen was another writer who had written an exhortation to martyrdom (his own father had been martyred, it was said). Now the authorities hunted him down and captured him. The learned old man was slung into prison and mercilessly tortured, but his captors refused to give him the death that he had written so approvingly of.

At this point in the narrative we must leave Dionysius and Cyprian in hiding, and poor Origen with his tormentors, shut in an iron collar with his flesh subjected to flaying claws. Sadly he was to remain in that miserable state for some time.

Qitmir

The persecution was a major shock to the developing Christian church and various tales concerning it persisted into later times. The most interesting legend is the story of the so-called 'seven sleepers of Ephesus' (variants have three, five, eight or nine of them). These devout young men refused to renounce their faith and so gave away their worldly possessions and retired to a cave outside the city. This angered the emperor who ordered the mouth of the cave to be sealed off to suffocate those within (a most unlikely story given that Decius probably never went to Ephesus). Over 250 years later, in the reign of Theodosius II, the cave was re-opened by the landowner who was astonished to find the seven alive and well! For their part, they thought they had slept but a single night. One of them stumbled into town to buy food and was astonished and delighted to see beautiful Christian churches adorning the streets all around. He tried to buy bread with an ancient and obsolete coin bearing the image of Decius, which raised suspicion, and so was brought before the Bishop of Ephesus to explain himself. The bishop was convinced by his story and thus the legend was born: accounts circulated rapidly and the existence of a church in the city dedicated to the sleepers is attested from as early as the sixth century. The miracle became included in the summary of Decius's reign as recorded by later Byzantine chroniclers such as George Cedrenus who accepted it as a true wonder. It also spread rapidly among Syriac and Arab writers and found its way into the Qu'ran (early seventh century) in the Surah Al-Khaf, which adds the detail that the sleepers were accompanied by a faithful dog called Qitmir who slept through that long night with his forelegs out-stretched at the cave entrance.[18]

Marauders on the borders

There are indications that security problems arose in Gaul in the year 250. A series of inscriptions dedicated to the emperor have been found in the vicinity of Mainz (Roman Mogontiacum) and Heidelberg which have been interpreted as indicating fighting on the Gallic frontier, and two coin hoards in Alsace terminate at this time. An enigmatic statement in one late historical source tells us that Decius 'suppressed a civil war which had been fomented in Gaul' which might indicate another short-lived rebellion in one of the legions in the face of the security threat.[19]

Evidence from coin hoarding in the area of the upper Danube points to another incursion in that sector the same year which could fit an emerging pattern of coordinated raiding on different parts of the frontier. It is also likely that the Carpi raided Roman Dacia again, having recovered after Philip's defeat of them, and that Decius made a visit to the province in person. That would fit with the prominence that the province received on his coinage. Additional evidence comes from an inscription of 250 that describes Decius as 'restorer of Dacia' and also founder of a new colony for military veterans at Apulum (now Alba Iulia in Romania). Apulum was a great legionary base that housed *legio* XIII *gemina*. The inscription does not entirely prove that Decius was there in person but it seems plausible that he would have visited the province in his first year as emperor if he judged that his power base in Rome was secure. Additional evidence that he or his generals campaigned in both Gaul and Dacia in 250 comes from milestones carved in the latter half of the year which describe him as *dacicus maximus*.[20]

In or around September there was more cause for celebration as Decius raised his younger son Hostilian to the rank of *caesar* to match his brother Herennius Etruscus. The ceremony may have taken place at Viminacium on the Danube, the place where Decius himself had been proclaimed the previous year and where a special medallion was minted in honour of the young prince. It seems the brothers shared the title *princeps iuventutis*, or Prince of the Youth from then on.[21]

Meanwhile, far to the south, there was trouble brewing among the tribes in Nubia in modern day Sudan. These people were variously known to the Romans as Blemmyes, Megabaroi, and Noubai, and there were also the cave-dwelling Troglodytes along the Red Sea coast. Pliny the Elder had claimed that the Blemmyes were headless, with their eyes and mouths in their chests, which perhaps reminds us how little some urbane Romans knew of what lay beyond the outer reaches of their empire, in the first century at least. The geographer Strabo, more accurately, and with an element of pathos, described them thus: 'they are not too numerous, nor do they live closely together, for they inhabit a long, narrow and winding river valley [the upper reaches of the Nile]...Nor are they well prepared either for war or for life in general.' Nevertheless the Blemmyes seem to have grown in strength and numbers by the mid-third century: their kings, with their allies the Noubai, wielded significant military power which the Roman governors usually contained in the normal way via generous diplomacy mixed with the threat of military reprisals for bad behaviour. Important trade routes from India crossed through Blemmye lands and traders were generally allowed to travel to and fro while everyone profited from the general peace and security.[22]

Unfortunately this situation was seriously upset in 250, leading to warfare. It seems likely that the entire region had been destabilized by the first wave of plague which was followed by widespread famine when harvests went uncollected. The garrisons became seriously depleted and the Blemmyes raided the empire, causing enough of a problem for the event to be remembered in later times. Order was restored, but with biological warfare according to a seventh-century Byzantine source known as the *Chronicon Paschale* (or Easter Chronicle) which seems to have obtained its dubious information from some earlier, unknown source. It tells us that Decius 'brought from dry Libya poisonous snakes and dreadful hermaphrodites and released them at the Egyptian frontier because of the barbarians, the Noubades and the Blemmyes'.[23]

Chapter 4

Escalation of the Gothic War

Palimpsests and spurinyms

The lovely word palimpsest derives from the Greek to 'rub smooth' (*psestos*) 'again' (*palin*). In textual studies it denotes something that has been written on, cleaned, then written over again. That happened frequently in medieval Europe when neither papyrus nor paper was available and parchment made from animal skin was so expensive. Unwanted second-hand texts were frequently effaced and the vellum washed and re-purposed, but modern forensic techniques can often reveal what was written before. Sometimes the original text is of considerably more interest than the over-write, and very occasionally a scholar is lucky enough to find something really sensational.

That is what happened in 2008 when a team from the Austrian Academy of Sciences began work on a palimpsest found among the pages of a mundane Byzantine manuscript on ecclesiastical law held in the collection of the National Library in Vienna.[1] Someone in the thirteenth century had inserted some pages into this volume including a curse on book thieves. Although barely visible to the naked eye, four leaves – eight pages – of this inserted section had been re-purposed. In 2013, a technical and scientific team was able to recover the lines using a combination of multi-spectral imaging and digital enhancement, separating it from the much more obvious over-write (Plate 2). Ultimately, this led to the almost complete decipherment of all but two pages of the dense text. It was a very tedious and complicated task according to the scholars – but more than worth the effort.

What has been revealed are six pages from *Scythica*, a long-lost history of the Gothic wars of the third century written in Greek by the Athenian statesman and general Dexippus. This man lived through the period and even took an active part in the fighting. To their great credit, the team published preliminary transcriptions and images of the palimpsest as soon as they were able, making it available to a range of specialists so others could assist in the interpretation. They and other scholars have subsequently translated it into English which proves of enormous use in understanding the events that surround the great Battle of Abritus in 251 CE, and much else besides.

It was already known that the *Scythica* existed, not least because various Byzantine authors actually record having read it, and a series of other excerpts have come down to us independently, copied into other compendia. Fortunately, the new fragments were all previously unknown, and their content is extremely informative and exciting. Even so, most of the *Scythica* is still missing and we must hold on to the slender hope that more might be deciphered or discovered in some other ancient palimpsest.[2] What we now have, however, is enough to flesh out the bare-bones summaries and narratives of the war that were made by other Byzantine historians.

Scholarly research on the text (which has been dubbed the *Scythica Vindobonensia*, or Vienna *Scythica*) proceeded apace, culminating in a summary publication in 2020 which includes images of the entire text, an updated transcription of the Greek text, and many scholarly perspectives on the historical context.[3] We will make frequent use of this research in the coming pages. For now, however, one important side-effect of the discovery is worth expanding on – its corroboratory effect on the uniquely valuable Gothic history of Jordanes, another important source which has already been mentioned in passing.

Early in 551, a scholar called Jordanes made a summary (in just a few days, and from memory by his own account) of a history of the Gothic peoples that he had previously read twice but did not at that moment have access to. The source work had been written about thirty years earlier in twelve books by Cassiodorus, a senior figure in the court of the Ostrogothic King Theodoric the Great in Rome (reigned 493–526).[4] Theodoric himself had commissioned it, and because Jordanes described himself as being of Gothic descent, we can expect the result (which he titled *Getica*) to be broadly favourable to the Goths. Jordanes tells us that the Goths had kept their history alive orally – 'they sang of the deeds of their ancestors in strains of song accompanied by the cithara'. Some scholars have been deeply critical of the *Getica* because it contains very obviously mythic elements, not least the participation of Goths in the Trojan War and fighting ancient Egyptian pharaohs. Part of the polemical intention behind it was to present them as an ancient people with a deep history equivalent to, and on a par with, other nations. But events of the third century are less obviously mythological and most historians have regarded the *Getica* as containing valuable information about the period from a Gothic perspective.[5]

Much of the debate has focussed on the activity of various Gothic nobles from our period of interest, most notably King Ostrogotha and another leader called Cniva. The critical historians have been wont to regard Ostrogotha in particular as mythic or fictional, his name being some kind of heroic back-projection of the people who much later called themselves Ostrogoths ('eastern Goths'). Jordanes placed Ostrogotha as a grandson of King Amal who had given his name to the royal Amal lineage, and he was father of another King called Hunuil. The line of descent is then traced through many more generations all the way down to Theodoric the Great himself. Because of this apparent 'pedigree-making' it was confidently stated that the name Ostrogotha was a 'spurinym' (fake name) with 'no roots in Gothic oral history'. Cniva was considered by some to be a little more believable, although others also rejected him as a historical figure. The collateral damage in this debate was not just to dismiss the historicity of these individuals but everything Jordanes said they did.[6]

One curious piece of evidence that was sometimes overlooked in these discussions is an epic Anglo-Saxon poem called *Widsith*. This is a candidate for being the oldest surviving English language text, and some scholars think its original formulation could be as old as the sixth or seventh century. The poem is a kind of romp through famous kings and nations of the past that the bard Widsith (the name means 'Long Journey') claims to have visited. Our guide spent time with Huns, Goths, Vandals, Gepids, Saxons, Burgundians, Franks, Scots, Picts, Assyrians, Israelites, Indians, Egyptians, and so on, and even met Julius Caesar and Theodoric on his imaginary travels. One can almost sense the glow and crackle of a Dark Age hall as *Widsith* conjures up a larger world than the listeners could ever encounter, populated by peoples and heroes from far afield. For our purposes it is worth noting that among the many great names mentioned is 'Eastgota, the wise and virtuous father of Unwen'. Eastgota and Unwen are etymologically similar to the Ostrogotha and Hunuil of Jordanes, which coincidence led some scholars to think that the *Widsith* may record an independent oral tradition of a historical Ostrogotha that had made it as far as early Anglo-Saxon England. The poem concludes with the sentiment that 'he who wins fame has lasting glory under the heavens'.[7]

The stunning fact revealed by the Vienna Palimpsest is that (as we shall see in proceeding with the narrative) the actions of both Ostrogotha and Cniva are reported in detail by Dexippus of Athens who was their contemporary. It is as if some ancient British text from the sixth century had been found detailing the activities of a historical King Arthur, rather to the chagrin of those who had confidently proclaimed that he never existed. There can be no doubt that Ostrogotha and Cniva were real, live, flesh-and-blood characters. The upshot of all this is that the value of the *Getica* has undoubtedly been enhanced by the discovery of the Vienna palimpsest. It is appropriate to rein in some of the scepticism, which is not to say that we can now use Jordanes uncritically. Indeed there are significant points of difference between him and the new *Scythica* which are interesting to ponder.[8]

The Goths

The 'barbarian' confederation under King Ostrogotha was a far greater threat to the empire than the Blemmyes and other peripheral peoples. Although the Goths had been beaten back in 248, possibly, as we have speculated, by the ill-fated general Pacatian, they remained a substantial threat to the richly metalliferous province of Dacia and the provinces of Lower Moesia and Thrace to the south. Decius had a reputation for severity and was facing an ongoing financial crisis, so he was not about to resume paying their subsidy. That meant that more warfare was guaranteed.

Who exactly were the Goths? Naming the various trans-Danubian tribes and understanding their relation to each other is challenging, not least because groupings could disappear, amalgamate and split and be known by more than one name or even a nickname. Later historians tended to use ethnic terms more suited to their own times, while Dexippus, the Greek historian who wrote most about them in the third century, generally referred to all the northern 'barbarians' as Scyths. This was an archaic name, seemingly used in deference to Herodotus who wrote nearly a millennium before him, and it is most unlikely that anyone actually identified as a Scyth at the time.[9]

The tribal name 'Goth' or its variants had been in use since at least the first century, at which time it indicated a people who inhabited the southern shore of the Baltic Sea in an area that is now part of northern Poland. According to Jordanes, this people had earlier migrated from Scandinavia and of course there is still a large area of Sweden called Gothland. They called their new home on the other side of the Baltic 'Gothiscandzan', which, it has been suggested, is the root of the name for the modern Polish port city of Gdansk, although that idea is controversial. Their wandering was to continue in the second century at which time they moved *en masse* towards the area of the Black (Pontic) Sea following the river routes of the Vistula and Bug, eventually arriving in an area just beyond the imperial frontier. Here they thrived:

> Now the Gothic race gained great fame in the region where they were then dwelling, that is in the Scythian land on the shore of Pontus, holding undisputed sway over great stretches of country, many arms of the sea and many river courses. By their strong right arm the Vandals were often laid low, the Marcomanni held their footing by paying tribute and the princes of the Quadi were reduced to slavery. [Jordanes, *Getica* XVI, 89.]

This story receives some support from the archaeological record, notably the progressive expansion of the so-called Wielbark and Černjachov (or

Chernyakhiv) Cultures across the neck of Europe in the second century. Their arrival in the second century may well have disturbed the Marcomanni, another Germanic tribe who had previously inhabited the border zone beyond the Roman Empire. It has been argued that the press of this migration was the underlying cause for Rome's so-called Marcomannic Wars in the reign of Marcus Aurelius.[10]

Many modern historians baulk at the idea of ethnic groups moving into new homelands and displacing one another through violence and warfare. The spread of a culture does not necessarily entail great men leading entire peoples to new territories. It may be that it was fashion, language and ideas that were spreading – or memes if one prefers – rather than ferocious warriors. Particular suspicion attaches to the nineteenth and twentieth century tendency for tracing back the origins of distinct 'peoples' such as the Germans, Franks or English for nationalistic or political propaganda, a process that has been called ethno-fabrication.[11]

Clearly we must tread carefully in debates like these while trying to avoid a false dichotomy. People did move around in antiquity, sometimes in large groups (witness the amazing marches of the Vandals and Visigoths in the fifth century), and they frequently made war on one another and committed atrocities. Other people undoubtedly adopted and changed their languages, fashions and customs through time, and generally intermixed peaceably. The Baltic Goths of the first century were certainly not the undiluted ancestral pool for those who challenged Rome in the third, still less for later groups such as the Ostrogoths and Visigoths of the fourth and fifth centuries, or the Gothic kingdoms of the sixth. Nor are the Goths the only tribal grouping that crops up in the historical sources as having moved, geographically, from northern Europe to the fringes of the Roman Empire. Others included the Heruls, Vandals, Tervingi, Bastarnae and Sciri, all of which may have contributed to the Černjachov Culture. There were also other major ethnic groups in the area north of the lower Danube and Black Sea such as the aforementioned Carpi and various nomadic or semi-nomadic Iranian-speaking steppe tribes including the Sarmatians and Alans. These peoples might have intermixed and adopted Gothic ways or at other times they may have coordinated with them while retaining a separate identity.[12]

Argaithus and Guntheric

The normal Roman policy after an invasion of imperial territory was to mount a major expedition into *barbaricum* with the aim of punishing the guilty. The Romans excelled at the kind of unequal warfare in which superior drill, discipline, weaponry, tactics and logistics made up for weight of numbers. But achieving a professional military strike force was not something that could be undertaken quickly. Extensive planning was required; troop levies would be raised and the units earmarked for an expedition would require training and organization and be ready to move into the sector of operations in an orderly manner. Weapons, equipment, money and food would need to be stockpiled, then effectively deployed and defended in campaigning baggage trains. Large numbers of pack animals were required as well as cavalry mounts. Although the historical sources are silent on the matter, we can reasonably assume that Decius initiated such preparations as soon as he came to power.

For the time being, however, he had to rely on the frontier legions to hold their sectors. The province of Lower Moesia on the lower Danube remained the most exposed, having suffered from the recent incursions. Accordingly, Decius appointed one of his ablest and most trusted commanders, a man of consular rank called Caius Vibius Alfinius Trebonianus Gallus to the governorship there, and he very likely beefed up the strength of the frontier legions under Gallus's command.

But the Goths were not simply going to wait for a great Roman expedition to be formed against them. Once again they assembled large numbers of men in arms on the opposite river bank and launched another invasion across the Danube, seemingly in the spring of 250.[13] Jordanes summarizes the force thus:

> Ostrogotha, king of the Goths… led out three hundred thousand armed men, having as allies for this war some of the Taifali and Astringi and also three thousand of the Carpi, a race of men very ready to make war and frequently hostile to the Romans… Besides these tribes, Ostrogotha had Goths and Peucini from the island of Peuce, which lies in the mouths of the Danube where they empty into the Sea of Pontus. He placed in command Argaithus and Guntheric, the noblest leaders of his race. [Jordanes, *Getica* XVI, 90–91.]

Most historians consider numbers like 300,000 warriors to be habitual exaggerations. In this case, it may be a problem with the text itself, and an alternative reading of 30,000 is favoured by some.[14] However, given that the force seems to have been split into two commands, it should not be dismissed out of hand. Of the named tribes, the Taifali are a mysterious group, and historians are uncertain if they were Germanic or Asiatic (possibly Sarmatian) in origin. This is their first appearance on the stage of history, although they do re-appear in the fragmentary records of the later third and fourth centuries.[15] The Astringi were a group of Vandals (also known as 'Hasdingian' Vandals) and the Peucini were a tribe of Celts on the lower Danube. The 'island' of

Peuce was at that time a mound of deltaic sediments projecting into the Black Sea that has since been silted up and incorporated into the wider delta system. It was nominally Roman territory but may have been lawless since the destructive invasion of 248.

Archaeological evidence of destruction and the timing and distribution of coin hoards gives clues as to what happened but the evidence must be interpreted with caution. Destruction layers may have nothing to do with hostile action: fire was a frequent hazard in the Roman world. Coin hoards offer a precise location for an event but only an approximate date. If the youngest coin in a pot is of a particular year, such as 250, then it could have been buried then or at any time after, in principle (the date is technically called a '*terminus post quem*'). Interpreting the likely date of burial for a hoard relies on some factors that can be treated statistically and some that cannot. For instance a large collection of coins is more likely to include more up-to-date issues than a small one. But in periods like ours, when the administration was regularly debasing the money, people might have preferentially hoarded earlier issues. A single small hoard is not very informative, but multiple hoards in a particular area with similar termination dates are obviously more reliable.[16]

Argaithus (or Argaith) and Guntheric are Gothic names – the first means something like 'Oath of Command' in the Gothic language, and the second 'Battle Prince'. Argaithus may perhaps be identified with 'Argunt, the king of the Scythians' who, according to Julius Capitolinus, one of the supposed authors of the *Historia Augusta* 'was devastating the kingdoms of his neighbours' around the time of Philip's accession in 244. If so, it seems to indicate that Roman sources had some record of this individual independent of the Gothic tradition. If he was a king in 244, he was subordinate to Ostrogotha in 250, at least in Jordanes's account.[17]

The fact that two men are named suggests a division of command with two major objectives. The evidence from hoarding indicates that their army penetrated the Roman frontier once again somewhere on the lower Danube (Map 4). There could be no permanent bridges or even roads in this unstable, low-lying and featureless maze, so getting the men and baggage across must have been a major undertaking which was presumably facilitated by the local knowledge of the Peucini tribe. It was possible: in the previous century the emperor Trajan had managed to take a Roman campaign army across the delta going in the other direction.[18]

Unlike the more spontaneous invasion of 248, this one seems to have been planned with great care and the cities themselves were targeted. The cities of Moesia and Thrace had all been provided with strong walls and fortifications by the Emperor Marcus Aurelius at the time of the Marcomannic Wars in the late second century, and so could attempt to defend themselves. Once across, the Gothic army seems to have advanced about 300km to lay siege to Marcianopolis (now Devnya, Bulgaria) in the Province of Moesia Inferior while, according to the chronology preferred here, a second detachment marched onward, skirting the eastern foothills of the Haemus (Balkan) Mountains and moved deep into the province of Thrace, besieging its capital and richest city, Philippopolis. These moves strongly imply that the Goths were once again able to temporarily neutralize the local Moesian legions, *legio* XI *claudia* and *legio* I *italica* upstream at Novae, along with their associated auxiliary units.[19]

The neutralizing of all these forces could have been achieved by bottling the troops up in their fortresses using overwhelming numbers rather than fighting pitched battles, which would fit with Jordanes's assertion that this was a very large-scale invasion and not merely raiding war-bands. The Goths may have calculated that the depleted forces facing them would concentrate in the big legionary bases and not sally forth until sufficient reinforcements had arrived in the sector, so their aim would have been to create sufficient time for plundering and then to get back across the Danube with a haul of loot and captives before that had happened.

Marcianopolis and Philippopolis were both major urban centres with splendid architecture and advanced civic facilities including great aqueducts, baths, temple complexes and trading emporia: far more sophisticated than anything that existed in the land of the Goths. Both cities had thriving industries, which at Marcianopolis included substantial workshops sculpting imported marble into statues and ornate pediments. Both had an active mint producing bronze coins for their local economies. Each city functioned as an administrative hub for a large agricultural hinterland that was no doubt systematically raided and despoiled by the invaders after most of the inhabitants had fled to the relative safety of the walled cities, either taking their transportable wealth with them or burying it in secret places. It seems that neither city had a significant garrison, so the defence had to be organized by the inhabitants. These citizens were probably well-dressed with fashionable hairstyles (the ladies) and neatly trimmed beards (the men) whereas the Goths were shaggy, wild-eyed desperados, at least if contemporaneous art is to be trusted. Rome must have suddenly seemed a very long way away. The terror of the situation is not difficult to imagine: if a city fell, the entire population would either be slaughtered or enslaved and dragged away into *barbaricum*. All portable valuables would be stolen, and everything left over destroyed.[20]

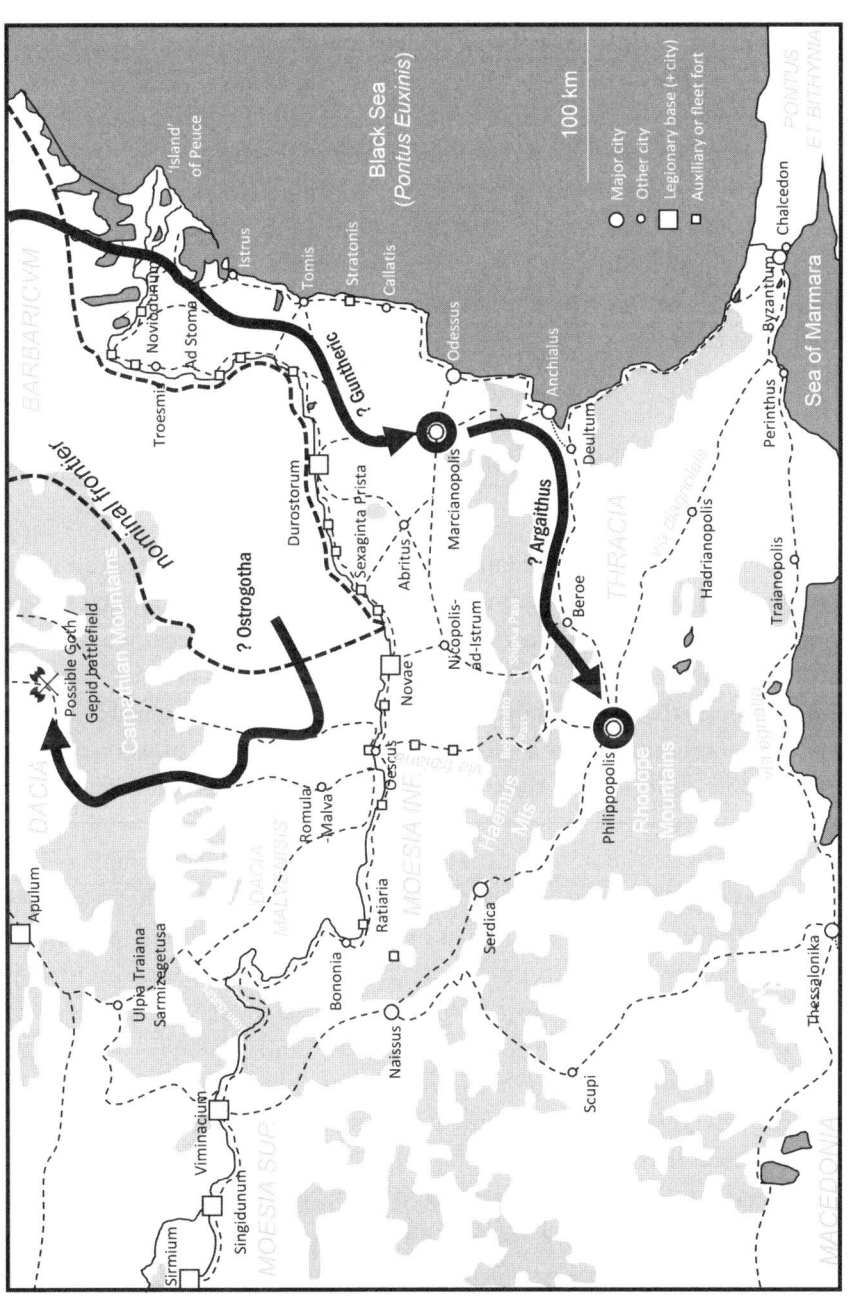

Map 4. Reconstruction of the invasion of Argaithus and Guntheric and the sieges of Marcianopolis and Philippopolis, 250 CE. Ostrogotha may have been campaigning simultaneously in Roman Dacia. The Battle of Galtis between Goths and Gepids is based on Jordanes.

Separate accounts of both sieges extracted from Dexippus's *Scythica* survive via a tenth century compendium of writings on siege warfare.[21] We will turn our attention first to Philippopolis. This had a population of about 100,000, making it one of the largest provincial cities of the empire. A traveller from the eastern provinces in the second century had called it 'the largest and most beautiful of all cities', and as Bulgarian Plovdiv it remains a beautiful place today with a claim to be one of the oldest continuously occupied cities of Europe. In Roman times it was furnished with the full range of monumental public buildings including a theatre, race-track, and three large aqueducts bringing fresh water into the city. Note that this Philippopolis is not to be confused with the town of the same name in Syria, previously discussed; this one was named after Philip of Macedon, father of Alexander the Great, rather than the recently defeated emperor Philip. An alternative name for it was Trimontium ('the three hills') after the rocky eminences on which it was built and around which its fortifications had been constructed.

We learn from Dexippus that the Goths first reconnoitred the walls looking for weaknesses and then launched an attack using skirmishers and arrow shot, but were beaten back. Then there was a lull while they built a range of siege equipment including leather-clad wooden cages, battering rams, ladders and wheeled towers which were fitted with drawbridges and designed to advance right up to the wall. One detail is that the ladders were extensible, using runners, like something from a modern hardware store. They were run out using ropes and pulleys until they were the right height to reach the top of the wall.

All this challenges some preconceptions about 'barbarian' armies which were long thought to be too unsophisticated for operating the necessary technical contraptions. Some academics have dismissed Dexippus's account as merely a series of well-worn 'tropes' in the style of the ancient Greek histories that tells us little if anything about what actually happened. But we should remember that the Goths had fought alongside Roman armies in the east for at least a generation and that a significant number of disaffected Roman soldiers (enough to have been recorded by Jordanes) had joined Ostrogotha after having been discharged following the recent revolt of Pacatian. And if the Goths laid siege to great cities at all, it seems scarcely credible that they would have done so without a viable strategy for success. Dexippus himself knew the enemy well from his own later military exploits and it is reasonable to assume that his intended readership would also have had a fair idea of what the Goths were capable of.[22]

To return to Dexippus's description: the resistance proved strong as the defenders dropped rocks and logs down on the ladders. They also managed to smash some of the advancing siege contraptions, along with the men within them, by dropping rocks 'as big as wagons' from the parapets (it was, and still is, a rocky city, with plentiful means of quarrying within the circuit walls). Other machines were burnt to the ground with torches, brimstone and burning pitch as the assault faltered and then failed altogether.

In desperation, the Goths then decided to build a giant mound against a weak point in the city wall. Construction began with a row of wooden stakes driven into the ditch at the base of the wall, then the space between this screen and the wall was filled up with 'dirt and all kinds of wooden stuff'. As the mound grew, the defenders augmented their own wall with wooden towers and planks to help maintain the height advantage. And then, one night:

> ... at a secluded spot, they lowered by rope from the wall a man who was both brave and noble, giving him a burning torch and a jar full of pitch, brimstone and other combustibles to set fire to the mound. And indeed he set fire to the beams supporting the mound and when the whole mass went up in flames the mound collapsed. Dexippus, *Scythica* fragment[23]

Unfortunately we don't know the name of this intrepid hero. The desperate Goths tried to rebuild their smouldering pile, and perhaps with an element of vengeance they resorted to killing all the sick and old prisoners and some of the pack animals and dumping the bodies onto the heap with other detritus. We learn the grizzly detail that 'three days later the bodies had swollen so much that they caused the mound to rise considerably'. The defenders countered this new threat by cutting a hole in their own wall and sapping the stinking mound from within. At this, the Goths gave up and withdrew.

Meanwhile at Marcianopolis (west of modern Devnya) the refined citizenry were faced with a similar terrifying prospect against massed barbarians. But as at Philippopolis, the walls, gates and towers were in good repair and the Goths were unable to succeed by direct assault so they set about piling up rocks ('like a wave'). Here we learn that the defence was led by a certain Maximus, otherwise unknown to history, whom Dexippus described as 'a man whose entire life was steeped in philosophy' but who was 'ready at that moment to show the behaviour suitable not just of a general, but a brave soldier'. Assaults on the walls were beaten off so the Goths resorted to a hail of javelins, arrows and rocks aimed at the defenders, but with little effect. They withdrew entirely for a few days, perhaps trying to lure the inhabitants out of the city, but Maximus was too wily to drop his guard. Soon the attackers returned, launching another failed assault and massing once again at the foot of the walls. The defenders had evidently been collecting rocks and missiles that had been fired into the city because at this point the *ad hoc* commander decided it was time to return fire. A furious rain of missiles caught the close-packed Goths by surprise and inflicted such severe casualties that they also decided to withdraw completely 'having accomplished nothing', at least according to Dexippus.

The Gothic commanders of both sieges knew that their window of opportunity was time-limited, being wary of other forces arriving in the sector and potentially cutting off their line of retreat as seems to have happened in 248. And Jordanes, who wrote from their perspective, tells us that the Goths also received payments from the local people to go away. They returned across the Danube with a significant amount of booty and slaves from the countryside and with their forces substantially intact.[24]

The Gepids

Why did King Ostrogotha not lead the invasion himself? Of course there are all sorts of possible reasons, but it may be that he himself was campaigning against Roman Dacia at the same time. The available histories make no mention of this but it fits the wider pattern and would have made sense for the Goths to launch simultaneous assaults in different areas to stretch the imperial defences. The raids into Moesia and Thrace were aimed at gaining booty from the empire, but the warfare in Dacia may have had the more exalted aim of permanently wresting control of that mineral-rich district from the Romans and bringing it within the Gothic confederation.

The uniquely valuable Gothic history of Jordanes tells us that the invasion of Argaithus and Guntheric was followed by a period of infighting between the forces of King Ostrogotha and a group called the Gepids under King Fastida. These Gepids were universally regarded as a branch of the Goths, but legend had it that they had been in the rear of the great pan-European migration and so were still concentrated far to the north, in the area of the Vistula river (in modern day Poland): the very name Gepid was derived from the Gothic word for something slow. This prejudice seems to have persisted into Jordanes's own time because he referred to them as 'slow of thought and too sluggish for quick movement of their bodies'. They were, nevertheless, jealous of the booty brought back by the raiders, and Fastida wanted to expand the Gepid homelands. Jordanes's account has no parallel among the Greek or Roman authors and so is presumably based on Gothic oral history. The tale starts with an exchange of ambassadors and a bout of negotiation that failed to resolve the Gepids' complaint, whereupon:

The Gepids hastened to take arms and Ostrogotha likewise moved his forces against them, lest he should seem a coward. They met at the town of Galtis, near which the river Auha flows, and there both sides fought with great valour; indeed the similarity of their arms and of their manner of fighting turned them against their own men. But the better cause and their natural alertness aided the Goths. Finally night put an end to the battle as a part of the Gepids were giving way. Then Fastida, king of the Gepids, left the field of slaughter and hastened to his own land, as much humiliated with shame and disgrace as formerly he had been elated with pride. The Goths returned victorious, content with the retreat of the Gepidae, and dwelt in peace and happiness in their own land so long as Ostrogotha was their leader. [Jordanes, Getica XVII.99–100.]

It has been suggested that the town of Galtis is 'Galt' which is still the German name for the Romanian town of Ungra on the Olt River (in Latin, Aluta) in modern Romania (located to the top centre of Map 4). If so, this was nominally inside Roman Dacia in the foothills of the Carpathian Mountains. This is evidence – admittedly weak – that Ostrogotha himself was assaulting the area in 250 while his subordinates were raiding south of the Danube. In any case, this Gothic infighting may have taken up much of the rest of the year, allowing the Romans in Moesia and Thrace something of a breather.[25]

Decius in Rome

In January of 251 (the third year of the new millennium, if anyone was still counting) Decius assumed his second consulship, this time alongside his elder son Herennius Etruscus. The first emperor Augustus had famously claimed to have found Rome built of brick but left it in marble. The city had been neglected of late, so in a first sign of his own intention to embellish the capital, Decius ordered construction of a new public bath complex on the Aventine Hill to be called, naturally enough, the Baths of Decius (*thermae decianae*). This district had a reputation for being rather rough and ready, hence the emperor may have decided the inhabitants could do with a sweet makeover. (The building no longer survives and most of what we know about the complex comes to us via accurate plans made in 1554 by the famous Renaissance architect Andrea Palladio.) Inscriptional evidence suggests that Decius also constructed a new *porticus* (elegant colonnade) in the ceremonial heart of the city near the Capitoline Hill and ordered repair and refurbishment of the Colosseum which had suffered fire damage after a lightning strike – something that was no doubt interpreted as another sign of the recent displeasure of the gods.[26]

The monetary system also needed attention after a long period of turbulence and inflation. The silver content of the double-denarius had continued to slide in recent years and the bronze sestertius was being struck at lower weight and often with much less care and attention than had been the case in the past. Decius showed his innovative side by ordering the issue of a heavy double-sestertius, with radiate crown (denoting a double), to be tariffed at four to the double-denarius. The reverse design shows *felicitas saeculi*, 'Happiness of the age', with Felicity carrying the horn of plenty. These large-flanned coins were made with great care and attention at the mint, and were a visual reminder of the prestige of the reforming emperor. The idea seems to have been to restore the old coinage system, albeit at twice the original face value. Decius also reintroduced an old bronze denomination known as the semis, worth just one sixty-fourth of the double-denarius, so there would be loose change as well. For reasons that are not entirely clear, however, these experiments in monetary reform failed and the old denominations were soon resumed.[27]

Another innovation ordered by the emperor was to open a new imperial mint in the north of Italy at Mediolanum (Milan). It seems this city was designated as a kind of mustering point where troops could be concentrated and made ready to move up to the Rhine or Danube sectors as desired. It was more economical to manufacture pay on the spot rather than bring it all the way up from Rome. Numismatists have inferred that the new mint operated with three *officinae* in addition to the six still in operation at Rome. Judging from the style, some of the engravers, and even some of the dies, seem to have translocated from Rome. This move is evidence that Decius was still preparing to inflict a mighty blow on the Goths when hostilities resumed.[28]

Intriguingly, the emperor ordered the Milan mint to produce an unprecedented series of coins honouring the deified emperors of the past. This had never happened before, so we can be sure the order came from the very top. All sorts of motives for it have been discussed by historians. Most plausibly, the intention was to remind the populace of the benefits of wise rule in happier times and of associating the current emperor with the virtues of all the good men that went before him. It also underlined the high status of the official imperial cult that Decius was so insistent upon: the deified emperors were expected to be worshipped everywhere alongside the so-called Capitoline Triad of Jupiter, Juno and Minerva. On another level, the coins may also have been designed as another collectable set following the success of Philip's millennium games series, although they were not numbered in the same way.[29]

Around this time the emperor was immortalized in marble by an unknown master sculptor. The portrait can be seen today in Rome's Capitoline Museum.

He appears every inch the stern consul of the old Republic, commanding and self-composed, but his intelligent eyes have a deep and mournful expression as if the pressures of the job sit heavily upon him (Plate 2). From what little we know of his character it is unlikely Decius ever took a moment to relax, but if he did, he could reflect with some satisfaction that virtually the entire population of the empire had sacrificed at the altars of the gods. Never in history had there been such a universal display of piety and common purpose. The plague in Egypt had peaked, and although details are sparse, there is no indication that it had spread much further. Certainly it had not taken hold in Rome, which was what the authorities would have dreaded most. The marble quarries were busy once again, supplying public works in the city centre, and the provincial road networks had been restored. The Blemmyes of Nubia had been defeated and the Goths beaten back across the Danube for a second time having failed to capture any significant towns. No new military setbacks were reported from either the Rhine or Persian fronts. Most importantly, the army, after a prolonged and rigorous regime of training, was now spoiling for a fight when the campaigning season began. The fury of the gods, so evident of late, might just have been assuaged.

Chapter 5

Ostrogotha Takes the Initiative

Oescus

Winter was harsh in the continental climate of free Gothia, a time of ice and snow when thoughts normally turned to survival rather than warfare. Food for concentrations of men and pack animals was hard to come by, few animals stirred in the forests, and men would be needed on the farmsteads to sow seeds and tend the livestock when the frosts finally receded. Then it generally took time for warriors to amass in sufficient numbers for a new campaign to be launched. But this winter Ostrogotha seems to have kept his huge army intact, perhaps profiting from grain and fodder stripped from the farms of Roman Moesia and Thrace the previous year. His master stroke was to launch a new campaign in the depths of winter and in an unexpected quarter, apparently catching the Romans entirely by surprise.[1]

Upstream of the delta, the Danube was a wide and formidable obstacle for any invading army that could not control the waters (Plate 2). The Romans had a network of spies, but even if an attempted crossing successfully began in secret, the alert would soon have been raised and passed down the forts and watchtowers so that the river fleet would arrive on the scene in a matter of hours. A small war-band might cross the river at any time, but getting an army across dry-shod was out of the question.

But there was a chink in this defensive system. Nowadays the Danube rarely freezes in its lower reaches below the Iron Gates gorge, but before about 1950 it did so every year like clockwork, with the maximum ice thickness occurring in late January. In 251, the Goths seem to have taken advantage of the annual freeze by crossing about 200km upstream of the delta where they were probably expected to strike. Key to the new invasion strategy was to seize the river crossing at Oescus in Upper Moesia, one of three main umbilicals that connected Roman Dacia with the rest of the empire (Map 5). There was no permanent stone bridge at Oescus; instead the crossing may have used a bridge of barges or a tethered ferry system, at least once the thaw had set in. There was an old fortress there which may have housed a small garrison, but the legion that had once occupied it had vacated over a century before. An auxiliary fort at Sucidava on the north bank opposite Oescus was probably occupied at the time by a cohort of mounted archers (*cohors* I *cilicium milliaria equitata sagittariorum*) who are attested by inscriptions. It seems the Goths managed to overwhelm these defences by sending a force across the ice and securing the river crossing intact, establishing a line of communication over the Danube.[2]

Oescus itself was a major urban centre with many fine public buildings. The site is now totally deserted, and perhaps because of its isolation in northwest Bulgaria it is one of the most evocative Roman places to visit. The ruins lie in farmland near a village called Gigen which can only be approached via many miles of severely potholed roads. The archaeological park can be found behind a rusty iron gate at the village perimeter. The visitor can wander entirely alone through acres of rough ground and spoil tips littered with ornamental architecture on the grandest scale: enormous marble columns recline beside their huge drum-like bases among the bushes; ornately decorated capitals and architraves that once graced elaborate colonnades are strewn about in their hundreds and there is even an intact and inscribed temple pediment lying at a drunken angle in the grass (Plate 2). The remains of great temples dedicated to the Capitoline triad (Jupiter, Juno and Minerva) and to Fortuna lie at the centre of the complex. Many of the better known Roman sites around the empire probably once had a similar air of magnificent desolation before the visitor centres were built. One hopes Oescus will retain its lonely appeal as this author knows no better place to open a copy of Gibbon and contemplate the glory that was Rome.[3]

After securing Oescus, the Gothic strategy seems to have been to split into three substantial divisions. One army, under the leadership of Ostrogotha himself, and possibly working once again in coordination with other tribes including the Bastarnae and Carpi, seems to have remained on the north bank of the Danube and invaded Roman Dacia once again.[4] A second detachment, which according to Dexippus numbered 70,000 men and was led by a chieftain called Cniva proceeded downstream along the south bank to attack the legionary fortress of Novae (now Svishtov, Bulgaria). (Cniva apparently means 'knees' in Gothic, which is not a particularly heroic name but with its hard 'C' it sounds better in English.) Novae was home to *legio* I *italica* and it seems likely that the regional commander Trebonianus Gallus would have concentrated his forces there, bringing up *legio* XI *claudia* from Durostorum, the river fleet and whatever auxiliary forces were in the area. Cniva's intention seems to have been to eliminate the Roman threat by force of numbers as had seemingly been achieved the year before. This gave the third force under an unknown leader ('Div. 3' on Map 5) a free hand to despoil the hitherto untouched districts of Lower Moesia that lie between the Danube at Oescus and the Haemus Mountains to the south. There is no further mention of Argaithus and Guntheric, so perhaps they had been sidelined after their unsuccessful sieges of the previous year.[5]

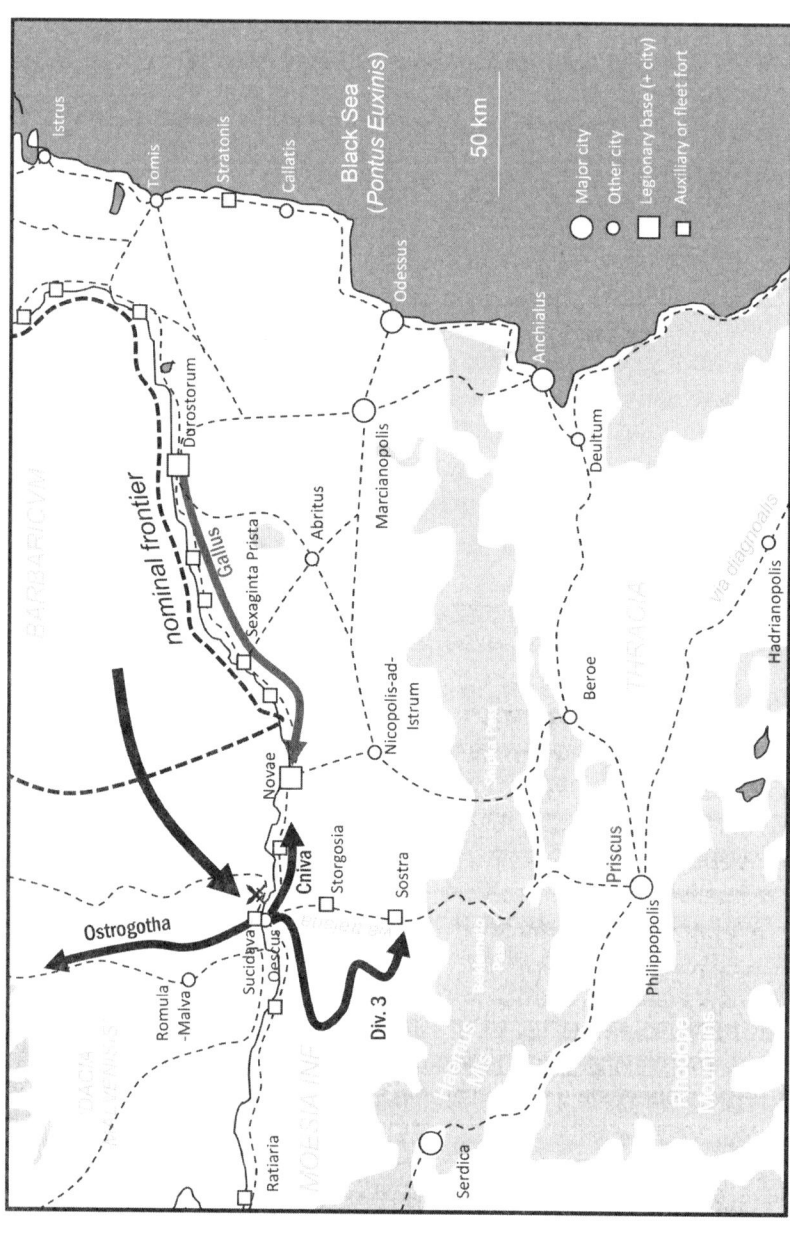

Map 5. Reconstruction of the opening moves on the Danube in 251 CE according to the interpretation preferred here. The Goths began operations in midwinter with a surprise attack on the key crossing point at Oescus. Ostrogotha then marched into Roman Dacia while Cniva on the south bank divided his force. He led one division toward the legionary base at Novae, leaving the other division ('Div. 3') free from interference to plunder part of Moesia. In response, Trebonianus Gallus, the *dux* (regional commander) concentrated his forces at Novae.

This invasion may account for the existence of a hoard of over 3,000 silver coins that was found in 1922 in a vineyard on the outskirts of the fine modern city of Pleven in northern Bulgaria, about a day's ride south of the Danube. The coins span well over a hundred years but they include three of Hostilian which must have been minted in Rome after September 250, defining the closure date for the hoard. Pleven hosted a Roman military posting station called Storgosia manned by a detachment from *legio* I *italica*, so new coin issues probably circulated there very quickly. It seems likely therefore that the owner buried the treasure when the garrison was evacuated, sometime around January of 251. Like all other hoards that have been discovered in modern times, whoever buried it never came back to collect.[6]

News of the invasion may have reached Decius in Rome by about the middle of February and likely precipitated a hurried departure. The Romans may well have been primed for an early start to the campaigning – but not this early. It took time for the war machine to swing into action; and also for the emperor and his elite praetorians and other imperial troops to move up to the sector. Weeks of worry and frantic preparations lay ahead, but it was also, one suspects, a time of great anticipation. There must have been many in the military who welcomed the prospect of a showdown with Ostrogotha and a chance to solve the chronic security problem on the Danube front with decisive military victory in the accustomed Roman style. From what we know of the emperor, that would certainly have included him.

The revolt of Valens

At about this time there was (apparently) another short-lived revolt within the empire about which very little is known. Aurelius Victor states that 'when Decius had left Rome as quickly as he could for that reason [i.e., to wage war on the Goths] Julius Valens seized the imperial power at the insistence of the common people'. The much abridged *Epitome de Caesaribus* says: 'In this man's time [i.e., Decius], Valens Lucinianus was made *imperator*'. Hence the name of the usurper was probably Julius Valens Lucinianus, although some historians suspect a scribal error and prefer to read 'Licinianus' which is a more common name that could be senatorial and would imply some degree of high level support. Based on Victor's bald statement above, most historians have dated the attempted coup to around March of 251 and placed it in Rome.

It is a peculiar circumstance, however, that anyone should attempt to usurp in the capital when the legitimate emperor was at the head of a substantial army and could very well do an about-turn to restore order by force. Moreover, it is generally thought that the younger prince Hostilian was resident in Rome, and he certainly survived the incident. Nor is there any explanation of why the people should have been so upset with Decius as to want to replace him.[7]

Another source, the oft-maligned *Historia Augusta*, says that at this time a certain Valens 'was killed after he had ruled for a few days in Illyricum', so perhaps the disturbance was somewhere on the upper Danube and not at Rome. That would make more sense: the panic caused by the Gothic invasion may have prompted one of the Illyrian legions to rebel. Either way, the power bid failed, for reasons that are lost in time. Valens never controlled a mint and we know nothing more about him except a rumour, probably fictitious, that he was the uncle or great-uncle of another obscure rebel of the Valens family in the following generation.[8]

Communion and excommunication

The troops along the Danube were not the only ones with worries to contend with that winter. The Christian state-within-a-state had suffered serious damage in the persecution of 250. A number of the most senior church leaders had been executed while others like Dionysius of Alexandria and Cyprian of Carthage had survived only by going into hiding. It was a matter of grave concern and sadness to the surviving bishops that so many Christians had willingly sacrificed to 'pagan' gods to obtain their certificates. In the stern version of Christian orthodoxy of the day, to deny Christ, even under extreme duress, was akin to the death of the soul. Everyone with a certificate had self-excommunicated themselves, by definition. Only the faithful could expect salvation and there was a much smaller number of these than there had been just a few months previously.

It is quite likely, however, that many who considered themselves Christians did not adhere to such an uncompromising interpretation of the faith. It has been pointed out that there were strong parallels between the Christian view that the world was in decline, awaiting the second coming of Christ, and the prevalent Roman one, based on the Stoic philosophy, that the world was in its old age, awaiting a new beginning. Some with a more tolerant view of the wider religious practices of the empire may not have had a problem in sacrificing to 'pagan' gods and praying to Christ as well if that would help fill the fields with healthy crops, stem the plague and reverse the fortunes of the empire. We must remember that surviving Christian writings are heavily biased towards what was considered acceptable in later centuries and any advocates of a less exclusivist version of the faith would have been edited out of the record long ago.[9]

Ill-tempered wrangling descended on the surviving Christian community about whether the 'lapsed' – those who had sacrificed – might be readmitted to the church. A common view was that the sin of apostasy was so great that to allow the lapsed back into 'communion' was out of the question: God's final judgement would be their only appeal. Interestingly, however, the strongest support for taking a softer line came from some of those who had suffered the most in the persecution, a group who became known as the 'confessors'. These men and women had stood firm before the magistrates and jeering crowds and refused to deny their god, and many could show scars of torture. Some of them began to use their newly acquired moral authority to argue for a general amnesty. The church was not all righteousness, fire and brimstone: a benign substratum of brotherhood and forgiveness was also strong, especially among the laity and those who had been most steadfast in upholding the faith.[10]

Cyprian's correspondence and sermons from the period survive intact, giving us direct access to the controversy. He initially took a harsh line: God alone could judge the lapsed, except perhaps in cases of extreme penitence where some might be re-admitted to the church, but only on their death beds. But he was also having to justify his own continued existence, having gone into hiding. Had he not previously enlarged at length on the joys of martyrdom only to run away from it, in stark contrast to Fabian, Bishop of Rome, and many others? Was he a hypocrite, or worse, a coward? Cyprian's defence was that as a senior person his survival had been necessary for church cohesion, and that to go into hiding was itself a form of personal sacrifice. He used his best rhetorical skills to link those who had died – and were thus universally respected as martyrs by the faithful – with those who had suffered torture and confiscation, those who had been banished by the authorities, and those who had been forced into hiding: all were martyrs in different ways. Cyprian even went so far as to argue that by staying alive to serve his brethren and voluntarily foregoing instant unification with Christ, his was the greater sacrifice. Not everyone was convinced and it has been noted that there are elements of sarcasm in the replies he received from the confessors in Rome with respect to this argument.[11]

Worse still, a group of presbyters within the Carthaginian church started to defy Cyprian's hard line by ministering to some of the penitent lapsed, and they were backed by some of the local confessors. A deacon called Felicissimus was the ringleader. It is perhaps not coincidental that several years earlier this same group of presbyters had opposed Cyprian's consecration as bishop in the first place. Cyprian excommunicated Felicissimus. Felicissimus excommunicated Cyprian. There was now a rival church with a more tolerant approach to the lapsed and they were flocking to it.

Under growing pressure from Felicissimus, Cyprian took the substantial security risk of calling an assembly of the African bishops in Carthage to debate the problem of the lapsed and agree a party line on re-admission to the church. By the time this group assembled it was the Easter feast of 251 (which was in late March that year). Just as Cyprian had argued that there were degrees of martyrdom, so the delegates decided to recognize degrees of apostasy. At the lowest level there were the *libellatici* who had never sacrificed but instead had obtained their certificates by bribery or forgery or by some other means. Many of these claimed to have clear consciences for they had simply outwitted the authorities. Another large group had been persuaded to respect the sanctity of the pagan altars by publicly praying at them for the health of the emperor and the communal good but without actually sacrificing – this was a middle ground that some local authorities seem to have encouraged in defiance to the strict instruction of Decius's decree, presumably in order to prevent more of a bloodbath. These were called the *thurificati* after the word for burning incense. Most egregious were the *sacrificati* who had gone all out and eaten the sacrificial meat, whether willingly or out of terror and coercion did not seem to matter. One reason for the passion aroused by this debate is that the early Christians did not necessarily deny the existence, or even the power, of the 'pagan' gods. To sacrifice to them was to honour demons, often ones with prodigious influence among the sinful. Hence sacrificing was much more culpable than simply indulging in a meaningless ceremony.

As the bishops listened to the testimony of the confessors, and the sincerity of many of the *libellatici* and *thurificati* became evident through their tragic stories, so Cyprian softened his line. He insisted that only a lawfully elected bishop (such as himself) had the power to re-admit the lapsed, but nevertheless assured his flock that he would give due weight to a suitable recommendation from the confessors. At the same time he doubled down on his attack on Felicissimus using fire and brimstone sermons to assert that God's church, in principle, could no more be split than God himself, and that he (Cyprian) alone was God's supreme representative in Africa.

Similar arguments also raged in Rome. Following Fabian's martyrdom at the beginning of the persecution crisis there had been a kind of interregnum in the nascent papacy lasting over a year – unsurprisingly, perhaps, because to be elected Bishop of Rome under the nose of Decius would have been to take on a suicidal role. But as the active persecution subsided and the emperor left the city on campaign, two rivals emerged for the exalted position: the strict Novatian and the more accommodating Cornelius. Both were formally consecrated by rival groups in March 251, creating another schism. In what might be regarded a deft political move (if one were to be cynical about the actions of avowed men of God guided by the power of prayer), Cyprian and the African bishops chose to recognize the moderate Cornelius, thereby forming a powerful middle-ground alliance. Cyprian condemned Novatian despite having so recently taken a similar hard line on the lapsed himself. Meanwhile, the laxist Felicissimus and a minority of African bishops consecrated their own candidate, one Fortunatus, as bishop of Carthage. Cornelius condemned Fortunatus. Novatian condemned both Cyprian and Fortunatus and consecrated his own man, the hard-liner Maximus as a third contending Bishop of Carthage who was, unsurprisingly, condemned by everyone else. In response Cyprian and his followers softened their line on the lapsed even further, making their position now almost indistinguishable from the faction of Felicissimus and Fortunatus, who nevertheless remained left out in the cold. All this manoeuvreing can be reconstructed thanks to the extensive correspondence between the parties that was lovingly transcribed and copied by scribes down through the centuries.[12]

Some may have wanted to appeal to the authority of the greatest Christian theologian of the age, Origen of Alexandria, but he was still being kept alive under appalling conditions by his tormenters in Caesarea, Palestine. The Roman governor there had decreed that Origen was to be released only if he publicly renounced his faith which, of course, he refused to do.

Pride

Before we leave the Christians for a time, an intriguing aspect of Decius's persecution that has profound repercussions for the cultural landscape of the modern world is recorded in a very late source, a Byzantine chronicler of the eleventh century called George Cedrenus who had access to information otherwise lost to us. It was the custom across the empire for respectable women to go about in public with their heads modestly covered. Not to do so was the mark of a prostitute. The first century apostle Paul even went so far as to instruct that a woman who prayed with her head uncovered should have it cut off (the hair, that is).[13] But Cedrenus tells us that Decius ordered that all Christian women must remove their headscarves:

> He mandated in Rome that the Christian women not go out with the head covered, thinking through this shameful legislation to draw them toward idolatry. But with uncovered heads they went out more eagerly, considering that which seemed a dishonour among men a glory on behalf of Christ. Whence, to the present, observant Christian women go out

uncovered, but the Jews and unfaithful cover themselves. [Cedrenus, p. 466.19–467.5.][14]

By the 'unfaithful' Cedrenus meant the Muslims who were the long-term enemies of Byzantium in which he lived. This response of the Christian women is reminiscent of other oppressed minorities in more modern times who have responded to social stigmas by embracing them as badges of honour.

Novae and Nicopolis

As we have seen, the Roman response to the invasion of Moesia was organized by the recently appointed provincial governor, Trebonianus Gallus, who had gathered his forces at Novae, a major stronghold on a bluff overlooking a great bend on the Danube's south bank. It is now an archaeological park. The excavated remains on display there include the *principia* (headquarters) and parade ground as well as the treasury and a building that is interpreted as a kind of junior officers' mess. The walls were very substantial with towers and buttresses. Novae also boasts one of the best preserved military hospitals (*valetudinarium*) anywhere in the Roman world. That facility would now be needed.[15]

Gallus led out his combined force. The total number of men at his disposal was probably around 10,000 but he may have been substantially outnumbered. Little is known of the confrontation except that Cniva's Goths were driven off. There is archaeological evidence of destruction just outside the fortress wall that may date to this episode: parts of the extramural settlement including the necropolis and Mithraeum were destroyed, as well as a fine peristyle building in which several statue bases were found. A desecrated bronze head of the deified Emperor Gordian III, with ears cut off, was found in modern times in the bed of a local river, presumably having been tossed into the waters by some defiant Goth. The curtain wall of the fortress was partly dismantled and rebuilt in the mid-third century, possibly after damage caused at this time. From these meagre clues it appears that the Goths under Cniva were unable to take the fortress but, equally, Gallus was not strong enough on his own to defeat them decisively in battle.[16]

The Goths' general tactic seems to have been to pin down the legions by force of numbers while other groups marauded the countryside in search of slaves, food and other portable wealth. Similar trials of strength may have been occurring in the province of Dacia to the north as Ostrogotha's force raided there (according to the scenario preferred here), but unfortunately the historical sources give us almost no further information. There were two main legionary bases in Dacia at that time, *legio* XIII *gemina* at Apulum (where Decius had set up his new *colonia* of retired veterans just the year before) and *legio* V *macedonica* further north at Potaissa. All we can infer now is that neither the combined legions nor King Ostrogotha and his allied tribes were able to achieve a sufficiently decisive victory to have made its way into the historical records.

Having been repulsed from Novae, Cniva's army moved south to lay siege to the rich and hitherto tranquil haven of Nicopolis ad Istrum (near modern Nikyup, Bulgaria) which was just 50km or so to the south.[17] This city had been founded and named the 'City of Nike [Victory] near the Danube' by Trajan after the conquest of Dacia. (Note that this is a different city to the Nicopolis in Seleucia, previously mentioned in connection with the revolt of Jotapian.) A large statue of its founder, the emperor Trajan, dominated the forum. A century later it had prospered and grown into a major commercial and cultural centre with all the trappings of a sophisticated imperial city.

Nicopolis was abandoned in ancient times and became overgrown and totally forgotten, only to be rediscovered in the nineteenth century. Most of the city still lies unexcavated under acres of pock-marked terrain, but the outline of the walls and city blocks are all very clear from the air. The central civic area has been excavated and constitutes another superb archaeological site. Excavations over the years have revealed a large range of monumental buildings and official residences. The most interesting of these is an apparently unique heated basilica which boasts twenty-eight shops and a large meeting hall. According to its surviving inscription it was proudly, and, as far as we know uniquely, called a *thermoperipatos* which means something like 'a warm walk-about', the nearest thing the ancient world has to a modern shopping mall. Contemplating these remains, one is very forcefully reminded, once again, of the contrast between the 'civilized' lives of the inhabitants and the 'barbarians' that sought to destroy them. Fortunately Nicopolis had stout walls and the defenders may have been assured that help was on its way.[18]

Because of this point in the action, probably still in the early spring of 251, Decius and the main imperial field army arrived on the scene, much earlier than the Goths had expected. His arrival drastically altered the balance of forces in the sector. We do not know the composition of this army, but because it had moved up from Rome it was likely formed around a core consisting of the praetorians and imperial horseguard together with the elite Roman-levied *legio* II *parthica*, all re-modelled and re-trained after these forces had been on the losing side at Verona. To these were probably added vexillations (detachments) of picked men from a wide variety of other units, including specialist auxiliary cohorts. Decius's line of approach was most likely along the Danube where a combination of roads and downstream river transport could move an army very efficiently.

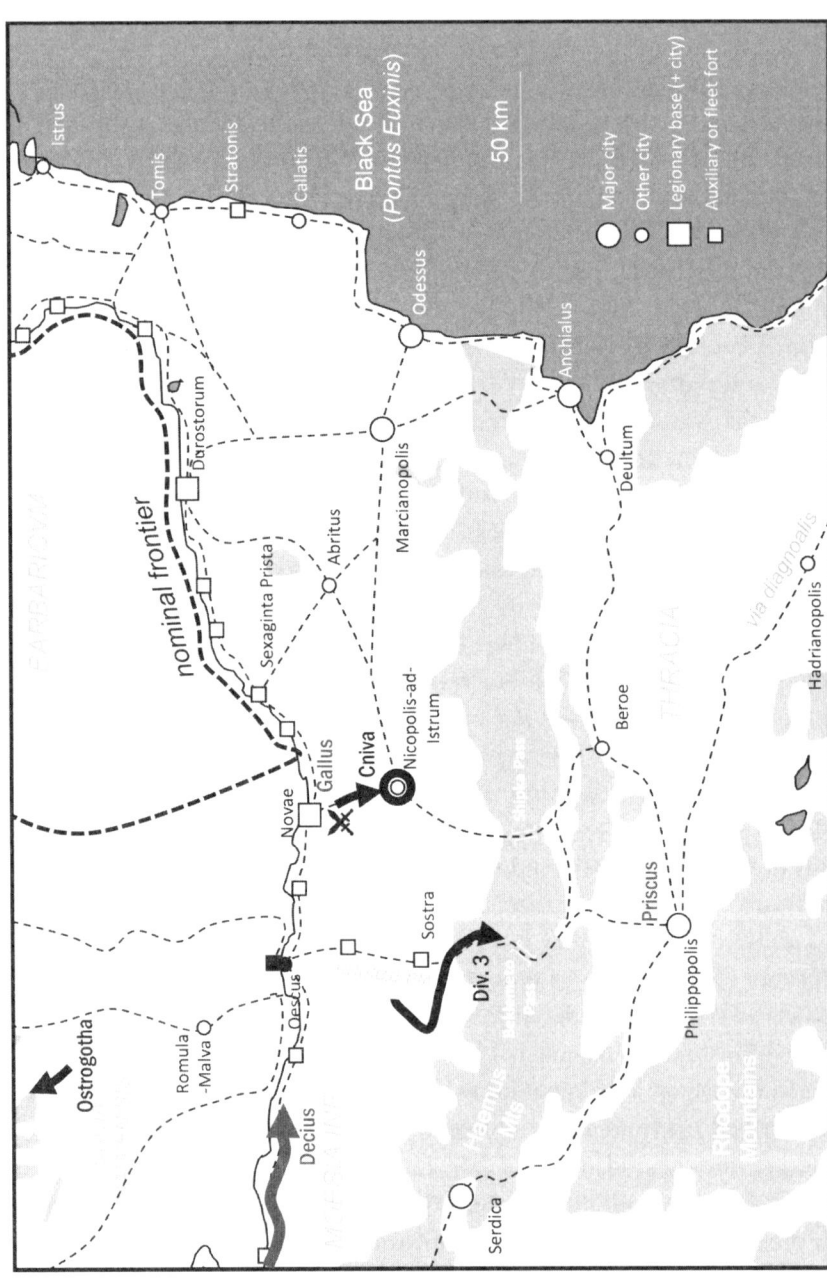

Map 6. The Battle of Novae, 251 CE. Cniva was repulsed by Gallus and moved on to besiege Nicopolis as Decius and his powerful strike force arrived in the area.

News of his arrival may have spurred the Gothic division raiding in Moesia to move south across the Haemus Mountains via what is now called the Beklemeto Pass ('Div. 3' on Map 6). The *via traiana* was equipped with various fortified posting stages but the auxiliaries who normally manned them would have been more like a sleepy police force than something able to tackle a mass invasion numbering tens of thousands of men. At least they would have been able to raise the alarm. It became increasingly obvious that the rich city of Philippopolis was to be the target once again. Evidently the invaders thought it was vulnerable despite having failed to capture it the previous year.[19]

The emperor's first move was to re-capture the crossing at Oescus and in doing so he drove a wedge between the forces of Ostrogotha, currently attacking Dacia in the north (according to the reconstruction preferred here), and those in the south. There is evidence for significant destruction at the old fortress at Oescus from about this time and it may be that the damage was caused when the Romans re-took the place from its temporary garrison of Goths rather than at the time of the initial surprise assault across the frozen river some weeks earlier. Decius had re-taken the strategic centre ground: he could now move rapidly to any point of the compass along good road networks with a force that, in theory at least, was more than sufficient to defeat any of the Gothic hordes in pitched battle, or even all three combined.

Time was of the essence, so after what was probably an instant decision, Decius marched east and fell upon Cniva's Goths at an unknown location near Nicopolis (Map 7). He may even have achieved tactical surprise; in any event the siege was raised and a very substantial defeat was inflicted on the enemy. According to one late source, the Goths lost 30,000 men, but they were not totally destroyed and the remainder – perhaps half the initial force – fled south across the Haemus Mountains where Cniva was able to regroup. Decius's timely arrival could explain why Gallus had not moved against Cniva earlier: the decisive engagement at Nicopolis may have been reserved for the emperor in person along with his elite force.[20]

Nicopolis was Decius's first significant victory and it is probable that he was awarded a second imperial acclamation on the occasion (the first, as was usual, had been awarded to him by the Senate on his accession). He was thereafter styled as IMP(ERATOR) II in inscriptions and formal documents. Long-serving and militarily successful emperors could notch up strings of such acclamations on their curriculum vitae (his hero Trajan, for instance, got as far as IMP XIII during two decades at the helm). Decius was laying out his stall as a warrior-emperor in the old mode, skilled in warfare and able and willing to personally command troops in battle. In later times the idea of an emperor taking to the field at the head of an army was considered a danger

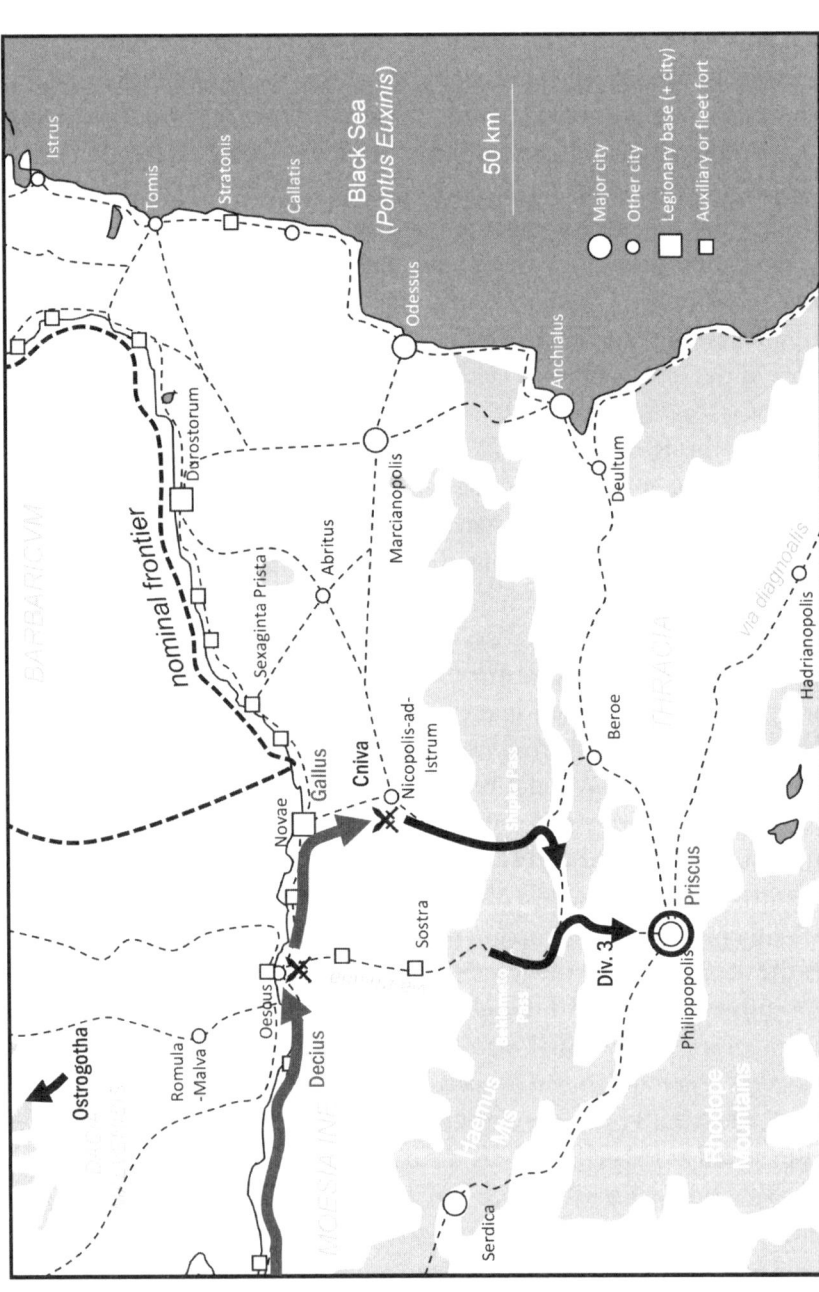

Map 7. The Battle of Nicopolis, 251 CE. Decius re-captured Oescus then attacked Cniva who then retreated south across the Haemus by the Shipka Pass. The third Gothic division began to besiege Priscus in Philippopolis.

to the state, but as Decius and his soldiers well knew, it was that kind of leadership that had made the empire great in the first place. We can imagine the troops assembling in the forum of Nicopolis acclaiming their victorious emperor, followed by a lavish victory party thrown by the grateful citizens.[21]

The road south of Nicopolis along Cniva's line of retreat gently ascended through foothills of the Haemus Range at first, and then steeply up to the summit at what is now called the Shipka Pass. Once in the frozen mountains, Cniva would probably have temporarily thrown up a defensive line to cover his retreat. It is unlikely he would have been able to keep any of his siege engines or heavy equipment in the flight.[22]

It may be wondered why Decius allowed a substantial force of Goths and their commander to slip away over the mountains at this time. Possibly the Roman army was tired and strung out after its rushed departure and long march and needed time to rest and re-equip; equally likely is that Decius needed to take a moment with his high command to properly assess the wider situation including what was happening with regard to Ostrogotha's force. For him, Cniva's Goths were fleeing in the right direction – that is, deeper into imperial territory while he was blocking their exit route. Still key to the whole theatre of war was the crossing point at Oescus. The ice would likely have melted by now, but the crossing still had to be defended and it appears from later events that Decius entrusted that role to Gallus. His job was to hold the position from threats both north and south and, above all, not to let any barbarians escape back across the river.

It must have seemed only a matter of time before the two Gothic armies south of the Haemus joined up. Decius may not have been especially concerned about that prospect. His strategy was to try to bring about pitched battles in which the opposition could be annihilated. Concentrations of the enemy were not to be feared, and in fact were preferable than having to mop up dispersed war bands. Decius also knew that by this time, Philippopolis had been strengthened by a large contingent of Thracian auxiliary troops under the command of one Titus Julius Priscus who was then serving as provincial governor of Thrace (not the same person as the aforementioned Gaius Julius Priscus, brother of the previous emperor Philip).[23] Exactly when the auxiliary force arrived in town is not clear but it may have been mustering there in preparation for the year's hostilities. We do not know the precise unit or units commanded by Priscus but inscriptions from various places on the Danube refer to units of Thracian cavalry (*ala* I *thracum victrix*), infantry (*cohors* I *thracum syriaca*) and archers (*cohors* I *thracum sagittaria*) so it may have included some or all of these.

Letter to Philippopolis

The emperor's immediate concern at this juncture, according to Dexippus, was that the Thracian auxiliaries in Philippopolis might take matters into their own hands and sortie out to confront the invaders rather than allowing a siege to develop. There were impeccable precedents for this bold strategy but it was also very risky and defeat of the garrison troops would have been a disaster, potentially leading to the immediate sacking of the city. Even a victory by Priscus might have been undesirable for Decius, who according to Dexippus 'was afraid of the power growing in Thrace, worried that it might prompt some radical change in the empire's condition'. This is a curious phrase, but it should be remembered that Priscus's forces were ethnic Thracians, and Philippopolis was their most ancient city, having once been the core of a proudly independent civilization. A victorious Thracian army, in the enthusiasm of a victory over the Goths, and decrying the lack of security provided by the Roman state in recent years, might attempt to make Priscus their *de facto* king and secede from the empire, such was the parlous state of loyalty at that time. This is the context of a letter to the Thracian garrison at Philippopolis which survives as a fragment of Dexippus's *Scythica*.

Although the letter purports to be a real document delivered by imperial courier, that is most unlikely; instead it was Dexippus's way of spicing up his narrative, along with invented speeches and other such devices. Some modern historians are critical of their ancient predecessors for inserting 'fake' material into their accounts, but it must be emphasized that their histories were meant to be dramatic and mostly designed to be read aloud. They were judged for their style and verve as well as the strict accuracy of the content, and a certain amount of inventive license was permitted, even expected, to give a sense of immediacy to the narrative. Imagined speeches and letters are also an economical way to explore the situation from different points of view. So, according to Dexippus, Julius Priscus assembled the entire citizenry at the race-course to hear the emperor's letter. It so happens that the curved end of the race track which would have housed the governor's box from which he would have spoken can still be seen in Plovdiv city centre (Plate 3).

The letter is worth quoting at length, not least because it contains some fascinating descriptions of the enemy as rendered in this lively translation by J. McInerney:

> 'Preparations have been time-consuming for this expedition, since I have been occupied with both our recent victory [at Nicopolis] as well as the rest of the war, and my guess is that the barbarians, given that they have

been scattered so far afield, have arrived before we have and will attack you. It behoves me, therefore, through explanation and exhortation to state publicly the course of action you should follow to ensure the highest degree of safety to yourselves and compliance to my wishes.

[…]

For I am told that, somewhat intemperately emboldened by your numbers and exuberance, you hope thereby to inflict a stunning reversal upon the enemy, a typical mistake made by those inexperienced in war. … Safer is the man who trusts in reason than he who climbs into the chariot of ignorance and charges off blindly into the unknown.

[…]

Keep this in mind, and don't go looking for a fight with an opponent when you lack support but your enemy is at full strength, equipped with a considerable cavalry and a large army of both heavy and light infantry. Furthermore, the enemy has a fearsome amount of military expertise, and inspires dread thanks to his physical appearance and his habit of banging his arms, and is more than capable of scaring the living daylights out of those who meet him in battle for the first time with his extravagant yelling and screaming. Would that you did not endanger yourselves, facing such an enemy, especially when you could take cover in safety behind your walls!

[…]

If anyone is pained by the loss of delightful houses and villas and the other trappings of wealth, let him note two things: first, that pain, at least in so far as it concerns the loss of buildings, is minor and can only be perceived for a short time, while we will soon be in a position to prevent their total disappearance and will be able once again to restore an abundant supply of public monies to this end.

[…]

We have abandoned neither preparation nor planning for the saving of your community, and you may expect our arrival in a few days with a force. You should remain inside the walls while we occupy ourselves with the business of winning the conflict outside. This promise is the truth, as the events at Nicopolis have already shown, without wishing to boast. In battles of such magnitude, when events occur too quickly to allow a clear view of the right course of action, one must employ such advisors and helpers as can explain the situation, demonstrating their experience of events and ...' [Dexippus, *Scythica*, fragment.][24]

... and there the fragment ends. But its purport is very clear: the Thracians were to man the walls and await the imminent arrival of the imperial army even if that meant watching their rich country estates burn. There is considerable archaeological evidence for the destruction of villa estates in the region during the mid-third century, so that is no doubt exactly what happened.[25]

The Battle of Beroe

Thus it was that after regrouping and analyzing the wider strategic situation, Decius set about crossing the Haemus Mountains via the Shipka Pass, following in Cniva's wake in the hope of forcing battle and relieving the garrison at Philippopolis. Only when Cniva and the other Goths in Thrace had been crushed would he once again move north for the final confrontation with the forces of Ostrogotha.

Crossing the mountains was a difficult manoeuvre for the army because the way was steep, narrow and winding. The Shipka Pass sports over a hundred switchbacks both going up then coming down. Even the modern metalled road can only take two vehicles abreast. An army on the march needed innumerable wagons to carry supplies, food for men and animals, construction equipment, artillery pieces and ammunition, each of which was capable of breaking an axle or losing a wheel and causing delays behind. The standard procedure, therefore, was to send a strong mounted vanguard ahead to check for ambushes and secure the exit point onto the plains beyond. The summit was cold and windswept, still a barren snowfield even in springtime, and men would have rested wherever they could, waiting in turns to move and halt. Eventually, the head of the column started to debouch from the hills in good order onto the Thracian plain below.[26]

But then disaster struck. Cniva had appreciated the strategic potential of this place and calculated his moment perfectly, attacking the Roman army in the vicinity of the city of Beroe (now Stara Zagora in Bulgaria). According to Jordanes's history of the Goths:

> While he [Decius] was resting his horses and his weary army in that place, all at once Cniva and his Goths fell upon him like a thunderbolt. He cut the Roman army to pieces and drove the emperor, with a few who had succeeded in escaping, across the mountains again to Euscia [Oescus] in Moesia, where Gallus was then stationed with a large force of soldiers as guardian of the frontier. [Jordanes, *Getica* XVIII, 102.][27]

This account implies that Decius never made it to the safety of the city walls of Beroe. Strategically, the likeliest interpretation is that the Goths attacked the vanguard on the plain while the main force was still strung out on the high pass behind them. With these troops routed, Decius could hardly continue to drip-feed men down the mountain to be massacred by the Goths, so he had no option but to perform an about-turn and extricate as many as he could, abandoning part of his force at the foot of the mountains in clear sight of the bulk of the army. While Jordanes may well have exaggerated the extent of the Gothic victory, it was certainly a humiliating setback for Decius.

If this interpretation of the Battle of Beroe is correct then the most likely location is not adjacent to the city itself but about 45km to the north-west where the Roman road comes down on to a wide agricultural plain that is known today as the 'Valley of the Thracian Kings' because of the many pre-Roman burial mounds. This is where the modern town of Shipka nestles against the lower slopes of the Balkan (Haemus) range (Plate 3). A battle at this location would explain why the Roman force was camped out resting their horses and had not simply entered the safety of the city walls. Beroe, being the nearest city, could still have given its name to an engagement at this spot (Map 8).[28]

Beroe was a significant city in its own right, with the usual public buildings and porticoed halls. The partially restored forum can be seen in an elegant city park in the heart of modern Stara Zagora. There is no historical or archaeological evidence that it was ever taken or even besieged by the Goths who evidently by-passed it. It may be relevant that although the city had once had a mint, the production of coins had stopped a couple of decades earlier, implying, perhaps, a reduced status and little in the way of imperial treasure in the city. The walls, however, were nevertheless formidable. So Cniva probably ignored the place and moved toward the far more valuable prize of Philippopolis where he could link up with the other Gothic force (see Map 8).

The passage above from Jordanes is of great use in confirming that Gallus was stationed at Oescus which made sound strategic sense, especially if Ostrogotha's army was north of the Danube as this author thinks likely. After a long and humiliating retreat, Decius was forced to regroup there where he still held the strategic high ground and could summon more reinforcements to restore his army's strength. That would take months, however, during which time the citizens of Philippopolis and the auxiliary force under Julius Priscus would have to hold out against Cniva's Goths. And here, perhaps, we can see the rhetorical force of the imagined letter to the city in Dexippus's story. Decius had ordered the Philippopolitans to allow their town to be encircled and besieged for what was supposed to be just a matter of days before he

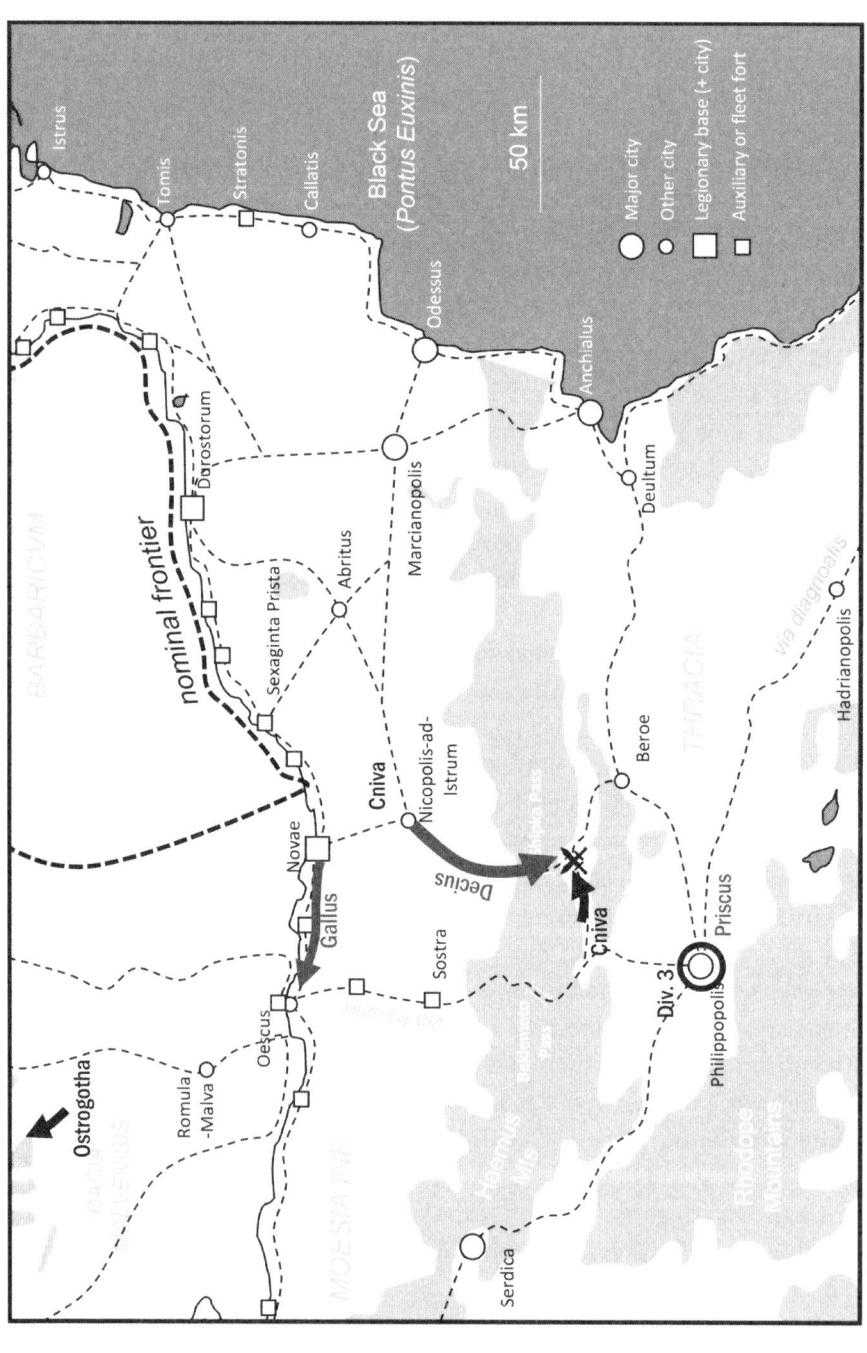

Map 8. The Battle of Beroe, 251 CE. The Third Division of Goths under an unknown commander commenced the siege of Philippopolis. Gallus was ordered to Oescus to hold the crossing. Decius crossed the Haemus Mountains via the Shipka Pass but his vanguard was destroyed by Cniva in the vicinity of Beroe.

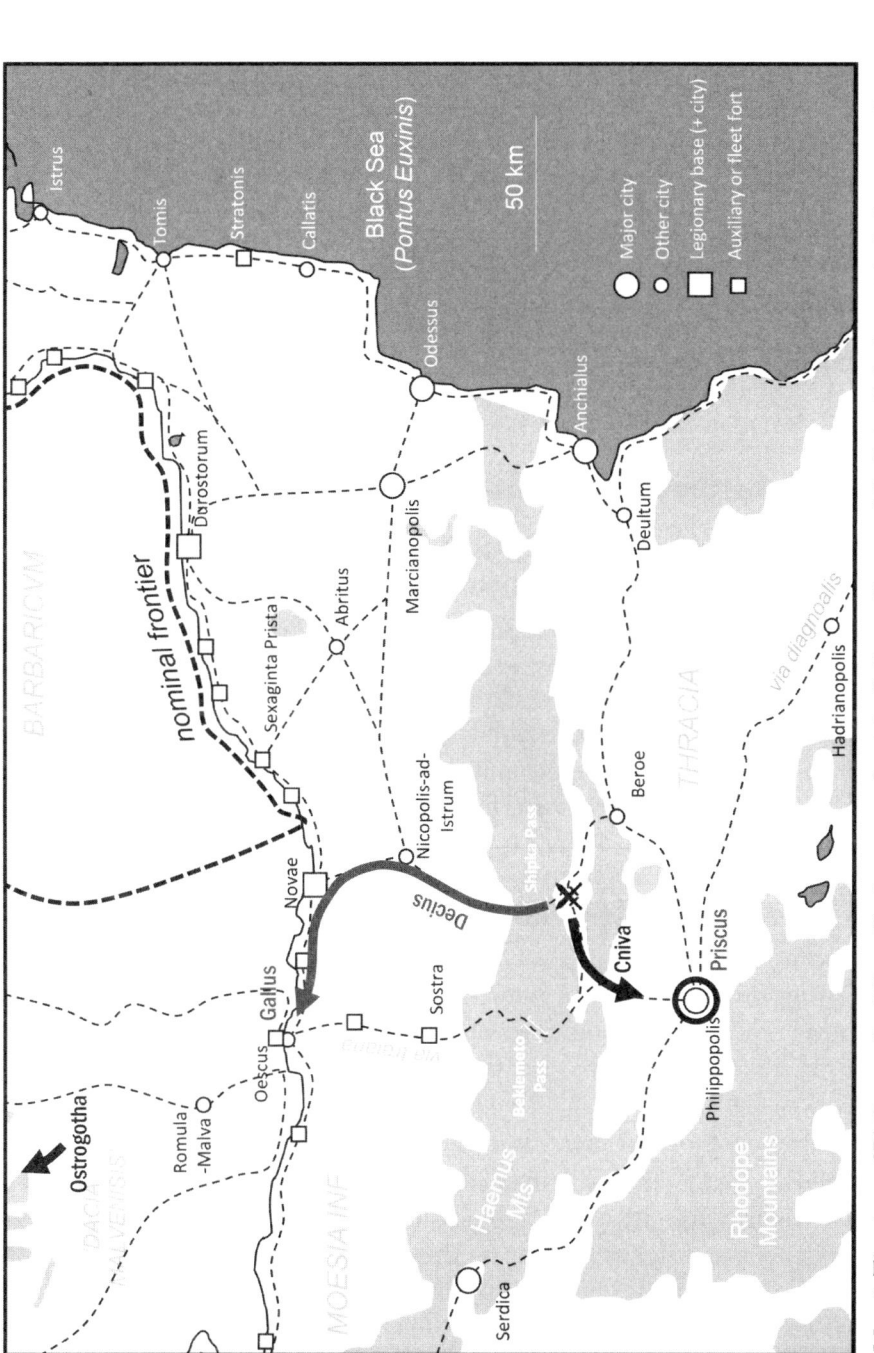

Map 9. The siege of Philippopolis, 251 CE. Decius retreated to join Gallus at Oescus while Cniva linked up with the besieging force.

came to the rescue. Now it would be months, if at all. And to reach the city the imperial army would either have to take a long detour or repeat the risky manoeuvre of crossing the mountains into an area controlled by a Gothic army.

It was probably in this interlude, in the spring of 251, that Decius decided to elevate his elder son Herennius Etruscus to the rank of *augustus* or co-emperor. It was a welcome distraction and an excuse for another donative to raise morale. Gold coins of Decius celebrate *victoria augg* ('Victory of the two emperors') which presumably refers to the Battle of Nicopolis. Intriguingly, the new coins of Herennius as *augustus* feature the legend *victoria germanica* ('Victory over the Germans') which either indicates that the Goths were regarded as Germans by the regime or refers to some otherwise unknown victory won by a general on the Rhine frontier at that time.[29]

Five hundred darics

Philippopolis held out valiantly for a considerable time, just as it had the previous year. The situation was far from hopeless because this time it had been reinforced by the Thracian auxiliaries. This is the historical setting for three new fragments of the *Scythica* that have been re-discovered in the Vienna palimpsest. The first of these fragments, which consists of two pages, describes the Gothic assault. Here we learn that the invaders initially encircled the town but then pretended to withdraw, building a secret camp a little distance away where they 'refrained from lighting fires at night, fearing that they might be seen'. Indeed it would have been easy enough to conceal an army behind a prominent hill to the west of the ancient city. This interlude may have corresponded with the arrival of Cniva himself after his victory at Beroe.[30]

During the lull there was some sort of rebellion against authority inside the town – perhaps relating to tensions between the city magistrates and the garrison after it had become clear that Decius was not riding to the rescue any time soon. Believing that the siege had ended, some of the townspeople gave themselves over to merriment 'as if the war had ended and they had achieved a splendid victory'. But an unnamed traitor took advantage of the situation and stole out of the city to the Gothic camp. This man promised to return to Philippopolis and signal at night 'in the place where the fortifications could be climbed most easily'. Next we learn that 'five men, who had volunteered out of zeal and in hope of money, were sent out by Cniva by night as scouts to check what had been reported and to test the arranged betrayal.' They saw a light high on the ramparts and everything looked good.

Cniva then planned his attack, offering '500 darics for the first man to climb the walls and for the second three hundred'. It is a very odd term: the daric was an ancient Persian gold coin no longer in circulation. Perhaps Dexippus was consciously using archaic terminology as part of his formal style but if that was not the case, and insofar as historians have considered what he may have meant, two views have been proposed. The first is that the daric was just a flowery way of referring to gold coins in the hands of barbarians, and that they must have been Roman gold aurei. The second theory is that Dexippus was referring to 'barbarian' gold coinage – crude imitations that were occasionally manufactured in eastern Europe; and perhaps Cniva had a supply of these. But a third and perhaps more obvious possibility is that the darics were contemporaneous Sassanian gold coins. It so happens the Persians had just recently reintroduced gold after a gap of hundreds of years (Plate 3). Scholars think they were not used in general circulation but rather for prestige purposes as ceremonial gifts and to compete with Roman gold coins (being considerably heavier). So perhaps Cniva was being bank-rolled by Persia, indicating that Philip's decision to cut the Gothic subsidy had brought about a new alignment of the world order, much to the detriment of Rome.[31]

The Gothic force advanced quietly at night as the inhabitants continued with their drinking. A stealthy assault was made on the identified weak point of the defences. This, we learn, was

> ...by the race-course of the stadium, a low fortification built on rock, not hard to climb at all points, and they found the guard to be not very numerous. Well, scrambling up this rock at this point and fixing sharp iron in many places on this fortification... they got over it and arrived inside. Dexippus, *Scythica* Fragment[32]

Given the rewards, one wonders if there was an unseemly rush to be first over the walls, but if there was, order was maintained and the Gothic commando force killed the few sleeping guards and lit their own torch to signal a breach of the defences. Cniva ordered a further 500 picked men to advance with ladders and ascend the walls. The general alarm was eventually raised but the Goths already inside the city managed to fend off the counter-attack by blocking the narrow entrances to the guard towers. At this point the fragment ends.

An attack near the racetrack might have been invented for dramatic effect, not least because it is the very place that Priscus is supposed to have previously read out his letter from Decius. But the description fits very neatly with archaeological reconstructions of the city (Map 10) which shows the racetrack in the north-west with one side built into the craggy hill beside it (now called Nebet Tepe, and a public park; it is one of the three hills which gave the city its alternative Roman name of Trimontium). The perimeter wall enclosed the summit of this hill, but the ground was too rough and rocky there for building, so the sector would have been relatively quiet at night (Plate 3). If the Goths scaled the rocky hill and seized control of the wall at this point they could easily have defended the spot while infiltrating their entire force. The outnumbered garrison could have retreated to the walled citadel at the ceremonial heart of the city and fight it out there, but they would know for sure that the game was up.

In 2017, archaeological excavations on Nebet Tepe hill revealed the ruins of a defensive tower that was apparently destroyed in the mid-third century, possibly, we may speculate, in the first phase of the Gothic assault described by Dexippus. Among the charred remains was a small barrel of wheat, possibly fodder for the animals. This clue, and the fact that the circumstantial details of Dexippus's recently discovered account fit the layout of Philippopolis very well, support the idea that his was not simply some made-up or formulaic

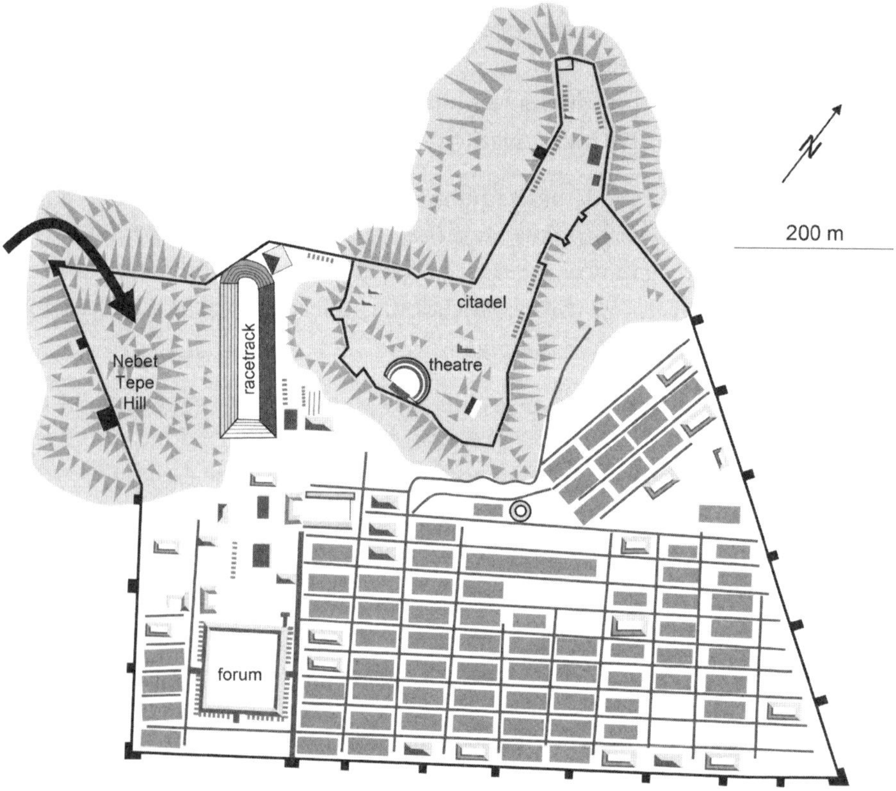

Map 10. The assault on Philippopolis, 251 CE. Urban plan based on Mateev (2016). Arrow shows the suggested Gothic attack up Nebet Tepe hill.

account of the conflict as had once been thought. It appears to be an accurate narrative written by someone with military experience who had been close to the action at times for an audience that would have included well-informed individuals.[33]

Faced with the choice of surrender or death, the governor Priscus entered negotiations with Cniva. The result was that he and his substantial force of Thracian auxiliaries switched sides and joined the Goths. It was a desperate move, but the men may have reasoned that they themselves had been betrayed by the emperor after being ordered to stay within the walls and then he had failed to come to the rescue. Aurelius Victor tells us that Priscus was proclaimed emperor on the spot by his auxiliaries and that when the news reached Rome, the nobility (senate) declared him an enemy of the state.[34] Tragically, the townspeople were not to be spared. The fourth century historian Ammianus Marcellinus, who had access to Dexippus's *Scythica*, wrote that a hundred thousand died 'unless the histories are false'.[35] The negotiations may have allowed some time for the frantic burial of valuables. No fewer than fifteen coin hoards from around this time have been dug up in modern Plovdiv, four of them with very up-to-date issues bearing the image of Decius. Some of the coins are fused and burned. Even more poignantly, a 2018 excavation in central Plovdiv at a property near the ancient theatre turned up a destruction layer from this time. In it were the skeletons of a young man, a young woman with bracelets clutching a votive statue of Venus, and a child with a spearhead in its chest.[36]

Chapter 6

The Road to Abritus

The hypothetical Battle of Romula

The second newly discovered fragment of Dexippus picks up the story after the fall of Philippopolis. Some intervening text is evidently missing, possibly just a few pages.[1] We learn that a general alert had gone out across Greece and Macedonia, and for the first time we hear of a Greek force moving up to defend the famous strategic pass at Thermopylae (composed of 'Athenians and Boeotians with an army, and a select band of Spartans') and further defences being organized along the border country between Thessaly and Macedonia led by one Ptolemaios the Athenian. The reference to Greek soldiers with archaic-sounding names is fascinating, not least because specifically Greek units rarely served in the Roman military. They must have been organized on an ad hoc basis by the local authorities who now appreciated that they were cut off from imperial support and terrified that the barbarian horde might soon move south and fall upon the rich and cultivated cities of Greece.

The fragment then goes on to explain that King Ostrogotha heard that 'the Scythians [Goths] were holding Cniva in the highest regard, and were celebrating him in song, as is their ancestral custom.... whereas they were holding himself in less esteem, charging him with cowardice and failure in his tactics'. It is an evocative image and moreover evidence of the way Gothic oral history of the sort alluded to by Jordanes was actually created. From it we can infer that the raiding in Dacia (if that was indeed where Ostrogotha was stationed) was not proceeding quite so well as intended. So Ostrogotha marched quickly at the head of his substantial force, this one allegedly composed of 50,000 men according to the new palimpsest. The objective may have been to punch through Oescus and link up with Cniva, facilitating the latter's escape along the *via traiana* (which, presumably, had been the original plan before Decius intervened).[2] A smaller Roman force drawn from the legions of Dacia may have shadowed Ostrogotha's army, as subsequent evidence suggests.

The narrative continues by examining the point of view of the emperor himself:

> Decius was concerned about the wrongdoing of the auxiliary troops and the capture of Philippopolis. And when the army was gathered, about 80,000 men, he wanted to renew the war if he could, as he thought the situation was favourable to him – even though he had lost the auxiliary force – but also to liberate the Thracian captives and to prevent them crossing to the other side. [Dexippus, *Scythica* Fragment.][3]

The loss of the auxiliary troops refers to the garrison of Philippopolis under Priscus. By 'crossing to the other side' the text implies that Decius wanted to prevent the Goths taking their captives beyond the Danube where they would be distributed as slaves. The passage is the only information we have to indicate the size of Decius's army. It is a useful detail because, if it is to be even half-believed,[4] it shows that it was still a major force after the defeat on the plain of Beroe. Decius had evidently summoned substantial reinforcements, and if Jordanes is reliable, the mustering point was at Oescus, a convenient place for new troop detachments to assemble. Next we are told that Decius built a trench and encampment at an unknown place called Hamisos where he seems to have waited for developments.[5] Then we learn that 'when the advance of Ostrogotha's force was reported to him, he [Decius] thought that he should encourage his soldiers, as a good opportunity arose'.

At this point we are treated to a speech by the emperor himself, or at least the beginning of it. Of course, it largely reflects the imagination of the historian, but being newly discovered it is worth reproducing, not least because it hints at the severe old emperor's stoicism:

> Men, I wish the military force and all the provincial territory were in a good condition and not humiliated by the enemy. But since the incidents of human life bring manifold sufferings (for such is the fate of mortals), it is the duty of the prudent men to accept what happens and not lose spirit, nor become weak, distressed by the mishap in that plain [presumably a reference to the Battle of Beroe] or by the capture of the Thracians – in case any of you has been disheartened by these things. For each of these two misfortunes offers arguments against your discouragement: the former was brought about by the treachery of the scouts rather than by any deficiency of ours, and the Thracian town they took by ambushes rather than through prowess, having failed in their attacks. And weak… [here the fragment ends]. [Dexippus, *Scythica* Fragment.][6]

At least one major engagement took place after this, although the circumstances remain obscure. Either the Romans attempted to eject the

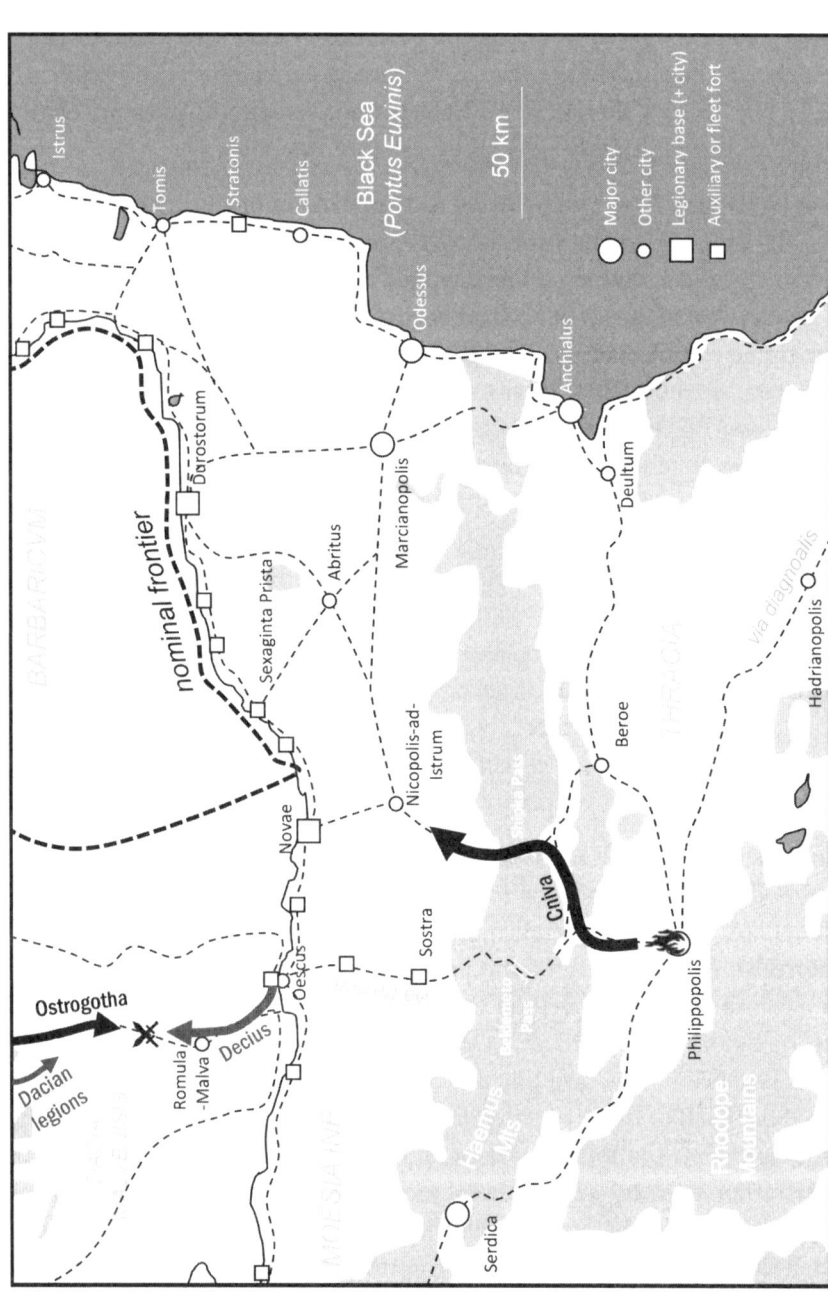

Map 11. Suggested background to the 'hypothetical Battle of Romula', 251 CE. Ostrogotha moved south tracked by the Dacian legions while Decius blocked his approach somewhere before Romula-Malva and fought a defensive battle there. Ostrogotha's advance facilitated Cniva's flight from Philippopolis.

Goths from Philippopolis or, more likely given the developing trajectory of Dexippus's narrative as revealed by the new fragments, a battle took place between Decius's imperial troops and Ostrogotha's advancing relief force. Ostrogotha would not have been able to cross the Danube in the face of the imperial army, so if he was indeed campaigning in Dacia, it seems likely that Decius would have moved north to confront the Gothic king after delivering the speech above. On the opposing bank from Oescus the *via traiana* heads north up the floodplain of the Alutus (modern Olt) river past the town of Romula-Malvensis into central Dacia (modern Romania). These strategic considerations lead to the suggestion that if a confrontation between Roman emperor and Gothic king took place, it was most likely somewhere here (Map 11). Because the circumstances surrounding this inferred battle are so obscure, it is referred to here as the 'hypothetical Battle of Romula'.

We can infer that the battle was at least a partial success for the Romans because the Gothic armies never linked up. Moreover it would seem a fitting way for Dexippus's narrative to develop, in which Decius had suffered setbacks but encouraged his men to make another effort. This fragment of Dexippus is the last we hear of Ostrogotha and his army. Jordanes implies that he died about this time, although he does not mention the circumstances. Of course, he (or Cassiodorus before him) was keen to show the Goths in the best light, especially Ostrogotha who was allegedly of the noble Amal bloodline and a direct ancestor of Theodoric the Great who had commissioned the Gothic history. Hence it is entirely plausible that Ostrogotha may have been killed or captured in this battle.[7]

At this point another historical source may be relevant in shedding light on the course of the battle itself. The Byzantine emperor and military strategist Maurice (ruled 582–602), who may have benefitted from reading Dexippus's full account, stated that Decius used the tactic of feigned retreat to great effect against the Scyths (i.e., the Goths), allowing him to kill many of the enemy. That description does not fit any other battle in the war. Maurice does not give further particulars, but in the same context he goes on to describe the use of caltrops (iron spikes) and concealed pits as ways in which a killing ground can be prepared in advance. With Ostrogotha advancing rapidly, as the aforementioned fragment suggests, it would have been a perfect opportunity for Decius to employ such tactics against him.[8]

Disastrously for the Romans, however, the young co-emperor Herennius was apparently killed in the engagement. This is mentioned in Jordanes's abbreviated summary:

In the battle that followed [i.e., after the capture of Philippopolis] they quickly pierced the son of Decius with an arrow and cruelly slew him. The father saw this, and although he is said to have exclaimed, to cheer the hearts of his soldiers: 'Let no one mourn; the death of one soldier is not a great loss to the republic', he was yet unable to endure it, because of his love for his son. [Jordanes, *Getica* XVIII.103.]

Ostrogotha's advance may have been a tactical defeat for the Goths but it could have succeeded in its main objective of giving Cniva the opportunity to break away from Philippopolis and re-cross the Haemus range into Moesia unmolested, apparently beginning a race to the border. According to Jordanes, Decius was now determined to annihilate Cniva's remaining Gothic army and win the war, swearing 'death or vengeance'.[9]

Decoding the Great Ludovisi Battle Sarcophagus

In 1621 a monumental marble sarcophagus was dug up on the site of an ancient burial ground outside the Porta San Lorenzo in Rome. All commentators agree that it dates to the time of the Gothic wars in mid-third century. Known as the Great Ludovisi Sarcophagus after its original owner, the wealthy art-collecting Cardinal Ludovico Ludovisi, it is carved from a huge block of the finest marble in unrivalled super-deep relief with sublime artistic accomplishment and consummate technical skill (Plate 4). Originally, it would have been even more impressive than it is now because subtle traces on the surface show that it was selectively highlighted with gold leaf. It depicts a chaotic and crowded battle scene in which Roman troops are busy trampling and slaughtering 'barbarians', as the Romans saw them. The enemy are shaggy and bearded, with wild expressions, while the Romans appear calm and determined. Every detail commands attention, and the overall composition is magnificent. Among the action is a Roman *tubicen* or trumpeter, blowing hard, and a *cornicen*, or horn player, with his instrument curved around his head. The latter figure has been interpreted as a Roman, but his hair is long and it is possible he is a barbarian youth, especially as he seems just about to be apprehended by the Roman soldier standing behind him. Whatever the case, he and the trumpeter seem to project the very din of battle.[10]

This great work of art reminds us how the Romans viewed themselves and their enemy in this time of crisis. It also gives us some conception of the military kit worn by the respective armies, at least as idealized by sculptors in Rome. The Romans carry shields and wear helmets and body armour; both chain mail (*lorica hamata*) and scale armour (*lorica squamata*) are depicted. The senior officers have crested helmets of various styles while the more junior ranks have plain helmets. They all carry the famous Spanish stabbing sword or *gladius*, the traditional weapon of the Roman infantryman. The barbarians are also armed with swords and shields but mostly fight bare-headed and in some instances bare-chested too. Some of them wear trousers, a form of dress generally associated with northern barbarians.

The central figure is a serene but confident young man mounted on a splendid horse with lion-skin saddle, his cape flowing out behind him. He is depicted charging through the mêlée with right arm raised and the palm of his hand open. This man is not participating in the mayhem, indeed his sword is sheathed. He is widely interpreted as the departing spirit of the deceased, the raised hand being a gesture of valediction: a young Roman commander killed during a battle against northern barbarians on the very point of victory.

Whoever was interred within the sarcophagus must have been extremely rich. We do not know for sure who he was; indeed historians debate whether the carving was intended to depict an actual battle or if it was just a stylistic representation suitable for the burial of any man with military pretensions. A number of other, earlier, battle sarcophagi exist with some similar motifs and overall composition, although none is so finely crafted. Hence it is possible that a workshop in Rome produced such works in advance, leaving the central figure unfinished for whichever rich patron might come along to purchase it.[11]

And yet, beyond the superb quality, there are features that lead one to think that this sarcophagus is not a generic production. Most commentators have focused on the main scene on the front, but the lid (which has become separated from the rest and is now at a museum in Mainz) offers additional information. It shows a young man sitting on a raised chair, flanked by Roman soldiers and legionary standards, receiving submission from a group of barbarians who are apparently handing over their children as hostages. This sort of scene is familiar from Roman art, but only victorious generals could dictate peace terms in this way. The man has similar features to the horseman on the front panel, and despite the fact that he wears no insignia, the motif appears to befit the status of an emperor and not just some regional commander. There is also a woman depicted on the lid, bearing a scroll who, it has been noticed, is a good likeness for the Empress Herennia Etruscilla as depicted on another surviving bust in the British Museum (see Plate 4) and as seen on her many coins. It may be relevant that a later inscription describes the empress as *mater castrorum* ('Mother of the Camps') which indicates that she had, at some point, accompanied the army on campaign. The scroll could represent her carrying news of the victory back to Rome.[12]

Closer inspection of the main figure reveals that he has an incised 'X' in the centre of his forehead. This clue led one art historian in the 1950s toward an intriguing interpretation. She noted that there are two other third century busts of unknown young men with similar features and an 'X' on the forehead, and suggested they were images of the same person who must therefore have been an important personality. The mark, she argued, could represent an initiate of the cult of Mithras, although that has been disputed. More significantly, she also claimed that a similar 'X' on the forehead could be seen on some coins of Hostilian, the younger son of Decius. Hence in her interpretation, it was a real-life scar on the head of that prince. This theory was cautiously welcomed by experts at the time and seems to have taken hold, such that the Great Ludovisi individual is usually identified as Hostilian by modern commentators and is widely depicted as such across the internet.[13]

Unfortunately, however, it is far from certain that any coins of Hostilian with an 'X' on his forehead actually exist. None has been illustrated and the standard catalogues make no mention of them. Perhaps the cited examples were just scratched. But the main problem with the identification as Hostilian is that he did not die in war and, as far as we know, never fought a battle; his fate will be discussed later. A more likely figure is surely his older brother, Herennius Etruscus, who did die fighting according to all the histories. If so, it would seem to be a magnificent tribute to a prince who had promised so much for the empire but perished heroically and was enrolled among the gods.[14]

An important part of the composition which, to this author's knowledge, has not received particular scrutiny, is a tableau to the left of the central figure where there is a mounted barbarian wearing a soft 'Phrygian cap' which flops forward over his head. He is the only foe on the front panel shown alive and well, riding a fine horse and slashing at a Roman soldier below. The Phrygian cap may appear a little comic to modern eyes, but it had particular significance to the ancients. It is normally associated in Roman art with eastern 'barbarians', especially Persians, and was well known as part of the costume of the Persian god Mithras, for example. Within the empire, it – or something closely related – also became associated with freed slaves who were awarded their woollen 'cap of liberty' (*pileus*) on manumission. There seems to have been a certain conscious irony that free peoples outside the empire and freed slaves within it wore the same headgear. But, tempting as it may seem, the figure on the sarcophagus does not have anything else that marks him out as Persian. His facial features and shaggy beard are similar to all the other northern barbarians.

Less well-known is that the Phrygian cap was also associated in Roman art with barbarians north of the Danube. In discussing Trajan's conquest of Dacia at the beginning of the second century, Cassius Dio recorded that the noblest class of Dacians were known as 'cap-wearers' (Latin, *pileati*) – in their own language they were *tarabostes*. This elite included none other than Decebalus, King of the Dacians, who is depicted on Trajan's column wearing a soft cap, even in a battle scene. Perhaps to the wearers it symbolised not only their noble status but also defiance of Rome, freedom, and a contempt of death. All these qualities were admired by the Romans, of course, because it made them worthy adversaries.[15]

The sarcophagus has occasionally been interpreted as a battle between Romans and free Dacians (Carpi). The problem with that is that one would expect the enemy to be equipped with the vicious curved sword or *falx* which was synonymous with Dacian warriors in Roman art: they are not. Another possibility is that they are Goths. It so happens that the Phrygian cap was also associated with Gothic nobility and kingship, albeit in a later age.[16]

Directly below this rider is another individual in a Phrygian cap, almost identical, but depicted as a captive with hands cross-tied on his knees. It is the most poignant mini-scene of all, as a Roman soldier lifts his chin, apparently weighing the prisoner's fate in the balance while at the same time protecting him with his shield. It was common in Roman sculpture to present a visual narrative in which the same individual could occur more than once. The friezes that wind around Trajan's Column, for instance, are like a cartoon strip where important individuals crop up again and again. So it is proposed here that the two individuals on the front relief marked out by the Phrygian cap may have been intended to represent the same man: none other than the barbarian commander who, the sarcophagus seems to be telling us, rode bravely into battle but was captured.[17]

More individuals of interest are the well-attired Roman officers who are shown side-by-side defending themselves with shields around the captive. They wear spectacular helmets with intriguing designs. The man guarding the captive wears a helmet decorated by feathers and capped by the head of an eagle. The man to his right (our left), who is shown defending against the postulated barbarian commander, has a plumed helmet on which a lioness is apparently shown being set loose to trample a serpent. The serpent represents the enemy, as was traditional in Roman art. It is proposed here that these two men might symbolise officers of the two Dacian legions, *legio* V *macedonica*, symbol the eagle, normally based at Potaissa, and *legio* XIII *gemina*, symbol the lion, normally based at Apulum. Some other men on the sarcophagus, including the one in the extreme top left, have helmets decorated with the Capricorn, a symbol that was used by several legions, the nearest being *legio* I *adiutrix* based at Brigetio on the Danube in Upper Pannonia. It is quite plausible that this legion had moved up into Dacia to support the other two legions during the ongoing war and so participated in the same battle.[18]

In summary, then, the Great Ludovisi sarcophagus does not look like a generic production but appears to have been intended to honour a particular young man of imperial status who died fighting the barbarians, while at the same time being credited with a substantial victory. The only candidate that fits this description is the young prince Herennius Etruscus, recently raised to the rank of *augustus*. The victory may have involved taking prisoner of the enemy commander who could be none other than King Ostrogotha himself. This capture may have been achieved by men of *legio* V *macedonica* who were possibly fighting alongside their colleagues from *legio* XIII *gemina* and *legio* I *adiutrix*. Victory was followed by some sort of peace treaty when the surviving enemy offered their children as hostages. (Of course, if the prince died in battle he could not have negotiated a treaty afterwards, but the point of the imagery was to credit him with the success.) News of the Victory was carried back to Rome by his mother, the Empress Herennia Etruscilla, along with the body. In other words, the sarcophagus fits well with the hypothetical Battle of the Romula, a significant Roman victory which was nevertheless tinged with tragedy. The Dacian legions may have marched south on the tail of Ostrogotha's advancing army, possibly harassing the advance and then engaging them from the rear as they approached Decius. It may even be that Herennius had been placed in command of that force during the campaign.

This is all conjectural, of course. The best hope we can have of gaining solid information comes from the lid which has a central panel that must originally have been painted with an inscription but is now totally blank, presumably having faded away. It is just possible, however, that modern spectral imaging techniques might recover the lost text; it would certainly be worth the attempt.[19]

The traditional Roman practice with captured enemy commanders was to strip them naked and force them to grovel for mercy at the feet of their conqueror. They would be reserved for humiliation in the final triumphal parade through the streets of Rome, after which they would be ritually slaughtered, unless the emperor was inclined to clemency. Unfortunately for Ostrogotha, Decius was the ultimate traditionalist, and he is unlikely to have been in a merciful frame of mind after losing his elder son and heir.

Pestilence strikes Carthage

Meanwhile, on the other side of the empire, despite all attempts by 'pagans' to appease the gods and the fervent prayers of Christians alike, the great plague started to fan out across the western world from its foothold in Alexandria. When it struck Carthage the event was documented in the writings of two Christians to be preserved for posterity. These were Bishop Cyprian, whom we have previously met describing the events surrounding the persecution edict, and his deacon and biographer Pontius. The latter's account is the most graphic that we have of the effects:

> Afterwards [that is, following the edict of Decius] there broke out a dreadful plague, and excessive destruction of a hateful disease invaded every house in succession of the trembling populace, carrying off day by day with abrupt attack numberless people, every one from his own house. All were shuddering, fleeing, shunning the contagion, impiously exposing their own friends, as if with the exclusion of the person who was sure to die of the plague, one could exclude death itself also. There lay about the meanwhile, over the whole city, no longer bodies, but the carcasses of many, and, by the contemplation of a lot which in their turn would be theirs, demanded the pity of the passers-by for themselves. No one regarded anything besides his cruel gains. No one trembled at the remembrance of a similar event. No one did to another what he himself wished to experience. Pontius, *Life of Cyprian* 9

Just like Bishop Dionysius of Alexandria, the Carthaginian Christians regarded the disease as sent by God as a test of faith – their theology demanded as much – and Cyprian wrote an entire sermon entitled *De Mortalitate* ('On the Plague') which survives intact. He was evidently responding to complaints from among his flock as to why God was letting the righteous suffer alongside with the rest. Surely a loving and all-powerful God would answer the prayers of his own people? Cyprian's answer was that the Christians should in fact rejoice and embrace the benefit of the occasion because they should be eager to depart the world. Those who died would be revered almost as martyrs because their suffering was akin to that of Jesus, and moreover they would enjoy eternal life much sooner than would otherwise be the case. Non-Christians who succumbed under identical circumstances were, by contrast, destined for eternal suffering.

It was a stern creed, but Cyprian did not rejoice in the death of unbelievers and Pontius records that he busied himself caring for diseased non-Christians as well as for his own flock, helping them as best he could and praying for them on their death-beds at a time when even their own families had deserted them. In this he was following the example of Jesus himself who had ministered to the sick. For once, Cyprian's actions exemplified the more charitable and sympathetic undertones that made the new religion so attractive to its many converts.

For the modern reader there is frustratingly little detail about the disease itself in Cyprian's long and moralizing sermon, but almost as an afterthought a vital passage occurs. As if in parentheses, he includes important incidental details on the symptoms of the disease which makes him the best eyewitness we have from a medical point of view. Because of that, it is as the 'Plague of Cyprian' that the epidemic has generally become known. It is a long sentence with a terse framing clause which can be separated from the significant content with dashes as follows:

> This trial – that now the bowels, relaxed into constant flux, discharge the bodily strength; that a fire originated in the marrow ferments into wounds of the fauces [the arch at the back of the mouth]; that the intestines are shaken with continual vomiting; that the eyes are on fire with the injected blood; that in some cases the feet or some parts of the limbs are taken off by the contagion of diseased putrefaction; that the weakness arising by the maiming and loss of the body, either the gait is enfeebled, or the hearing is obstructed, or the sight darkened – is profitable as a proof of faith. [Cyprian, *De Mortalitate*: Treatise 7.14.]

Modern researchers think that these details and the appalling mortality rate recorded by other writers most closely fit the symptoms of a haemorrhagic fever brought about by a filovirus like ebola rather than, for instance, a variola virus like smallpox, a virulent influenza, or a bacterial disease like bubonic plague.[20] Some of the infected survived, to be sure, just as they have done in more recent ebola epidemics (typically about half of those infected, but in some outbreaks a mere ten per cent according to the World Health Organization), but for those poor individuals in whom the virus really took hold, the reality was a rapid dissolution of the bodily tissues and organs in a ghastly bout of viral meltdown.

Cyprian's sermon reads as if it was delivered at the height of the crisis but it is difficult to date precisely. There is, however, a comment made in passing that may refer to the latest news, hot off the press, of the capture of Philippopolis and the enslavement of its people by the Goths:

> Thus, when the earth is barren with an unproductive harvest, famine makes no distinction; thus, when the invasion of an enemy any city is taken, captivity at once takes all…and the disease of the eyes, the attack of fevers, and the feebleness of all the limbs is common to us with others, so long as this common flesh of ours is borne by us in the world. [Cyprian, *De Mortalitate*: Treatise 7.8.]

News of the disaster at Philippopolis would have spread throughout the empire in a matter of months. No other major city of the empire had suffered this awful fate in many generations.[21]

Cyprian's account implies that the plague was accompanied by food shortages and starvation. That is hardly surprising given the unharvested crops and the inevitable disruption to the trade networks. To the righteous it really must have seemed that an apocalypse had been unleashed on the world. Cyprian himself was confident that he was living through the end times, and took comfort from many scriptural passages that prophesied widespread suffering and chaos before the second coming and the triumphant final victory of Jesus over the forces of the Devil.

Meanwhile, on the Danube frontier, where the plague had yet to surface, the Gothic war was building towards an apocalyptic finale all of its own.

The Great Battle of Abritus

It was now around April of 251. Despite the military setbacks and the death of his son and co-emperor, Decius still had the strategic upper hand. If our interpretation is correct, Ostrogotha's force had been soundly defeated and Decius knew that Cniva's Goths would be making for home, encumbered by their captives and booty. Decius controlled the river border and especially the crossing at Oescus where the incursion had first begun. The twelfth-century Byzantine historian John Zonaras tells us that the Goths 'were hard pressed and offered to surrender all their loot if they were allowed to withdraw' but that the answer was a firm no. As Count Zosimus, writing much earlier about the beginning of the sixth century, put it, Decius 'endeavoured to cut off their retreat to their own country, intending to destroy them all, to prevent their ever again making a similar incursion'. In doing that he would rescue many of the captured citizens from a bleak future in the lands of the Goths, in part redeeming his failure to support their city in its hour of need (although by harsh convention any re-taken plunder would be the property of his victorious army rather than the wretched people from whom it had been stolen in the first place).[22]

Cniva seems to have crossed the Haemus Mountains unmolested, most plausibly via the Shipka Pass, the same route as he had used on the way south. He successfully reached the plains of Lower Moesia with booty and captives still intact. He probably skirted Nicopolis and began a dash (if the trundling movements of laden wagons can be described as such) eastward in the direction of the Black Sea coast and the delta of the lower Danube where it would be possible to cross back into Gothia with the help of local guides from the marshes.

Returning now to the south bank at Oescus (if indeed he had ventured north against Ostrogotha as we have suggested), Decius split his forces. In one of the more enlightening comments from the historical sources, Zonaras tells us that Decius 'posted Gallus, one of the men of the senate, on the route of the barbarians, ordering him not to let them pass'. The obvious way to accomplish that would have been for Gallus to use river transport and alight at the fortress at Durostorum which was directly in the path of the Gothic flight while Decius pursued the foe overland. Presumably the men under Gallus consisted of his rightful command, namely the two Moesian legions (*legio* I *italica* and *legio* XI *claudia*) and their associated auxiliaries cohorts and the river fleet. Decius commanded the main field army which had been reinforced since the disaster at Beroe. The plan was to trap Cniva in a giant pincer movement (Map 12).[23] Decius probably had a smaller and more mobile army than Cniva with a higher proportion of cavalry, and of course it consisted almost entirely of elite troops, the cream of the empire. He was also unencumbered by booty and captives. When he caught up with Cniva he would have been confident of triumphing in a pitched battle.

The road east from Nicopolis went in the direction of Durostorum via a cross-roads at the fortified city of Abritus (which boasts a splendid archaeological site and museum, just two kilometres east of the modern city-centre of Razgrad). It was near this city that Cniva must have realized from his scouts that escape was now impossible. Wearily, after much foot slogging, his men were forced to turn and confront the force rapidly advancing toward them. The final showdown of an exceptionally bloody campaign had arrived (Map 13).

Cniva's main advantage, other than weight of numbers (if indeed that was an advantage), was that he had time to reconnoitre the land and select the field of battle. The coming engagement has been known since antiquity as the Battle of Abritus (or by the alternative spelling Abrittus). Naturally enough, it was long assumed that it was fought within sight of the city walls, but the true location was confirmed in 2014 by archaeologists from the Razgrad Regional Museum of History who placed it adjacent to the modern sleepy village of Dryanovets about 15km north-west of the city itself (43°35'16 N, 26°23'57 E).[24]

Cniva had chosen his site well for what may be termed both strategic and tactical reasons. By moving north-west from Abritus up the minor road toward the naval base of Sexaginta Prista he may have avoided being caught between the two Roman armies (see Map 13). On a tactical level, the battlefield exhibits a pronounced constriction in the landscape where a small river known as the Beli Lom flows sluggishly towards the distant Danube.

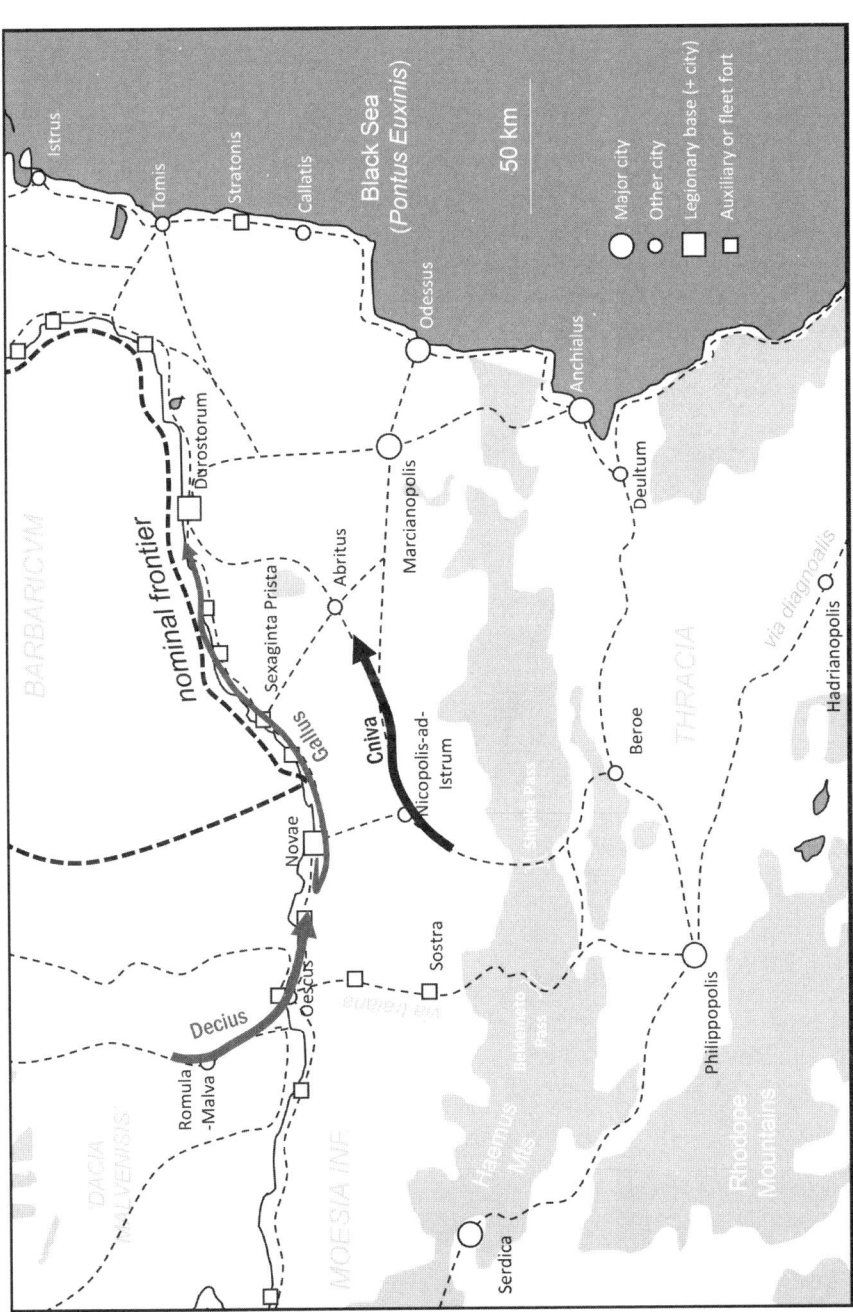

Map 12. The developing situation in Moesia prior to the Battle of Abritus in 251 CE. Decius started in pursuit of Cniva while Gallus was posted downstream to Durostorum to block the likely escape route.

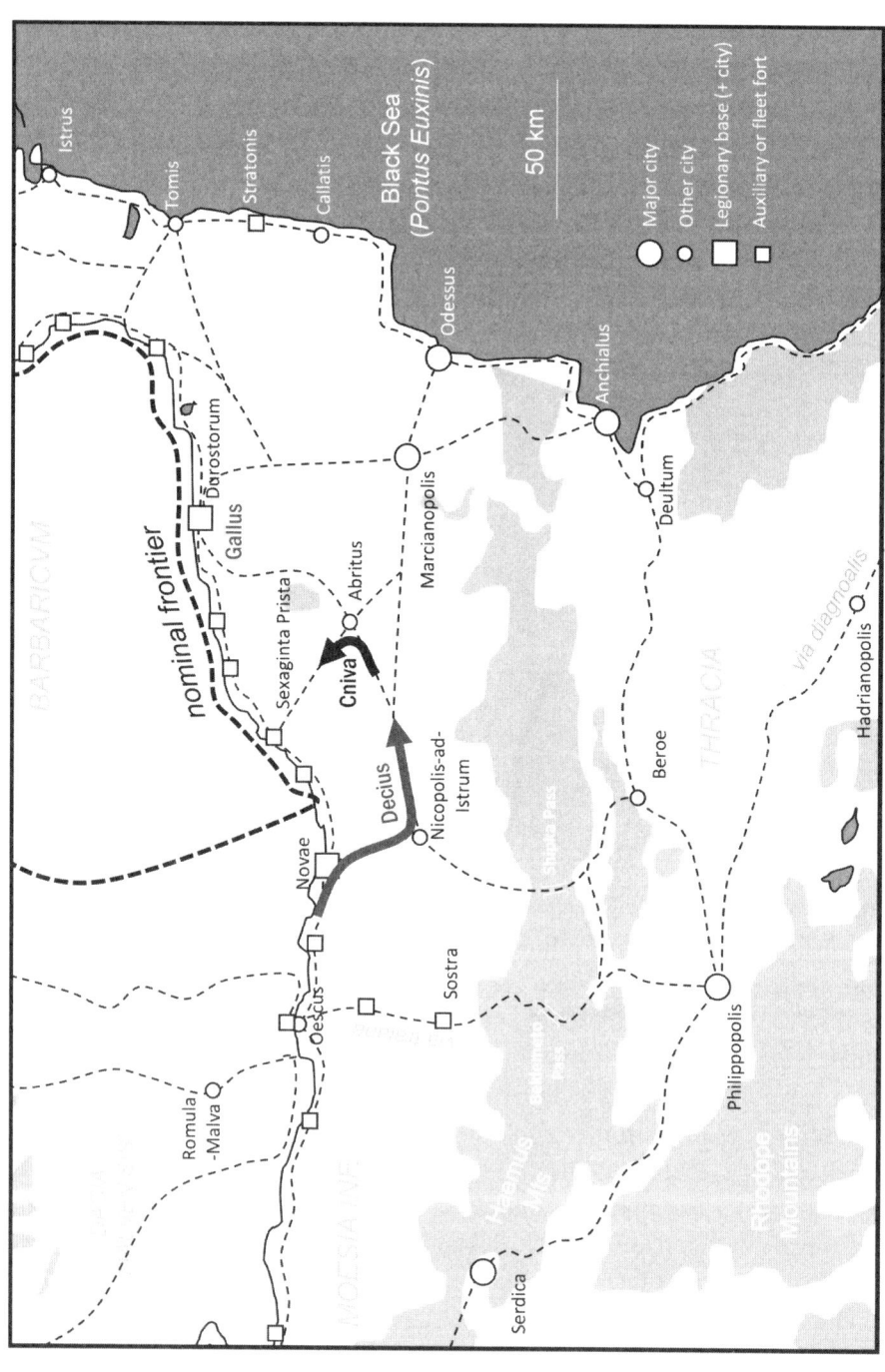

Map 13. The final move before the Battle of Abritus in 251 CE. Cniva avoided the Roman pincer by selecting a battlefield on the road to Sexaginta Prisca.

Its flood plain forms a flat valley floor a little over a kilometre across which, being fertile land, was probably farmed then as now. On the north-eastern side of the valley above the modern river channel there are steep cliffs with a wooded plateau high above (Plate 5). The converging hills on the south-western side of the valley, although less elevated, are covered in dense thorny scrub and are equally difficult to penetrate. At a stroke Cniva had reduced the Roman advantage in cavalry: outflanking manoevres would be impossible on one side (the Gothic left flank) because of the steep cliffs, and very difficult on the other. Even infantry would find it difficult to ascend the slopes in an organized fashion if the clifftops were lightly defended.

The Gothic practice was to drawn the wagons into a huge protective circle and make a camp at the army's rear.[25] Cniva may have stationed missile troops upon the heights, and perhaps even siege engines if he still had them, concealing them until the engagement began. He may even have set up a command centre upon the bluffs because they afford a perfect view of the battlefield, although his personal presence was probably required down on the plain to encourage the troops. The valley floor could have been staked out with sharpened poles as an anti-cavalry measure, and there may also have been time to create pits and traps and other obstacles as was often the case on ancient battlefields, just as Decius may have done in the previous engagement. In effect, Cniva was challenging Decius to smash through the centre of his army on a constricting piece of chosen ground (Map 14).

With the ground prepared and the Goths challenging battle, Decius would have approached from the south-east, the direction of Abritus.[26] Observing the enemy arrayed in a defensive position, he apparently camped overnight in the valley floor in an area known today simply as 'Poleto' (the field) (Plate 5). On visiting the site, this author observed several pieces of Roman pottery from the plough-soil including part of the base of a yellowish bowl and the rim of a reddish drinking vessel – from the last meals of the soldiers, perhaps. Much more exciting finds have been found by the villagers over the years and more recently by the archaeologists. These include several *spatha*-type long-swords and a *gladius* (Roman short sword), greaves (shin guards) and pieces of tessellated 'snakeskin' armour (*lorica squamata*) similar to that depicted on the Great Ludovisi Sarcophagus, and even tent poles. It seems the whole site is ripe for further archaeological investigations that may shed much more light on the events of that fateful day around the middle of May 251.[27]

The extremely brief historical sources contain rather few details about the battle, but one fact that is agreed upon is that Cniva drew his men up in three divisions. His weakest troops were likely in the front and centre, the elite to the rear. Perhaps for once we can use this information, combined

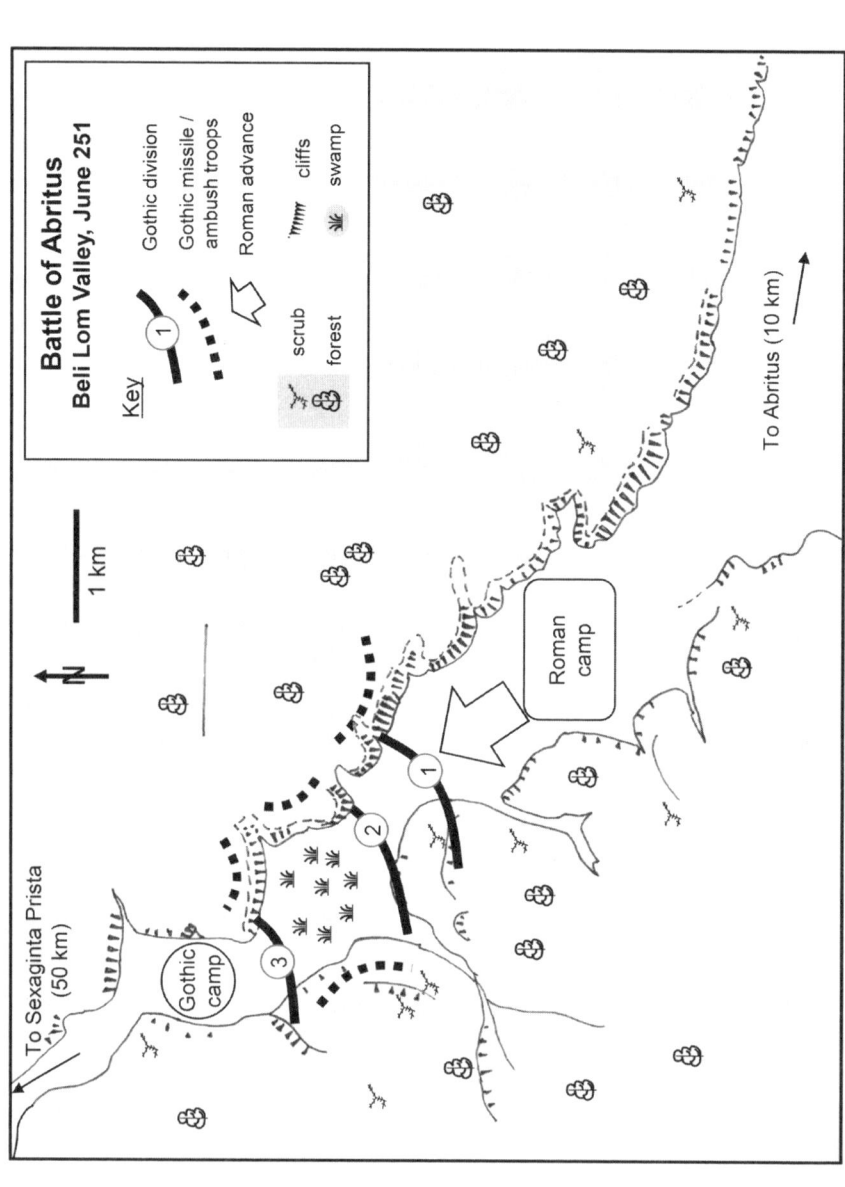

Map 14. The battle of Abritus, 251 CE. According to this author's interpretation, the three divisions of the Gothic army spread out across the progressively constricting valley with their left flanks pinned against the cliffs. The Roman army arrived from the direction of Abritus and attempted to advance up the valley, destroying the enemy in the process.

with what we can divine from the topography of the battlefield, to offer an estimate, however rough, of the size of Cniva's army. The valley is a little over a kilometre across at the likely point of Cniva's front line. If each division was ten men deep standing a metre apart (a standard estimate for ancient armies), that equates to about ten thousand men in each division. Multiply that by three and one gets thirty thousand infantry, to which can be added an unspecified number of cavalry, artillerymen and skirmishers, plus whatever number protected the camp and guarded the captives. By this admittedly very rough estimate the army probably numbered in the mid tens of thousands at least, which is entirely consistent with the sort of numbers indicated in the various historical sources.[28]

The historical accounts also say that there was a swamp or bog between the second and third line, hidden from Roman view (see Map 14). This was the key to Cniva's defensive tactic. It so happens that a small tributary joins the Beli Lom at Dryanovets, cutting across the valley floor. According to local knowledge there was also a lake here in olden times, long since drained. It was very probably an oxbow lake which is a typical feature of meandering rivers (the Beli Lom is now confined within substantial levees to keep it to a straight course). Oxbow lakes are usually filled with reeds, silt and sludge: very difficult terrain for both horses and foot soldiers encumbered with armour.

On the day of battle, with outflanking manoeuvres ruled out by the topography, Decius had little option but to use his army as a giant battering ram, relying on the infantry to scatter the enemy with their superior training, weaponry and discipline. Ancient history shows time and again that professional armies could defeat much larger forces of less well-trained enemies. Large numbers could actually act as an encumbrance on the field because they are difficult for a commander to control. No matter how brave individual men are, panic can easily spread from one poorly-led unit to another, precipitating uncontrollable rout. A well-equipped and disciplined army can act like a buzz-saw when deployed against such a force and suffer surprisingly few casualties in the process. That, at least, was the military doctrine that the Romans habitually relied on. Decius had the additional advantage that he could choose his moment to close ranks and begin the engagement. As a traditionalist, there can be little doubt that he made sure his men had full bellies, encouraged them with speeches, and used divination to confirm that the auspices were good.

There is no mention in the accounts of night fighting so we can assume the battle occurred in daylight. If it went the normal way for ancient engagements it would have started with a hellish din raised by both sides to intimidate the other. No doubt the Goths indulged in the banging of weapons and extravagant yelling and screaming that Decius had described in his letter to Philippopolis. Another possibility is that the Romans advanced in silence to emphasize their discipline, which can be even more intimidating. Initial contact involved skirmishing along the lines and exchanges of missile and artillery fire. Then, on the orders of the emperor as relayed by the senior field commanders, selected units would have advanced to close contact behind ranks of shields, their standards held proudly aloft. When the distance closed to just a few metres there would have been a final massed throw of javelins followed by a rush to hand-to-hand combat.[29]

Fighting would have been shield against shield accompanied by methodical stabbing and kicking, a trial of bodily strength and stamina. Room to manoeuvre was at a premium. Exhausted men were rotated out of the front rank to catch breath if they were lucky enough to emerge uninjured. Roman archers poured missiles over the heads of the infantry to weaken up the lines beyond. Gothic archers may well have appeared on the heights showering death and injury from above. The confined valley with its steep walls would have magnified the din as trumpets and tubas blared out above the shouting and screaming. On the Roman side, at least, the battle would have been carefully choreographed as fresh units were ordered into contact, all in an orderly and disciplined way under the watchful eye of their field officers.

Eventually, and perhaps inevitably, the Gothic front line began to crumble under the pressure, allowing the Romans to advance over the dead and wounded and evacuate their own casualties to dressing stations in the rear. More units were ordered forward to exploit the situation. The historical sources agree that soon enough the second Gothic line was also put to flight. All that could have taken many hours, but despite the intense pressure Cniva's army did not collapse into rout. Cniva may have attempted to pin his flanks with his better troops so as to envelop the advancing Romans, using his larger numbers to best advantage. Meanwhile the Roman commanders may have begun to receive reports of the boggy central zone that the men at the front were moving in to.

It may have been at about this point in the action that someone at the Roman camp buried a substantial stash of money. We know this because in 1952 a lucky farmer unearthed a pot containing about 30 gold and over 500 silver coins. It was probably the property of a senior officer. Interestingly, some of the gold coins are rather rough-and-ready in comparison to regular issues and it has been suggested that they may have been army pay minted by a mobile treasury while on campaign.[30] The owner never came back. Perhaps, then, this hoard records the moment in the battle when the Roman army was literally getting bogged down and Decius decided to gamble all by moving forward with his elite praetorians, cavalry units and bodyguard. Like Napoleon committing the Old Guard at Waterloo, it was a do-or-die move intended to bring the battle to its final phase.

Unfortunately for Decius, his group also encountered the treacherous bog. Cniva had probably stationed his own elite behind the killing zone, presumably slightly raised and on dry ground, and had concealed more men in ambush on both flanks. By the time the emperor arrived, the ground was no doubt running with as much blood as water. At this moment the ambush was sprung and the troops on the flanks made a sudden charge. The result was a mighty slaughter. It is ironic, perhaps, that Decius had previously urged the garrison at Philippopolis not to 'climb into the chariot of ignorance and charge off blindly into the unknown'. He seems to have done exactly that. The site of Decius's last stand is probably in or around the village of Dryanovets, 2–3km up the valley from the Roman camp (Plate 5).[31]

As the sympathetic account of the pagan historian Zosimus concludes:

> Proceeding therefore incautiously in an unknown place, he and his army became entangled in the mire, and under that disadvantage were so assailed by the missiles of the barbarians, that not one of them escaped with life. Thus ended the life of the excellent emperor Decius. [Zosimus, *New History* I.15.]

Abritus was to be ranked among the greatest ever defeats for the Roman army. Christian writers were not as sympathetic as Zosimus. Lactantius, for instance, wrote that 'stripped and naked, he [Decius] lay to be devoured by wild beasts and birds – a fit end for the enemy of God'.[32]

The fate of Marcianopolis

On 10 November 1929 man called Pavel Todorov was building an extension in his back yard in the tiny Bulgarian village of Reka Devnia when he stumbled across two huge clay jars full of silver coins. It was the largest hoard of Roman silver ever to be found anywhere in the empire. About 20,000 coins had already been dispersed before the museums at Sofia and Varna stepped in to acquire the rest. Numismatist N.A. Mouchmov was able to make a detailed catalogue of the remaining 80,000 pieces. They span an impressive age range of almost three hundred years. The oldest were minted by Mark Antony in 32 BCE. The youngest were coined in 251 CE, the fateful year of the Battle of Abritus, and feature both Decius and Herennius Etruscus. The Reka Devnia treasure is so large that it has sometimes been used as a yardstick to assess the frequency of the various issues of imperial coins that were in circulation across the centuries. If a specialist wants to know if a particular reverse design was common or rare, they often look at the relative numbers in this hoard.[33]

Despite the academic interest, there is frustratingly little published discussion of the hoard's context and the reason for burial. It is clearly not an official or military treasury because that would only have featured the most recent issues. It does not look like a sensible way of banking money either, because none of it has been changed into gold, a much more portable form of wealth. Common issues are common, and rare ones are rare, and although this may seem a mundane fact, it may turn out be a major clue to its origin: a hoard like Reka Devnia could only accumulate if small amounts of silver were being siphoned off almost continuously from whatever was in circulation, but the fund was never dipped in to, the money never spent.

When did this hoarding start? Not at the time of the very earliest coins, that is clear: they are relatively few and might have been in circulation for many years. Instead, it seems to have begun accumulating sometime early in the second century, probably in the reign of Trajan (98–117 CE) who is represented by over 5,000 pieces.[34] It is to be hoped that a statistical treatment of the coins together with a study of wear patterns might one day nail the date more precisely. But if it began, say, in the Year 110 CE, there was still 140 years of patient accumulation to go, putting it beyond the capacity of even the most dedicated and long-lived of hypothetical misers.

Reka Devnia is not just any old village, it sits on a mound of archaeological debris that once was the ancient city of Marcianopolis. This is the place that Dexippus tells us had held out so valiantly against the Goths the previous year under the philosopher-turned-soldier Maximus. Fortunately for us, Mouchmov conducted excavations at the discovery site soon after the coins were dug up, finding that the jars containing them had been hidden beneath the floor of what appeared to be a rather modest cellar room. But in the adjacent river bed, he found a Corinthian capital and a large marble column and other ornate items which were interpreted as coming from the colonnade of a splendid public building, possibly a temple.[35]

These facts may add up to give us a picture of the context of the great hoard. Marcianopolis was founded by the Emperor Trajan soon after 106 CE who was busy in the area planning the local economy and infrastructure after his victory in Dacia. The story goes that the emperor's sister Marcia sent her maid to fetch water from the river but she dropped the gold flask and it washed away. Fortunately for the maid, it was eventually found downstream, which was taken as a positive sign from the gods. Trajan chose the spot for a new city and named it after his sister.[36] A temple was founded and the money soon started to trickle in. It may have been donated in relatively small amounts by pious visitors over many years, each offering up a prayer. That would explain why the Reka Devnia hoard is so representative of the silver currency as a whole and why it was never spent, being inviolate and protected by the priesthood for generations.[37]

Mouchmov also made the important observation that the building housing the treasure had been destroyed by fire, with burnt rubble lying all around. The year 251 is the *terminus post quem* of the hoard – the earliest possible date for the burial and the destruction of the putative temple which could, in principle, have happened any time after that.[38] But because there are so many coins, it seems likely that it was also that year the hoard was lost. Presumably the priestly authorities were either killed or captured and nobody who survived the catastrophe knew anything about the money that lay beneath the charred ruins. Hence the real significance of the Reka Devnia treasure appears to be that it points to a thoroughgoing sack of Marcianopolis by the Goths in the same year as Abritus. The city went into rapid decline in the mid-third century until being re-established a couple of decades later. Hence it seems likely that Cniva or one of his generals moved against it after destroying the Roman imperial army and before retiring across the Danube. Marcianopolis is only about 100km east of Abritus and may even have been targetted out of spite for its resistance the previous year. Unfortunately, however, the relevant part of Dexippus's history that might have described the eventual sack of the city is missing.

Gothgeld

Another fascinating coda to the Battle of Abritus comes from numismatists Aleksander Bursche and Kirill Myzgin.[39] Bursche noticed that hundreds of gold aurei in the names of Decius and his family and their immediate predecessors have turned up in 'barbarian' territory over the years. Some of these coins hail from great aristocratic or royal collections going back hundreds of years. Now they mostly reside in museums, ranging from Denmark to Poland, Ukraine, Belarus and Russia. Bursche diligently set about recording them, plus every known mention of such a piece in the antiquarian literature. The original findspot of most of the coins is unknown, but similar examples have been turning up in increasing numbers in the twenty-first century thanks to the rise in the number of active metal detectorists and improvements in their machines (especially for gold discrimination). The tally as of 2020 was around 500 finds.[40]

The (literally) striking fact is that virtually all of them are pierced with a hole above the emperor's head (Plate 5). The holes are of fairly uniform size, all made with a circular punch banged in from the obverse side. This shows that although they are now dispersed over a huge area, they belong to a single group. It is very tempting to think that they are war booty, carried by warriors returning from the campaign. A simple knotted leather strap is all that would be needed to make a striking pendant. Perhaps they were handed out as medals on the battlefield of Abritus by Cniva himself.

Back in 'barbaricum' some of the pieces were cut up into quarters or even smaller fragments and deposited in the ground. This fits with the known Germanic ritual of burying weapons and artefacts taken from the enemy in war. Cutting up the coins and offering them to the gods may have been a way of ritually destroying the power of the enemy. But many warriors must have kept hold of their trophies because at least two are known to have come from the graves of men who were interred with them, along with weapons and other artifacts. Some are partly melted, presumably in the fierce heat of funeral pyres. Possession of such an ornament would have marked a man out as one of the heroes of Abritus for the rest of his days.[41]

The pieces that have been discovered must be a minute fraction of what was originally taken at Abritus. Bursche estimates that the total haul may have amounted to many tonnes of gold. At 4–5 grams each, that equates to hundreds of thousands of gold pieces, perhaps somewhere in the ballpark of the half million that Philip had used to pay off Shapur after the defeat at Mishik in 244. Decius may have been sufficiently confident, foolhardy, or untrusting of his subordinates that his field army went into battle with a huge mobile exchequer in the rear, gold being the most readily transportable form of wealth.

Even more fascinating is the distribution of the known findspots of the holed aurei when put on a map. These form a great arc which extends through Poland and across to western Ukraine and Belarus. Bursche and Myzgin point out that this area corresponds well with the so-called Wielbark and Černjachov cultures of the second and third centuries, as recognized by archaeologists, which has often (though controversially) been identified with the Goths: the fit is very striking when the two are overlaid. Particularly noticeable is the abrupt termination of the distribution on the west bank of the Dneiper River, beyond which was apparently not Gothic territory.[42] The conclusion seems inescapable: the army at Abritus was drawn from a vast but politically and culturally well-defined area that extended all the way from the Baltic to the Black Sea. This, then, is tangible evidence for the existence of the land of 'Gothia' mentioned in Shapur's inscription at Naqsh-i-Rustam.

We know very little about the military organization of the Goths of the third century because they left no written records. Each year the call must have gone out to young men from all over the area to congregate for war. They would have travelled vast distances along the river systems of the Vistula, Oder and Dneiper, and on arrival they needed to be housed, fed, equipped, drilled, trained, and organized. The distances they covered in campaign and the fact that they were able to defeat an elite Roman imperial army in pitched battle suggests that by the time they took to the field, they were far from the stereotypical disorganized and undisciplined rabble often envisaged. All that organization was achieved without a monetary economy or centralized record keeping, so it presumably relied on the tribal hierarchies and the promise of plunder. Abritus was a stunning military achievement for this non-literate culture, and of course a massive inducement for the younger relations of the veterans to join up and seek their own fame and fortune by raiding the Roman Empire in future years.

Writing of the battlefield in the sixth century, Jordanes remarked: 'This place is to-day called the Altar of Decius, because he there offered strange sacrifices to idols before the battle'.[43] But the gods, it seems, had not been listening.

Part II

Gallus to Valerian, 251–260 CE

Chapter 7

Gallus

Peace in our time

Insofar as Decius is remembered at all as a military leader, his failure at Abritus was his defining moment: 'incompetent and embarrassing' according to one recent assessment; 'monumentally foolish' according to another.[1] And yet on the morning of battle he must have been brimming with confidence. The war had been long and arduous; there had been both victories and defeats, but he had finally gained the strategic upper hand. Cniva's desperate offer to hand over all the captives and booty in return for a safe passage home was just that. The Gothic chieftain, possibly now a king, had been forced to offer battle against an elite Roman army, the last thing he would have wanted to do.

If Decius had won a stunning victory that day, he would have dictated harsh peace terms on the surviving Gothic elite which would have meant once again enrolling their forces in the Roman army and boosting its strength, deterring any Persian threat. As *gothicus maximus*, greatest victor over the Goths, and with the full backing of the Senate and People of Rome, he would have been in a position of strength unparalleled by any emperor for at least fifty years. And as a new *optimus princeps*, he could turn his attention to rebuilding the economy and prestige of the empire. His brutal suppression of the Christians would have continued unabated, perhaps to the extent that the religion may never have re-surfaced. Ten years later, a long and glorious reign might have culminated with a march on Persian Mesopotamia, re-incorporating it into the empire as had been achieved over a century before by his hero Trajan.

Instead, a new and much more uncertain future lay ahead. Trebonianus Gallus was proclaimed emperor by his troops on the spot without bothering to wait for a decision from the Senate. It has been suggested that this occurred in the fortress at Abritus where the defeated Romans may have re-grouped and which seemingly never fell to the Goths. Unsurprisingly, however, rumours of betrayal began to spread, focusing on the shadowy figure of Gallus who had not been on the field of battle nor ridden to the rescue, but profited from the disaster. The story can be found in two of the ancient sources. It was alleged that Gallus had made a secret deal with the Goths and even pointed out the battlefield to them, along with its bog, and then sent messages to Decius encouraging him to attack on unfavourable ground. On the face of it, it is a most unlikely tale, but if the ultimate source of the information should turn out to be the well-informed Dexippus, then we would need to give it more credence than it currently appears to deserve. With hindsight, however, the defeat is probably best assigned to the inspired generalship of Cniva and a new level of organization and martial ability among the Goths.[2]

In the immediate aftermath of Abritus, the reality was that Gallus with his border force was not strong enough to challenge Cniva's victorious army. Of course he could have sallied forth, but he and his men would very probably have suffered the same fate as Decius, making the situation ever worse. The sensible thing to do, while he retained some leverage, was to preserve the remaining border forces and enter negotiations. The first and most pressing problem was to secure the provinces of Moesia and Thrace from further attacks: a peace treaty would be needed, however humiliating the terms. Perhaps then Cniva's great army would disperse and the recent annual ritual of mass Gothic incursions from across the Danube would come to an end. The key element of the treaty would have to be renewal of the annual subsidy which had so unwisely (as it turned out) been terminated by Philip just a few years before. The Persian threat had not diminished and it was by now patently evident that the Roman Empire could not afford major hostilities against Goths and Persians simultaneously.

The historical sources agree that a peace treaty along these lines was indeed agreed. The Goths were allowed to return home across the Danube unmolested. Not only did they get to keep all their plunder from Philippopolis and the other ransacked cities of Moesia and Thrace, plus the gold from the imperial treasury, but they could now look forward to receiving annual payments to secure their new 'friendship' with Rome. We do not know the scale of the agreed subsidy, or how it compared with what had been paid previously, but given the circumstances it must have been an eye-watering figure: *vae victis*, or woe to the vanquished, as the old saying went.[3]

And so it was that Gallus managed to achieve a degree of stability on the border. It is likely that the treaty was concluded on a personal level between him and Cniva in the Germanic way rather than on a 'state' level. Personal alliances and guarantees meant more in times of near chaos than binding international treaties. Peace would also have suited Cniva: he had won the war and secured enormous riches for his men. He was not, however, of the Royal Amal line, and Ostrogotha had at least one surviving son (called Unwen according to the *Widsith*, or Hunuil according to Jordanes). Cniva's priority was probably to secure his status and stabilize his realm, and perhaps also to demand fealty from King Fastida of the Gepids.

We must not imagine that Abritus was necessarily a terminal disaster for the Roman Empire. It still mantled the entire Mediterranean, a huge and prosperous area largely untouched by warfare, if not the recent plague; traders still plied the seas, the imperial bureaucracy functioned adequately, and the provinces were producing food, wealth and manpower. The task for Gallus was to steady the ship of state and ride out the storm. The cost of agreeing peace was permanent damage to his reputation among the hard-liners in Rome, and all the later chroniclers, for whom any dealings with the barbarians short of inflicting mass slaughter was a sign of deficiency. The peace was shaky, to be sure, but in reality it was a significant achievement under the circumstances. The new emperor was undoubtedly demonstrating diplomatic talent in playing a difficult hand.

The dreadful news of Abritus reached the capital between 9 and 24 June, by which latter date Decius had been deified at the behest of a solemn senate.[4] That still left one male member of the imperial family standing, the younger son Hostilian *caesar* who was in the city together with his mother Herennia Etruscilla. Gallus, still in Moesia, did the decent thing and declared Hostilian co-emperor, awarding him the rank of co-*augustus*. In reality he had little choice: he could hardly depose Hostilian and his mother remotely and expect them to quietly disappear. Recognizing Hostilian as equal to him in rank, if not in actual power, was probably necessary to avoid yet more civil war. And by being seen as the person to offer Hostilian the promotion, Gallus earmarked for himself the implied seniority, as indeed befitted his age and experience. He also raised his own son Gaius Vibius Volusianus, or Volusian, then aged about 21, to the rank of *caesar*.

At some point in the autumn, Gallus entered Rome to a formal, if not exactly joyous, welcome (*adventus*, as recorded on some of the coins). Every effort was made to apply a positive gloss on events. At least the new man was another very traditional type of emperor: an Italian aristocrat and senator of consular rank who had excelled in his public duties. He had been hand-picked by Decius for the vital governorship of Moesia, which must indicate that he was considered to be of the highest ability.

To cement the new reality, Gallus declared himself the adopted son of Decius[5] and his own son, the young prince Volusian, married one of Decius's surviving daughters whose name, unfortunately, is not known. Arranged marriages like this had been a fact of life for centuries among the ruling elite. Whether or not the two made a happy couple was irrelevant: the royal wedding would have been a welcome diversion in Rome during very dark times. Gallus's wife, and Volusian's mother, was a lady called Afinia Gemina Baebiana, but quite sensibly there was no move to give her the title of *augusta*.

Having two emperors from different families was one thing, but two leading ladies may have been seen as a step too far.[6] The net result of this diplomatic manoeuvring was that a new imperial dynasty emerged with Gallus as the de facto senior *augustus*, Hostilian his colleague, and Volusian the true heir apparent with a new wife and an empress as his mother-in-law.

A major empire-wide recruitment drive must have been ordered to make good the battlefield losses. Evidence from the early issues of the new coinage shows that as well as a range of standard types there seems to have been a distinct effort to promote the cult of the war god Mars as guarantor of peace (*marti pacifero*). That there was a crisis in the gold supply after the loss of the treasury at Abritus is demonstrated by the coinage itself. The average weight of the aureus dropped instantly from 4.31 g to 3.58 g and a new 'double aureus' weighing 5.86 g was introduced, showing the emperor wearing a radiate crown. This was a bold, impressive and beautiful coin, but of course it was not twice the weight of the old aureus, or even the new one. It has been argued that from this point on, the gold coinage was not used much as regular currency but rather as a store of wealth, by weight. Evidence for this is twofold: from now on individual gold coin finds become very rare in comparison to the earlier history of the empire, and later Roman gold coins rarely show much wear.[7]

At Rome, the silver content of the double-denarius was maintained, but those minted at Antioch are often in poor quality metal.[8] The bronze sestertius continued to be struck from well-engraved dies but the weight was diminished with the result that some of the pieces are more square than round. All this is more evidence that the concept of the face value of the coinage was holding, at least in the eyes of the state, but drifting away from its intrinsic value in metal. Inflation was the inevitable result and by implication a drop in purchasing power and living standards for all those tied in to the monetary economy of the empire.

There seems to have been disagreement between the great mints about what the senior new emperor looked like: at Rome he is slightly jowly with a long nose but at Antioch he is more of a block-head. A bronze bust in the Vatican Museum in Rome may be the best likeness: it shows Gallus with rather soft and thoughtful features, sunken eyes, and a slightly hunted expression (Plate 6).[9]

Universal pestilence

Recall that the 'plague of Cyprian' seem to have made its first appearance in the historical record in the letters of Dionysius, bishop of Alexandria, in the year 249, more or less at the end of Philip's reign. Drought, plague and other disasters were generally attributed to the anger of the gods, hence reports of the contagion spreading in Egypt may have been one of the reasons that Decius had ordered his universal edict of sacrifice early in 250. It hadn't worked. In Carthage the plague evidently hit later, following the persecution according to the testimony of Bishop Cyprian, hence it seems to have peaked there early in 251. Carthage was but a small step from Rome and it appears that the disease took hold in the Eternal City soon after Gallus arrived in the summer of that year, hence his is the name most associated with it in the various later chronicles that record the calamitous event. The epidemic had become a pandemic. One writer, Orosius, describes it as an 'unusually relentless and grave pestilence' and that 'there was almost no province of Rome, no city, no house, which was not attacked and emptied by this general plague'. He tells us that it also affected animals, killing the livestock and 'corrupting the waters and infecting the pastures with contagion'. Human to animal transmission is plausible with an ebola-like disease, although there is no evidence that domesticated animals have ever shown symptoms of ebola and died in modern times. If Orosius is reliable on this point it could be a significant warning from the past of what a filovirus pandemic could one day inflict on us again.

Like any virus that has jumped the species, the plague of Cyprian would have been evolving fast. Every infected person is a vast incubator of virions and the more people infected, the more mutations occur. Less infectious variants fade away while more infectious strains gallop ahead. The brute logic of natural selection is that viruses adapt themselves to the environment they happen to find themselves in. In this case, the contagion was optimizing itself to spread in the conditions then prevailing in the Roman Empire. Various Byzantine accounts of it seem to rely principally on a sadly lost history of Philostratus of Athens who witnessed the plague. According to this testimony it seems to have spread more rapidly in the cooler months when people were in closer proximity; one source tells us that it had an annual cycle 'starting in the autumn and abating with the rising of the Dog Star'. Another describes it as 'a great pestilence, which moved out of the east toward the west, and no city was spared from this destruction… The disease was transmitted through the clothes or simply by sight'. It caused a greater mortality than ever known before and 'denuded many of the cities of their inhabitants'.[10]

The chroniclers George the Monk (ninth century) and Cedrenus (eleventh century) report the event in the same way, virtually word for word, both relying on some earlier Christian source which is lost:

> a pestilential disease began destroying the human race to the point of annihilation. For from the earth and the sea certain vapours arose, and

in addition to these, winds and breezes blew from the rivers and an exhalation from the harbours, so it was deemed that the dew was the effluence or corpses. From this, then, unremitting plagues and grave and incurable diseases afflicted the earth, and limitless and numberless became the destruction of mankind, with the result that the majority of the dead were abandoned unburied… For there was not a household in which there was not one dead and reeking, and the harsh people of the gentiles, avoiding the transmission of the sickness and of death, cast people out unburied or even half-dead. George the Monk, *Chronicle* 465.12–466.15[11]

One of the more graphic accounts of the disease comes from the fourth century life of Gregory Thaumaturgus ('the Wonderworker'). Before examining this, let us first take a moment to consider this interesting character. As a young man, Gregory had been converted to Christianity by the famous theologian Origen (who, at this point in our narrative, is still in grim detention). He was later elected bishop of his home town of Neocaesarea in Pontus (on the Black Sea coast of northern Turkey) even though there were just seventeen Christians in the place at the time. By his good works and many miracles he turned Neocaesarea into a Christian powerhouse. He went into hiding during the Decian persecution so as to avoid making sacrifices. He is also distinguished as the first person in history to report seeing a vision of the Virgin Mary and thereby contributed to her growing cult.

The plague in Neocaesarea struck after the persecution, possibly also in 251, reportedly killing over half the population. It 'fell abruptly upon the people, penetrating faster than they expected, feeding on their houses like fire, so that the temples were filled with those laid low by the disease who had fled there in the hope of a cure, and the springs and streams and cisterns were full of those burning with thirst because of the weakness brought on by the disease.' It is interesting to read (and in a Christian source too) that the people fled to the pagan temples. In fact it was the obvious thing to do to seek help. Some of these establishments were associated with healing, such as shrines to Aesculapius or Salus, and may have functioned as hospitals for the public good funded by charitable donations. Burning thirst is, incidentally, another significant symptom of haemorraghic fever.[12]

The effect in Rome, the world's greatest metropolis, was extreme. The *Historia Augusta*, possibly at this point citing a lost passage from Dexippus, says that 'such a great plague arose in both Rome and the cities of Greece that in one day 5,000 people died of the same disease', a claim that is within the bounds of possibility and consistent with a 50 per cent mortality rate.[13] The most prominent victim in the capital was the young co-*augustus* Hostilian, son of the deified Decius. He seems to have died around the end of August 251, just ten weeks or so after his father fell in battle at Abritus. That, at least, is the official version of events as recorded by later Latin chroniclers. Unsurprisingly there is a suspicion that he was murdered by Gallus, but historians mostly accept the explanation of plague. It is a reminder that the great pathogen was almost as much a threat to the lives of the wealthy elite as it was to the ordinary folk. Gallus's son Volusian was promoted from *caesar* to *augustus*, probably after the funeral and deification of Hostilian, and he is attested as such by late summer. It is no wonder then that a prominent theme on the coinage of Gallus and Volusian thereafter was the health of the remaining emperors.[14]

There is an unusual development in the coinage from this time that may relate to the death of Hostilian. Numismatists have noticed that for a short period all six *officinae* engraved a prominent star in the background of their reverse design (Plate 6). This is the only time such a thing happened during the whole run of Roman imperial coins and no written source refers to it. It must have been ordered from the top. The frequency of these pieces suggests that the practice continued from about August to October inclusive, after which the designs continued just as before, without the star. There is no known astronomical event from this time: it does not coincide with Halley's Comet for instance, and there is no evidence of a nova or supernova in the meticulous records kept in China. Hence it has been suggested that perhaps the star represents a period of mourning for the soul of the deified emperor Hostilian, now taking his place in the firmament. Meanwhile the Empress Herennia Etruscilla seems to have retired from public life and no more coins were minted in her name.[15]

Aurelius Victor records the interesting detail that Gallus and Volusian 'won popular favour because they meticulously and assiduously arranged the burials of all the poorest folk'.[16] Jordanes goes even further by claiming that

> They reigned amid universal peace and favour. Only one thing was laid to their charge, namely the general epidemic. But this was an accusation made by ignorant slanderers, whose custom it is to wound the lives of others with their malicious bite. [Jordanes, *Getica* XIX, 106.]

Gallus and Volusian did not flee the city but sat it out, managing the situation and dealing with the rumours as best they could. With the Danube frontier experiencing an uneasy peace (a man called Marcus Aemilius Aemilianus had been posted there in command of the troublesome Moesian troops previously commanded by Gallus), the new emperor was able to see out the rest of the disastrous year 251 in the palaces of Rome. Then, as the New Year dawned, he and Volusian took the consulship as was normal for emperors in their first year.

The Christians were still mightily unpopular in many quarters because of the plague. One of the magistrates in Africa called Demetrian was actively denouncing them as responsible for all the ills of the world. This spurred Bishop Cyprian, now apparently out of hiding and going about his normal business, to pen a spirited defence. The two men were in agreement that the world was showing signs of final decay. As Cyprian put it, there was less heat in summer, less rainfall in winter, less water in the springs, less fruit on the trees, less precious metal in the hills, fewer boats on the sea, a decline in fair dealing in the market place, and a general moral collapse: 'individual and particular elements in the world have begun to run out, when already half the world is in eclipse and at its final end.' But of course in Cyprian's eyes this was not the fault of the Christians but evidence that the one true God was angry at all the evident sin in the world and the foolish worship of idols. The vengeance of God was at hand. It had all been foretold in the scriptures by the doomster prophets whom he quoted at length with evident satisfaction.[17]

Gallus must have continued to enact anti-Christian measures of unknown nature because we find him listed as a persecutor in later Christian accounts. He was certainly of the traditional religion. From the very first emission of his reign there was a new and unprecedented focus on Juno Martialis ('Juno of Mars', she being mother of Mars), her temple, an elegant, garlanded rotunda, being depicted on the coinage. It is likely, therefore, that this entirely new design was ordered by the incoming emperor. It has been suggested that Juno Martialis, who is elsewhere apparently depicted with shears for the cutting of hair, was in some way connected to hygiene and protecting the people from the dangerous miasmas that were blamed for spreading the plague. We do not know what public health measures were enacted during the pandemic but a focus on personal hygiene and the cutting of hair may have been part of it.[18]

Another new theme that appears on the coinage for the first time is *apollo salutaris* (Apollo the Healer), reminding us once again that not all who contracted the disease died, although many of the survivors were permanently debilitated. Apollo was a Greek god, not a Roman one, but he had reputedly helped save Rome from an outbreak of plague as far back as 433 BCE. Now dedications to him appeared in military contexts across the empire, including for instance on Hadrian's Wall in Britain, suggesting an imperial decree was enacted to sacrifice to Apollo and help stem the pestilence.[19]

But if the emperors hoped that their pious dedications would bring respite to the troubled empire, they were soon to be disappointed. In the spring of

252 two major calamities occurred. The first was the assassination of King Khusrov II of Armenia, a key Roman ally in the east, which was followed by a massive Persian invasion of his kingdom, and the second – perhaps inevitably – was that the Goths broke their vows and attacked the empire once again. Although these things occurred simultaneously, we will have to deal with the problems one at a time, starting in the east.

Treachery in Armenia

In Persian eyes, the Kingdom of Armenia (under long-term ruler Khosrov II) was a powerful rebel state that harboured the remnants of the old Parthian royal house and as such was an existential threat to the Sassanian dynasty; not only that, they had a regular habit of invading Sassanian territory and plundering the countryside. As the Armenian historian Agathangelos put it, the Armenians had 'attempted to eradicate, destroy completely, extirpate, and overthrow the Persian kingdom and aimed at abolishing its civilization… for ten years they made continual incursions in this manner, plundering all the lands which were under the suzerainty and authority of the Persians.' But now the balance of power had shifted. Shapur aimed at outright conquest of Armenia although nobody could pretend that would be easy given the extensive mountainous terrain and the powerful, well-organized and experienced military backed by the might of Rome.

Evidence for what happened comes from an entertaining story from the fifth century Armenian history of Agathangelos. The story concerns an Iranian (Pahlavi) nobleman called Anak. He was descended from the old deposed Parthian royal house, but unlike others of his family he had remained in Persia and was now a senior figure at Shapur's court. His ambition was to recover his ancestral status by becoming satrap (local ruler) of Pahlav under Shapur's wider dominion. To achieve this aim, he offered to kill King Khusrov, and then in the succeeding mayhem Shapur could invade and subjugate the Armenian kingdom. Shapur sealed the deal as follows: 'if only you settle this account loyally, I shall return to you your native Parthian land, your own Pahlav, and I shall honour you with a crown and make you famous and honoured in my kingdom and call you second to me.'[20]

Towards the end of 251, Anak posed as a refugee, pretending to flee the Persian court to exile in Armenia 'along with his brother, his household, their wives and children and all his retinue'. The asylum seekers finally made their way through the war-torn borderlands as far as Khusrov's winter capital, the city of Khalkhal near the Caspian Sea coast (now in northern Iran). There they were welcomed with open arms and given full royal protection:

> ...and for the whole duration of that winter they passed the days of chilling winds and ice in cheerfulness. But when the warmer days of the southerly winds arrived to open the gates of spring, the king departed from those regions. They descended to the province of Ayrarat, to the city of Valarshapat. And while they happily relaxed there the king decided to gather an army and invade Persian territory. [Agathangelos, *History of the Armenians* I. 30–31.]

It was at this point that Anak and his brother made their move. Having arranged to meet the king in private, they attacked him with daggers and fled on horseback, heading for Persian territory. When the mortally wounded king was found, a great hue and cry was raised and the palace guard split into groups and tried to cut off the assassins' flight. Anak and his brother had mistimed their move: the Araxes (modern Aras) River was by now in full spate with the melting of the winter snows and the fugitives were easily cut off at a bridge, apprehended and then 'cast into the river'.

In his dying breath the king ordered the massacre of the assassins' entire families and their retinues, even though they had all been wholly innocent of these designs. 'From among the children they left not even those too young to know their right hand from their left. Likewise they exterminated the female side of the family by the sword.' But the nurses managed to hide and rescue two of Anak's infant sons of whom one was spirited away to Persia and the other to the Roman Empire. It now sounds like we are going to scroll forward a few decades and the brothers, not knowing their past, will meet in combat and between them somehow decide the fate of the world. Unfortunately the surviving account ends there, so we do not know how it ends, unless and until Hollywood picks it up one day, that is.

Anak's treachery reads more like a historical romance than actual history but it may contain a grain of truth. Certainly the spring would have been the ideal time for an assassination, just before the marching season began, and the removal of the royal court from Khalkhal to Valarshapat (near modern Yerevan) would have been a serious blow to any such plan, it being about 800 km further north and far distant from Persian territory. The brothers would hardly have been confident of escaping over such a huge distance, nor are they likely to have intentionally left their entire families behind to be slaughtered. A clandestine assassination, sadly botched, seems the most likely interpretation. Whatever the truth, Khusrov indeed died around this time, to Shapur's great delight.

> And it happened that when the Persian king heard of all this he greatly rejoiced, and he made that day a great and joyous festival and carried

out many vows to the [Zoroastrian] fire-temples. He assembled an army and hastened to make incursions throughout the regions of Armenia. He brought into captivity many men and beasts, old men and infants, youths and children alike.... Then the Persian king came and imposed his own name on Armenia, and set the Greek [i.e., Roman] army to flight, pursuing it to borders of Greece [i.e., the Roman Empire]. He had ditches dug to fix the frontier. [Agathangelos, *History of the Armenians* I. 35–36.]

This abbreviated account is virtually all we have to record what was a seismic event at the time. The 'Greek' (i.e., Roman imperial) army mentioned by Agathangelos must have been a legionary force under an unknown commander who was treaty-bound to try to prevent a Persian annexation. The best positioned force was *legio* XII *fulminata* at Melitene in Cappadocia with whatever auxiliaries it could muster. We can imagine these troops mobilizing as soon as the Persian invasion got underway, but as the Armenian army collapsed they were unable to prevent the conquest.

It seems likely that the much fought-over Roman border city of Nisibis was taken by the Persians as a prelude to this invasion. This city had switched between Persian and Roman control in previous conflicts, most recently being recaptured by the Romans during Gordian's invasion just eight years earlier. In the tenth century, Eutychius of Alexandria, one of the first Christian writers to use Arabic, and also known as Sa'id ibn Batriq, related a curious story about the capture of Nisibis which begins with Shapur being angered on seeing the defensive refortification of the city. Perhaps this had been conducted in contravention of the peace treaty agreed with Philip. After being frustrated by a prolonged siege, Shapur ordered his men to pray for victory (presumably to the Zoroastrian fire god Ahura Mazda) whereupon 'the city wall was split from top to bottom and a gap opened up which men could enter'. The entire garrison was slaughtered, everyone else was enslaved, and Shapur carried off 'a great quantity of wealth'.[21]

The conquest of Armenia in 252 was a major victory for Shapur – finally he had destroyed his great enemy. The remnants of dissident Parthian and Armenian royalty fled to Roman territory. Rome's most important ally had fallen and the Persian presence now loomed menacingly over the Roman east. Some historians have suggested that Shapur may have followed this victory up with an immediate invasion of the empire, but that seems unlikely given that Armenia was a huge, mountainous area and would have taken considerable time and manpower to subdue. It seems best to interpret Agathangelos's statement that Shapur 'had ditches dug to fix the frontier' to mean that he intended to hold Armenia for good and adopted a defensive posture, for now at least. He placed his son and heir Hormizd in charge of Armenia, no doubt with instructions to crush any stirrings of dissent, and returned to Persia.[22]

This was terrible news for Gallus and the strategists in Rome. Their forces in the east were in a relatively weak and demoralized state. With the buffer state of Armenia now out of the equation, the entire eastern empire now faced an existential threat. An empire-wide call went out to raise detachments for a new eastern campaign, but this must have been a most difficult task when the army simultaneously had to make good the losses of Abritus and of any men who had succumbed to the ongoing pandemic.[23]

Sacrilegious barbarians

North of the Danube, the victorious Goths still commanded a major force and, six months on from Abritus, they were eagerly expecting first payment of the annual tribute and not in a mood for quibbling. Unsurprisingly, a row broke out. According to Zonaras, they 'came to receive these things, and, saying that what was given to them was less than what had been promised, departed under threats'. Perhaps there was a problem with the weight or precious metal content of the coins the Goths were being offered (which is quite likely if the payment was being made in the new reduced-weight gold coins), or perhaps it was just a pretext for war. Treaty or no treaty, the Goths could see the empire was in a weakened state and many of the young fighters may have been itching for an excuse to re-invade.

Subsequent events are very obscure and the accounts offered by the ancient historians are sparse and divergent, but if we follow the most detailed version given by Zosimus, which was probably based on a lost part of Dexippus's *Scythica*, it seems that a Gothic army crossed the lower Danube once again in 252, and ravaged 'the whole of Europe quite unhindered'. This claim is less astonishing than it at first seems once it is appreciated that Europe or 'Europa' was a relatively small district of eastern Thrace bordering on the great city of Byzantium, later made into a Roman province of that name. It corresponds approximately to that part of modern Turkey that lies west of the Bosporus. It is most unlikely that the Goths besieged Byzantium itself which was in a great defensive position and had formidable walls even then, but the minor cities and farmland of the area were plundered for the first time.[24]

The fact that the Goths were unhindered suggests that the local frontier legions, especially *legio* XI *claudia* at Durostorum, whose zone of control this was supposed to be, were unable to stop the incursion. By the time they reached Europa the Goths had already come over 500km as the crow flies suggesting that they were probably using water-borne transport, a tactic which we know they were to adopt in subsequent years. The Roman Black Sea fleet (*classis pontica*) was evidently unable to prevent this happening.[25]

With the months dragging by, and still no sign of a response from Rome, the marauders made a wholly unexpected (and possibly initially unplanned) move by crossing into Asia Minor. Before them lay the whole of Anatolia, an entirely new territory to exploit, and one that had been peaceful and prosperous for generations. It was virtually undefended except for whatever militias the towns and cities could raise. Zosimus tells us that the Goths plundered as far as Cappadocia, Pessinus, and Ephesus (Map 15).[26] To achieve this in any reasonable time frame they must have split into smaller units, the most obvious solution being for one group to despoil the Black Sea coastline of Bithynia and Pontus as far as Cappadocia (which was an additional thousand kilometres each way), another to go south along the Aegean coast toward Ephesus (a large and populous city that was not destroyed at this time and so may have beaten off the raiders), and still another to attack far inland to the historic city of Pessinus.

An interesting relic of these times is an inscribed stone slab from the city of Stratonicea which lay a little beyond Ephesus to the south. The city was not attacked, but the inhabitants were evidently terrified of a repeat attempt and so consulted the nearby hilltop oracle of Zeus. Fortunately the great god was still listening and was able to give a comforting reply, as documented in the inscription:

> Oracle of Zeus Panêmêrios. The city under the instruction also of Serapis, asks through Philokalos the son of Philokalos, *oikonomos* [City Treasurer] whether the sacrilegious barbarians will attack the city or its territory in the coming year. The god gave his oracle: 'I see that you are troubled but am unable to understand the cause of this. For I have arranged neither to give your city for sacking, nor to make it slave from free, nor to deprive it of any other good things.'[27]

Given these movements it seems inevitable that the invaders were using boats for transport, coasting up and down the Black Sea littoral, the Sea of Marmara, and the Aegean. From the inclusion of Pessinus in the list of places attacked it is clear that they were not just seaborne raids, because the city is far inland. This must have been achieved by long-distance mounted raiding that took advantage of the excellent road network, and it was conducted with complete impunity. All this must have taken months. The plan was presumably for the raiders to congregate once again at their crossing point at the Dardanelles – where they must have used boats – before marching back the way they came.

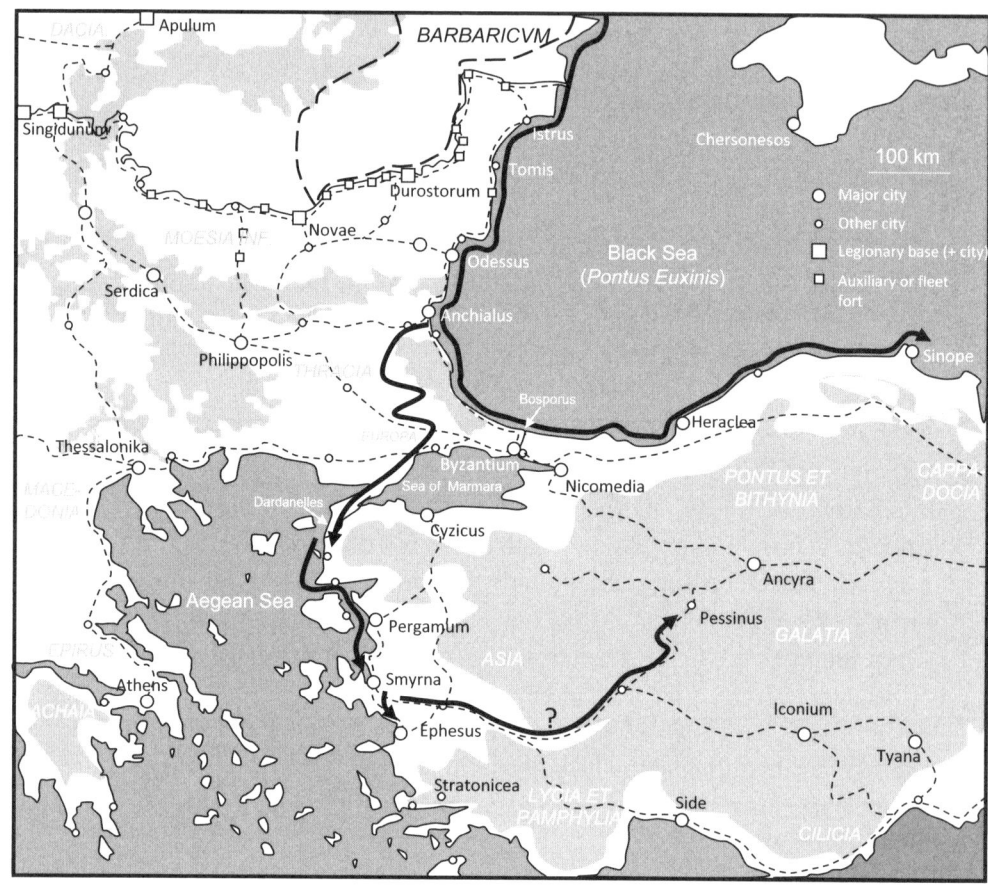

Map 15. Barbarian raids into Thrace and Asia Minor according to Zosimus, probably 252 CE. The distances covered and the places raided imply attacks by both land and sea.

When they eventually re-crossed the Danube into Gothia they would thumb their noses at the impotent garrison of Durostorum.

But it was not to be. While the raiding was going on, the new military governor of Moesia, Aemilian, was exhorting his troops to take action. Just as Decius had picked Gallus, so Gallus must have selected Aemilian for his loyalty and martial ability in this most important posting. According to Zosimus, he 'did his best to encourage his troops, who did not dare resist the successful barbarians, and reminded them of their Roman honour'. Zonaras also alleges more venal motives by promising 'that he would give to the soldiers all that had been given to the Scythians, if they would engage in war with the barbarians'. The Goths would be absolutely loaded with plunder, and very likely off their guard. Both Zosimus and Zonaras agree that Aemilian caught the enemy by surprise on their return trek, probably somewhere in

Thrace. There had been plenty of time to prepare a trap. The result was a great slaughter of the Goths: all but a few were killed and the Romans 'collected much booty from them'. The balance of power in the Danube sector had once again shifted dramatically.[28]

But Aemilian was not satisfied with this great victory. Seizing the day, he took his men over the Danube directly into the land of the Goths, and, as Zosimus relates 'destroyed every obstruction and, contrary to every expectation, freed Rome's subjects from their tormentors'. Zonaras, too, briefly records this excursion and we must presume that both historians got their story from Dexippus's *Chronicle*. In any case it was no mean achievement: Aemilian must have known from scouts and spies where the main Gothic camp was. By taking the war to the enemy (which, after all, had been the original intention) he inflicted a major blow that must surely have disrupted any further military preparations underway at the Gothic court, wherever it was.

By this time, according to the most plausible chronology, it was late in the year 252 and the marching season was coming to a close. Aemilian returned to his command centre in Moesia with his reputation greatly enhanced and his soldiers overjoyed. Novae was his most likely centre of operations, the base of *legio* I *italica*. They and their colleagues from *legio* XI *claudia* must have felt fortunate indeed to have missed out on the slaughter at Abritus and now be lauded as victors over a great Gothic army while massively enriching themselves in the process. Ancient armies generally had a semi-independent piratical edge to them, something that is seen throughout Roman history and not just in the third century: there was no way central government was going to relieve them of their booty and nor would there be any attempt to return any of the loot to its rightful owners.

A few details about Aemilian, the victorious governor, are known. He was an African, supposedly born on the island of Girba (modern Djerba, a tourist resort off the coast of Tunisia). He was also described as a Moor, which may mean he was of ethnic African descent and had dark skin. Some of the sources put him at about forty years of age, others in his early fifties. Another thing we are told is that he had seditious intentions and, flushed with his success and with his troops fully behind him, he himself began plotting for the imperial throne…

Tomb Raiders

Meanwhile, the Christian church was still deeply split, with the rival bishops in Rome and Carthage still struggling for supremacy. Many of those cast out of the church for having sacrificed were still clamouring for re-admittance but the hard-liners persisted in excluding them so they were driven to alternative congregations. Even the more moderate bishops such as Cyprian of Carthage (having now softened his line) and Cornelius of Rome were insisting on long periods of penance and privation before any of the lapsed could be re-admitted.

Cornelius had so far experienced rather a short period in high office, dogged by the rigorous 'anti-pope' Novatian and his supporters. It seems there may have been some competition between the rival factions for possession of the holy relics of the city. This apparently began when the Novatianists took into safe keeping (or stole, depending on your perspective) the bones of Saint Silanus, one of seven deeply revered brothers who had been martyred for their faith in the time of Antoninus Pius (reigned 138–161 CE). Perhaps in response to this (and if we are to believe a story in the *Liber Pontificalis*, the 'Book of the Popes'), Cornelius asked a woman called Lucina, one of his flock and apparently a wealthy lady with estates dotted around the city, to take possession of the bodies of the greatest of all the saints, Peter and Paul. The bones were taken from their plots on the Appian Way and re-buried near to their respective execution places, it being a Christian tradition to inter martyrs close to the site of their ultimate triumph. No doubt the new burial plots would be tightly guarded by the Cornelian faction.[29] Accordingly, Paul was re-interred on a patch of Lucina's land on the road to Ostia near where he had been beheaded. Peter, on the other hand, was moved across the Tiber. Cornelius buried him where a small Christian shrine already stood close to the race-track there, which according to tradition was the site of his inverted crucifixion back in the reign of Nero (54–68 CE). This episode accounts for the later position of St. Peter's Basilica which now occupies the centre of the independent Vatican State: the high altar supposedly stands directly above the spot that Cornelius laid him to rest.[30]

Cornelius had been praised by Cyprian for his bravery in accepting the bishopric of Rome while Decius was still emperor. After Abritus the Christians may have hoped for a milder regime, but it was not to be. Soon enough the well-meaning Cornelius was arrested and brought before a magistrate whereupon he refused to deny his faith. He was banished to a nearby coastal village called Centumcellae (now Civitavecchia) where he sent and received letters, including from Cyprian, and ordained priests. This activity was, however, against the terms of his exile, so Cornelius was brought before the emperor who ordered him to be beaten upon the mouth (presumably, this was the punishment for sedition) and taken to the temple of Mars to worship. If he would not do so he was to be beheaded on the spot, which is of course what happened. According to the *Liber Pontificalis*, 'his body was taken up at night by the blessed Lucina and the clergy and was buried in a crypt in her own garden, near the cemetery of Callistus on the Via Appia'.³¹

Scroll forward to 1852 when an exciting new academic discipline called archaeology was emerging. One of its early practitioners, a young man called Giovanni Battista De Rossi, was exploring a vineyard beside the Appian Way. It was a region outside the city limits with many ancient tombs which had been ransacked for hundreds of years for its ancient artworks, marble, and other precious items. Very little was left other than debris and the ruined masonry of once well-appointed tombs and temples. Among the rubble De Rossi found a broken marble slab with the neat inscription …NELIUS MARTYR preceded by part of a letter that could have been the top of an 'R'. Believing that he may have found the tomb of Cornelius mentioned in the *Liber Pontificalis*, he asked for an audience with Pope Pius IX and, showing him the inscription, suggested that the Vatican should buy the land and fund a proper excavation. The Pope listened in silence and, when De Rossi had finished his appeal, dismissed him with a contemptuous wave of the hand and just four words: "Sogni di un archeologo!" ("Dreams of an archaeologist!").

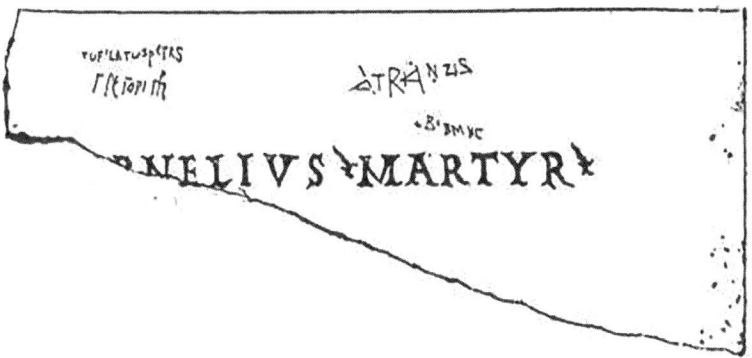

De Rossi left the audience downhearted, but Pope Pius may have hurried off to consult his Book of Popes to remind himself just who his obscure and distant predecessor Cornelius was, or possibly to check the state of his wine cellar. Whatever the reason, De Rossi later received a message that the Pope had indeed purchased the vineyard and allocated him an excavation fund. The digging soon revealed a large vaulted crypt which was then systematically excavated. Within it was a tomb on top of which a broken marble slab with the letters 'CO' and part of an R, with EP^S beneath (short for *episcopus*, or bishop) was discovered. The pieces fitted together perfectly. Not only that, but the walls were decorated with ornate sixth century frescoes, one of which depicted Cornelius himself alongside Cyprian of Carthage. Pope Pius was naturally keen to see the results of the excavation. It was a great formal event and when De Rossi showed him the restored slab he did so with a flourish, saying 'Sogni di un archeologo!'[32]

It was unusual for Christian inscriptions to be rendered in Latin in the third century, Greek being the generally preferred medium of the early church. So it might be wondered whether the inscription on the grave was original, from the time of the bishop's death, or later, from the time the frescoes were painted. But the great Roman archaeologist Rodolfo Lanciani who preserved De Rossi's story thought the text was contemporaneous and pointed out that the burial place in Lucina's garden was on the ancient plot of the *Gens Cornelia*, one of the great patrician families of Rome with roots stretching back to the early Republic. There were scores of distinguished consuls on the record, the greatest of all being Publius Cornelius Scipio Africanus who had defeated Hannibal at the Battle of Zama in 202 BCE. The austere slab and Latin inscription was of an antique style that befitted one of their number. Lanciani proposed, therefore, that Cornelius, bishop and martyr, was one of the last of this noble line.[33]

Cornelius was replaced as Bishop of Rome by a man called Lucius who was immediately arrested and banished. He was no doubt careful not to be caught receiving correspondence.

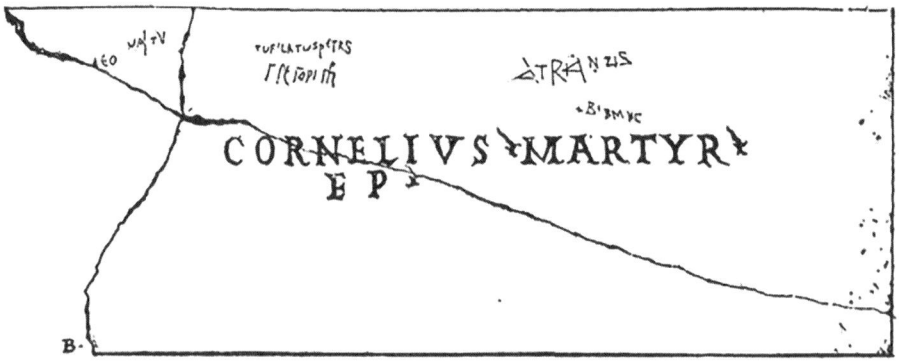

Chapter 8

253: World in Flames

Surprise attack on Antioch

Gaius Vibius Afinius Trebonianus Gallus Augustus witnessed the dawning of 253 CE in Rome. All things considered, he may well have been in an optimistic mood. Even Bishop Dionysius of Alexandria, who had every reason to be critical, admitted that 'his reign was prospering and things were going according to his mind'. If the sequence of events as reconstructed here is right (and we have to admit that it may not be, such is the paucity of sources) he had successfully seen out a whole year at Rome in which a major victory had been scored over the Goths by his general Aemilian and, despite military failure in allied Armenia, the Roman borderlands in the east were still intact. The plague still raged, but its peak appeared to have passed. The surviving people of Rome seemed content with the new imperial dynasty that had handled the contagion pretty well. In the New Year celebrations the status of Volusian was enhanced by making him senior consul for the first time. Tradition was also respected by the raising of a distinguished senator, Lucius Valerius Poplicola Balbinus Maximus (about whom not a lot else is known), to be his colleague.[1]

Unfortunately, another great disaster of unprecedented proportion was about to unfold. The scene was the east, and treachery was once again at the heart of the matter. The story this time focuses on a man called Mariades.[2] He was an eastern nobleman from the ruling class of the great imperial city of Antioch on the Orontes and was, reputedly, something of a rake. According to a story told much later by John Malalas, he was

> … expelled from the council through cooperation between the whole council and the people, because of deficiencies in his administration of chariot-racing: he had not bought horses for whichever faction it was that he led but had embezzled the public funds that were set aside for the hippodrome. [Malalas, *Chronographia* 295–296.]

Naturally the people would be upset if their favourite charioteers had to race with substandard nags. Another source tells us that Mariades robbed his own father of most of his gold and an enormous amount of silver. It seems that he then took to the hills. An obscure verse from the Thirteenth Sibylline Oracle refers to 'a bandit from Syria' who may be our man. Whatever happened, he somehow crossed over to the Persian Empire and offered his services at the court of Shapur. There he encouraged the King of Kings to invade his own homeland and, offering insider knowledge, suggested a cunning plan for the capture of his home city. His revenge on the council and people of Antioch would be served hot.[3]

So it was that in the marching season of 253, using the recent failed Roman intervention in Armenia as his *casus belli*, Shapur himself led a formidable army into Roman Mesopotamia. What happened next was pure disaster from the Roman perspective, so much so that it goes virtually unmentioned in their histories. For the details we have to turn once again to Shapur's great inscription at Naqsh-i Rustam which is rendered in both Persian and Greek:

> And the Caesar lied again and did injustice to Armenia. We marched against the Roman Empire and annihilated a Roman army of 60,000 men at Barbalissos. The nation of Syria and whatever nations and plains were above it, we set on fire and devastated and laid waste. [*Res Gestae Divi Saporis* 10–12.]

Barbalissos has been identified as modern Qal'at Balis in Syria, deep in Roman territory. If the number of 60,000 men on the Roman side is even half correct, the force there must have consisted of many legions and their associated auxiliary cohorts. A major Persian victory was achieved with the result that the Roman east was now open for plunder, and Mariades's home, the great metropolis of Antioch on the Orontes, was the main target.

Shapur evidently caught the citizens of Antioch totally by surprise, if there is any truth in a dramatic story told by the fourth century soldier and historian Ammianus Marcellinus:

> For it happened one day at Antioch, when the city was in perfect tranquility, a comic actor being on stage with his wife, acting some common scene from daily life, while the people were delighted with his acting, his wife suddenly exclaimed: 'Am I dreaming or are the Persians here?' The audience immediately turned round then fled in every direction while trying to avoid the missiles which were showered upon them. [Ammianus Marcellinus, *History* XXIII.5.3.]

Another version tells us that 'unexpectedly and suddenly he [Shapur] seized the height that commanded the theatre, and with his arrows shot and massacred that great crowd of spectators'.[4] This story has been dismissed as inconceivable – the Persians could not possibly have reached the centre of Antioch undetected – but judging from archaeological maps, the ancient theatre (*theatrum caesaris*) backed on to Mount Silpios at the eastern edge of the great city, using its slope as part of the construction. If a Persian commando force had approached over the mountains rather than along the Orontes Valley, as would seem necessary to attain the element of surprise, they might well have appeared at this very point. The soldiers could well have been spotted first by an actor on stage while the audience, with their backs to the mountain, were oblivious. But to achieve surprise at this point the Persians must have scaled the formidable city wall which was set back high up on Mount Silpius. The historical sources make no mention of this happening, but a comment made in the sixth century by the biographer of the Byzantine emperor Justinian may be of relevance. Referring to a re-fortification of his own time, he wrote 'In ancient times its circuit-wall was both too long and absolutely full of many turnings, in some places uselessly enclosing the level ground and in others the summits of the mountain, and for this reason it was exposed to attack in a number of places.' Perhaps this was one such occasion. This, then, could have been the essence of Mariades's plan – to penetrate an outlying sector of the city wall in secret and launch a surprise attack on the civic centre. If so it worked perfectly.[5]

The summary of these events given by Malalas in the sixth century makes no mention of the theatre but it does state that Antioch was captured during the evening, which fits with the idea of a theatrical performance. It goes on to tell us that the great city was plundered and set on fire. The entire neighbourhood was torched and many of the citizens were taken captive. Centuries later, one writer was to lament that Antioch had no noble buildings to boast of because the insolent Persians had once burnt them all.[6]

The traitor Mariades must have relished the sight of his fellow citizens being dragged away into slavery but his joy was not to last. Rather than rewarding him, Shapur had him executed for the crime of betraying his own city, which was considered shameful behaviour even to the Persians. He perished, either by being burned alive (according to Ammianus) or decapitated (according to Malalas): true or not, the story provides a strange insight into the moral values of the ancient world.[7]

Devastation across the east

The destruction of Antioch, the effective capital of the eastern empire, was an unprecedented disaster for the Romans. But it was not to be the end of the troubles. The rout at Barbalissos had left other cities and districts entirely at the mercy of the Persian army which was, for now, virtually free to operate as it pleased. After recounting the victory at Barbalissos, Shapur's great inscription at Naqsh-i Rustam continues:

And in the campaign we took the following fortresses and cities from the nation of the Romans: the city of Anatha with its surrounding territory – Birtha Arupan – Birtha Asporakan with its surrounding territory – Sura – Barbalissos – Hierapolis – Beroea – Chalcis – Apamea – Rephanea – Zeugma – Ourima – Gindaros – Larmenaz – Seleucia – Antiochia – Cyrrhus – another city by the name of Seleucia – Alexandretta – Nicopolis – Sinzara – Chamath – Ariste – Dikhor – Doliche – Dura – Circesium – Germanicia – Batna – Chanar – and from Cappadocia: the city of Satala with its surrounding territory – Domana – Artangil – Souisa – Souid – Phreata, a total of thirty-seven cities with their surrounding territories. [*Res Gestae Divi Saporis* 12–14.][8]

The militaristic Sassanian dynasty seems to have reformed the Persian army, albeit along traditional lines, resulting in a large, highly organized force with a fearsome cavalry contingent drawn from the nobility. The basic unit of up to a thousand men was the *drafsh* (literally, banner), each of which belonged to an army division (*gund*) of around 12,000 commanded by a senior officer known as a *gund-salar*. Roman historians had been somewhat disparaging of the old Parthian military in pre-Sassanian times, but from now on they are unanimous in praise and fear. It seems appropriate to refer to this professional army by its Persian name: the *spah*.[9]

The impressive roll call of conquered territories has sent historians scurrying for their atlases. Building on much previous geographic research on this topic, the various locations are here put on maps with an attempt to derive a plausible route and strategy for the campaign. In agreement with previous suggestions, it seems obvious that after the major victory at Barbalissos, the army must have fragmented into a series of sizable divisions. How exactly that was accomplished, and in what order, is not recoverable with certainty. Nevertheless, in reconstructing the most likely course of events, it is as instructive to consider the developing strategic situation and the places that are not mentioned (and so presumably were not captured) just as much as those that are.[10]

Well before the decisive encounter at Barbalissos, the Persians crossed into Roman territory and hostilities commenced at the outpost of Anatha, a fortified town that had probably only been taken into Roman hands as little as a generation before. The rather nervous garrison stationed there would have been no match for a full-scale invasion: it was first on Shapur's list and first to fall, very likely at the beginning of the campaign season around March 253. Birtha Arupan, next on the list, has been identified as the ruined fort at Qreiye in eastern Syria. This was built in the early third century as a base

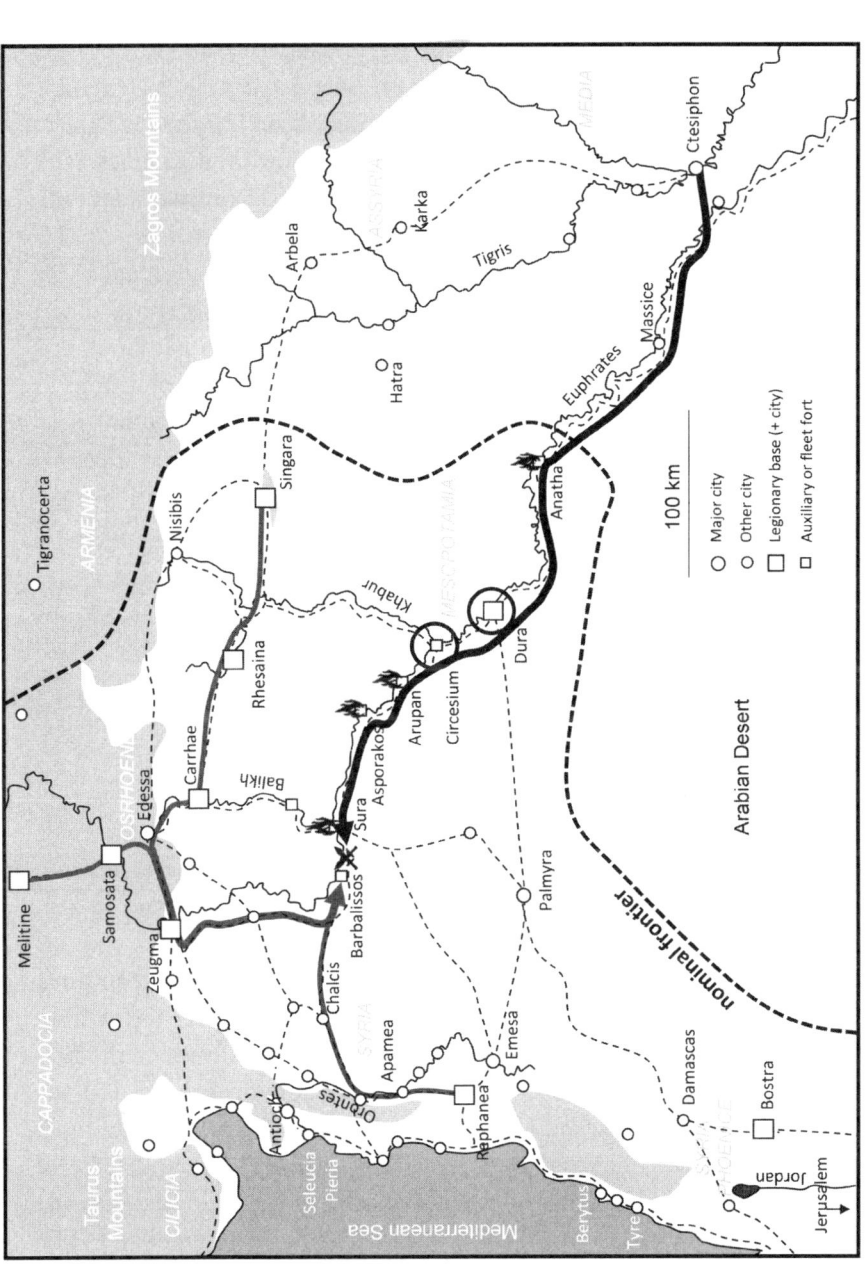

Map 16. The Battle of Barbalissos, 253 CE. Shapur advanced up the south bank of the Euphrates, probably besieging Dura and Circesium and destroying smaller forts. The Romans gathered their forces at Barbalissos in an attempt to block the route into Syria.

for a unit of auxiliary camel corps who presumably made full use of their mobility as soon as they saw the enemy marching on them – by trotting off in the other direction. The fort was destroyed and never re-occupied. The great fortified city of Dura-Europos and the fortress at Circesium lie between Anatha and Arupan, but feature much later on Shapur's list, so it is possible that the Romans decided to leave garrisons in position forcing the Persians to lay siege. Dura ('the stronghold') in particular was a hard nut to crack with its strong circuit walls and protected by deep natural wadis on two sides with the river on a third.[11]

A great invasion up the Euphrates can hardly have been unexpected so we can be confident that the Romans would have war-gamed the situation. Their strategy seems to have been for most of their other forces in Mesopotamia to fall back towards Syria, with the aim of concentrating as many troops as possible at a defensible spot for a decisive battle. The legions of northern Mesopotamia probably withdrew into Syria using the crossing at Zeugma which explains why the location of the battle was so far back in Roman territory. Such a concentration of force would have been necessary to stand any chance against the *spah*.

Shapur's march apparently continued up the southwest bank of the Euphrates via Sura to Barbalissos where the armies clashed. The exact location is not known: if it was directly beside the river it may lie under the modern reservoir known as Al Assad Lake. There may even have been a naval element to the battle. We do not know who commanded on the Roman side. One possibility is the senior commander of the Euphrates (the *dux ripae*, or Duke of the Riverbank) who was normally based at Dura and was responsible for security on the frontier. The office holder under Gallus was an equestrian named Julius Julianus who is attested in two inscriptions from Dura in 251, but about whom nothing more is known.[12]

The Roman army likely consisted of the combined forces of between three to seven legions backed by large numbers of auxiliary and border forces from all along the frontier. Legions that might have been involved, with their main bases (see Map 16) are: *legio* IIII *scythica* (Zeugma), *legio* XVI *flavia firma* (Samosata), *legio* III *gallica* (Raphanea), *legio* XII *fulminata* (Melitine), *legio* III *parthica* (Rhesaina) and *legio* I *parthica* (Singara). A total force of 60,000 men is just about possible if every soldier in Syria and Mesopotamia was mobilized, but of course the numbers may have been exaggerated. The Roman army was certainly not annihilated because all these proud legions lived to fight another day. But we do know that the Romans suffered a major defeat because Syria was left largely at the mercy of the attackers.

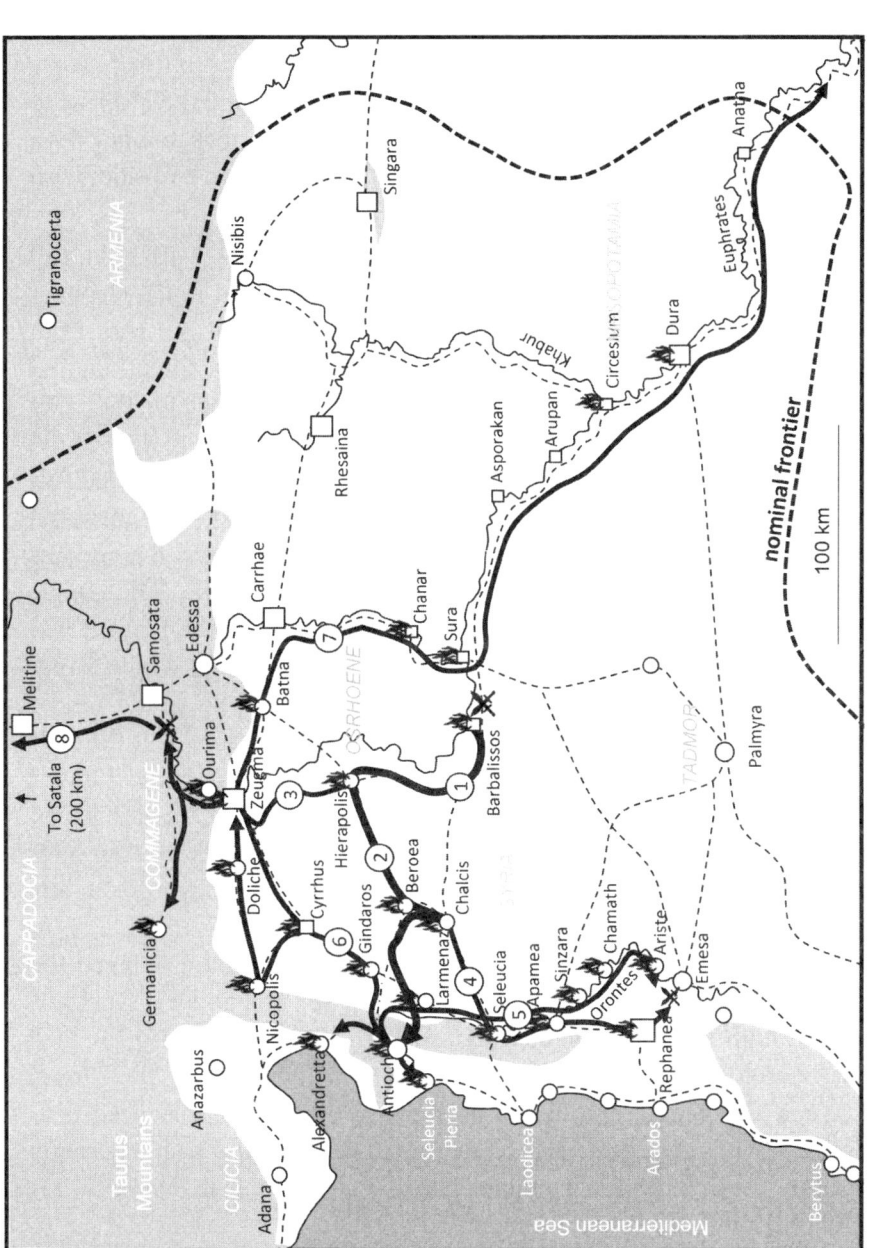

Map 17. Reconstruction of the Persian invasion of 253 CE after Barbalissos based on the roll call of conquered territories in the *Res Gestae Divi Saporis*. Phases 1 to 8 of the campaign discussed in the text are numbered.

In the immediate aftermath of battle, the *spah* probably moved up the Euphrates to Hierapolis (modern Manbij; then as now an important road junction) where Shapur took stock of the situation (Route 1 on Map 17). Hierapolis means 'holy city', and it was home to a great temple and oracle dedicated to the moon goddess Atargatis. This had been described over a hundred years earlier by a visitor called Lucian of Samosata, one of the most lively and prolific writers of the ancient world. It is worth digressing for a moment on the temple because it gives us an insight into the traditional religious life of the area.

Lucian reports that when he visited, the temple was ablaze with gold, full of gilded statues and all kinds of other treasures, gems from India, elephant tusks and so on; and the air was infused with a delightful fragrance from Arabia. He describes witnessing a sacrifice with more than three hundred priests in attendance all wearing white robes and caps except for the chief priest who wore purple and gold. There were also 'pipers, flute players… and women frenzied and fanatic'. The temple complex featured a large sacred fish pond where the pampered fish grew to enormous size and even answered to their names. Devotees who wanted to register petitions with the goddess would have to swim out to an altar in the middle of the lake. The temple precinct was the site of orgiastic rituals, and to emphasize the point it was fronted by two prodigious phalli, each about ten metres high. Once a year during a special festival these were climbed by priests who would render prayers from aloft for paying customers. Lucian witnessed this himself because he described their mode of ascent: 'the man throws round himself and the phallus a small chain… As he mounts he jerks the chain up his own length, as a driver his reins. Those who have not seen this process, but have seen those who have to climb palm trees in Arabia, or in Egypt, or in any other place, will understand what I mean'.[13]

It might be expected that the invading Persians would have stripped the temple of all its wealth, but that is not necessarily so. The goddess Atargatis was held in high esteem, as well as fear, in Persia, where she was identified with her Zoroastrian equivalent Anahita. She was the deity of the Moon, water, crops and beauty, but also a powerful war goddess who needed to be appeased with gory trophies: Shapur's father Ardashir had reportedly displayed the severed heads of conquered kings in her temple in Persia. So it is likely that Shapur left Hierapolis undefiled to retain divine favour and not to spook his army. Had the invaders been Goths it would have been a different story. It is also worth noting that during the march, Shapur must have passed by the tomb of Gordian III near Circesium. We know it was not destroyed because it was still in existence over a century later.

Positive evidence for the tolerant religious policy of Shapur comes from the so-called 'Kaaba of Zoroaster', a cubic religious building, possibly a fire temple, at the ceremonial complex of Naqsh-i-Rustam in Iran. An inscription on the monument recalls the deeds of the Mobed (Zoroastrian high priest) Kirder (also spelled Kartir or Kirdir) who accompanied Shapur's army into Roman territory:

> There too, at the command of the King of Kings, I reduced to order the priests and fires which were in those lands. And I did not allow harm to be done them, or captives made. And whoever had thus been made captive, him indeed I took and sent back to his own land. And I made the Mazda-worshipping religion and its good priests esteemed and honoured in the land. [Inscription of Kirder at the Kaaba of Zoroaster.]

It is even said that the great Prophet Mani accompanied Shapur. He was the founder of an important (for a while) composite religion with Indian and Christian elements known as Manicheism. Not every religion was respected, however. Shapur seems to have destroyed the temple of Jupiter Dolichenus at Doliche on the Euphrates, signalling the death-knell of that particular cult across the empire. Possibly this was because the Roman high god was anathema to the Persians.[14]

Taking the order of fallen territories in Shapur's inscription as a guide, from Hierapolis it is likely that he launched an immediate attack in the direction of Antioch, the greatest prize of all, sacking Beroea (the modern city of Aleppo) and Chalcis *en route* (Route 2). This accords with the account of Malalas who states that it was at Chalcis that the Persians broke into the Province of Syria.[15] Then, as we have seen, acting on the advice of the traitor Mariades, he probably launched a stealth attack across Mount Silpios, catching the citizens of Antioch unawares. To achieve this rapid advance he would have made full use of the splendid high quality road network between Antioch and Chalcis, parts of which survive today.

The list of fallen territories suggests that Shapur split his army twice before arriving at Antioch, sending divisions (perhaps each comprising an army group or *gund*) in pursuit of the retreating Romans with orders to harass the enemy and destroy their bases. One such group could have gone north from Hierapolis along the Euphrates to attack the legionary base at Zeugma and secure the crossing point and control of the upper river (Route 3). Another could have split off at Chalcis to go south towards the fortress at Raphanea (Route 4) with the aim of destroying it. This would have disrupted any attempt by the Roman forces in the south to regroup and perhaps join up with other legions that might be planning on coming up from Judaea or even further afield. Both groups were successful in these objectives, which probably entailed siege works and must have taken considerable time. The first army group may then have gone on to attempt to reduce the legionary base at Samosata, the old capital of Commagene and headquarters of *legio XVI flavia firma*. If so, they were unsuccessful, because it does not appear on Shapur's list and so, presumably, the Roman survivors were finally able to hold out within the walls there. The city of Germanicia, which lies at the end of an isolated spur in the road network, may have been a supplemental target for this division.

After the sack of Antioch, the Persians likely fragmented further to pillage the entire area. The only constraint they had was to withdraw by the year's end with as much booty as could possibly be extracted. One division appears to have gone south along the Orontes (Route 5), taking the wealthy city of Apamea (if it had not fallen already) a splendid ruin today with its famous great colonnade and theatre – and several others, perhaps linking up with the column besieging Rephanea and aiming for the wealthy city of Emesa which, however, held out in its defence (as is described further below). The maritime cities of Seleucia Pieria (port of Antioch) and Alexandretta were pillaged, but the coastal zone further south seems to have escaped unmolested. The rest of the army under Shapur himself may have eventually retired from the Antioch district and re-grouped at the strategic crossing point of Zeugma (Route 6). No doubt an efficient system was devised for exporting the miserable captives and portable wealth of Roman Syria, using the Euphrates as a conveyor belt.

Towards the end of the year, the bulk of the Persian army may have retired via the territory of Osrhoene (Route 7) which would account for the presence of Batna and Chanar on the list. The major city of Edessa and the fortress at Carrhae evidently held out if they were attacked. The last contribution of this force may have been to attack Circesium and Dura which appear towards the end of Shapur's list. However there must be serious doubt that Dura actually fell to the Persians because it was not destroyed; nevertheless its rich and fertile agricultural hinterland would have been devastated.

The final five cities named on Shapur's inscription are described as being in Cappadocia. The locations of three of them (Domana, Souisa and Satala) are known, and they form a cluster over 300km to the north of the rest. For this reason most historians think they were attacked in a second parallel invasion that year, perhaps launched out of newly conquered Armenia under the leadership of Shapur's son Hormizd.[16] However there are two reasons to think that interpretation may be wrong. The first is a historical snippet that says Shapur 'captured the whole of Syria and burnt down many other cities as well as Antioch the Great, and that… he passed through Cappadocia into Persian territory'.¹⁷ The second is the aforementioned inscription of the Zoroastrian High Priest Kirdir which says:

> I, Kirder, underwent much toil and trouble for the *yazards* [priests] and the rulers, and for my own soul's sake. And I caused many fires and priestly colleges to flourish in Iran, and also in non-Iranian lands. There were fires and priests in the non-Iranian lands which were reached by the armies of the King of Kings. The provincial capital of Antioch and the province of Syria, and Cilicia; the provincial capital of Caesarea and the province of Cappadocia, and the districts dependent on Cappadocia, up to Pontus, and the province of Armenia, and Georgia and Albania and Balasagan, up to the 'Gate of the Alans' – these were plundered and laid waste by Shapur, King of Kings. [Inscription of Kirder at the Kaaba of Zoraster.]

Not all of this plundering necessarily happened in one campaign but it would have made sense for Shapur himself to end the year by moving into Armenia, sacking a few Cappadocian cities on the way for good measure (Route 8). He would then have exited the Roman Empire into newly conquered Armenia, apparently then moving up through the northern kingdoms to the heights of the Caucasus. The 'Gate of the Alans' in Kirder's account is the Darial Pass in the centre of the Caucasus Mountains, now on the border between Russia and Georgia. Such an operation would fit with his main priority which must have been to cement permanent control over Armenia.¹⁸

Mosaics, mosaics, mosaics

Around the year 2000, a new Euphrates dam was threatening part of the archaeological remains at the site of Zeugma on the river's west bank, so a rescue excavation was rapidly organized. It revealed a series of luxurious riverside residences, some of which had been owned by retired veterans from the Roman army. Part of this area was sealed by what archaeologists call a 'destruction layer' in which many buildings were burned or collapsed. The excavations produced hundreds of scattered coins. The most recent of these are silver tetradrachms from the mint at Antioch featuring Trebonianus Gallus dated to 252–253. These pieces would have had just enough time to make their way up from Antioch in someone's purse as Shapur's army was closing in from the south. Recently harvested almonds in the same deposit prove that it was high summer when Zeugma fell. Thus the destruction layer is solid physical evidence for the damage boasted about by Shapur on his famous inscription.¹⁹

Some of the excavated houses indicate stupendous wealth, as indicated by the many superb mosaics (Plate 6). Nevertheless the city, or at least the excavated part, had been in decline for some time. According to the archaeologists, 'spacious homes were diminished by blocked doorways and colonnades converted to solid walls; latrines went out of use and painted plaster walls were scrawled with graffiti'.[20] Some of the most opulent rooms were being used for storage. There is no doubt that Zeugma had been experiencing economic problems, but for how long is difficult to establish. It stands to reason, however, that the wealth of the region must have suffered greatly since Persian hostilities had begun about twenty years earlier, back in the time of the Emperor Severus Alexander. Caravan trade along the old Silk Road out to the distant east (and ultimately China) was instantly curtailed at that time and the whole area had become even more militarized than it had been before.

The destruction layer concealed many other finds including a wide range of domestic materials and, in some of the houses, weaponry. In one room in what became known as the 'House of the Helmets' there were three helmets, two spears and a sword plus a fine gold finger ring featuring a Capricorn, symbol of *legio* IIII *scythica*. Shields and armour and an antique gladius or stabbing sword were found in other riverside houses. Whether this had anything to do with the defence of the town in 253, or was just old or defective equipment left lying about, is unclear.[21]

As for the mosaics, they form a world-class heritage collection that equals anywhere in the Roman world, and are now the focus of a specialist museum at Gazientep in Turkey. Many people tend to think of mosaics as quintessentially Roman, but in fact the tradition began in the east before the empire even arrived. The mosaics of Zeugma span a wide range of ages from the third century BCE to the third century CE. Some of the finest date to around the year 200 CE, including two that are signed by the master artist Zosimos of Samosata (not to be confused with Zosimus the historian). They give us a vivid image of the riverside luxury that came to an abrupt end in 253. But the irony is that if it were not for the destruction layer that seals them, they would not survive today.[22]

Local hero

As mentioned above, the city of Emesa managed to withstand an attack by the southern Persian army group after it had sacked the city of Apamea and other local towns. Two rather enigmatic historical sources and an obscure rock inscription are thought to refer to the defence of Emesa, and numismatic evidence adds more of interest. The first source, the riddling Thirteenth

Millennium celebration coinage. 1–6, collectable animal designs, SAECVLARES AVGG; SAECVLVM NOVVM; ROMAE AETERNAE.

Bronze sestertius of Philip 'The Arab'.

The rebel emperors Pacatian (celebrating the Year 1,001) and Jotapian.

Page of the Vienna Palimpsest in plain light (left) and the same, spectrally enhanced (right).

Decius.

The Danube near Oescus.

Ruins at Oescus.

A libellus from the Decian persecution in Alexandria.

North end of the circus (racetrack) at Philippopolis (central Plovdiv). Decius's letter to the townspeople was supposedly read out here by Julius Priscus.

Persian gold dinar of Shapur I.

Shipka, Bulgaria, proposed as site of the Battle of Beroe. The vanguard of the Roman Army descended from the Haemus mountains and was attacked on the plain by Cniva's Goths.

'Nebet Tepe' Hill west of the race-track in Plovdiv. The Goths secretly climbed up at night and entered the city alerted by a traitor, according to a new fragment of Dexippus's *Scythica*.

The Great Ludovisi Battle Sarcophagus.

The Battlefield of Abritus.

Photograph 1: the Roman camp.

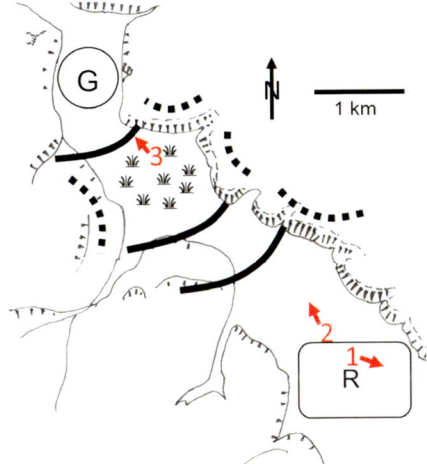

Key to photographs (see text).

Photograph 2: the Roman advance.

Photograph 3: Decius's last stand?

Pierced gold aureus of Decius.

Trebonianus Gallus

Coin of Volusian with a star in the reverse field.

Aemilian.

Excavation in progress at Zeugma.

Valerian: restorer of the human race.

Gallienus: Five times greatest victor in Germany.

Silbannacus.

Salonina: Eternal Rome.

Artificial mound at Manole, Bulgaria, under excavation.

The Paris cameo.

Shapur I ('the Great').

Odaenathus, Lord of Tadmor.

Rock carving celebrating Shapur's victories over Philip (kneeling) and Valerian (captured).

Coin of Sponsian, Hunterian Museum, Glasgow.

Regalianus and Dryantilla.

The Augsburg Victory Altar, 260 CE.

Macrianus and Quietus.

Postumus.

Sibylline Oracle, contains a few lines which refer to armed resistance of the Persian invasion of 253:

> Then there will be a rout of the Romans; but immediately thereafter a priest will come, the last of all, sent from the sun, appearing from Syria, and he will do everything by craft; the city of the sun will arise, and around her the Persians will endure the terrible threats of the Phoenicians. [*Oracula Sibyllina* XIII, 150–154.]

The City of the Sun is the old Phoenician city of Emesa (modern Homs) which was very rich in Roman times and home to the famous cult of Elah Gabal (literally, god of the mountain, but also a sun god and all-round supreme deity).[23] The second source is Malalas who has the following curious account:

> He [Shapur] captured all the regions of the east as far as Emesa in Phoenice Libanensis, and destroyed burnt and plundered it and killed everyone. The priest of Aphrodite, called Sampsigeramos, came out with a force of countrymen armed with slings and went to meet him. The Persian emperor, Shapur, noticing his priestly costume, ordered his army not to shoot at them nor to attack or fight them, and he received the priest as an ambassador for his country. While the emperor Shapur was conversing with the priest, seated on a high platform, one of the countrymen hurled a stone from his sling at him and hit the emperor Shapur on the forehead; he died immediately on the spot. A disturbance broke out and his army heard of his death. Because they supposed that the Romans had arrived, they all fled towards the limes [frontier], pursued by the farmers and the priest Samsigeramos, and they abandoned all their plunder and disappeared. [Malalas, *Chronographia* XII.26.]

What are we to make of this? Shapur was certainly not killed at this time and it is most unlikely that the Persian army group would be routed by a group of farmers armed only with slings. Nevertheless, it could be that the Persian general (*gund-salar*) leading the southern column was killed during negotiations, something that might fit with the Sibyl claiming that the priest 'will do everything by craft'. It is also possible that the Persians may have been panicked by the threat of a new Roman army moving up from Judea in the south (perhaps *legio* X *fretensis* which was based at Jerusalem) and so decided they were too exposed and it was time to withdraw, dumping anything that was not especially valuable.

Finally, the above-mentioned rock inscription is from a village on the edge of the desert near the modern Syrian city of Hama. It reads (in part) 'Year 564 when the men exposed themselves to Nemesis, the Hero called upon

Kronos, and victory was given to him.' The Seleucid Year 564 equates to the period from the autumn of 252 to the autumn of 253 CE. In Greek mythology, Nemesis was the goddess of fortune. Kronos was a Titan, father of Zeus, who might be identified with Elah Gabal. It has been suggested that the inscription commemorates the site of a battle where the Persians were expelled and that 'the Hero' was the priest Samsigeramos of Malalas's account.[24] Samsigeramos was in fact the name taken by several members of the royal house of Emesa who were also chief priests of Elah Gabal. Their religion had been described by Herodian a few years earlier:

> A huge temple was erected to this god, lavishly decorated with gold, silver, and costly gems. Not only is this god worshipped by the natives, but all the neighbouring rulers and kings send generous and expensive gifts to him each year. No statue made by man in the likeness of the god stands in this temple, as in Greek and Roman temples. The temple does, however, contain a huge black stone with a pointed end and round base in the shape of a cone. The Phoenicians solemnly maintain that this stone came down from Zeus; pointing out certain small figures in relief, they assert that it is an unwrought image of the sun, for naturally this is what they wish to see. Herodian, *History of the Empire* V.III.4–5

It has been suggested that the Emesene temple described by Herodian was not at Emesa itself but further south at the holy city of Baalbek, in mountainous country where its spectacular ruins can still be seen. The stone is depicted on various Roman coins, including in the process of being drawn on the back of a chariot where it appears to have been as much as two metres high, although that could be the artist's license. The consensus among historians is that it was a meteorite, and if the size is even roughly correct it would be one of the largest ever known. Its fall to Earth would have been accompanied by a blinding flash of light and a substantial blast wave, a most impressive demonstration of the power of Elah Gabal, if anyone had witnessed it.[25]

After the Persians were repulsed, the mint at Emesa began producing coins in the name of Uranius Antoninus, one of the Emesene Royal family and priestly elite, and because of this he has tentatively been identified with the Sampsigeramos in Malalas's account.[26] It is fascinating that the city took this bold step without any reference to the legitimate emperor in Rome. But with the east in turmoil, the city authorities may not have known if Roman authority would ever be restored, such was the calamity suffered at the hands of the Persians.

One of the coins of Uranius Antoninus conveniently bears the date 565 of the Seleucid Era (which ties it to 253/254 CE). These coins are almost the only evidence we have of how the upstart regime presented itself. Uranius is shown as a soldier in imperial Roman garb with a laurel wreath and cuirass without a hint of eastern or priestly attire or attitude. Most common are silver tetradrachms with Greek legends which style him as *autokrator*, the equivalent of the Latin *imperator*, denoting supreme military command. He also minted gold and silver coins with Latin legends which, rather modestly, just give his name in full but no titles: L[VCIVS] IVL[IVS] AVR[ELIVS] SVLP[ICIVS] VRA[NIVS] ANTONINVS. It is questionable if he made a direct claim to be *augustus*, a rival emperor. The most common reverse legend is *fecunditas aug* (fecundity of the emperor), which may signify a desire for a good agricultural yield following the devastation inflicted by the Persians brought about through the divine offices of the *augustus*. But who this *augustus* was – whether Uranius or whoever was officially recognized by the Senate in Rome – is left unstated. Another coin has the legend *saeculares augg* with two Gs signifying *two* emperors, and a column inscribed with COS I (consul for the first time). The coin seems to perpetuate what by now must have been the rather jaded hope for the dawn of a new Golden Age under two emperors. Is Uranius here granting himself the high office of consul? And who are the two *augusti*? There is no simple answer.[27]

One thing these coins do tell us is that there was no shortage of bullion in Emesa. The gold aurei were struck to the old pre-Abritus weight standard and not only that, there is a low variance in weight which tells us this was a careful and deliberate policy. The first issue of 'silver' coins was struck to the debased standard of just fifteen per cent, making them dull and lifeless to look at, but the second issue was almost pure silver. This would obviously have made Emesene coins highly prized and would have projected a visual representation of the wealth of the city and the prestige of the separatist regime across the devastated east.[28]

Aemilianus augustus

Early in 253, at about the time Shapur was moving up the Euphrates, the commander on the lower Danube Aemilian rebelled against all lawful authority, his troops declaring him emperor. His reasons for doing so can only be a matter of speculation. Booty captured from the Goths may have given him the necessary financial resources. Perhaps the historical sources are right that he was puffed up by pride at his success against the Goths, that he despised Gallus and believed that the empire would be better off in his own hands. Maybe Gallus really had been guilty of double-crossing Decius at Abritus and now the army chiefs decided it was time to exact revenge. Or, as Jordanes implied from his Gothic perspective, Aemilian may have been terrified of the Gothic army that was being prepared against him in reprisal for his raid, and that the only way to save his sorry skin was to strike for supreme power. Whatever the motive, rebel he did.[29]

We can infer that Aemilian secured the support of all the legions on the lower Danube and not just the ones under his direct control because he was able to march directly on Rome through Pannonia (indeed some of the historical sources refer to him as commander of the Pannonian legions). Hence there must have been some serious plotting among the regional high command. Aemilian's first recorded act was to issue coinage in his own name from one of the Balkan mints, but he did not stick around there for very long.[30] Relying on speed in an attempt to catch Gallus unawares, he marched on Rome. In doing so he was following a well-trodden path most recently taken by Decius.

It so happens, however, that as Aemilian began his march, detachments of troops were gathering at Castra Regina (Regensburg), headquarters of *legio* III *italica* in the Province of Raetia in the early stages of preparation for the planned eastern campaign, possibly with the intention of wresting control of Armenia back from the Persians. Gallus sent a desperate message for assistance to the governor of Raetia, Publius Licinius Valerianus, or Valerian as he is known in English. Valerian heeded the call, but was unable to prevent Aemilian crossing the Julian Alps and entering Italy. Gallus mobilized whatever troops he had at his disposal in the capital but these may have been unusually weak given that the imperial forces of Decius had recently been annihilated at Abritus, and that too may have figured in Aemilian's calculation.[31]

Aemilian's army marched past the Po delta, down the coast to Ariminum (Rimini), then took the *via flaminia* across the Apennines in a dash for the capital. Gallus and his son Volusian bravely marched out to meet them. The armies met high in the hills at the town of Interamna Nahars (modern Terni). The sources disagree as to whether a battle actually took place. According to Aurelius Victor the imperial forces didn't rate their chances and so Gallus and his son 'were cut down by their own soldiers who hoped for greater reward from Aemilius [sic], to whom victory came without labour or losses.' Zonaras, on the other hand, says that 'when the armies had engaged in combat, Gallus' men were beaten, and being beaten they attacked their own emperor'. This may fit with another writer, Jerome, who records that both Gallus and Volusian were killed 'in Forum Flaminii [modern San Giovanni Profiamma] or, as some believe, at Interamna'. Perhaps they fled to Forum Flaminii after the defeat and were killed there.[32]

Whatever happened, this was the bloody end of the reign of Gallus and Volusian. The fourth century historian Eutropius's verdict was that 'they

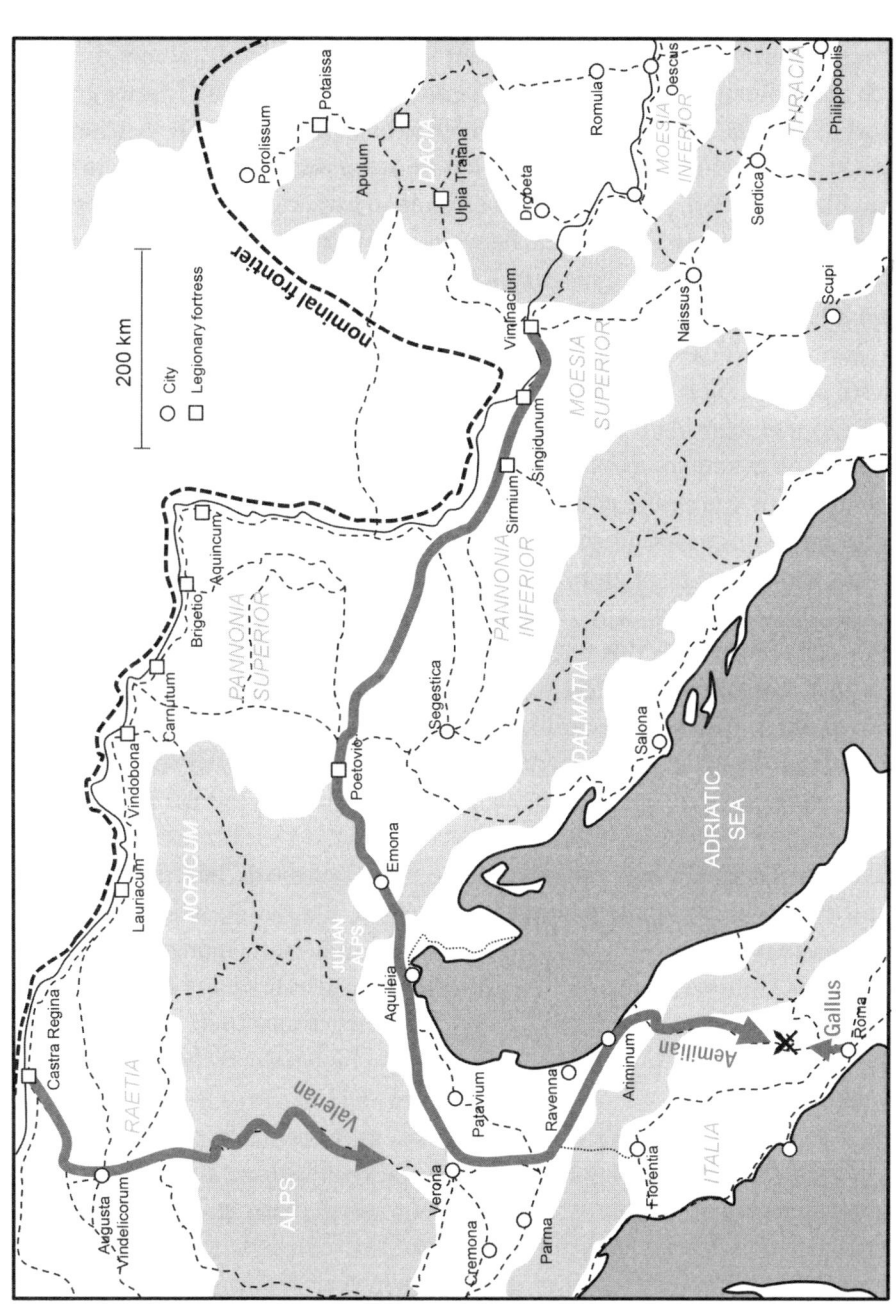

Map 18. The Battle of Interamna Nahars, 253 CE. Aemilian marched on Rome and Gallus marched out of the city to meet him. Valerian was unable to intercept the rebel.

achieved nothing remarkable at all; their reign was notable only for plague, diseases and afflictions', which seems rather harsh given the difficult hand they had been dealt.[33]

Every emperor for the last forty years had died violently, sometimes in battle but more often murdered by those around him, and usually after rather a short reign. Aemilian must have intended to buck this trend. The Senate had recently declared him a public enemy, but he acted with great courtesy to that venerable institution, writing to them offering to leave the regular government of the empire in their hands while he would 'fight as their general' in Thrace and against the Persians. This may have caused temporary uncertainty as to whether Aemilian intended to actually take the throne. It also indicates that by this time both Aemilian and the authorities were aware of serious problems in both sectors. The empire desperately needed a strong military leader and Aemilian was their man. In reality, of course, the Senate had no choice but to accept his offer and yes, it became clear that he did intend to be emperor, and so he made his triumphal entry to the city.[34]

The great mint started making coins for yet another new emperor, his portrait showing a hard and determined man as befits the situation (Plate 6). There was still enough in the imperial treasury to afford a cash bonus for the troops – we know this because some of the coins record the decennial vows that the soldiers took on the occasion, the idea being that it would be repeated every decade of Aemilian's glorious reign henceforth. Some of the coins honour his wife, the new empress, naming her as Gaia Cornelia Supera and showing her with the elaborately plaited, looped and pinned hairstyle of the day.[35]

The existence of a new empress in the palace begs the question of what happened to the previous incumbent, Herennia Etruscilla, wife of Decius, or indeed that other noblewoman, the wife of Gallus and empress who never was, Afinia Gemina Baebiana. The historians are utterly silent on the matter, so one can only hope that these sophisticated ladies and their retinues were permitted to quietly exit from the back door of the palace as the new arrivals moved in.

As Aemilian and his wife settled into their new residence, the Senate sent out messengers to the provinces in the usual way informing them that a new man was in charge, the most obvious result being that regional mints also started to produce coins in Aemilian's name. These include the great mint at Alexandria, an unspecified mint in the province of Dacia (evidently secure from Gothic attacks), and several places in Asia Minor. It is noteworthy that none of the Syrian mints did the same, the area being at that time under attack by the Persians. Careful study of the coin evidence dates Aemilian's accession to the late spring of 253, at about the time that Antioch was being attacked.³⁶

The core of Aemilian's army was probably *legio* I *italica* from Novae. They and their long-standing colleagues from the eleventh had avoided the disaster at Abritus and gained glory and booty through victory over the Goths under Aemilian's leadership. Now, presumably, they followed the triumphal route during the formal proclamation of their hero and then enjoyed strolling about the metropolis spending some of their previously acquired riches. Everything looked secure for Aemilian except for one thing. Out of honour or sheer personal ambition, Valerian, the governor of Raetia who had been summoned to the aid of Gallus, made the drastic decision to ignore the new political reality and march on Rome at the head of his scratch army. This of course made *him* the new enemy of the state.

Valerian on the march

Valerian's command consisted of *legio* III *italica* from Raetia and a heterogeneous collection of detachments (called vexillations after the military flag they marched under, the *vexilla*) which had been summoned from legions far and wide for the planned eastern campaign. Some had come up from Africa, others probably from Spain, Gaul and Britain. These men now marched on Italy, presumably crossing the Alps via the Brenner Pass at about the same time as Aemilian was entering Rome. Evidence for this is that the new mint at Mediolanum (the one set up by Decius before the Abritus campaign) never minted coins in Aemilian's name.³⁷ From there Valerian's army moved south in good order, following the same route that Aemilian had so recently taken. The emperor set out to confront this force, just as Gallus had done. By now it was late summer. Once again, two armies converged on the *via flaminia*, this time meeting about 15km closer to Rome than the previous confrontation at Interamna. The *Epitome de Caesaribus* gives us the precise place, a bridge near Narnia [modern Narni]. Aemilian may have judged this to be a better defensive position than had been selected by Gallus. Unfortunately for him, however, the result was much the same as before.³⁸ Zonaras has the most detailed account:

> Then, in fact, those who served with Aemilianus, when they had recognized that they were no match in battle for the army of Valerian, judging that it was not pious that Romans destroy and be destroyed by one another, that wars be joined between men of the same race, and otherwise reckoning, too, that Aemilianus was unworthy of the realm

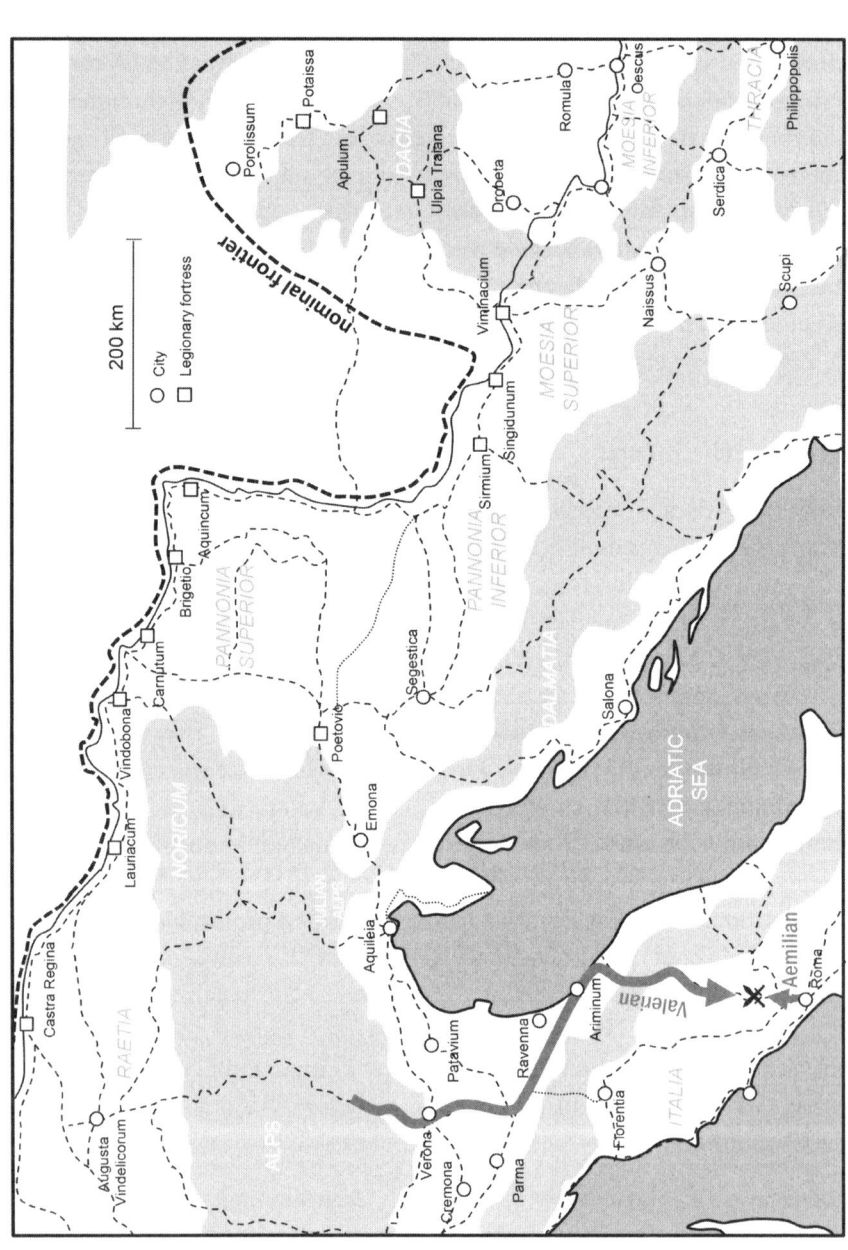

Map 19. The Confrontation at Narnia, 253 CE. Valerian continued his march and met Aemilian just a little south of the previous battle at Interamna Nahars.

both as ignoble and grovelling, and, to be sure, considering that Valerian was better suited for the rule because he would, for certain, assume affairs in a more authoritative fashion, killed Aemilianus, who had not yet reigned four months and was forty years of age. They submitted themselves to Valerian and entrusted the empire of the Romans to him without a fight. [Zonaras, *New History* XII.22.]

And so Valerian assumed the throne in identical fashion to his predecessor, sometime around September of 253. The senate enthusiastically applauded yet another man whom they had so recently outlawed.

A numismatic conundrum

In the 1930s the British Museum acquired a unique and puzzling artefact: a coin minted in the name of an entirely unknown man called Silbannacus, naming him *augustus*: IMP(ERATOR) MAR SILBANNACVS AVG(VSTVS) wherein the 'MAR' could be the name Marcius, Marius, Marinus, or something else (Plate 6). It had been found at Lorraine near the river Rhine. The name Silbannacus appears to be Celtic and may be a corruption of Silvannacus. The unique reverse type shows the god Mercury, a deity who, it has been observed, was especially honoured in Gaul. The coin is well made and the style was deemed about right for the year of Rome's millennium or a few years after.[39] Based on these few clues, it was suggested that Silbannacus may have been a regional commander in Gaul, possibly of auxiliary troops who rebelled against Philip the Arab around the time that Pacatian and Jotapian had made their bids for power, and was successful enough to get to the point of minting at least one decent coin. Another theory had him as a rebel against Decius, which would account for the troubles in Gaul as recorded by Eutropius and previously discussed.[40] Absolutely nothing else was known about Silbannacus and none of the historians mention him. He was so obscure that even Trebellius Pollio, the alleged writer of the 'Thirty Tyrants' in the *Historia Augusta* – which includes some very dubious padding and dredged-up material to get the total up to the desired number of thirty – never mentioned him. Some experts speculated that the coin may be an elaborate fake, but the museum specialists were adamant that it was genuine.

And there the issue stood until 1996 when a second coin emerged, this time having been discovered near Paris. It was minted using the same obverse die as the British Museum specimen but with a different reverse, showing Mars 'Propugnator' (Mars the Combatant, or Champion). This coin shed new light on the mysterious Silbannacus. Numismatist Sylviane Estiot pointed out that the reverse type and its abbreviated legend are known only from the issues of Aemilian, minted at Rome,[41] although a precise die match for it has not so far been found, and that both the style and metal of the two Silbannacus coins are typical of the Rome mint. The British Museum specialists had originally suggested the same about their coin, which was part of the enduring puzzle. Estiot therefore deduced that Silbannacus must have very briefly controlled the mint at Rome, possibly just for a day or two but long enough for at least two different types of coin to be hammered out. Estiot suggested that Silbannacus could have been one of Aemilian's loyal lieutenants who briefly controlled the city when his death at Narnia became known. These unusual pieces must then have somehow got into circulation and travelled to Gaul, possibly in the purses of soldiers from Valerian's army who were sent back to their bases after a spell in the capital. According to this scenario, we can imagine that when news of the assassination of Aemilian reached Rome, Silbannacus was briefly proclaimed emperor before reality sank in. Silbannacus may have stepped down gracefully or, more likely, was executed on Valerian's arrival.

There are a few loose ends to this story, however. The first is the strange reverse design of the original find. Mercury was a relatively unusual subject for Roman coins and this is the only example in the entire run of imperial issues that links the god with the legend *victoria aug* (Victory of the Emperor). Mercury was the fleet-footed 'messenger of the gods' who could run like the wind.[42] Close inspection shows the god with his winged helmet and his usual caduceus (serpent-entwined staff). The caduceus is the ancient symbol for a herald, that is, someone carrying news or dispatches. That much is normal, but when so depicted he generally holds a sack of money in his other hand, symbolic of his role as the patron of merchants and trade. Indeed, that very design had recently appeared on some coins of Herennius Etruscus.[43] In this single instance, however, Mercury carries the winged symbol of Victory who proffers the laurel wreath and stands on an orb. This confirms that the legend is not some mistake on the part of the engravers, as did occasionally happen but was integral to this original design.

A last clue is that the die appears very well made and is above the normal run of engraving. Compared with the regular Mercury issues of Herennius, the figure of the god is very clear down to the wings on his helmet (not usually shown), the way his arms wrap around the nicely symmetrical caduceus to hold the rounded boss at its base, and the delicate folds in his traveller's cloak. The tiny Victory that he holds is perfectly clear although just a few millimetres high. Thus it appears to be the work of a master engraver of the kind who normally made the dies for the gold aurei, which perhaps fits with the fact that this was a new design that other engravers were to emulate in due course.

From all this it seems fair to conclude that the reverse die was specifically chosen to convey the swift arrival of news of a great imperial victory. Could it be that it was ordered by the departing emperor on the eve of battle in anticipation of his success? When the enemy army was closing in, the decisive fighting was expected to take place just a few days' march from the city. When the inevitable news arrived at Rome, carried by an imperial messenger, there would be great rejoicing. The coin would be extremely appropriate for such a moment. The reverse type of the other coin, Mars the Champion (*propugnator*) may also allude to the expected battle, with Mars, god of war, fighting as champion of the city. The expected victory failed to materialize, of course, and the die may have been discarded, but not before Silbannacus had had his brief moment in the limelight.

Silbannacus has always been described as a usurper, that is, someone who attempted to seize power illegally. Estiot wrote that the time and place of Silbannacus's usurpation were now decided: Rome in the late summer of 253; that is, after the fall of Aemilian and before the declaration of Valerian. But the term 'usurper' is questionable. The Roman mint was most unlikely to have produced such coins without senatorial approval, because that would have been treason. As a contributor to the online forum 'cointalk.com' who styles himself 'Julius Germanicus' wrote in 2018: 'Unless nobody else has done so yet, I hereby proclaim the obvious: Silbannacus was no usurper, but indeed the 43rd legitimate Emperor of Rome!' He surely has a point.[44]

But there is another possibility that seems worth raising, namely that Silbannacus may have been a senatorial emperor *before* Aemilian; that is, after Gallus and Volusian had been assassinated at Interamna a few months earlier. That would fit with the story of Aemilian sending a letter to the senate at that time. In the words of Zonaras, he 'wrote to the Senate, promising that he would rid Thrace of barbarians, that he would campaign against Persia, and that, *having turned the realm over to the Senate*, he would do everything and fight as their general' (my italics). A similar phrase is found in a surviving fragment of text from the 'Anonymous Continuator of Cassius Dio' who says 'After he had been acclaimed sovereign, Aemilianus wrote to the Senate: "*I leave the realm to you*, and I strive in every way as your general"' (my italics). Perhaps the Senate had mistaken these modest words as indicating that Aemilian did not desire the imperial purple, and so they quickly appointed one of their own (Silbannacus) but were rapidly disabused of the notion when Aemilian and his army got to hear about the move.[45]

From the numismatic evidence it seems equally plausible that Silbannacus was emperor before or after Aemilian. We can hope that a final answer will come from a study of die linkages spanning the latter actions of Gallus and Volusian through the short reign of Aemilian and on to the early issues of Valerian. Or perhaps another Silbannacus coin will be dug up somewhere by some ultra-lucky metal detectorist. If two such pieces made it into circulation, there surely must have been others…[46]

Ransoming the Christian Virgins

The civil war of 253 and the troop movements associated with the troubles in the east may have precipitated an upsurge in violence all along the frontiers. Little is known of what happened on the Rhine, but subsequent events suggest the area experienced major security problems, with the depleted local legions presumably coping as best they could. The fleet protecting Britain (*classis britannica*) disappears temporarily from the archaeological and written record about this time and an increase in coin hoarding in that province may be evidence of heightened raiding and lawlessness there. A major rearrangement, or rather imperial contraction, occurred in the province of Africa. It is difficult to date precisely, but it was around this time most of the forts that had been built on the desert frontier during the reign of Septimius Severus (193–211 CE) were abandoned, which meant the coastal cities became more insecure and prey to nomadic raiders.[47]

There was also trouble in Numidia, probably in the hill country west of Carthage that included the militarized cities of Cirta and Lambaesis (modern Algeria). The only reason we know about this is a surviving letter from Cyprian, bishop of Carthage, to the bishops of Numidia concerning an unspecified number of their brethren who had been captured by barbarians, presumably desert dwellers from the south. Cyprian was especially concerned for the welfare of the virgins, but interestingly he refers not just to the lust of the captors but also their contagion, possibly indicating that they may have been harbouring the plague. Quoting the Christian maxim that people should do for others what they would do for themselves, Cyprian's letter enclosed the enormous sum of a hundred thousand sestertii (equivalent to a thousand gold aurei) which had been collected by the church of Carthage for their ransom. This probably included some of Cyprian's own personal fortune which, since his conversion, he had been liberally distributing to the needy. In return he asked that the Numidians remember the subscribers in their prayers. The money was specifically to redeem captured Christians; whether there were pagans held alongside them is not mentioned.

Another small snapshot of African history can be reconstructed for the eleventh day before the Kalends of November in the year of the Consuls Volusian and Maximus (i.e., 22 October 253). On this day an inscribed altar stone was set up at the far frontier fort at the oasis of Gemellae on the fringe of the Sahara Desert (now the village of M'Lili in modern day Tunisia, probably a variant of the same name). This outpost was on the very edge of the Roman Empire about 600km from Carthage across mountains and parched scrubland. The stone records the arrival of a well-travelled detachment (probably cavalry) from *legio* III *augusta* under the command of centurion Marcus Flavius Valentus and his *optio principis* (first officer) Lucius Voluminis Cresces. These men (the inscription tells us) had just returned to Gemellae from Raetia (modern Switzerland). From this it is reasonable to infer that a vexillation from *legio* III *augusta* had been summoned for the impending eastern war, and had travelled up to the mustering point in Raetia, but had then been incorporated into Valerian's army for the more urgent task of defeating the upstart emperor Aemilian. Once Rome was secure they were sent back to Africa, perhaps because the new emperor had been alerted to the difficulties that had brewed there during their absence. There is just enough time for them to have done all this and made their way back up to the desert frontier. The stone is dedicated to Victory. Whether they were celebrating Valerian's victory at Narnia or their own efforts against the local barbarians to regain control of the area (and perhaps rescue any remaining captives) is not clear.

Thermopylae 253

There is a final twist to the story of the chaotic year of 253. With Aemilian's Danubian legions nowhere to be seen, a new horde of Goths had no problem entering the empire, swatting aside whatever feeble remnants of the Roman military that may have tried to stop them. Not a single regular legion was held in reserve in the entire Balkan Peninsula. The countryside of Thrace and Moesia was despoiled once again although there may have been little to take as the area had suffered so grievously in previous years. We have already seen that the Goths liked to vary their tactics and line of attack. This time they set their sights on the rich provinces of Greece. The Greek inhabitants (the Hellenes as they called themselves) were forced to rely on their own initiative and resources. At this moment of crisis, some sort of renewed spirit of Greek nationalism seems to have stirred. Until recently we knew nothing about this episode except for a few meagre sentences in the summary histories of the Byzantine writers Syncellus and Zonaras who may have taken their material from Dexippus's *Scythica*. Happily the source text seems to have been found in one of the new fragments of the Vienna palimpsest, so now we know more of the story – although it is fair to warn the reader that the dating of the events to which the fragment refers is disputed by specialists and may belong to a later year.[48]

In any case, an extraordinary council was held, possibly under the auspices of the Panhellenion, a federation of the Greek city states. Dexippus tells us that three generals were appointed for the defence. In overall command was Marianus, the governor of Achaea (otherwise unknown) who represented the Roman imperial administration. He was supported by two senior Greeks, Philostratus of Athens (described as 'a man versed in speech and though') and Dexippus of Boeotia (the area west of Athens).[49]

There were several prominent Athenians called Philostratus (or in Greek, Philostratos) in the second and third centuries and historians have wrestled with disentangling their possible identities. The one in the new fragment is probably Lucius Flavius Philostratus who is described as *archon* (chief magistrate) later in 266/7 on an inscribed marble slab that was discovered in 1933 mortared into the lining of a cesspit in Athens city centre. This Philostratus went on to write a history of his own, focusing on the war in the east, which only survives in a few fragments (we have cited him previously in connection with the plague and as recording that Shapur returned from his victorious campaign through Cappadocia). It is just possible that 'Dexippus of Boeotia' was none other than our principal historian referring to himself in his younger days. It is generally acknowledged that Dexippus the historian was involved in military matters, after which he retired from public life and wrote his *Scythica* as well as a world history and other works. The current consensus, however, is that Dexippus of Boeotia was another person, possibly a close relative.[50]

As we have already seen, the Gothic armies were not undisciplined hordes but organized forces arranged in marching columns with a hierarchical command structure and a knowledge of siege warfare. They struck first at the great city of Thessalonica, hoping to breach the walls, sack the place, and carry off the people, but the defenders managed to hold out for an indeterminate number of days. A short account is recorded in a rare fragment from an otherwise lost history by one Eusebios, a citizen of that city:

> The people of Thessalonica did not remain idle in this situation, but having armed themselves with whatever was at hand, having resisted, they pushed back those who tried to enter the city and in the course of the struggle itself they captured a number of barbarians. For many people of the city who had been captured this led to liberty because the

barbarians, in order to free their own, gave back many of those they took. [Eusebios of Thessalonica, *Fragments of History* 14.][51]

A separate fragment seems to relate to the siege of another town somewhere in Macedon. The most likely candidate for this is Amphiopolis, a town on the *via egnatia* that was significant enough to have minted its own coins on occasion. Here we learn that the attackers were using fire arrows so the defenders dug basins beside their artillery pieces and rigged fire engines using lead pipes to dowse the flames.[52]

Frustrated by the delay at Thessalonica, the Goths held a council of war at which opinions were aired in the democratic manner of the Germanic tribes. Lured by tales of fabulous rich temples full of gold and silver to the south, and probably aware that Roman armies were busy marching against one another in Italy and so were not likely to intervene, the Goths agreed to cut their losses and proceed in the direction of Athens, intending to sack the famous Acropolis, the greatest prize of all.[53]

The Thessalonians had won some valuable time for their compatriots, however. The antique curtain wall of Athens, unused and unnecessary for over three hundred years, was hastily rebuilt with whatever materials were at hand, and a new fortified line was constructed over the Isthmus of Corinth in a desperate attempt to seal off the cities of the Peloponnese peninsula (the Roman province of Achaea) in case the invaders by-passed Athens. But the Greeks well knew from their own long history that any army marching on Athens from the north would first have to get through the pass of Thermopylae which is where they decided to make their first stand.

At Thermopylae (literally, the Hot Gates) the landscape constricts between the muddy shoreline of the Euboean Sea and the rugged heights of Mount Oeta (Map 20). Every Greek knew that long before, at this very spot, three hundred elite Spartan hoplites under King Leonidas had led a blocking force against hundreds of thousands of Persians. On that occasion, seeing the heavily armed Spartans arrayed against him in such a highly defensible place, the Persian King Xerxes had offered them a deal: lay down their weapons in return for an amnesty and a guarantee of Spartan independence. The Spartans had fought epic wars against Athens and other Greek city states and might well have thrived as a satellite to a wider Persian Empire, but Leonidas refused the offer. His response, very roughly translated, was 'if you want our weapons, you'll have to come and get them.' His men inflicted great losses on the Persians but were ultimately outflanked and cut down, virtually to the last man. Nevertheless the heroic sacrifice of the three hundred enabled the combined Greek states to prolong the war and eventually prevail.

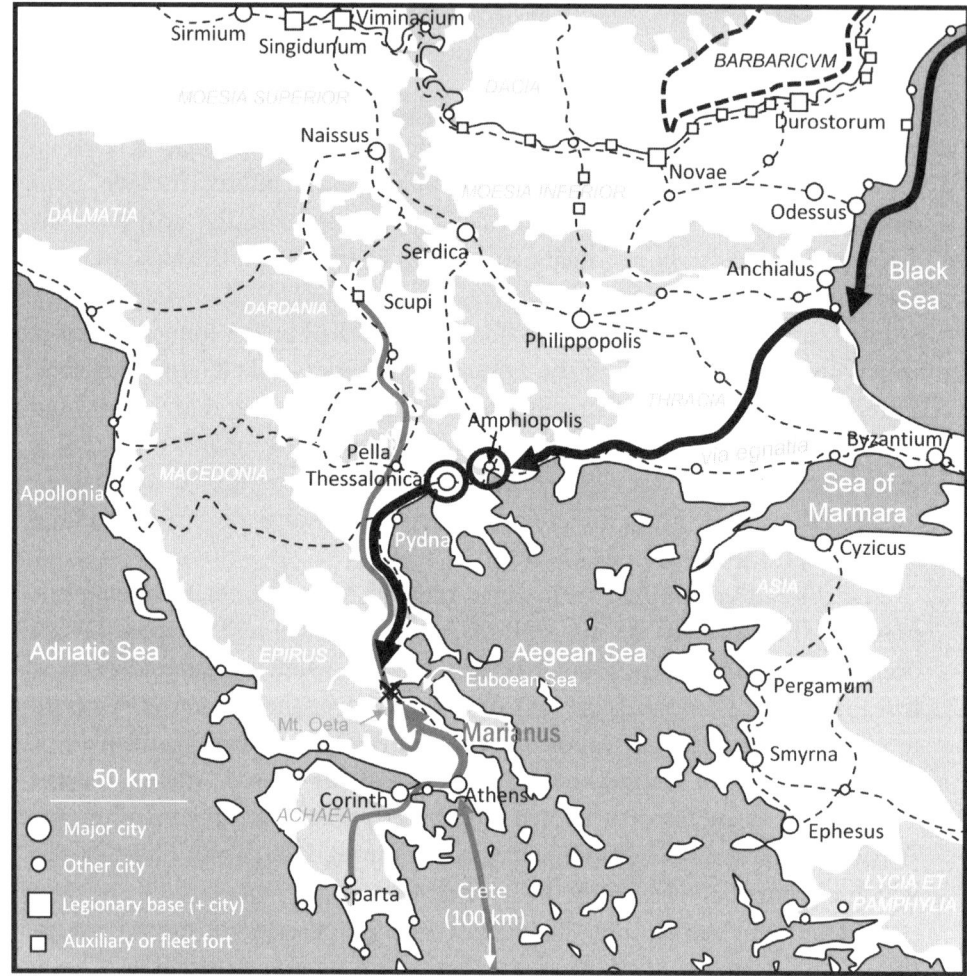

Map 20. Siege of Thessalonica and Battle of Thermopylae, probably 253 CE. How and where the Goths entered the empire is unknown, but naval transport seems probable. The most likely route from Thrace was along the *via egnatia*. Marianus led a scratch force from several Greek cities. Reinforcements from Scupi and Crete are based on the dubious *Historia Augusta*. The siege of Amphipolis is conjectural, based on Eusebios of Thessalonica.

That was in 480 BCE and so it was already ancient history, but the same strategic location was to be fought over again and again. It was of vital significance in the so-called Lamian War of 323 BCE, in which a Macedonian army was defeated by a Greek coalition occupying the pass. And then in 191 BCE a Roman army under the consul Manius Acilius Glabrio had won a great victory there over the Seleucid King Antiochus III. More recently, a combined force of New Zealanders and Australians managed to significantly delay a German armoured column at Thermopylae during the invasion of Greece in 1941.[54]

It was at this famous place that Marianus stationed his hastily arranged force, ordering them to set about rebuilding and re-manning the perimeter wall that stretched across the narrow plain. 'Some carried small spears, others axes, others wooden pikes overlaid with bronze and with iron tips, or whatever each man could arm himself with.' Here it is worth noting that an especially dubious passage in the *Historia Augusta* also refers to the defence of Thermopylae by the Peloponnesians, who were assisted by a force from Dardania (the area of Scupi, to the north) consisting of a thousand raw recruits, two hundred regular soldiers and a hundred and sixty cavalry. To these were added sixty Cretan archers. All that may be fiction, but such an emergency deployment, even to the extent of shipping a small detachment of archers from the island of Crete, is conceivable under the circumstances.[55]

Returning to the new fragment of Dexippus, Marianus addressed them as follows (at least as imagined by the writer):

> O Greeks, the occasion of our preservation for which you are assembled and the land in which you have been deployed are both truly fitting to evoke the memory of virtuous deeds. For your ancestors, fighting in this place in former times, did not let Greece down and deprive it of its free state, for they fought bravely in the Persian Wars and the conflict called the Lamian War, and when they put to flight Antiochus, the despot from Asia, at which time they were already working in partnership with the Romans who were then in command. So perhaps it may be good fortune, in accordance with the heavenly power [*daimonion*] that it has been allotted to the Greeks to do battle against the barbarians in this region... But you may take confidence in both your preparation for these events and the strength of the region – as a result of which, in previous attacks you seemed terrifying to the enemies. On account of these things future events do not appear to me without hope, as to better... [Dexippus, *Scythica Vindobonensia* 192^v-193.^{r}][56]

Unfortunately, at that point the page finishes and the account cuts off. A significant engagement must have occurred and according to the much abbreviated Byzantine summaries, the Greeks were successful in their defence of the pass. The Goths, frustrated by successive failures at Thessalonica and now Thermopylae, and not wishing to run the risk of being cut off by a relieving force, withdrew to their homelands once more, carrying much booty.[57]

Chapter 9

Restorers of the Human Race

Downturn

About 20km along the Rhine east of Basel in Switzerland lies the ruined Roman city of Augusta Raurica, now an archaeological park. It was named for the local Gallic tribe, the Raurici, and it is a typical example of the way the Romans literally civilized conquered peoples by providing them with towns featuring all the regular amenities including a forum, temples, theatre, amphitheatre, public baths and an aqueduct. As the empire grew, so the frontier receded and the city boomed, plugged into the wider imperial network and benefitting from the *pax romana*. Augusta Raurica was particularly famed for its cattle breeding and exports of cured meats, a delicacy enjoyed far afield. But then around the middle of the third century, disaster struck: a great earthquake destroyed many of the finest buildings in the city and most of the population left. Some people struggled on, but the town never regained its prosperity. Public buildings not brought down by the quake became overgrown with weeds and slowly fell into ruin.[1]

Or so the story goes. Recently the earthquake theory has attracted scientific investigation because planners in Switzerland are concerned about the ongoing risk of rare but high-impact seismic activity. Detailed geophysical surveying and paleoseismicity studies were undertaken but failed to find any hard evidence for such an event. The earthquake may have been more metaphorical than real. Instead, it seems, the city suffered from a sudden economic collapse, likely caused by panic, plague and exodus.[2]

The fate of Augusta Raurica is an extreme example of the rapid economic decline that set in all the way from the Rhinelands to the Black Sea as well as in much of the rest of the empire. The legions were repeatedly being ordered to supply military detachments of their better troops for foreign and civil wars, reducing their strength which they may have found increasingly difficult to make good. Those vexillations moved long distances, placing a huge, if transient, burden on the law-abiding communities in their path. Imperially sanctioned demands for food and the billeting of soldiers could easily cross the line into extortion and robbery. Meanwhile, fear of the once mighty and disciplined Roman army seems to have diminished, both on the part of would-be invaders from outside the empire and bands of robbers and cut-throats within it. The highly organized frontier defence system began to crumble as raiders dared attack and destroy the border forts, degrading the defensive infrastructure.[3]

As a consequence, large and small-scale raiding was on the increase, much of it never recorded in the written records. Intriguing evidence comes from the bed of the Rhine where loot dating to our period is occasionally dredged up. One such hoard from Neupotz in south-west Germany consists of domestic metalwork: platters, jugs, strainers, cooking pots, knives and so on, in sufficient quantity that it must have required wagons to transport it. Just a few miles upstream at Hagenbach, another hoard comprises silver items and votive offerings, some of which have inscriptions that prove they were looted from as far away as the foothills of the Pyrenees. For some reason these valuable caches ended up in the river, possibly thanks to violent if belated interventions by the *classis germanica*, the Rhine river fleet.[4]

Previously undefended settlements across much of the empire began to build stone walls, towers and gateways, including in distant provinces like Britannia, where the city of Londinium was one of many places to be furnished with new fortifications. Coastal forts were built along the North Sea and Channel coasts of Britain and Gaul, perhaps in response to increased piracy on the shipping lanes and coastal raiding. Major industries that relied on safe long-distance transport by road, river and sea, such as the famous decorated red-slipware potteries of Gaul (*terra sigillata* or 'Samian Ware') went into terminal decline.

Life went on, of course, but the economic malaise described by contemporaneous writers like Cyprian was real and evident in the reduced weight and quality of the money in people's purses. Former imperial silver coins had been almost pure, but by now the content was below thirty per cent and dropping all the time.[5] Inflation set in as people began to hoard the old coins and require more of the new ones to pay for their goods and services. The resulting lack of spending power completed the vicious circle of economic decline. Another trend of the period is the steep decline in public inscriptions. Previously, any self-respecting civic building would have boasted a prominent dedication naming some proud and ambitious local magistrate who had funded it for the public good, but from mid-century they become much harder to find. There seems to have been little enthusiasm for major new religious buildings either.[6]

Despite all this, historians have questioned whether there was indeed a 'crisis' in the Roman Empire at this time. Contrary evidence can be assembled and simplistic assumptions challenged. Town walls, for instance, might be expressions of civic pride and prestige rather than insecurity. The end of

Samian Ware production in Gaul might just be a matter of changing fashion. Archaeology shows that some places appear to have thrived when the empire was supposed to be in direst trouble, so an alternative narrative featuring a largely tranquil third century can be posited. Or one can argue that the empire had never been stable, either politically or militarily, so the middle of the third century was nothing remarkable. Such debates are entertaining but can soon become sterile, so we will return to our narrative, but not before briefly considering another hot question: whether climate change had anything to do with the situation.[7]

Climate

The role of climate in dictating the course of ancient civilizations from Asia to Mesoamerica has attracted increasing attention in recent years, for understandable reasons. Slowly changing weather patterns, often unseen and unremarked in the historical record, may have shaped the historical trajectory in ways that are only now amenable to study with scientific techniques. Obviously we cannot directly measure something like the temperature, sunshine, precipitation, or the length of the growing season in the past, but we can measure all sorts of things that would have responded to such factors. Tree rings, ice cores, stalagmites, slow-growing clam shells, corals, lake deposits and sea-floor sediments: all these were mutely recording their environment in various ways that are now amenable to study using a battery of laboratory techniques. These are the so-called climate proxies, and they have generated a large and technical literature.[8]

The climate of the Mediterranean region is very sensitive to North Atlantic sea surface temperatures and in particular the balance of high and low atmospheric pressure between what is called the Azores High and Icelandic Low. This shifting balance is known as the North Atlantic Oscillation which affects the wandering path of the jet stream that in turn controls storm tracks, temperature, precipitation and cloud cover over a vast area. The formation of deep waters in the North Atlantic helps drive the global ocean overturning circulation which affects the strength of the surface currents that bring heat and moisture to Europe. The whole delicate system is influenced by gradually shifting background conditions associated with the Earth's orbit as well as varying solar irradiance and the sunspot cycle; human-influenced factors like deforestation also affect moisture balance and run-off. Transient events like large volcanic eruptions can inject vast amounts of aerosols into the stratosphere causing severe cooling ('years without a summer') associated with widespread crop failure.

It so happens that the climate system was remarkably stable during the period when the Roman Empire was growing. Solar activity was fairly constant and there were no major volcanic eruptions on the planet after one that seems to have occurred in the portentous year of Julius Caesar's assassination in 44 BCE. Glaciers were in retreat in the Alps and modest warming was underway. The resulting benign conditions favoured the cultivation of grapes and olives (so vital for the economy) across the Mediterranean. North Africa was much wetter than it is now, with elephants living in the forested slopes of the Atlas Mountains and extensive irrigation schemes supporting huge and fertile farming operations. Areas that are now semi-arid wastelands were able to supply much of the grain and olive oil that sustained Rome and its armies. The Nile rarely failed in its rhythm of annual flooding, having been distinctly erratic in the few centuries BCE. The Levant was similarly blessed with abundant precipitation as the Dead Sea reached its high stand. These conditions correspond to what has been called the Roman Climate Optimum. When all the indices are aligned, the peak of the Climate Optimum corresponds with the high-point of the empire around the middle of the second century.

But then things started to change. General cooling set in that continued into the third century, as can be seen in all kinds of proxies. A spike in sulphate aerosols deposited in a Greenland ice core tells us that a major volcanic eruption occurred somewhere in the world around 235 CE, possibly depressing global temperatures for several years and affecting crop yields. Tree rings from the Alps record another sharp cooling in the decade from 243–253 CE which was followed by a solar minimum around 260 CE. The same records also reveal a general increase in variability from year to year, something anathema to farmers who are tied to one place and must plant in anticipation of the seasons. Precipitation in places as far apart as the central Mediterranean and France became more variable, causing alternating years of flood and drought. The Nile became less reliable in the 250s and there seems to have been a general drying out in North Africa as aquifers became depleted (something which Cyprian had remarked upon as evidence of the wrath of God).

Was any of this responsible for the disasters that beset the Roman Empire? It is of course difficult to establish any kind of direct link. All we can really say is that climatic and political instability went hand in hand. People who go hungry are likely to cause trouble, whether they be the city mobs of Rome or barbarians far beyond the borders.[9]

Another new regime

The new emperor Publius Licinius Valerianus was a senator from 'a reasonably distinguished family' and a former suffect (replacement) consul.

He is believed to have been born around the year 193 CE and thus was about sixty years old on his accession, quite an advanced age for the time.[10] The convoluted circumstances surrounding the rebellion of Aemilian meant that the throne had fallen into his lap. This was something he had not desired and only consented to as a public duty, at least if one can believe the account in the *Historia Augusta*. But some historians have wondered whether Valerian might have had the opportunity to cut off Aemilian's advance and chose not to do so, leaving Gallus to his fate and then moving in with a more powerful force to claim the ultimate prize. Had he played a game that was more crafty than honourable, as the distinguished numismatist Harold Mattingly suggested? That is something we may never know.[11]

One thing Valerian had in his favour was that he had a son of about forty years in the prime of life and fit to command armies, a man called Publius Licinius Egnatius Gallienus, and he in turn had three promising boys of about fourteen, twelve and five years of age known as Valerian (the younger), Saloninus and Marinianus.[12] The emperor's first act was to appoint Gallienus as *caesar*, the heir apparent, and together they set about repairing the state. Valerian's wife, Mariniana, had died before his accession so in traditional style she was consecrated as a goddess and celebrated on a special issue of coinage.

Valerian and Gallienus wisely focused on securing their regime in Rome, spending the rest of 253 in the capital and no doubt trying to do their best to re-order the military after the disruption of the most recent civil war. The rebellious Moesian legions were posted back to their bases at Novae and Durostorum under new, trusted, leadership, and tasked to seal the border against the Goths once again. The main focus of recruitment was to re-build the field army for deployment in the east while the military planners did their best to ascertain a full picture of the disaster that had unfolded there.[13]

One of Valerian's first acts was to consecrate the memory of Trebonianus Gallus who was henceforth to be regarded as a god. This of course fitted his narrative as the man's avenger. Unexpectedly, however, he issued an amnesty for the Christians who had been exiled or imprisoned by Gallus. Later tradition has it that he received Christian leaders with hospitality and friendliness. Bishop Lucius of Rome was allowed to return from exile and the old theologian Origen was finally released from his prolonged imprisonment. His health was ruined, however. According to a later account, he had been stretched four notches on the rack, dislocating bones and tearing muscles and sinews. The fact that he had not died a martyr adversely affected his theological legacy in the centuries to come.[14]

By the New Year celebrations for 254 at the very latest, Valerian raised Gallienus to *augustus* as his equal, and the two men shared the consulship as would be expected for two new emperors. Gallienus's wife Cornelia Salonina was made first lady, with the title of *augusta*. Little is known of her background other than some regional coins from Asia Minor give her the Greek name Chrysogone (golden-born).[15]

With a map of the empire spread out before them (one imagines) the emperors developed a joint strategy for asserting their authority and protecting it against the multiple threats being faced. Valerian would travel to Antioch where he would restore the city and mastermind the recovery of the eastern provinces. Gallienus would set up an imperial administration at Viminacium, capital of Upper Moesia, the best place for receiving rapid intelligence from both the Rhine and Danube frontiers. When his boys came of age they would be placed under the protection of loyal generals and fly the flag for the dynasty in places that the senior emperors themselves were unable to visit. Hopefully that would curb the endemic problem of serial rebellion wherever an emperor was absent.

Another key decision taken early on was to reform the army hierarchy. There would be no place for amateurism henceforth: instead, experienced career soldiers would be promoted to high command. The regular legions and auxiliaries would hold the borderland in the normal way, but it was by now crystal clear that a concentrated strike force was needed, held back from the frontier and ready to mop up raiders as well as repel mass invasions. Indeed, both emperors would build a substantial field army around themselves, one in the east and the other the west, and if the situation allowed they could be combined to bring overwhelming force to bear against a foreign foe. Valerian's army would have responsibility for restoring order in Syria and Mesopotamia and discouraging further Persian aggression, but it would also be able to move up in to Cappadocia and the rest of Asia Minor if necessary. Gallienus's army stood poised to sweep down the Danube as far as Byzantium if the incursions of recent years were to be repeated, but could equally campaign in the troubled area defined by the headwaters of the Rhine and Danube (the so-called *agri decumates*) and all along the Rhine up to the North Sea.[16]

Sometime in 254 the emperors clasped hands (the event being shown on their coins) and went their separate ways. This might have happened in Rome, but it seems likely for various reasons that first the pair travelled together overland as far as Byzantium which was the effective dividing line between their dominions. Logic would suggest that they would have campaigned against whatever Gothic threat remained in the war-torn districts of Thrace and Moesia and indeed both emperors claimed the title *germanicus maximus* that year. The emperors may then have entered negotiations once again with Cniva (assuming he was the Gothic king) to end the war. The Goths had done extremely well out of the plunder of course, but the fighting had not all gone their way. Aemilian had inflicted a major defeat on them and the Greeks at Thermopylae might also have caused significant losses.[17] A renewal of the shaky peace treaty and subsidy along the lines previously agreed by Gallus would fit the facts, but the truth is we have very little evidence of what happened on the Danube front in 254. Just possibly, however, one very large clue has recently been unearthed inside a mysterious mound at Manole in Bulgaria.

Puzzle of the Manole Mound

About 20km east of Plovdiv (ancient Philippopolis) lies the sleepy town of Manole, the chief claim to fame of which is, or rather was, that a local sheep pasture contained ancient Thrace's largest burial mound. Circular in cross section with gently concave earthen flanks and a circular depression at the summit, the mound had the appearance of a small grassy volcano. Much of it was subsequently removed in a series of excavations beginning in 2018. Nobody predicted what was discovered within.

Burial mounds are a common feature of Bulgaria's countryside, most dating to the first few centuries BCE, and those that have been excavated scientifically have proved a rich source of archaeological information about the wealthy elite of the so-called Odrysian Kingdom that flourished in Thrace before the Roman conquest. Manole was exceptional, however. Not only was it by some distance the largest such structure – at 23 metres tall and about 140 metres across it was more of an artificial hill than a mound – but it also appeared, at first sight, to be undisturbed. Perhaps the sheer size of the structure had put off prospective tomb raiders, or so it was hoped.

Funding was obtained to establish a visitor centre and support a series of archaeological investigations. Careful excavations along the periphery began to turn up significant finds. A series of ritual pits were found with sacrificial offerings including pottery vessels and a few Roman era coins. It would not have been unusual for a prestigious site such as Manole to have been to be the focus of religious devotion for centuries. The most intriguing object was a bronze figurine which was described as being typical of the Goths. Had a Gothic warrior visited the site at some point after its construction and made an offering?[18]

A bold decision was made to excavate downward from the top, partly to determine whether the structure had ever been robbed. At five metres down the archaeologists encountered a large 7 by 7 metre square of masonry, which to everyone's surprise was found to be of Roman construction in a style indicative of the mid-third century. Scanners indicated that the structure penetrated downward for at least several metres but even then it would only be occupying the upper part of the mound! Confusingly, however, it was not a tomb, but rather a solid mass of stone.

Geophysical surveying started to throw up unexpected results: the masonry, substantial though it was, appeared to be sitting directly on top of another, even bigger building. Sure enough, several metres further down, the diggers encountered a neat row of tiles, beneath which the footprint of the structure expanded significantly. A lot more digging and another such enlargement was found. For the first time people began to wonder whether they were excavating some kind of tower that went all the way to the original ground level. Rather than belonging to the ancient Thracians, the entire edifice appeared to be of Roman construction and very well built (Plate 7).

The excavators announced that the structure they had unearthed was so grandiose as to have no direct analogies in the whole empire. The closest comparison was to the so-called 'tower tombs' known from some of the eastern provinces like Syria. The team began to speculate that the 'tower' as it came to be called, might mark the tomb of a Roman emperor.[19] By 2020 the digging had gone all the way down to the original ground surface but, to everyone's surprise, the structure was found to be completely solid inside. The Roman engineers would build up a few courses and then augment the mound around the stonework as they progressed. When the structure was finally completed, the mound was greatly enlarged and topped with a final flat-lying layer of rubble. With investigations continuing there is still the possibility that more might be found beneath: subterranean chambers perhaps, so the tomb theory is still a possibility, but the most likely explanation now seems to be that the Manole is neither a tomb nor a tower but rather an enormous solid foundation. But for what?

At the time of writing, the preferred explanation appears to be that the tower and mound supported a giant statue, possibly of bronze, that was at some point carefully demolished and melted down. 'We are talking here of a huge monument,' one archaeologist said, and one that would have been visible across the Thracian plain for miles around.[20] But this author would like to propose a slightly different option. The structure seems rather over-engineered for a statue base, even a very large one. Instead it could have been intended as the foundation for a great victory column.

The ground at Manole is soft alluvial gravel laid down by floods in the upper reaches of the Maritsa River, a most unstable substrate, so a large column would require something like this to support it. It would also explain why the courses of masonry were so well made despite being immediately buried: it was necessary to provide a stable weight-bearing platform. The earthen mound would have helped distribute the weight of the column. If that was the intention, the monument was never finished because no trace of the hypothetical column has been found, not even a tiny fragment. Perhaps the engineering was at fault, and despite all precautions, the edifice sagged slightly to one side. It may be pertinent that the area east of Plovdiv is one of the most seismically active parts of Europe and subject to repeated tremors. An earthquake could have destabilized the structure before completion. Alternatively, perhaps the money, or the luck, of the emperor who commissioned it ran out, and the project was simply abandoned.[21]

So much for the archaeology, but who built the monument and why? The first pertinent fact is that Manole lies on the *via diagnonalis*, the great imperial highway linking east and west. Close by the mound was a Roman posting station (*mutatio*) called Sernota ten miles out of Phillipopolis and the first place a traveller would change horses and have a bite to eat. What better place for a public monument, and one that would also have been visible from the centre of Philippopolis.[22]

If the structure at Manole really dates to mid third-century as the reports have suggested, then it is possible it was intended as a victory monument to commemorate the Gothic War. It is fair to ask what the Romans thought worth celebrating, given that Decius had been killed at Abritus with most of his army and Philipoppolis had been devastated by Cniva's barbarians. On the plus side, the citizens of Philippopolis, the lucky ones at least, had been freed from captivity by Aemilian and peace had subsequently been restored. The needs of propaganda demanded that the Romans claim final victory. So perhaps it was in 254 that the work was commissioned, after Valerian and Gallienus had negotiated a new treaty of friendship with Cniva. Despite the fact that it was never finished as intended, the people who had lost loved ones in the fighting could still come out of the city and make humble offerings to the gods. And one day, perhaps, someone made a quiet memorial to one of the Gothic warriors killed in the fighting by burying a home-style figurine.

Imperial business

Valerian set up his court in the ashes of Antioch where his first problem was to deal with the rebel Uranius Antoninus in Emesa. The situation was probably resolved diplomatically. Recall that despite minting coins in his own name, it is doubtful if this man had ever actually claimed the title of *augustus*. He and his supporters could justifiably have pointed to the need for strong local command when threatened by Persia and with civil war in Italy the previous year (*imperium*, which he had claimed). Uranius had defended his city well and was also chief priest of the powerful sun religion of that place. Perhaps, then, he was allowed to step aside with honour while publicly professing his loyalty to the new emperors and the Senate and People of Rome.

The mint at Antioch resumed its activities, striking double-denarii in comparatively good quality silver which must have been shipped in especially for the purpose.[23] Previously, emperors had often boasted of being the restorer (*restitutor*) of one province or another; now Valerian was depicted as *restitutor gener humani*, 'Restorer of the Human Race' (Plate 6). A coin shows the emperor advancing confidently, wearing his radiate crown and holding an orb, symbol of his worldly dominions, while his other hand is outstretched as if reaching forward to protect the troubled provinces. Gallienus issued an identical type in his own name from the mint at Viminacium where the old regional mint had been upgraded. The message was clear, and potentially reassuring, but could the new men live up to such a grandiose claim?[24]

The imperial treasury was used to set in motion repairs all over the eastern territories that had been devastated the previous year. We can imagine the dutiful emperor touring the area while receiving two cheers from the half-starving populace – those lucky enough to have escaped Persian enslavement. Like Decius before him, Valerian may have found cold comfort in the austere philosophy of the Stoics at this difficult time. His travels probably took him to the very far eastern border and the fortress city of Dura-Europos on the Euphrates. Dura was certainly back in Roman hands by 30 April because an official document was issued there on that date.[25]

At this time, the vulnerable western 'desert' wall at Dura was strengthened with a steep glacis (external sloping bank) all the way along its length while the road that previously ran along the inner side of the wall was entirely filled in with rubble as the adjacent buildings were either demolished or requisitioned as part of the defence network. These works had the fortuitous effect of preserving some wonderful archaeology including a synagogue and the earliest known example of a Christian church. The effect was to create a great sloping rampart about fifteen metres thick with only the top of the pre-existing wall protruding. Now the entire circuit wall was immune to artillery and battering rams: the only way through would be a mad assault over the top of the defences, which had enfilading towers all along their length, or to burrow beneath. There can be no better testament to the fact that Valerian expected the war to continue and that he intended to hold the pre-existing frontier.[26]

There are some stories in the *Historia Augusta* attributed to Flavius Vopiscus of Syracuse that relate to this time. One of them refers to a senior officer of obscure birth but great zeal and courage called Aurelian. It was a common name, so to distinguish him he was nicknamed *'manu ad ferrum'* (literally, 'hand to iron', but more poetically, 'sword in hand' according to David Magie's acclaimed translation). This man is credited with restoring the frontier on the lower Danube and capturing cattle, horses and slaves. His boss, Ulpius Crinitus (otherwise unknown) was so impressed that he formally gave thanks to the senior emperor Valerian for giving him such an efficient deputy at the public baths in Byzantium. Such a thing could have happened before Valerian made his way east. Another story relates to a promising young man called Probus who, despite being a beardless youth, was put in charge of a military detachment sent to Gallienus by Valerian from the east. This exotic command included six cohorts of Saracens (desert-dwellers from the north-west Arabian Peninsula) and a company of Persians from 'Artabassis the Syrian'. Presumably these Persians, if they ever existed, had been captured as prisoners of war, but nothing else is known of Artabassis. Both stories are very doubtful because Aurelian and Probus were eventually to become emperors in their own right and it was clearly tempting to invent a back-story for them.[27]

We do not know where Gallienus wintered in 254–5, although most likely it was his new base at Viminacium. Valerian was definitely in Antioch because an inscription records his presence there on 18 January.[28] When it came time to elect the new consuls in Rome it seems that neither emperor was there to suggest replacements, so the senate by default voted both emperors back in to office as consuls for the second year running. The leading senator at the time was an old patrician who had been consul over twenty years before called Lucius Valerius Maximus. He had then been one of twenty distinguished men who had been appointed by the senate to look after the affairs of state during the Civil War of 238 (the so-called 'vigintivirate' of that year). Now he was appointed City Prefect and got on with the job of administering the metropolis. Not a lot more is known about him.[29]

In 255 a grand bridge over the River Pyramus was completed at Mopsuestia in Cilicia at the extreme northeast corner of the Mediterranean Sea and dedicated in the emperor's name at the imperial expense. The proud occasion is shown on a locally produced medallion which boasts a particularly inventive design. It shows the river god Pyramus reclining on his bridge above a veritable torrent of water with triumphal gateways at each end and the letters Δ-Ω-Ρ-Ε-Α in the five arches below. These spell out the Greek word for 'gift'. The bridge was on a major east-west route and would have facilitated a quick march by Valerian's imperial forces from Antioch up in to Asia Minor if the occasion required, so it very much fits the new imperial defence strategy. The site is close enough to Antioch (165km) that it is tempting to think that Valerian would have cut the ribbon in person.[30]

The Borani

There is no solid evidence that the Goths had signed a peace treaty, but no major attack was launched in 255, or at least not across the Danube. Instead, it seems, the Goths and their allies turned their attention to the northern and eastern shores of the Black Sea which was outside formal Roman territory. This fascinating region has always been at the crossroads of civilizations. In ancient times it had been alternately dominated by Assyrians, Scythians, Medes, Persians, Greeks, and Romans. Somehow, however, the old kingdoms there had managed to retain nominal independence for much of the time by signing declarations of friendship with the great powers. One such place was the so-called Bosporan Kingdom centred on the Crimea and the shores of the Sea of Azov where Roman army units were regularly posted to help bolster the defence.[31] Another was the kingdom of Colchis which dominated the eastern coastline of the Black Sea along the stretch where the looming Caucasus Mountains come down to sea level.

Colchis was a land of mystery and romance, the onetime reputed destination of Jason and his Argonauts in their quest for the Golden Fleece. The main town in Roman times was Pityus, having originally been founded as a Greek trading emporium. It was equipped with an old and substantial fortress, but with the rise of tensions in the mid-third century the inhabitants evidently began to feel exposed. Archaeology has revealed that a new city wall was hastily constructed to make a second, outer, line of defence and, presumably at the request of its citizens, a Roman garrison consisting of a detachment from *legio* XV *apollinaris* was installed to protect this allied power.[32]

Around the year 255 a mysterious group called the Borani, possibly allied to the Goths but under their own leadership, attacked the Bosporan Kingdom. Zosimus called them a 'nation', fit to be mentioned alongside the Goths and Carpi, and says they originated beside the Danube. The ethnic identity of the Borani has, however, long puzzled scholars, not least because there is no distinct archaeological culture that can be associated with them, and they have variously been described as Germanic, Gothic, Sarmatian, Alan, or even Slavic. A recent study sees them as a mixed parcel of renegades, runaway slaves, robbers, destitute townspeople, orphans, and deserters from both sides of the wars who had been forced to look to their own devices during the tumult

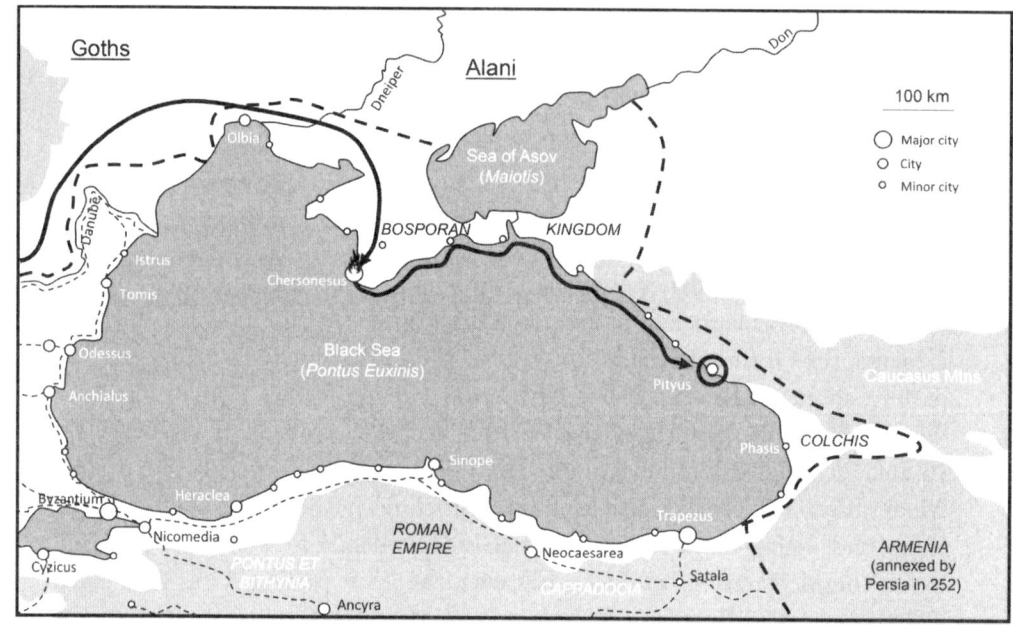

Map 21. The attack of the Borani on the Bosporan Kingdom and Colchis, probably in 255 CE. The nominal borders of the Roman Empire, Bosporan Kingdom, Colchis, and Persian Armenia are shown, but were highly fluid at the time.

of the last few years. In other words, the homeless and stateless may have coalesced into a political force all of their own in the devastated borderlands and marshes of the lower Danube. The suggestion that their number could have included ex-Roman soldiers is interesting, and one wonders whether some of these might have been men cashiered by Decius for neglect of duty just a few years previously.[33]

Although it was a longstanding Romanized client state, the Bosporan Kingdom had seemingly been experiencing internal difficulties on the death of one of its kings. Numismatic evidence points to a power struggle between Rhescuporis V and King Pharsanzes, the latter apparently hostile to Rome and minting coins in 253–254. It has been suggested that Pharsanzes may have recruited outside forces to bolster his claim. Little is known of the fighting but it seems that parts of the Crimea were effectively annexed by the Borani at this time. Significantly, they also managed to seize control of a fleet that had been based in the Bosporan capital of Chersonesus. As Zosimus put it, the Bosporans were 'induced more through fear than good-will to supply them with vessels, and to guide them in their passage'. The Borani decided to use this newly acquired naval asset to launch a surprise attack on Pityus. Its isolated garrison was now to face an onslaught from the waves.[34]

The only account we have of this event is a highly abbreviated few lines by Zosimus:

> But Successianus, who commanded the army there, made so vigorous a defence, that the barbarians were routed, and in such dread lest the other garrisons hearing what was done might join with that of Pityus and totally destroy them, they hastened with the utmost speed to their ships, and returned home under great hazard, having lost many of their companions at the Battle of Pityus. [Zosimus, *New History* 1.32.]

When Valerian heard reports of this engagement he was so impressed that he sent for Successianus and, evidently liking what he saw in the young man, made him Praetorian Prefect. This was an astonishing promotion for a one-time commanding officer of a remote garrison beyond the imperial border, but it fits with the new regime's determination to promote on merit rather than social status in these difficult times. Zosimus tells us that Successianus was then put in charge of the repair and recovery of Antioch while Valerian moved on to confront other threats in the east.

Pipara

If we are right that Gallienus was occupied in Moesia and Thrace in 254, he must have turned his attention to the Rhine frontier in 255. The minting of coins suggests that he initially set up his administrative centre at the well-connected city of Augusta Treverorum (Trier) and later moved closer to the border at Colonia Agrippina (Cologne) to where the imperial mint was transferred. Military activities could equally have been conducted from the legionary base at Mogontiacum (Mainz) to the south. Inscriptional evidence shows new units appearing in the area at this time including detachments from *legio* VI *victrix* and *legio* XX *valeria victrix* from Britain suggesting that that relatively untroubled province may have lost more of its protection at this time.[35] A brief passage in Zosimus records what happened:

> As the Germans were the most troublesome enemies, and harassed the Gauls in the vicinity of the Rhine, Gallienus marched against them in person, leaving his officers to repel with the forces under their command any others that should enter Italy, Illyricum, and Greece. With these designs, he possessed himself of and defended the passages of the Rhine, at one time preventing their crossing, and at another engaging them as soon as they had crossed it. But having only a small force to resist an immense number, he was at a loss how to act, and thought to secure

himself by a league with one of the German princes. He thus not only prevented the other barbarians from so frequently passing the Rhine, but obstructed the access of auxiliaries [i.e., reinforcements]. [Zosimus, *New History* 1.30.2–3.]

By a combination of decisive military action on the river border and alliance with powerful tribal leaders, Gallienus seems to have stabilised the Rhine frontier which had hitherto been in a state of disorder. It was exactly the kind of policy pursued by famous leaders of the past such as Julius Caesar, and for Gallienus to accomplish it from a position of relative weakness was surely a success. Eutropius says that he 'achieved a great deal in Gaul and in Illyricum' by establishing a degree of stability for these beleaguered provinces. By this time his coins from the third issue at Rome were describing him as *germanicus max ter* (Thrice Greatest Victor over the Germans) and depicting a trophy of heaped up captured arms and armament.[36]

A curious passage in the *Historia Augusta*, allegedly penned by Trebellius Pollio, tells us that the emperor 'loved a barbarian maid, Pipara by name, the daughter of a king. And for this reason Gallienus, moreover, and those about him always dyed their hair yellow'. Elsewhere the same author says that he 'grew weak in loving a barbarian woman'. This would normally be dismissed as salacious invention except that Aurelius Victor independently refers to his 'shameful love affair with the daughter of Attalus, a king of the Germans, whose name was Pipa'. The *Epitome de Caesaribus* tells us of 'a concubine – Pipa by name – whom, when a portion of Pannonia Superior had been ceded through a treaty by her father, king of the Marcomanni, he had accepted in a kind of marriage'. Hence it seems possible that some of the Marcomanni were settled within the empire in Pannonia with some sort of conjugal link between Gallienus and Pipara being part of the deal. Gallienus remained married to the empress Salonina and continued to mint coins in her name, and Pipara (or Pipa) was never recognized as an official empress. Even so it seems that some of the Roman nobility were scandalized by such behaviour in an emperor just as they had been by Antony and Cleopatra hundreds of years before.[37]

As well as diplomacy, some of the credit for the successes on the Rhine and Danube may be due to the rising stars of the military firmament who surrounded Gallienus and were given regional commands – those subordinate officers mentioned by Zosimus in the passage above. One of these, according to the dubious testimony of Flavius Vopiscus in the *Historia Augusta*, was 'sword in hand' Aurelian who allegedly distinguished himself during a Sarmatian raid into the Balkans and 'with his own hand slew forty-eight men in a single day'. There may well have been fighting in Illyricum, but the inventiveness of Flavius Vopiscus seems without limit when he then tells us that Aurelian was given command of a mixed force of exotic eastern units including two hundred Ituraean bowmen [that is, from the area of the Golan Heights northeast of the Sea of Galilee], six hundred Armenians, one hundred and fifty Arabs, two hundred Saracens and four hundred auxiliaries from Mesopotamia. He was also allied with four Germanic chieftains named as Hariomundus, Haldagates, Hildomundus and Charioviscus and both he, and the dashing young tribune Probus, were at different times given command of the Third 'Felix' Legion as well. Unfortunately, that legion probably never existed until, for some reason, it was brought to life in the opening battle scene of the movie *Gladiator* in 2000.[38]

Tragedy at Trapezus

Lucius Valerius Maximus, the hard-working city prefect, was made senior consul for the second time in 256 to crown his illustrious career, serving alongside another patrician called Marcus Acilius Glabrio about whom nothing else is known except that he might once have served as governor in Africa. He may have been a very distant descendant of the consul mentioned in the previous chapter who had commanded an army at Thermopylae over four centuries earlier. These appointments are a timely reminder that not every decision that happened in the empire came from the very top. The Senate was still a most important administrative hub and not just for the city of Rome and its environs. It contained an enormous amount of hard-won experience and a strong patriotic core. Valerian and his predecessors Decius and Gallus were all rather conservative traditionalists (although capable of innovation) and relied heavily on the old aristocratic system of government to support them. The Roman Senate still stood at the top of a pyramid of delegation that extended right down through the provincial level to the towns, tribes and village councils, giving the system real resilience.[39]

Valerian or his generals campaigned along the eastern border zone with some success in 256 as the regime claimed a victory over the Persians. One significant achievement seems to have been the re-capture of the strategic city of Nisibis which would have done much to stabilize the situation. After two hard years putting the east to rights, Valerian seems to have decided that the administration there could be left to continue the process of recovery by itself (perhaps overseen by his Praetorian Prefect Successianus in Antioch) with security entrusted to the legions which must by now have been brought back up to acceptable strength after the disaster at Barbalissos. Accordingly, he travelled west and the two emperors were reunited. It is tempting to suggest that the meeting happened early in 256, in Rome. That year Gallienus's elder son Valerian reached adulthood (perhaps fourteen or fifteen years of age) and was raised to the rank of *caesar*. We do not know when this happened, but the tradition was to have a coming of age ceremony for the boys on a feast day called the Liberalia (17 March) when they would remove their childhood charm (the *bulla praetexta*) and dedicate it to the household gods. Then they would don the pure white toga of a man (*toga virilis*). This was a private ceremony in the home, but Valerian would no doubt have been keen to exhibit the new *caesar* and Prince of Youth. Perhaps the younger Valerian took pride of place at the head of his assembled age cohort of newly minted young men while the two emperors, his grandfather and father, presided, along with his mother the empress Salonina.[40]

The Borani had been repulsed from Pityus in 255 according to the most likely chronology, but it was not to be the end of the trouble in that area. Zosimus proceeds to tell us that the 'Scythians' (probably, this time, including Goths as is discussed below) procured more ships from the Bosporans, and launched new raids against the towns of the eastern Black Sea coast. Most likely this was in the summer of 256 when the weather was conducive to sailing. The initial attack was against Phasis (see Map 21 for location) where they despoiled a Temple of Diana and the historical palace of King Aeeta. Aeeta was the legendary figure who had owned the Golden Fleece according to Greek legend, so it is tantalizing that Zosimus should refer to his palace as somewhere still worth attacking in the third century.

The assault on the main citadel at Phasis was unsuccessful for reasons not given, so the raiders proceeded once again to Pityus, which did not have Successianus to organize the defence. This they captured second time around, and then proceeded back along the coast to the great and ancient city of Trapezus (Trabzon in modern Turkey). Unlike Pityus this city was formally part of the Roman Empire, indeed one of the most important places in the Province of Cappadocia. The summary provided by Zosimus tells the whole story in some detail for once:

> Having there [Pityus] seized on the castle, and turned out the garrison, they advanced forward; and as they had a large navy into which they put all the captives who were able to manage an oar, they sailed with favourable weather, which continued almost the whole summer, towards Trapezus. This is a large and populous city, and was then guarded by ten thousand men above the usual complement. When they commenced the siege of it, they did not therefore even imagine that they should succeed, as it was surrounded by two walls; but when they observed that the soldiers were

addicted to sloth and inebriety, and that instead of continuing on guard, they were always in search of pleasures and debauchery, they piled against the wall trees which they had prepared for the purpose of scaling it, on which their troops mounted in the night and took the city. The soldiers within were struck with consternation at the sudden and unexpected assault; some of them succeeded in escaping through the gates; the rest were slaughtered by the enemy. Having thus got possession of the place, the barbarians acquired an incredible quantity of money, besides a very great number of slaves, for almost all the inhabitants of the country had fled for refuge into that city, as it was strongly fortified. Having demolished all the temples and houses, and everything that contributed to the grandeur or ornament of the city, and devastated the adjacent country, they returned home with a great number of ships. [Zosimus, *New History* 1.33.1–3.]

A sad but interesting witness to the aftermath of this attack has survived via the archives of Christianity in the form of a letter written by Bishop Gregory of Neocaesarea (the aforementioned 'Wonderworker') to a neighbouring bishop, possibly of Trapezus, on the question of how to treat those among their Christian brethren who had been captured by the barbarians or had otherwise become involved in the raiding. Gregory assured his colleague that it is not a problem if prisoners had eaten meat supplied by their captors because 'it is agreed by everyone that the barbarians who overran our region did not sacrifice to idols' so the meat was clean. Any woman who had been raped should not be regarded as having sinned, with the proviso that she 'in her former life has shown herself pure and beyond suspicion', otherwise 'clearly the state of fornication is suspect even in times of captivity'. What seems to have concerned Gregory more is the theft and looting that followed in the wake of the barbarian raids, and the disconcerting fact that some of the Christians themselves had been involved:

> That in the time of the invasion, amid such grief and lamentations, some should go so far to regard the crisis that brought ruin to all as the opportunity for gain for themselves, is the work of men impious and hateful to God, and their wickedness is beyond all measure. Therefore it seems right to excommunicate such men, lest wrath should descend upon the whole people. [Letter of Gregory the Wonderworker.][41]

More startling still is that Gregory condemned his fellow Christians who 'have become so thoroughly barbarized as even to put to death men of their own race by the gibbet or noose, and to point out roads and houses to the barbarians, who were ignorant of them'. Gregory also condemned those who 'found in the fields or their own houses objects left behind by the barbarians' and kept hold of them in place of property which they themselves may have lost, remarking that although 'the Borani and Goths worked on them deeds of war', such men were 'Borani and Goths to others'. This comment is very valuable as a contemporaneous source specifying the identity of the 'barbarian' enemy. Gregory's final comment was that 'those who fulfil the commandment [of God] should fulfil it without any ambition for base gain, demanding reward neither for the giving of information, for returning a runaway slave, for restoring lost property, nor recompense of any kind'. Slaves were slaves, even to the Christians, and needed to be rounded up so that order could be restored.

Concord of the Emperors

In August 256 it seems that Valerian and Gallenius were both at Colonia Agrippina (Cologne), the capital of Germania Inferior. The city's defences received a makeover including a restored gateway inscribed with the names of the two emperors. A medallion from around the same time with the obverse legend *concordia augustorum* ('Concord of the Emperors') and reverse design *adventus augg* ('Arrival of the Two Emperors') shows them riding together in full armour at the head of a procession fronted by the winged figure of Victory. Given the martial theme, it is possible that the emperors had assembled the might of their combined imperial strike armies on the Rhine for a joint campaign against the 'barbarians' – generally identified as Franks and Alemanni in the later sources – who had been causing all the trouble there. Whoever they were, the enemy were not the more peaceful tribes just beyond the Rhine with whom Gallienus had recently negotiated friendship. Nothing more is known about the campaign that followed except that the Romans claimed at least one, and probably two, more victories in the name of both emperors as advertised on the coinage which now read *germanicus max v* (Greatest Victor over the Germans for the fifth time) and show a trophy of arms with tied prisoners beneath. Were these victories major engagements or just minor skirmishes? We don't know. Twenty years earlier, the emperor Maximinus Thrax had fought a string of successful battles deep in Germania but only claimed the title *germanicus* once: inflation may have been setting in with regard to victory titles and acclamations. Not everyone may have been pleased by this development. The rich landowners of the empire were expected to celebrate each claimed victory by donating gold to the imperial treasury so a victory proclamation was essentially a tax on the wealthy elite, something that was now being repeated again and again.[42]

Yet another imperial mint was opened around this time, probably at Augusta Treverorum (Trier) in the Rhineland while the Cologne mint still operated. It was in line with the new policy of focusing money production closer to the troop concentrations. Not only would a ready coin supply ensure prompt payment for the regular legions stationed along the river frontier, but it would also fund the cavalry strike force that Gallienus was building up.

Inevitably, this decentralizing policy, with the emperors away on campaign most of the time, tended to lower the prestige of the capital. Perhaps mindful of this, Valerian was back in Rome again by 10 October where a dated rescript in his name was issued. It seems probable that he wintered there and that Gallienus joined him too. The two men could have taken some satisfaction at the progress of their regime and the string of victory titles and imperial acclamations that had been notched up. Most of the borders had been secured including, most importantly, the Persian frontier which had experienced a period of uneasy peace ever since Shapur had dragged his booty and captives eastward in 253. The lower Danube appears to have been peaceful also, possibly after the conjectured treaty with the Goths. Apart from ongoing outbreaks of plague, the great crisis that had gripped the empire seemed to have abated to some extent. Nobody could have claimed the dawning of a new Golden Age, but a corner may have been turned.[43]

Chapter 10

Turbulence

Persecution renewed

The year 257 probably opened with both emperors in the imperial capital, sharing the consulship once again and perhaps for once being able to focus on non-military matters. Their workload was huge and no doubt they made many important decisions, but the only one that comes down to us is that they elected to renew the persecution against the Christians. As we have seen, Valerian had been well-disposed towards the religion at the beginning of his reign, offering its leaders an amnesty, but that now changed dramatically.

The Bishop of Rome at the start of Valerian's reign had been a man named Lucius, whom Gallus had exiled from the city but Valerian had permitted to return. This man had died soon after, in March 254. He is not counted among the martyrs in church records and the cause of his death is unknown. His successor was a man called Stephen who seems to have gone about his duties unmolested for several years, indulging in theological correspondence with bishops far and wide, including with Cyprian of Carthage. It was a mini boom-time for the church and many new converts were apparently made across the empire, some from the highest social circles.

Despite this, the surviving correspondence shows that another unseemly row broke out within the senior hierarchy, this time concerning two Spanish bishops who had obtained certificates during the Decian persecution and who were also alleged to have invoked the traditional gods on other occasions. They had been ejected from office and two replacements elected, but Stephen, in his widely accepted role as senior bishop, agreed to hear their case and decided to reinstate them. The new bishops refused to step down, however, and received the powerful backing of Cyprian and the assembly of African clergy. This now set Cyprian at odds with the bishop of Rome. To make matters worse, another set of rival bishops also emerged in Gaul backed by different groups in Rome.

All these splinter groups were busily baptizing converts and the question arose as to whether such people were to be regarded as part of the Christian community if they had joined the church in good faith. Cyprian, backed by Dionysius of Alexandria, said no: there was only one true church and any baptisms conducted outside it must, therefore, be the work of demons, however innocent they might seem. Stephen disagreed, and moreover started excommunicating communities that Cyprian and his followers regarded as genuine. It was this kind of power struggle between senior bishops that was ultimately to lead to the rigidly hierarchical structure adopted by the Catholic Church and the medieval notion of the infallibility of the papacy in Rome.[1]

But renewal of the persecution put an end to the internal arguments for now. A century later it was claimed that the reason for Valerian's change of policy was that the leader of the Jewish community in Egypt had persuaded him to crack down on the Christians, although there is no evidence Valerian was ever in Egypt and the story must be doubted. Another person who gets the blame (from the contemporaneous testimony of Dionysius of Alexandria) is Valerian's finance minister (*a rationibus*) Fulvius Macrianus who is supposed to have conceived a hatred against the Christians for the ongoing misfortunes in the realm. This man had the ear of the emperor and, according to Dionysius, managed to turn him to the dark side.[2]

Bishop Stephen died in August 257, probably of natural causes although a much later legend has it that soldiers sent by Valerian had intruded upon a religious gathering and beheaded him as he sat on his papal throne. He was replaced by a man called Sixtus II. In the same month Valerian issued a new empire-wide edict, the text of which is lost, but the gist of which was that a new sacrifice was required, but this time it was not for all the citizens, just for those suspected of being Christians. Christian leaders (bishops and presbyters) were to be exiled from their communities and forbidden to conduct ceremonies in public or in private. If they broke this rule they were to be punished further.[3]

As usual, the severity of the persecution depended on the temper of the regional authorities. Cyprian was banished to the pleasant coastal town of Curubis (modern Korba, Tunisia), about 100km from Carthage, where he continued to run his diocese *in absentia*. The situation in the neighbouring province of Numidia was far worse, with many Christians committed to work in the mines. Sentencing to the mines (known as *damnatio ad metalla*) reduced the victims to a state of miserable slavery, where they were to face vicious beatings and imminent death. Interestingly, however, Cyprian was able to write to them and receive replies, carried by messengers who were able to buy access to the condemned, presumably by bribing the mine owners. The unfortunate individuals are nine bishops named as Nemesianus, Felix, Lucius, another Felix (not a lucky name, apparently), Litteus, Polianus, Victor, Jader, and Dativus. These senior men were imprisoned with an unspecified number of presbyters, deacons, and lay brethren. Cyprian encouraged them to embrace their situation by drawing an analogy between the wooden clubs with which they were being beaten on a daily basis and the cross on which Jesus had been crucified. And what a wonder it was, he remarked, that more metaphorical gold and silver (that is, the condemned men) was being taken in to the mines rather than out of it![4]

One could be forgiven for thinking that the condemned themselves might not have appreciated such a message from Cyprian in sunny Curubis-on-sea. But three replies to the letter are preserved, the first from Nemesianus and three of the others, the second from Lucius, and the third from one of the Felixes along with Jader and Polianus. These groups were evidently in different mines. Only the last letter gives us the location, which was 'the mine at Sigua' (modern Sigus in Algeria) where there was a copper mine. All three letters express love and gratitude to Cyprian and remark that his message had helped strengthen them in their hour of suffering and end by bidding him a hearty farewell. They all looked forward to impending death with courage and even optimism.

Another man who came before the courts at this time was Dionysius of Alexandria. An intriguing letter of his tells of the trial itself, in which he and four of his colleagues were arraigned before the deputy prefect of Egypt, a man called Aemilianus (probably the distinguished equestrian Lucius Mussius Aemilianus). After being ordered to worship the gods who preserved the empire, Dionysius replied that surely it was normal that each person worships the gods which they themselves approve; that he and the other Christians worship only the one true God, and moreover they pray to him continually for the good of the empire and the well-being of the emperors. For this they were banished to Cephro (in the west of the Nile delta) and banned from holding assemblies or entering cemeteries. Dionysius ignored the order and, according to his own testimony, made new converts at Cephro. The authorities responded by sending him to 'a rougher and more Libyan-like place' called Colluthion.[5]

Devastation in Bithynia

Zosimus details another Black Sea raid that happened around this time. He records that the Scythians (Goths) had been impressed with the success of the Borani at Trapezus and were determined to emulate them by raiding down the west coast to find more places that had not yet been plundered. The Roman Black Sea fleet (*classis pontica*) is still nowhere mentioned, hence the Goths were able to build a fleet at leisure in their own territory using captured Roman citizens as slave labour assisted by 'others who through necessity had taken up their abode among them'.[6]

Unusually, the attack occurred in winter, most likely that of 257/8. The fleet set off past the mouth of the Danube accompanied by a land army which 'marched as quickly as they could along the shore'. The force passed the cities of Tomis and Anchialus without attacking them, presumably because they were fortified. Eventually they approached Byzantium, arriving at a place called 'the Lake of Phileatina', and 'finding that the fishermen of that lake had concealed themselves and their vessels in the neighbouring fens, they made an agreement with them, to put their land forces on board the fishermen's boats, and sailed forward in order to pass the strait between Byzantium and Chalcedon.' Phileatina (alternatively Phileas or Philiae) is an ancient Thracian town on a small headland on the Black Sea, identified with modern Karaburun. The Lake of Phileatina is modern Lake Durusu about 40 kilometres northwest of Istanbul (Map 22). The fact that the Goths needed to make an agreement with the fishermen implies that they required their nautical skills and not just the boats.

The Goths were taking a substantial risk by sailing the length of the Bosporus (which is about 25km long and just a kilometre or two wide) past Byzantium which was ordinarily supplied with a substantial garrison and fleet. One can only assume that the forces there were in a state of complete disarray and the Goths knew it. One thing the invaders had in their favour was the surface current, which always flows from north to south thanks to the salinity difference between the Black Sea and Sea of Marmara. They landed at Chalcedon at the southern end of the strait opposite Byzantium. What happened next was a disgrace, according to Zosimus:

> And though there was a guard from Chalcedon as far as the temple which stands at the entrance of the Pontus, which was strong enough to overpower the barbarians, yet some of the troops marched away under the pretext of meeting a general whom the emperor had sent there, and others were so terrified that when they first heard of it they fled with all possible precipitation. The barbarians then crossed over, took Chalcedon without opposition, and got possession of an abundance of money, arms, and provisions. [Zosimus, *New History* 1.34.3.]

Urged on by someone called Chrysogonus (the name is Greek, the same, it so happens, as that of the Empress Salonina so this was presumably a local informer), the Goths then marched to the great city of Nicomedia, provincial capital of Bithynia et Pontus, which was undefended. The citizens fled at their approach but 'the barbarians still were astonished at the vast quantity of valuables they found'. Then the cities of Nicaea, Cius, Apamea and Prusa fell in quick succession. Nicaea was another great city, chiefly now famous for being

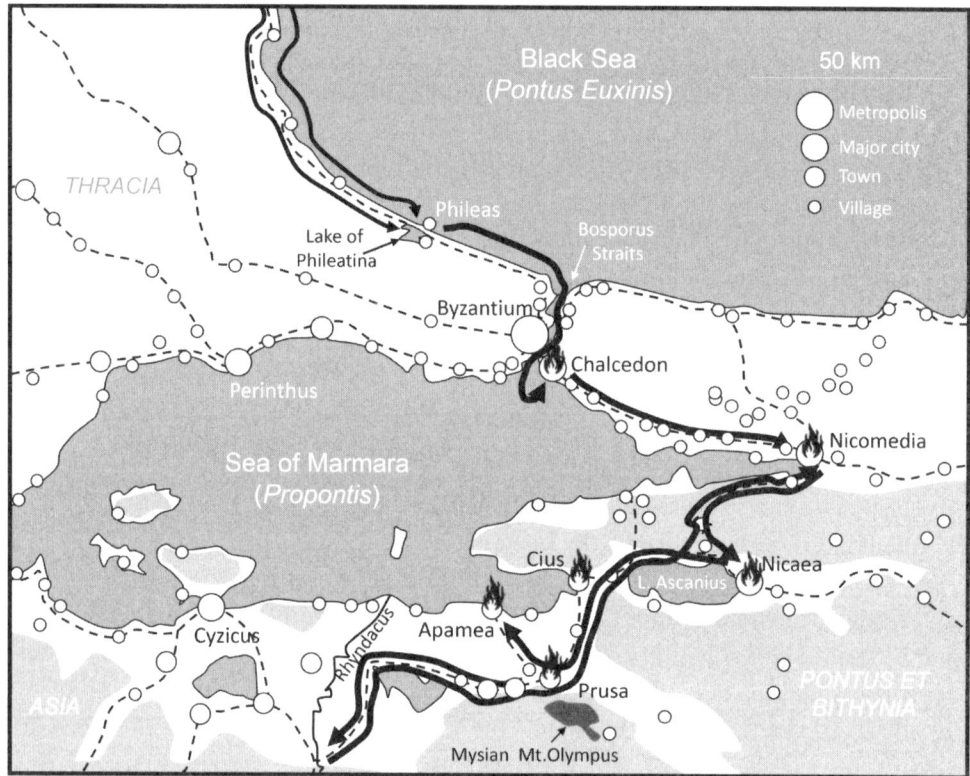

Map 22. The Gothic raid on Bithynia probably in 257/8 CE as described by Zosimus, The map shows all the known settlements in this densely populated area and the cities which are said to have been sacked.

the site of the First Ecumenical Council where the so-called Nicene Creed of the Christians was later to be established in 325 CE. Apamea (otherwise known as Myrlea and not to be confused with Syrian Apamea which had recently been sacked by Shapur) and Cius were both coastal cities with *colonia* status and important enough to issue their own bronze coins. Prusa was something of a resort town, nestling at the foot of Mysian Mount Olympus (rising to over 2,500m above sea level), famous for its healing hot springs and hydrothermal baths. There were also several lesser towns and scores of villages in the area (see Map 22) which do not get a mention but presumably suffered the same fate. There is no doubt that by this time the raiders would have been laden with much of the wealth of Bithynia, but they had their eyes on an even richer prize: the Roman province of Asia to the west and in particular the great city of Cyzicus which was just a few days' march away.

By this time, news of the invasion had reached Valerian. Bithynia was in his agreed sphere of influence, albeit at the extreme western edge of it, about

1,000km forced march from Antioch. Nevertheless he mobilized his strike force and took it north into Asia Minor, presumably using the new bridge over the Pyramus at Mopsuestia which had been built for just such an eventuality. At the same time, we are told, he 'sent Felix to Byzantium'. From the context it seems that this Felix might have been sent ahead with a naval task force to regain control of the Bosporus and Sea of Marmara. His identity is uncertain but he must have been a senior officer and it has been speculated that he may have been Lucius Mummius Felix Cornelianus who had been consul for 237.[7]

Cyzicus was a trading emporium that dominated the Sea of Marmara (Roman Propontis) and was entirely undefended, but the people of the city had one hope: it had been raining heavily that winter and the River Rhyndacus (the modern Mustafakemalpasha), which defined the provincial border, was in spate. There was only one feasible crossing point at a place on the road from Prusa, probably a ford rather than a bridge. Zosimus does not mention it, but it seems likely under the circumstances that a citizen militia from Cyzicus would have attempted to defend the far bank, rendering any attempt to cross even more hazardous. Frustrated, the Goths were forced to turn back to Nicaea and Nicomedia, which they torched out of spite, then loaded up their wagons and returned home. It is unlikely they attempted to navigate the Bosporus against the current but, being still in control of the eastern side of the straits, they presumably dragged their boats to the northern end for re-embarkation.

The fact that the raiders managed to accomplish all this and get clean away without being intercepted by the garrison at Byzantium was another first order disaster for the empire. Felix, it seems, must have arrived on the scene too late. When Valerian got the news that the Goths had escaped he had no option but to perform an ignominious about-turn somewhere in Cappadocia. According to Zosimus, he 'returned after having done some injury to every city through which he passed' which seems to be a rare reference to the problems caused by marching armies as regards victualling and billeting. The new grand strategy forged by the joint emperors had failed on this occasion.[8]

Duel at Tower 19

As we have seen, Valerian had managed to shore up the eastern frontier after the disastrous invasion of the Persian army in 253 and had claimed a victory over the enemy, possibly relating to the re-capture of Nisibis. The new defence strategy had involved putting a strong garrison back into Dura-Europos, likely under the control of a new *dux ripae* (Duke of the Riverbank). It is not clear to what extent the wider area had recovered from the depredations of the

Persians but presumably the administration wanted people to return to their valleys and their farms and the presence of the Dura garrison was designed to give them the confidence to do so.

But then, in the spring of 257, the *spah* attacked once again. Archaeology has provided dramatic testimony of what happened and had no intention of by-passing Dura. The action probably began with an attempt to take it by surprise and then with standard weaponry such as rock-throwing artillery and rams, but the Romans were well-prepared for that and the assault failed. Excavated evidence of projectiles from outside the walls shows that the Romans deployed much defensive artillery which must have caused considerable casualties on the Persian side as a regular siege developed. Positive evidence that the initial assault failed comes from the fact that at least four major engineering projects were developed against the walls. This would have been done simultaneously to stretch the resources of the defenders within. One of these was aimed at the Great Palmyrene Gate that led out on to the desert caravan route towards the west. A second area of attack was at the southern corner of the desert wall where an enormous ramp was constructed as well as a series of tunnels. These works were subject to counter-sapping by the Roman defenders. More tunnels were developed against at least two of the towers on the desert wall, known to archaeologists as Tower 19 and Tower 21. It is probable that there were also attacks along the riverfront and surprise assaults elsewhere on the flanks to keep the defenders guessing.

Most of what happened during those weeks or months will never be known. However evidence of the bitter struggle at Tower 19 was uncovered in 1932–3. Excavations there were conducted by the French military archaeologist Robert du Mesnil du Boisson whose discoveries included a subterranean tunnel enclosing a pile of bodies which, in the desiccated conditions, still included parts of soft tissues including brain and hair. These were undoubtedly defenders because some of them carried Roman money in their purses. Close by in the tunnel network was the body of one of the attackers in full Persian armour, his helmet laid to one side. He was carrying sulphur and bitumen.[9]

Du Mesnil suggested how he thought the defenders had died and all the evidence has been re-evaluated more recently in the light of new investigations on the ground, resulting in a detailed reconstruction of events.[10] The Persians began by starting a mine about 40 metres in front of Tower 19. This was a most exposed position, so one presumes the works were begun in silence in the dead of a moonless night. The Romans would have flattened everything in the approaches to the ramparts during their preparations a year or two earlier, but the attackers may have found some sort of cover among the chambered tombs outside the walls (the Romans never buried their dead within city limits). The tunnellers benefited from the geology, wherein a hard layer of limestone that forms the plateau of Dura and acts as the foundation of the city walls is underlain by a much softer stratum of sand and clay that was easy to dig in. As the Persian mine progressed forward under this natural limestone roof, a large spoil tip began to develop beside the entrance to the sap which is still visible today.

The Romans, of course, had a shrewd idea what was going on, and in response to the threat they sank at least one counter-mine which ran from a demolished house inside their own defences towards the wall. The idea would have been to locate the Persian tunnel and, as silently as possible, infiltrate and destroy it. A dangerous game of cat and mouse developed in the confined and highly unstable spaces below the walls. Du Mesnil re-excavated the Roman counter-mine and found that in places it was still held up by the original timbers but elsewhere the timbers had burned and the tunnel had collapsed.

When the Persians were directly under Tower 19 they hacked their way upward through the limestone cap (no doubt a very noisy operation), ultimately reaching the defensive masonry which was built of cubic limestone ('ashlar') blocks. These were passed back down the sap and discarded on the tip. In doing this, the attackers eventually succeeded in undermining the corner of the tower which collapsed downward, only partially, but making it unusable for artillery support. The Persians then made a ninety degree turn to the left and methodically dug along under the wall line being careful not to bring anything down. The idea was to prop it all up with timbers which would later be fired to hopefully produce a sudden breach in that part of the wall which was no longer subject to enfilading fire from the tower. A major infantry assault would proceed through the gap.

It was the Persians who first detected the counter-mine rather than vice versa. Crucially, the Roman tunnel was at a higher level. The Persians prepared a noxious fire of bitumen and sulphur with the deliberate aim of poisoning and asphyxiating everyone in the counter mine. Hot air rises, and the updraft, enhanced with bellows, would have fed the fumes throughout the Roman mineworks. This was subterranean chemical warfare of a kind reminiscent of the Western Front in 1917. In the chaotic situation that developed it seems that nineteen of the defenders lost their lives – those were the bodies found by Du Mesnil. As the air cleared the Persians pulled them into a makeshift barricade, which suggests that they were under missile fire from up the tunnel. A brave soldier came forward to light another fire which quickly took hold, bringing down the tunnel roof along an extended section. Only one Persian seems to have died, the fire-starter himself, either having been shot by the defenders or because he was overwhelmed by his own noxious fumes. His last act may have been to take off his helmet in an attempt to draw breath. He never made it back to his comrades who closed off the works with a pile of mortared rubble, entombing him and his victims for posterity.

Having thwarted the Roman counter-measures, the Persian sappers then completed their task of undermining the wall. When the props were fired, it sagged alarmingly (as can still be seen today) but, being supported by Valerian's new earthen banks on both sides, it failed to actually collapse. The Persians were thus thwarted in this particular operation. But in the end it didn't matter: somewhere else, unseen to archaeology, the *spah* got through and the whole city was put to the sword.

Du Mesnil's discovery has been described as the holy grail of archaeology, one of those rare occasions where the vagaries of burial and preservation provide a direct link for us to a few minutes of time in the past. In this case, they were minutes of horror and desperation, which, unfortunately, is representative of what must have been happening across a large part of the empire in those years.[11]

The Lord of Tadmor

The Roman Empire had initially taken control of the eastern Mediterranean using a combination of lightning military campaigns and targeted diplomacy. It had been as much a question of absorbing a patchwork of pre-existing powers as it was of conquest. The royal families of many eastern cities had been incorporated into the system rather than being replaced, and as long as they had kept the peace, considerable military might as well as civil power remained in their hands. The practice of adopting Romanized names can often disguise the fact that official magistrates and even senators might owe their power as much to hereditary local influence as they did to a standard career orchestrated by the centre.

When the power of the central administration began to falter in the third century the old local elites began to re-assert themselves, albeit often in Roman guise. The problem was most acute in the east as the balance of power shifted towards Persia. Local powers either wanted a free hand to defend themselves or to enter diplomatic relations with the Sassanians. An early example was the Kingdom of Osrhoene, centred on the city of Edessa to the east of the Euphrates, which specialized in training and equipping archers that had been drafted into the Roman army in large numbers as auxiliaries. Osrhoene seems to have rebelled for a time in the 230s under the leadership of King Abgar X, or at least it became nominally independent, before being reincorporated with a renewed treaty. It then relied largely on its own strength to defend itself, as it had done successfully during Shapur's great raid in 253. The temporary 'revolt' of Uranius Antoninus in Emesa is another example of the secessionist tendency, as may be the earlier rebellion of Jotapian who hailed from the old Royal House of Commagene.

Another of the big regional powers in the east was the Kingdom of Tadmor, centred on Palmyra, the rich City of Palms, which had exercised considerable military power in its own right before being incorporated into the empire. In pre-Roman times, Palmyra had dominated the Hellenisic city of Dura-Europos, for instance, as well as many other Euphrates settlements. It was far distant from anywhere else, separated by huge tracts of desert, and so it is perhaps inevitable that it would have maintained a strong individualist streak. The military had been brought into the Roman imperial armies by treaty rather than conquest, and by the mid-third century it continued to project a strong military presence across much of the east which included, for instance, supplying men to *cohors* XX *palmyrenorum* (twentieth cohort, of Palmyrenes) at Dura Europos and probably protecting the trade caravans which underpinned the city's economy.

Inscriptions from Palmyra that probably date from the 240s refer to a man called Septimius Odaenathus (a Romanized version of Palmyrene 'Odainath') as both a member of the Roman Senate and Lord of Tadmor (*rš' dy tdmwr*) (Plate 7). This innovation must have been permitted by the central authorities. An inscription from 251 shows that by that time Odaenathus's young son Hairan was being honoured with a statue (dedicated by a visiting officer from *legio* III *cyreneica* from Bostra in Roman Arabia). The implication is that a ruling dynasty had been established (or re-established) at Palmyra. The city had escaped Persian attention in Shapur's great invasion of 253 and it may be instructive that in the following year a bilingual inscription in Palmyrene and Greek was dedicated by the Senate and People of Palmyra to a man called Julius Aurelius Oge 'who served and was well-pleasing to them in his office of *strategos* (general)'. This man may have organized the city defences at that time.[12]

Odaenathus saw the urgent need to bolster the military strength of Palmyra and recruited substantial new forces of desert nomads and heavy cavalry (*clibanarii*), all of whom were nominally part of the Roman army but may have been locally financed. Evidence of the independent diplomatic game played by Odaenathus is a short historical fragment which says that he sent to Shapur

> magnificent gifts and other goods which Persia was not rich in, conveying them by camels. He also sent letters expressing entreaty and saying he had done nothing against the Persians. Shapur, however, instructed the slaves who received the gifts to throw them in the river and tore up and

crushed the letters. 'Who is he', he declared, 'and how has he dared to write to his master? If then he wants to obtain a lighter punishment, let him prostrate himself again with his hands in chains. Otherwise, let him know that I shall destroy him and his people and his land. [Peter Patricius, Fragments 10.][13]

If Shapur's threat was the prelude to an attack on Palmyra, we know that it was unsuccessful. One late source tells us that 'Odaenathus, the Palmyrene *decurion* [a rather modest title meaning a local leader], collected a band of Syrian country folk and put up a spirited resistance. On a number of occasions he routed the Persians.' This account may well refer to later events, but a couple of clues suggest that his initial military success dates to 257. The first of these is that by April 258 Odaenathus was being described as 'illustrious consul' in an inscription raised by the gold and silversmiths of Palmyra. He was not, of course, *consul ordinarius* in Rome. Instead, it was an honorific title associated with the bestowing of so-called consular ornaments (*ornamenta*) by the Roman Senate, giving him the equivalent rank, which was as high as the empire could go in its honours system. The ornaments would have included a special throne, a spectacular bejeweled robe and a staff of office. The Lord of Tadmor had definitely achieved something notable in the eyes of Rome, and fighting the Persians with success would fit the bill.

The second clue is that around 257 coins were issued from the mints at Antioch and Viminacium in Valerian's name with the legend *victoria parthica* or similar – 'Victory over the Parthians' (i.e., Persians). Evidently, the Romans had managed to halt the Persian advance somewhere after Dura had been captured. The most economical solution that fits all these facts is that Shapur had followed up his success at Dura by launching a raid across the desert to Palmyra which was repulsed by Palmyrene forces. There was only one realistic route for such an attack, through desert terrain that the Palmyrenes knew intimately. If Odenaethus had been sufficiently cunning he would have prepared an ambush before even making his diplomatic overtures, anticipating the likely outcome. It was, perhaps, when Shapur realized that no further progress was possible that year, that he ordered Dura to be destroyed once and for all rather than occupying it. Instead, it seems, he turned back to his own lands harbouring a grudge against the Lord of Tadmor.[14]

Valerian and Gallienus must have spent the remainder of 257 in a state of tension. Although Shapur had been repulsed, Dura, the lynch-pin of the Euphrates defence system, had now been lost. Roman strategists knew that Shapur had his own border problems in far distant areas across the Sassanian realm to deal with, so the big question was: would the Persians renew the war, and if so, when?

Ingenuus

The new consuls for 258 were Marcus Nummius Tuscus and Mummius Bassus, both distinguished senators with previous consuls in their families. The emperors may have been in Rome again, but if so they soon departed to their previously agreed stations for the marching season: Gallienus apparently went to the Rhine frontier at Cologne, protecting the province of Gaul (his coins now started advertising him as Restorer of Gaul), and Valerian likely moved east again to assess the situation after the loss of Dura-Europos.[15]

The long string of claimed victories in the Rhine theatre as advertised on the coinage only gives one side of the picture, of course, and there may have been major military setbacks of which we are not aware. Certainly the war there seems to have been dragging on for several years without a decisive outcome. One possible reason for this is that some of the raiders were coming from deep inside 'barbarian' territory, perhaps from as far as the area beyond the River Elbe, making them very difficult to reach once they had exited the empire. If Cniva was maintaining his peace treaty obligation not to attack across the Lower Danube, as we have inferred, perhaps some of the men that had previously marched under his banner had simply diverted their attentions to the Rhine.

Despite the apparent hard work on the part of the two emperors, it is curious that many of the later historical sources were relentlessly critical of Gallienus, treating him like a pantomime villain. According to this characterization he was slothful, vain, greedy, perverted and cruel, and he was blamed on a personal level for all the ills of the empire, something that has affected evaluations of the man into modern times. Whether or not there is any truth in these attacks is hard to tell, but certainly they were played up as part of the rhetoric which tended to contrast 'good' emperors with the 'bad'. So it was in this context that 'Trebellius Pollio' in the *Historia Augusta* tells us of the next major development:[16]

> In the consulship of Tuscus and Bassus while Gallienus was spending his time in wine and gluttony and giving himself up to pimps and actors and harlots, and by continued debauchery was destroying the gifts of nature, Ingenuus, then ruler of the Pannonian provinces, was acclaimed emperor by the legions of Moesia, and those in Pannonia assented thereto. [Scriptores Historiae Augustae (Trebellius Pollio), *Tyranni Triginta* IX.1.]

We have met the Moesian legions several times before: *legio* I *italica* at Novae and *legio* XI *claudia* at Durostorum. The reason for the new rebellion was, we are told, an invasion by the Sarmatians combined with dissatisfaction with the rule of Gallienus who was at that time absent from the sector. The border necessitated a great concentration of military force to deter raiders, but at the same time it was spawning rebellion after rebellion against the centre led by commanders whose troops considered them to be more competent or successful than the emperors themselves. The new man, Ingenuus, was probably serving as *dux* (military leader) of the Danube frontier before he rebelled, and was described as 'much beloved by the soldiers'.

There may have been another more personal and compelling reason for this particular revolt. We know that the young *caesar* Valerian II, the bright hope for the future of the empire, died early in 258. A new issue of coins from the central mint in Rome immediately proclaimed him as a god. The prince had been posted to Pannonia to represent the imperial family there and had been under the protection of Ingenuus. The cause of death is not known, and it may be noteworthy that the plague was still rampant, but Ingenuus inevitably fell under suspicion. This can be inferred from an odd passage in a surviving fragment by the writer known as the 'Anonymous Continuator of Cassius Dio' in which the empress Salonina expresses her distrust of Ingenuus, whom Gallienus had promoted, and instructs a man called Valentinus to keep an eye on him. This appears to be a prelude to a murderous tale, but we do not know how it ends except that it must have been badly for Valerian II.[17]

Gallienus moved fast – even the almost wholly antagonistic *Historia Augusta* admits that he 'could still, when necessity demanded, show himself quick in action, courageous, vigorous and cruel'. Aurelius Victor tells us that at the time of the revolt he was 'strenuously attempting to turn the Germans out of Gaul' (probably still based at Cologne) but had to divert his army to Illyricum where he met the forces of 'Ingebus', which is presumably a copyist's error. The armies met at the Battle at Mursa (now Osijek in Croatia, a town on the imperial highway beside the Danube). Various other sources contain a similar account and name Mursa as the site of battle in which Ingenuus or 'Genuus' was slain. It must have been a quick campaign because Ingenuus never got round to minting coins. A rare coin type from the new mint at Cologne features Victory with the legend *Gallienus cum exer(citus) suo* – or 'Gallienus with his army'. These coins epitomize the new, developing, reality that military might was being concentrated in a highly professional mobile cavalry army attached to the emperors themselves.[18]

Details of the Battle of Mursa can be found in the History of Zonaras who introduces another important military figure of the time, the general Aureolus (not to be confused with the previously mentioned 'sword-in-hand' Aurelian). This man was from a humble peasant family from Roman Dacia but had joined the army, eventually rising to high position as 'attendant of the imperial horses' at which he did an excellent job, pleasing Gallienus in the process. The precise location of the battlefield at Mursa has not been located, but if Gallienus had the advantage in cavalry and approached from the west, it seems likely that Ingenuus would have pinned his right flank on the river. Aurelous was in command of the imperial cavalry where he 'battled nobly with his horsemen, annihilated many of Ingenuus's adherents and turned the remainder to flight, with the result that Ingenuus himself fled in desperation and in doing so was killed by his own guardsmen'.[19]

One peculiar tragedy of civil war is that it brings families into conflict. The Anonymous Continuator of Cassius Dio tells of a man supposedly captured by his own brother on the battlefield and brought before the emperor. Gallienus was inclined to pardon him, but the brother insisted that only the death penalty was suitable for a rebel, and carried it out himself.

The premature loss of the young prince Valerian II left the imperial family with two more bright hopes for the future, Saloninus (about sixteen years old) and his brother Marinianus (only about seven). Saloninus was raised to the rank of *caesar* and conferred with the associated title Prince of Youth. The coins that were henceforth minted in his name are very similar to the series that had previously been produced for his elder brother. With Gallienus occupied in Pannonia and Moesia, Saloninus was sent to Colonia Agrippina (Cologne) under the protection of a man named either Silvanus (according to Zosimus) or Albanus (according to Zonaras) to fly the flag on the Rhine frontier. It is unlikely that the prince would have been allowed anywhere near the fighting, which was being coordinated by another talented general called Marcus Cassianius Latinius Postumus.

At War with the Saints

> Son of life, Son of immortality,
> you who are in the Light,
> Son, Christ of immortality,
> Our Redeemer,
> Give us strength,
> Because they are searching for us
> To kill us. [Early Christian prayer.][20]

In January 258, the emperor Valerian, before leaving for the east, had ordered the Senate that the persecution of the Christians should be intensified. But a period of uncertainty seems to have ensued because of disagreement on the precise meaning of the order or how to carry it out. By now there were Christians even among the Senators of Rome who may well have tried to water down any proposed measures while the hawks among their number pushed for the hardest line possible. Lives and great fortunes were at stake. The only remedy was to petition the emperor at Antioch and ask him to clarify his intentions, resulting in a period of prolonged anxiety for the faithful as they waited for a response.

The emperor's reply, or rescript, arrived in the summer. It was harsher than perhaps anyone had expected: a second and more intense persecution was ordered, one that seems to have been intended to destroy the Christian community once and for all. It was so pitiless that later Christian writers identified Valerian as 'The Beast' prophesied in the Book of Revelation about whom it was written: 'And it was given unto him to make war with the saints, and to overcome them: and power was given him over all kindreds, and tongues, and nations'.[21]

Bishop Cyprian of Carthage had sent some of his followers to Rome to establish the exact content of Valerian's rescript as soon as it became known. He then relayed the information to Successus, one of the African bishops. It must have made uncomfortable reading:

> Cyprian to his brother Successus, greeting. …
>
> Valerian had sent a rescript to the Senate, to the effect that bishops and presbyters and deacons should immediately be punished; but that senators, and men of importance, and Roman knights, should lose their dignity, and moreover be deprived of their property; and if, when their means were taken away, they should persist in being Christians, then they should also lose their heads; but that matrons should be deprived of their property, and sent into banishment. Moreover, people of Caesar's household, whoever of them had either confessed before, or should now confess, should have their property confiscated, and should be sent in chains by assignment to Caesar's estates…
>
> Sixtus [the new Bishop of Rome] was martyred in the cemetery on the eighth day of the Ides of August, and with him four deacons. Moreover, the prefects in the City are daily urging on this persecution; so that, if any are presented to them, they are martyred, and their property claimed by the treasury. [Cyprian, *Epistles* 81.]

The text of Cyprian's letter, and the pattern of subsequent events, indicates that 'punishment' for bishops, presbyters and deacons often meant death. The *Liber Pontificalis* confirms that Sixtus was beheaded on the day that Cyprian names, along with six (not four) deacons whom it names as Felicissimus,

Agapitus, Januarius, Magnus, Vincentius and Stephen. The proceedings against the Christians seem to have been conducted like show trials. The gravity of the situation meant that they were handled in person by the senior man in Rome, the City Prefect Publius Cornelius Saecularis. His name suggests that he may have been a relative of Gallienus's wife, the Empress Cornelia Salonina. An even more intriguing possibility is that he might have been related to Pope Cornelius who had been martyred a few years earlier, which could explain why Valerian's edict specifically mentioned members of the imperial household: it all looks ugly and personal.[22]

According to later tradition, Cornelius Saecularis summoned the most senior surviving Christian in Rome, a man named Laurentius, and ordered him to surrender all the riches of the church to the imperial treasury. Laurentius asked for three days to comply, during which time he gave away as much of the wealth as possible to the poor and needy. The prefect was, naturally, incensed when he found out. Laurentius (St. Lawrence) then was martyred along with several of his brethren who are named in the *Liber Pontificalis* as the sub-deacon Claudius, Severus the priest, Crescentius the reader, and Romanus the doorkeeper.

Back in Africa, Cyprian briefly went in to hiding to avoid being martyred in his place of exile but willingly gave himself up to the authorities in Carthage in the knowledge that he would inevitably be executed there. He was brought before the proconsul Galerius Maximus, who offered him a chance to recant; he did not, of course, and instead publicly reaffirmed his faith. Being a Roman citizen of high status, he was entitled to be beheaded rather than thrown to the lions. His executioner received the princely sum of twenty-five *aurei* for his services. The Christians of Carthage came out in large numbers to witness the event, some asking to die with him, but to no avail: the death penalty was reserved for the hierarchy, not mere followers. At nightfall they took the body away to be buried in a cemetery on the Mappalian Way, the main route westward out of Carthage, a place where the modern Basilique de Saint Cyprien now stands. Cyprian's martyrdom assured that his many letters and sermons would be preserved ever after. The date was 14 September 248 and he had finally proved to his flock that he was no hypocrite.[23]

Cyprian's recent correspondent, Bishop Successus, suffered the same fate, as did many others among the clergy. Some gave themselves up, others were hunted down. We have seen that in Carthage the main body of the congregation remained free, but in other provinces the authorities applied these measures to ordinary worshippers. In traditionally bloodthirsty Alexandria, Dionysius tells us that 'men and women, both old men and boys, girls and old women, soldiers and civilians, every race and every age, some enduring scourging and fire, others the sword… have received their crowns [of martyrdom]'. Some names have come down to us via the great medieval compilation known as the *Acta Sanctorum* (Acts of the Saints) although plausible detail in that work is often mingled with miraculous events and happenings which are considerably less credible to the modern mind than perhaps they initially were. In Palestine, Priscus, Malchus and Alexander became 'food for wild beasts'. Bishop Fructuosus of Tarragona and his deacons Augurius and Eulogius are the first known Christian martyrs from Spain. These three were arrested on the night of 16 January 259, tried a few days later, condemned, and burnt in the amphitheatre as public entertainment. In Numidia, many more were executed in a purge that lasted well into the following year. The list of the deceased there includes Zeno, another Alexander, Theodorus and their companions (interestingly, all Greek names) followed by others who died as late as April or May of 259.[24]

Bishop Dionysius of Alexandria tells us an elaborate story about his own escape from the persecution in which a military policeman (*frumentarius*) came in search of him as he waited in plain sight at his home while the agent 'went round searching everywhere, the streams, the roads and the fields'. Later, Dionysius fled with many of his congregation but they were arrested by soldiers and he resigned himself to his fate. However, a wedding party, of all things, found out where they were being held (it is not clear whether they were Christians or just sympathetic citizens) and stormed the police station to free the captives. Dionysius was saved in spite of himself. According to his own story, he actually tried to resist his rescuers so that he could enjoy martyrdom but was nevertheless spirited off into hiding. His eventual fate is not known.[25]

As the purge of the Christian clergy reached its height, Gallienus was meting out equally severe military and political punishments against the interests of Ingenuus's defeated rebels in Moesia and Illyricum. This latest civil war meant that the whole Rhine and Danube frontier was again tense and stretched. The warlike 'barbarian' tribes on the other side were no doubt delighted by the infighting, with young men from all around drawn once again to the banners of their chiefs. Africa was also threatened despite the return of detachments from *legio* III *augusta* a few years earlier. An inscription dated to 258 records a man named Marcus Cornelius Octavianus who was given command of all the forces in the region with the new title of *dux per africam et mauretaniam*, probably to coordinate the ongoing war against the raiders from the mountains and deserts to the south.[26]

Valerian seems to have been based in Antioch when he sent his rescript concerning the Christians.[27] The legions previously devastated at Barbalissos back in 253 had probably been brought back up to strength once again, but pride and fighting spirit are harder to instill. Odaenathus of Palmyra provided welcome military power although he was perhaps becoming more of an ally in adversity rather than a subject who could be ordered to obey. Our only option to get more of a picture from the east is from the coinage produced at Antioch and Samosata. The issues for Valerian of 258 feature *pax augg* (peace guaranteed by the emperors), *virtus augg* (virtue of the emperors), *conservat aug* (Apollo who preserves the emperor) and *iovi conservat* (Jupiter who preserves) and, most interestingly, *religio augg* (religion of the emperors). It would be wrong to think of these messages as merely formulaic propaganda: the pair wanted the public to know that they were running the realm through a combination of their own excellence, their strict religious policy and the personal protection of the greatest gods, delivering peace in the process.

Chapter 11

Nadir

Gaul Overrun

259 was the year of the consuls Aemilianus (otherwise unknown; it was a common name) and Bassus, probably Pomponius Bassus, a man of a very distinguished family. No doubt these men were untainted with any suspicion of irregularity in the religious line. The ongoing confiscations of Christian wealth and property may have raised some extra money for the treasury and set a high moral tone, but there was little hard evidence as yet that the displeasure of the gods was assuaged. There was one reason to celebrate, however: Valerian's was by now the longest reign of any emperor for a generation. With the legions soon to be roused from winter quarters, the strategists may have hoped that this year, for once, the empire would be able to take the initiative in military matters.[1]

Valerian was by now about sixty-five years old, raising the question of if and when he might decide to retire, or perhaps even abdicate in favour of his son. No previous emperor had ever done that, but an orderly handover of power would surely be a mark of success for the regime. If he did harbour such plans, the death of his elder grandson Valerian II must have been a blow, so for now at least the power sharing would continue along the same lines as before. There has been some speculation that Gallienus and Valerian may have fallen out by this time, and while perfectly plausible psychologically given the stress the men were under, there is no firm evidence to support the idea other than that the coins of Gallienus from the mint in Gaul increasingly focus on him personally. In contrast, eastern mints in Valerian's sphere of influence always focus on the two emperors, whether celebrating their piety, virtue, or (perhaps tellingly) their concord. The same is true of the mint at Rome which was probably under Valerian's direct control.[2]

An important topic that is, nevertheless, difficult to resolve is the status of diplomatic ties between Rome and her potential enemies at this time. We can presume that at least some of the Marcomanni remained friendly having been re-settled in Pannonia by the 'Pipa' Treaty between Gallienus and King Attalus. The raid along the Black Sea coast into Bithynia the previous winter might seem to indicate that any putative treaty with Cniva had dissolved, but that is not necessarily so. It may have been more in the line of organized piracy rather than a 'state' level mass invasion of the type earlier favoured by Ostrogotha. That the raiders had requisitioned fishing vessels to transport some of their men suggests that the numbers cannot have been too vast. There is no evidence that the Goths had re-invaded in strength across the lower Danube during Valerian's reign, despite the chaos engendered by the Ingenuus revolt, nor do they seem to have harassed Dacia, so a shaky truce may still have been in operation.

Reconstructing the sequence of events is especially challenging for this period but subsequent happenings suggest that when the marching season began, Gallienus crossed the Rhine from Mogontiacum (Mainz) and attacked the people later known as the Franks. Rome was still struggling to hold on to the defensive border (*limes*) in the area of the Taunus Salient. It would have made good strategic sense for Gallienus to use his mobile strike army to push beyond this degraded border zone well into 'barbaricum' so as to take the fight to the enemy and export the devastation of war to foreign lands for a change. The campaign may have met with some success as the main coin type from the Gallic mint that year was once again *victoria germanica* depicting bound captives.[3]

Unfortunately, however, with Gallienus fully committed, a hammer blow was to fall in the southern sector of the *limes*, probably somewhere west of the fortress of Castra Regina (Regensberg), base of *legio* III *italica* which may have been under-strength because it is known to have sent vexillations to the east. This area had suffered badly five years earlier, in 254. Once again the culprits appear to have been a 'barbarian' collective consisting of groups variously identified as Alemanni, Iuthungi, Quadi, Sarmatians, Heruli, Vandals and Suebi (the reality or otherwise of these peoples as distinct groups, and their classification according to various ancient writers, is a matter of debate among historians). The pattern of events points to dispersed but coordinated action by multiple bands under different leadership as befits such a confederation. No fewer than twenty-six hoards terminating in 259 or shortly before are taken as evidence of a major disturbance and there was probably also widespread burial of other less easily dateable treasure.[4] As this new threat materialized, the governor of Germania Superior may have ordered a strategic withdrawal of the auxiliary garrisons from the forts along the *limes* rather than allowing them to be destroyed piecemeal. At the same time, presumably, he sent frantic messages to Gallienus that his mobile army was urgently needed in his sector.[5]

For what happened next we are indebted to a brilliant but neglected study published in the 1960s by Emilienne Demougeot who noticed that a large number of coin hoards across modern Switzerland and southern France also terminate in 259–260 (Map 23). Any one of these, taken alone, is weak

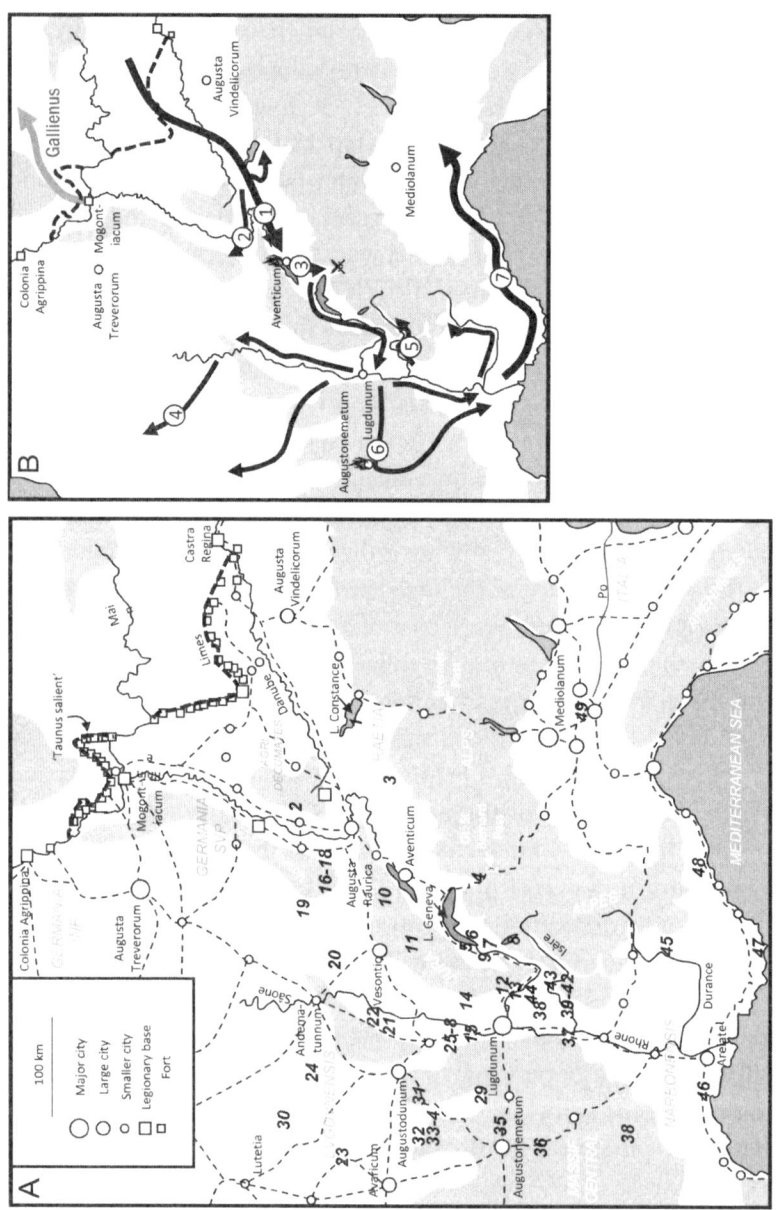

Map 23. The 'barbarian' invasion of 259 / 260 CE. A: Numbers indicate coin hoards catalogued by Demougeot (1962). Many other hoards in the area of the *limes* frontier and *agri decumates* are not plotted for clarity. B: Summary map based on written records and coin hoarding. It is speculated that Gallienus's main army was simultaneously involved in fighting across the frontier in Germania and so could not immediately respond. Numbers refer to phases of the invasion discussed in the text.

evidence for anything historical. Taken together, however, they paint a vivid picture of a wave of terror that spanned a huge area that has mostly, but not entirely, eluded written history.[6]

Using Demougeot's evidence we can infer that the invaders ignored Augsburg (Augusta Vindelicorum) on account of the city wall and possibly because remnants of the Roman military had re-grouped there. Instead, they headed up the Danube using the road network (Arrow 1 on Map 23B). The first of Demougeot's hoards (Number 1 on Map 23A) is at Gotthaus on the western shore of Lake Constance, which implies marauders fanning out among the rich villa estates of that region. Another group may have split off to the west to menace Augusta Raurica (Augst), although as we have seen, the former city may already have been largely abandoned as a response to regional insecurity and economic decline (Arrow 2). A particularly poignant series of hoards (Demougeot's 16–18) were found close together in valleys in the upland area now known as the Haute-Vosges (two in the small valley of the Thur above the modern town of Cernay). The fact that warbands dared to raid in the upper Rhine vally is the best evidence we have that Gallienus was otherwise occupied because this would have been his likely line of approach. One cannot help imagining that the rustic population inhabiting these places were either slaughtered or enslaved as the 'barbarian' raiders descended on them with little warning.

The main direction of the invaders, however, took them on to the area between the Alps and Jura known as the Swiss Plateau. This area was centred on Aventicum, the tribal capital of the Helvetii, with its surrounding town and villages. Aventicum is the beautiful modern town of Avenches which prides itself on a spectacularly well-preserved and indeed functional Roman amphitheatre in which rock concerts are frequently staged. Our source for what happened there is the seventh century Frankish *Chronicle* of Fredegar, who not only wrote proudly about the amphitheatre, but also says the city was burned in the reign of Valerian and blames the dissolute behaviour of Gallienus for the tragedy. The invaders are described as Alemanni under the leadership of a chieftain called Wibilus. Fredegar (if that was his name – it is Frankish, but only appears on some of the later known manuscripts, so the more cautious historians call him 'pseudo-Fredegar') was closely associated with Avenches and may have had access to local tradition, but it is fair to say the relevant passages are very muddled and seemingly confuse fifth and third century events and individuals. Nevertheless an attack on the city is perfectly plausible, indeed likely, given the circumstances.[7]

The invading 'barbarian' army, or at least part of it, may then have moved south (Arrow 3) with the intention of crossing the Alps via the Great Saint

Bernard Pass (between Mont Blanc and the Matterhorn). Here, 75km to the south of Aventicum nestling alongside the upper reaches of the Rhone between precipitous glacier-carved walls of rock sat the village of Auganum (now Saint-Maurice D'Aguane). It is noteworthy that one of Demougeot's hoards is from the village of Bex just a few kilometres north along the 'barbarian' line of approach. Here the invaders were repulsed, presumably by a force sent over the mountains and deployed there exactly for this reason. The battle must have been intense, as evidenced by a memorial to a senior commander (of unknown name, but with the high rank of *vir eregius*) who died in the fighting. With this route blocked, the main thrust of the attack diverted around Lake Geneva and down the Rhone valley towards Gaul.[8]

A series of Demougeot's hoards plot the likely path of the invaders to the major city of Lugdunum (Lyons) at the confluence of the Saône and Rhone. It was no doubt packed with refugees but was able to shut its gates and defend itself. Large numbers of coin hoards as well as temple loot and other treasures point to widespread panic in smaller settlements and rural areas along the entire length of the Rhone / Saône valley. Others extend almost as far north as Paris (Roman Lutetia) (Arrow 4) and up the Val d'Isère (Arrow 5). Another line of attack (Arrow 6) led deep into the undefended uplands of the Massif Central as far as Clermont-Ferrand. Here, the sixth century historian Gregory of Tours records an attack, and also names another 'barbarian' leader, in the following terms:

> In their time [Valerian and Gallienus] also Chrocus the famous king of the Alamanni raised an army and overran the Gauls. This Chrocus is said to have been very arrogant. And when he had committed a great many crimes he gathered the tribe of the Alamanni, as we have stated, by the advice, it is said, of his wicked mother, and overran the whole of the Gauls, and destroyed from their foundations all the temples which had been built in ancient times. And coming to Clermont he set on fire, overthrew and destroyed that shrine which they call 'Vasso Galatæ' in the Gallic tongue. It had been built and made strong with wonderful skill. And its wall was double, for on the inside it was built of small stone and on the outside of squared blocks. The wall had a thickness of thirty feet. It was adorned on the inside with marble and mosaics. The pavement of the temple was also of marble and its roof above was of lead. [Gregory of Tours, *History of the Franks*, 1.32.]

Some historians have doubted Gergory's account, partly because a better-attested Alammanic king called Chrocus is known from later times, as is another Vandal king of the same name. But it is noteworthy that Clermont-

Ferrand was Gregory's home town, so like Fredegar he could well have been privy to municipal archives or local knowledge passed down through the generations. It is interesting that Gregory, the Christian Bishop of Tours, should have recorded details of the destruction of a splendid 'pagan' temple with apparent disapproval. There has been some doubt as to the identification of 'Vasso Galatae' but the leading contender is a temple under the modern town centre. Archaeology has revealed traces of a richly decorated interior with black marble columns and confirmed that the roof was indeed made of lead. Gregory's account and later Christian tradition suggest that some bishops and other leading church members may have suffered death at the hands of Chrocus and his Alamanni alongside 'pagan' priests.[9]

The Romans might have expected the invaders to begin a systematic withdrawal across the devastated borderlands, dragging as many enslaved citizens and as much booty as possible. Worryingly, however, many of them decided to overwinter in the empire. They must have felt secure enough from reprisals from Gallienus's mobile army. Perhaps they also knew that Italy was barely defended: large numbers of the praetorians and imperial horseguard had been seconded to the two imperial armies, and *legio* II *parthica*, normally stationed near Rome, was with Valerian in the east. Coin hoards near the mouth of the Rhone and along the French Riviera as far as Nice indicate that some of the invaders by-passed the Alps and entered Italy via the coast road. Rome herself was now directly threatened by a foreign enemy for the first time in over half a millennium.

The eastern theatre

A particular problem affecting Valerian's forces in the east at this time was a resurgence of the plague. Zosimus says it attacked his troops after the abortive foray into Cappadocia and 'destroyed most of them', which sound like an exaggeration. Another source says it was the Moorish cavalry who were particularly affected. It was not some new disease: the historical sources agree that the affliction known today as the plague of Cyprian persisted. The army would have been a fine incubator, with so many men sharing cramped quarters. At least the soldiers had access to high quality medical care, although the military doctors (*medici*) would have had little in their armoury to fight hemorrhagic fever (if that is what it was) other than to isolate men and keep them hydrated. The mortality was terrifying and even many of those who survived would be unfit for further service. If the Romans had intended to launch a major counter-strike against Persia in 259, those plans were now put on hold.[10]

The fall of Armenia to the Persians in 252 and then the destruction of Dura-Europos in 257 would have forced Valerian to completely revise the defensive system in the east. Roman Mesopotamia was not to be abandoned, but it must now have been deemed largely indefensible against a major attack. Instead it was a kind of crumple zone in front of Syria, a province that must still be defended at all costs. Whether the population of Roman Mesopotamia realized this is not clear, but there were plenty of retired soldiers living along the Euphrates who must have had a shrewd idea of what the fall of Dura entailed for security in the region. The old battlefield at Barbalissos would mark the approximate forward position of a new defensive line between the strong and partially independent powers of Osrhoene in the north and Palmyra in the south. We know of little else of what happened in 259 in the east other than that the coins continued to invoke the protection of the gods and promote the concept of Eternal Rome.

Dawn of the *Annus Horribilis*

260 was to be known as the Year of the consuls Publius Cornelius Saecularis and Gaius Julius Donatus. The former was presumably being rewarded for his role in overseeing the purge of the Christians in which he had ordered the death of Bishop Sixtus and Deacon Lawrence among many others. Donatus was another former City Prefect who had distinguished himself in the persecutions. It was a great honour to be named *consul ordinarius* and for the year to be named after oneself. But these men may not have appreciated their names being forever linked in posterity to this particular year when large concentrations of 'barbarians' had filtered in to northern Italy from Gaul. Very little military might stood between the rampaging war-bands and the Eternal City herself which lacked defensive walls.

The City Prefect (possibly Marcus Nummius Albinus[11]) had no option but to raise a scratch home guard to face the advancing 'barbarians'. The general enlistment would have included various groups ranging from old veterans and soldiers on leave to paramilitary youth groups and volunteers. At least the civil service was sufficiently well organized and funded to supply these men with weapons and equipment. In the words of Zosimus,

> The Senate, seeing Rome in such imminent danger, armed all the soldiers that were in the city, and the strongest of the common people, and formed an army, which exceeded the barbarians in number. This so alarmed the barbarians, that they left Rome, but ravaged all the rest of Italy. [Zosimus, *New History* 1.37.]

Many of the senators had rich estates in the north and so must have been extremely dismayed by the situation. The only way Italy could be rid of these terrifying raiders was to wait for Gallienus. His army was urgently needed, and yet nowhere in evidence. Many of the later historians were relentlessly critical of Gallienus personally, blaming the parlous state of the western empire on his idleness and debauchery. Eutropius was typical in alleging 'cowardly inaction and despair'.[12] Aurelius Victor says that he frequented taverns and eating-houses and mixed with pimps and drunkards while maintaining his shameful love affair with Pipa. The *Historia Augusta* has much more along the same lines.

The best explanation, as we have seen, is to posit a Roman invasion into Germania in 259 in which Gallienus (or possibly his top general Postumus) had battled against the Franks. Reports of barbarian inroads into Gaul might have reached him when the army was already engaged and could only be shrugged off for the time being. The mobile army could not be everywhere at once, nor could it be continuously at war. All armies need periods of rest, repair and replenishment. It was not just the men who became exhausted, so did the pack animals, equipment, ammunition and food. Weapons needed replacing and new cavalry mounts had to be broken in. In any case, the high passes of the Alps could not be crossed in winter. So, when the fighting season ended, the army was apparently sent back to its winter quarters in Mogontiacum and other bases along the Rhine. Even so it was surely unwise for Gallienus to be seen (as was alleged) enjoying himself about town in the company of both his wife, the empress Salonina, and his blonde barbarian concubine, at a time when Gaul and Italy were being put to the sword.

Gargilius and the Rebel Faraxen

In scrubland outside the town of Sour El-Ghozlane in Algeria (Roman Auzia in the Province of Mauretania Caesariensis) lies the remains of a mausoleum dedicated to an individual called Quintus Gargilius Martialis. The inscription tells us that it had been set up on 25 March 260 by public subscription to commemorate a man regarded as a hero. It provides us with a detailed account of the career of a Roman knight (*eques romanus*) in the third century. His first command had been *cohors* I *asturum* (an auxiliary unit originally recruited from the Astures tribe in Spain) in the Province of Britannia, possibly based on Hadrian's Wall in the vicinity of modern Newcastle upon Tyne. He had then commanded a Spanish cohort somewhere in Mauretania Caesariensis, followed by a detachment of Moorish cavalry (*vexillationum equitum Maurorum*) based at Auzia itself. He seems to have liked the area because, on retiring from army life, he bought an estate and took up farming and writing. He served on the town council and as 'patron of the province' (*patronus provinciae*), which probably indicates that he was elected to a senior judicial role. He composed a series of works on agriculture including describing the medicinal value of various types of North African fruit and vegetables and a treatise on cattle husbandry, parts of which survive in later abridgements. Aelius Lampridius in the *Historia Augusta* tells us (independently, and perhaps unreliably) that he also wrote a biography of the Emperor Severus Alexander whom he may have admired in his youth, which work, if it ever existed, has unfortunately been lost.[13]

Shortly before his mausoleum was built, this worthy individual had been brought out of his pleasant retirement to lead troops against 'the rebel Faraxen and his followers'. Gargilius succeeded in capturing Faraxen who was later tried and executed. Another inscription from the legionary base at nearby Lambaesis appears to relate to the same campaign because it commemorates a string of victories against invading tribes called the Bavares, Quinquegentanei (the name means 'the five peoples'), and Fraxinenses. It refers to 'the capture of their very famous leader' who is not, in this instance, named, but is surely Faraxen. The tribes all appear to be Berber groups who had broken through the imperial frontier from their mountain homes to the south. Roman authority was restored, but the war did not all go their way. Gargilius was killed in an ambush by the Bavares, hence the mausoleum.[14]

Dust on the stars

The marching season of 260 in the east began with an event that the Romans dreaded above all: yet another well-organized mass invasion by the *spah*. Shapur's advisers must have been able to see the tottering state of the empire, and the possibility of emulating or even surpassing their great victory of 253 which had brought huge riches and masses of slaves into Persia, as well as unparalleled glory for the King of Kings. The Romans could hardly complain about such behaviour because when they themselves had been in the ascendency they had launched repeated raids into Parthian lands.[15]

A number of the great cities of the east had escaped destruction in the raid of 253, most notably Edessa in Osrhoene, Palmyra in Tadmor, and Emesa in Syria. Not knowing Shapur's target, it seems that Valerian's defensive plan began by concentrating a rapid reaction force at Antioch, but his troubles were compounded by the ongoing plague. Conscious of this, Valerian took the extreme measure of sending an embassy to Shapur offering gifts and an immense amount of gold if he withdrew. Shapur may have been tempted but,

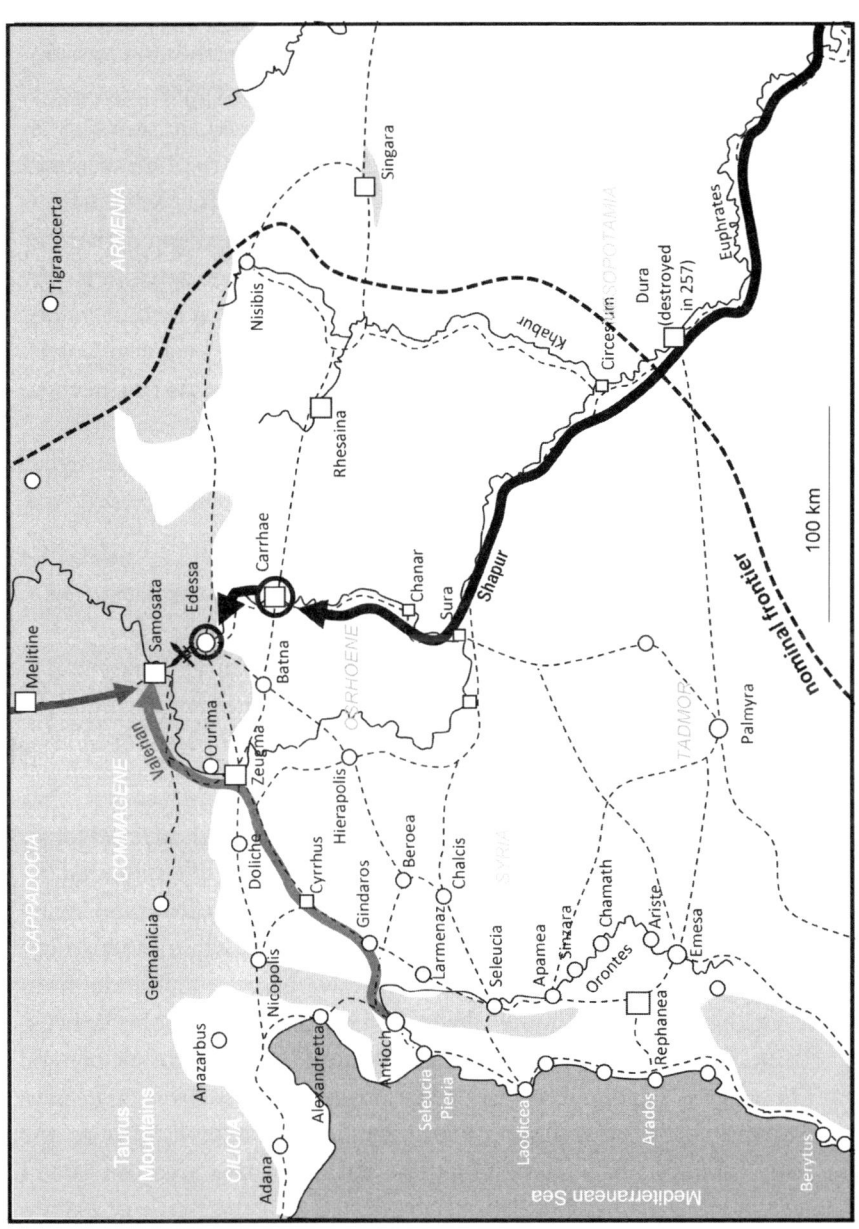

Map 24. The Battle of Edessa, probably 260 CE. Shapur advanced up the Euphrates to besiege Carrhae and Edessa. Valerian moved up to Samosata and the armies clashed somewhere in between. The Roman force from Cappadocia is based on the account of Firdawsi.

we are told, he kept the ambassadors waiting, presumably seeking further intelligence. When his spies reported back on the true extent of the plague he simply dismissed Valerian's ambassadors without reply.[16]

The crumple zone duly crumpled in a repeat of 253. But as Shapur approached the old battlefield of Barbalissos, he diverted north into Osrhoene up the Balikh River and immediately put the fortress of Carrhae and city of Edessa under siege. These places were strongly garrisoned, presumably by forces including the formidable Osrhoenian archers. Now the line of attack had declared itself, Valerian moved his army up to Samosata, headquarters of *legio* XVI *flavia firma*. His force may have been supplemented there by a second army that had been congregating at Melitene in Cappadocia. We are told that for a while he hesitated, unsure of the best strategy, but gained courage from reports that the garrison at Edessa had mounted vigorous sorties against the Persians, killing many and capturing much booty. At this news he decided to risk battle.

According to Shapur's inscription, a 'great battle took place beyond Carrhae and Edessa' against an enemy commanded by Valerian himself. It lists the size and composition of the Roman army, as follows:

> There was with him a force of seventy thousand men from the nations of Germania, Raetia, Noricum, Dacia, Pannonia, Moesia, Istria, Hispania, Mauritania, Thracia, Bithynia, Asia, Pamphylia, Isauria, Lycaonia, Galatia, Lycia, Cilicia, Cappadocia, Phrygia, Syria, Phoenicia, Judea, Arabia, Mauritania [again], Germania [again], Lydia and Mesopotamia. [*Res Gestae Divi Saporis* 20–23.]

The quoted force is slightly larger than Shapur claimed to have previously defeated at Barbalissos. There is no particular reason to doubt this, nor the various nationalities listed, which are consistent with a mixed army consisting of up to ten eastern legions augmented by German and Mauritanian light cavalry auxiliaries. The German forces might have been detachments from the Rhine legions or perhaps, more likely, men captured during the fighting on the Rhine frontier who had been moved across the empire as pressed troops. The phrase 'beyond Carrhae and Edessa' suggests, from a Persian perspective, the battle took place somewhere northwest of Edessa as the Roman army advanced from Samosata. The terrain in this area consists of gently undulating plains and low hills. The actual site of the Battle of Edessa has yet to be found.[17]

Very few reliable details of the confrontation survive but one thing we do have is a Persian epic called the *Shahnameh* or 'Epic of the Kings', written about the Year 1000 by Firdawsi, the great national poet of Iran. It is clearly highly stylized, reminiscent in its way of Homer or Virgil, and perhaps no more historical. Nevertheless, elements of Persian oral tradition may have been incorporated into the account as we know that Firdawsi used sources which transmit contemporaneous information from the Royal Annals. The geographic details are fanciful, but whether the text might preserve some memory of the battle or was entirely the work of the poet's imagination the reader can decide:

> Out of Cappadocia there marched an army from whose dust the sun itself grew dark, and another army marched out of Paluina [unknown], in command of which was a prince named Bazanush. He was a proud knight of illuminated spirit and much valued by the Caesars, a lasso-thrower, great in fame and lofty of dignity. As the clamour of the drums arose on either side, that noble warrior stepped forth from the heart of his army, while from the foe there came out a gallant nobleman whose name was Garshasp the Lion. He was a brave knight who, on the day of the combat, feared nothing, whether it was a raging elephant or a man that stood opposed to him. The two warriors wrestled together in their struggle and their dust dropped on to the stars. Many were the devices by which they attempted to satisfy their rage but neither could be overcome by the other. At last the entire armies on either side clashed together like mountain against mountain. From the great clamour caused by the trumpets and Indian gongs you would have thought the sky dislodged from its place. In the midst of his army the warrior Bazanush was taken captive with bleeding heart, and of the Rumis [Romans] in Paluina ten thousand were killed among the battle ranks, a thousand and twice three hundred were made prisoners and panic seized the heart of the remaining warriors. [Firdawsi, *Shahnameh* 25.][18]

Zonaras simply tells us that the Persians were 'many times more numerous' than the Romans when battle began. If true, it fits with the general Roman policy of fielding highly trained, armed and disciplined forces against greater numbers. The tactic hadn't worked for Decius at Abritus, however, and now it failed again. Their army was not, however, totally destroyed (on this point, at least, Zonaras and Firdawsi agree) and it seems that Valerian himself along with part of his force managed to cut themselves out and reached the temporary haven provided by the walls of Edessa which the Persians once again put under siege.

The most senior official in the east who was not with Valerian's army was the finance minister Fulvius Macrianus (the same man who was blamed for having turned Valerian against the Christians). Macrianus probably set about assembling a relief force at Samosata, bringing together whatever remnants of the army fell back in retreat and others not previously involved. That, however, would take time, which was a somewhat precious commodity as far as Valerian was concerned. At Edessa the besieged Roman army was afflicted by famine and 'in a mutinous mood'. The city had an excellent water supply but food must have run short very quickly in a city that housed both its regular garrison and remnants of the imperial army including, presumably, many wounded and possibly some afflicted by the plague.[19]

Valerian attempted to parley with Shapur, once again offering more money for a conclusion to the war. The poet Firdawsi says that

> He, the Caesar, would send all that he possessed if no further pain was inflicted. He would obey any command concerning tribute and send numbers of his kinsmen as hostages… Shapur stayed till the Caesar had sent him as tribute and tax ten ox hides filled with gold and Caesarian dinars, to which he added many valuables more. [Firdawsi, *Shahnameh* 25.]

The King of Kings demanded that the final negotiations be conducted man to man. The Emperor of the Romans, fearing mutiny and hopeful of striking a deal, agreed. He appears to have led a high level delegation into Shapur's camp under flag of truce and was promptly taken captive. That, at least, is the version of events reported by several of the Latin chroniclers. Shapur's inscription makes no mention of underhand dealings, but does say that 'we took him prisoner with our own hands as well as the other commanders of the army, the Praetorian Prefect, senators and officials'. The prefect in question may have been Successianus, hero of the first battle of Pityus and Valerian's right-hand man in Antioch.

A beautiful jewel known as the Paris cameo (Plate 7) appears to commemorate this event, albeit in a stylized way. It shows a Persian king grasping the hand of a Roman soldier whose sword is drawn for combat. The gesture indicates capture in battle. The Roman wears a laurel wreath and so the identity of Valerian seems assured. The cameo is of a style consistent with a third century date and so is thought to have been commissioned and probably owned by Shapur himself.[20]

Shapur's next move was to dispatch one of the high ranking Roman officials (a man called Cledonius) to Samosata to summon Macrianus for further talks. The finance minister supposedly declared 'is any one so insane that he would willingly become a prisoner of war instead of being a free man'. He urged Cledonius not to go back either, but the loyal official voluntarily returned to captivity in accordance with the vow he had taken. It is likely that Valerian and his entourage were then sent back to Persian lands as high level hostages to be ransomed.[21]

It is not clear what happened to the starving garrison at Edessa after Valerian's capture. One source implies that they thought the emperor had betrayed them, charging him with cowardice and voluntarily surrendering himself to the enemy. Subsequent events suggest that the city held out under whatever senior military command remained there, most probably the Osrhoenian nobility. Perhaps Shapur decided to avoid a costly assault on a well-protected city full of elite troops, even if they were short of food. And there may also be some truth in Firdawsi's story that Shapur had already tricked the Romans into handing over most of their treasury.[22]

Shapur must have been well satisfied with capturing Valerian and might have called an end to the campaign but there was still the lure of much plunder and he wanted to exploit his military advantage to the utmost. Therefore he marched against Samosata, an obvious thing to do because it was the last stronghold between the Persians and the largely unprotected lands to the west; moreover it was itself a rich city that had been undamaged in 253. Macrianus seems to have evacuated by the time the Persians arrived, abandoning the city to its fate and taking with him as many troops as were remaining. That circumstance, coming as it did soon after defeat in battle, put large areas of the east once again at the mercy of the invaders.

Invasion of Cilicia and Syria

After the Battle of Edessa there follows another sorry list of cities torched by the Persians:

> Samosata with its surrounding territory, the city of Alexandria with its surrounding territory, – Katabolon, – Aigeai, – Mopsuestia, – Mallos, – Adana, – Tarsus, – Augousta, – Zephyrion, – Sebaste, – Korykos, – Agrippiada, – Kastabala, – Neronias, – Flavias, – Nicopolis, – Kelenderis, – Anemourium, – Selinos, – Myonpolis, – Antiochia, – Seleucia, – Dometioupolis, – Tyana, – Meiakarire, – Comana, – Kybistra, – Sebastia, – Birtha, – Rhakoundia, – Laranda, – Iconium; all these cities together with their surrounding territories are thirty-six in number. [*Res Gestae Divi Saporis* 26–24.]

They only add up to thirty-three, so presumably some are missing and a few – such as Katabolon – remain unidentified. Once again the best way to reconstruct events is to plot the cities on a map (Map 25), in this instance also using a final clue given to us by Syncellus that the coastal town of Pompeiopolis

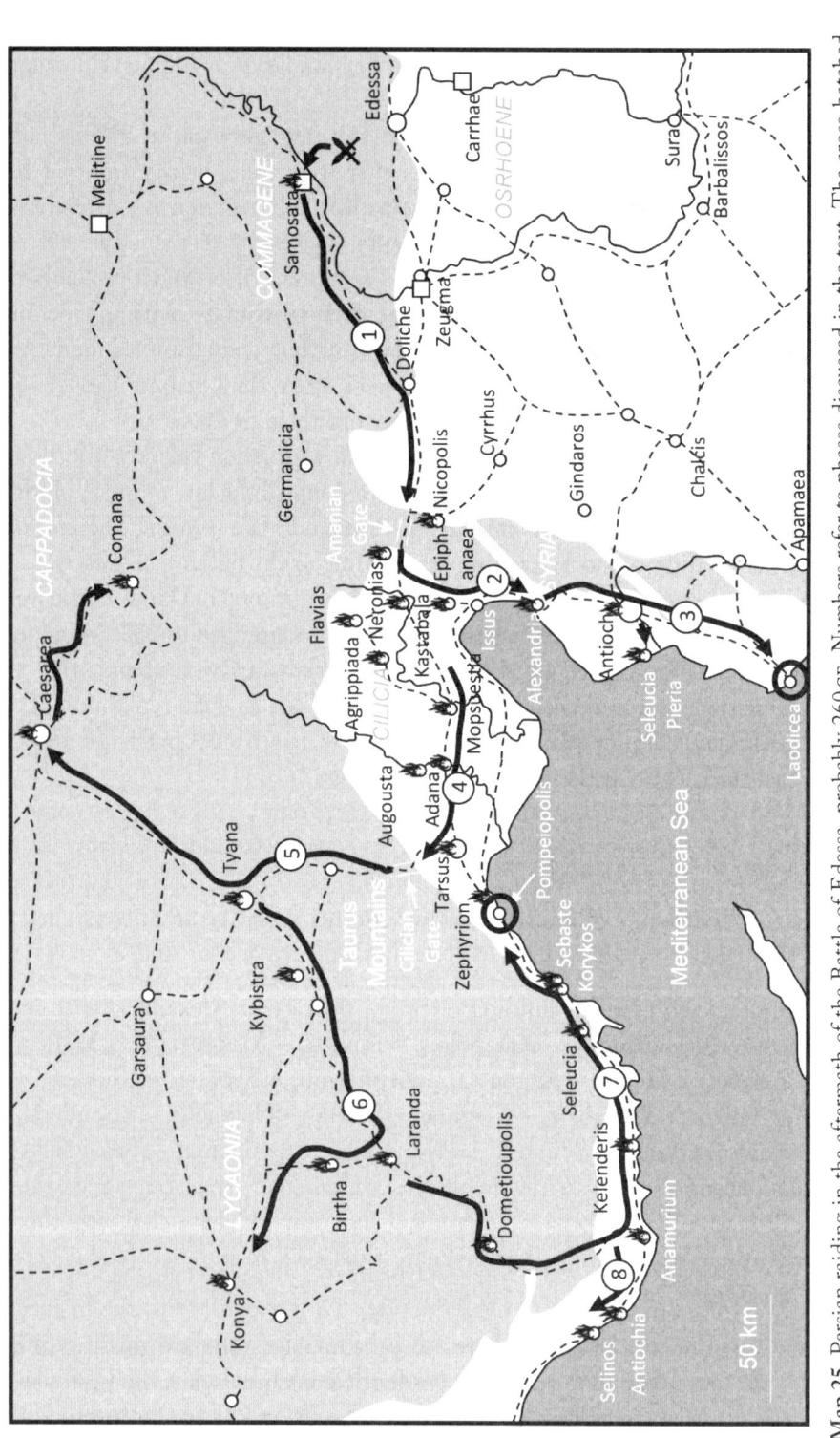

Map 25. Persian raiding in the aftermath of the Battle of Edessa, probably 260 CE. Numbers refer to phases discussed in the text. The cross-hatched area is that previously despoiled in 253.

was put to siege by a Persian army group after they had devastated the upland area of Lycaonia. Unlike the campaign of 253, the order in which the cities are listed makes little sense, but the main line of attack can be made out clearly enough. The intention was evidently to ransack fresh areas that had not suffered from the previous incursion. The list includes the major cities of Tarsus, Tyana and Caesarea in Cappadocia (called by its alternative name of Meiakarire on Shapur's list) as well as a number of other cities that were significant enough to have been minting their own coins during Valerian's reign: Aigeai, Mallos, Mopsuestia, Adana, Augousta, Sebaste and Agrippiada (also known as Anazarbus).[23]

From the map we can infer that after celebrating victory and recovering from battle, the *spah* marched fast towards the north-east corner of the Mediterranean (Arrow 1 on Map 25), crossing the Amanus (modern Nur) mountains by the pass known as the Amanian Gate. Cilician Nicopolis (modern Islahiye), which had been sacked in 253 was unlucky enough to suffer a repeat attack, being situated near the eastern end of this strategic pass. This is where the empire's main western highway ran, disgorging beyond onto the coastal lowlands of Cilicia. Several of the Roman sources report that the Persians dispersed, and given that most or all of the listed cities were protected by walls, a series of simultaneous stand-offs may have developed across Cilicia in the weeks after the battle of Edessa.[24]

Alexandria is not, of course, the great Egyptian city but a port north of Antioch also known as Alexandretta or Little Alexandria (Arrow 2). A contentious question is whether the Persians then made a second attack on the great metropolis of Antioch on the Orontes. Most of the ancient authors are clear that this did indeed happen and both Syncellus and Zonaras are unambiguous about it, but modern commentators have doubted it given that it was well protected by walls and was the likely rallying point for Macrianus after the Battle of Edessa. The Antioch on Shapur's list could be 'Little Antioch' (Antiochia ad Cragum) a small but spectacular site on a steep promontory on the Mediterranean coast of Anatolia. The two places may have become confused, it is argued. It has even been suggested that the destruction of Antioch on the Orontes was by now a kind of historical necessity for any historian describing a disaster in the east, and so can be dismissed.[25]

However there are good reasons for thinking that Antioch the Great *was* attacked for a second time beyond the fact that it accords with the historical record. A second sacking would have been a massive blow to Roman prestige in Syria, a significant consideration for the Persians. Valerian had expended a great deal of effort restoring the city since 253, as had been advertised on the coinage for years. The main imperial mint in the east was in the city, striking good quality silver in huge quantities, and so it would have been worth taking again. A move in the direction of Antioch would explain why Alexandretta was sacked, as is generally agreed, otherwise why was a detachment sent in that direction? The Seleucia on the list mentioned after Antioch could be one of several places of that name, but the city and naval base at Seleucia Piera would make sense as a target. The main Roman resistance appears to have been in the mountains of Syria rather than at Antioch, as is discussed in the next chapter. Finally, a passage in the Babylonian Talmud, often overlooked by historians in this context, but referring to the same invasion, says 'the walls of Laodicea were shaken by the noise of the arrows'. There were several cities of this name in the Roman east, but the one nearest the scene of action and known to have had a Jewish community is a port city which dominated the wealthy coastal zone south of Antioch. It had not suffered in 253, and so would have been a tempting target. To get to Laodicea by any sensible route the Persians must have passed by Antioch the Great (Arrow 3). Laodicea is not on Shapur's list, however, and so, presumably, was not captured.[26]

All this suggests that a substantial Persian army group, possibly a *gund* of 12,000 men, was diverted south into Syria while Shapur and the main army headed west onto the Cilician Plain. The greatest city in that district was Tarsus, chiefly known today as the birthplace of St. Paul. This was approached via Valerian's convenient new bridge at Mopsuestia. After despoiling Tarsus and all the other settlements in the area (Arrow 4), Shapur seems to have made a kind of base camp in the vicinity, a place where the loot could be stockpiled, captives herded, and non-combatants quartered. He then personally led a slimmed-down army northwards through the valley known as the Cilician Gate into the high and dusty mountain passes of the Taurus with his sights set on the rich cities of Tyana (birthplace of the sage and miracle-worker Apollonius), and beyond that Cappadocian Caesarea (Arrow 5). Before or after the fall of Tyana a separate army group was diverted west towards the cities of Lycaonia (Arrow 6), seemingly with orders to move south and return via the Mediterranean coastline (Arrow 7). The most distant city mentioned on Shapur's inscription is Selinos, about 300km along the coast from the marshalling ground at Tarsus (Arrow 8) suggesting that this group fragmented again too.[27]

Zonaras preserves an account of the siege of Caesarea (the capital of Cappadocia; a very populous trading city and significant hub of the road network; now the city of Kayseri) in which the defence was led by a brave and intelligent man called Demosthenes. The defenders held out behind their walls for some time. Unfortunately an unnamed physician was captured by the Persians and tortured, at which point he divulged a weak point where they could get into the city. A night assault at this location succeeded. Demosthenes, however, refused to surrender in the chaotic street fighting that followed:

> After he had been encircled by many Persians who had been ordered to take him alive, he mounted his horse, grasped his naked sword, and flung himself into the midst of the enemy. After he laid many low, he escaped from the city and managed to get away. [Zonaras, *Extracts of History* XII.23.]

Demosthenes was one of the lucky ones. Caesarea had for long been home to a substantial Jewish community. The Babylonian Talmud states that 12,000 Jews died in the massacre there. Large amounts of booty and huge numbers of individuals were marched out of the city gates destined for the slave markets of Persia. The historical accounts accentuate the brutality of Shapur in his poor treatment of the captives as he herded them in droves with barely enough food and water for life. At one point he allegedly slaughtered a large number of them and dumped their bodies into a ravine so that the baggage train could cross. Of course, this could be mere propaganda, but it was mountainous country and bridges may have been destroyed to hamper his movements.[28]

Valerian had claimed to be under the protection of Jupiter the Best and Greatest. Despite that, he had been captured, and his regime had conspicuously failed in its most basic role of providing security to law-abiding, tax-paying citizens in the east and west. Even the Eternal City was under threat. There can be little doubt that the year 260 was the lowest point thus far in the history of Imperial Rome.

Chapter 12

Disintegration

The Battle of Mediolanum

When the Alpine passes finally began to clear, Gallienus and his elite force, now rested, set off southward to rescue Rome. The young prince Saloninus was left on the Rhine to represent the imperial regime there, while the general Postumus was likely given overall command as *dux* of the Rhine frontier and ordered to continue the war against the Franks as well as he was able.

Although Rome avoided attack for now, the fact that such an event had very nearly come to pass must have been an enormous moral shock. The dissatisfaction expressed by various historical sources with Gallienus seems to have been shared by the commanders of his army, resulting in a high-level conspiracy, as related again by Zosimus:

> It was at this time, that Cecrops, a Moor, Aureolus, and Antoninus, with many others, conspired against him, of whom the greater part were punished and submitted. [Zosimus, *New History* 1.38.1.]

The identity of Cecrops is uncertain but it is possible that he was originally from Mauretania and now commander of a contingent of Dalmatian light cavalry in Gallienus's force. Aureolus was also a senior cavalry officer who, as we have seen, had led the line at the Battle of Mursa and put the army of Ingenuus to flight. Antoninus was presumably another high-ranking officer. The conspiracy evidently became known to the emperor, which would normally mean death, but Gallienus was hardly in a position to execute all his senior commanders while retaining the loyalty of the rank and file. The punishment may have been limited to reprimands and fines. It was hardly an auspicious start to the campaign.[1]

The direct route south would have been via the Great Saint Bernard Pass. Zonaras claims that by this time the barbarian hordes in Italy numbered 300,000 men, a number difficult to believe but easy to exaggerate. With a mere ten thousand at his disposal, we are told, Gallienus routed a major concentration of them in the vicinity of Mediolanum (Milan) and the mopping up operation began. The surviving 'barbarians' fled hither and thither hoping to escape, but of course they were deep within the empire, laden with plunder and captives, and faced a long trek back to safety with the mountains in between. It was probably a gleeful time for Gallienus's troops because any re-captured treasure was traditionally retained by the men, and captured 'barbarians' would be sold as slaves. The hunters had become the hunted.[2]

At some point around this time Gallienus must have received word of his father's capture. We do not know what he made of it. One school of thought is that he was delighted at the news; the old man was now finally out of the way and the empire was his, and his alone. Certainly the mints stopped issuing coinage in Valerian's name almost immediately, just as if he was dead, and that order must have come from Gallienus personally. Another view is that Valerian's capture was considered just another disaster to add to the list. In due course he would have to be ransomed, freed or avenged, but only after other more urgent matters had been dealt with first.[3]

To add to the general woe, a new wave of the killer disease began to spread in Illyricum, described as 'more dreadful than any that had preceded it'. Perhaps this was the same contagious new variant that had recently afflicted Valerian's troops in the east. Some towns there were shunned even by the marauding barbarians, escaping destruction, so that 'even the sick deemed themselves fortunate'.[4]

Ballista bolts

The senior surviving Roman official in the east, Fulvius Macrianus, seems to have taken to the hills and organized a guerilla war. This is the gist of a verse of the Thirteenth Sibylline Oracle that describes a 'well-horned hungry stag' who kept to the mountains while devouring 'serpents'. Aramaic for stag is *mqrw* which sounds like Macrianus, and is typical of the sort of riddle enjoyed by the Sibyl. The fact that Macrianus is described as 'well-horned' implies that he had assembled a substantial force under his command. The most likely interpretation is that he harried Persian forces trying to export captives and riches eastward through the Amanus range, a potentially lucrative operation for the men under his command. It is doubtful that he took the field in person because he is described as being lame in one leg.[5]

According to Syncellus, there was also another source of resistance:

> The Persians became dispersed here and there by their greed for booty. They were on the point of capturing Pompeiopolis on the coast, having laid waste to much of Lycaonia, when Callistus came upon them unawares with ships and a Roman force consisting of men who in their flight had chosen him as leader. He captured the harem of Shapur with much wealth.

Returning with his fleet to Sebaste and Korykos [Corycus], he wiped out a force of three thousand Persians. Shapur was greatly distressed by this and he withdrew in haste and in fear. [Syncellus, *Chronography* p. 57.]

The name 'Callistus' is thought by some to be a scribal error for 'Ballista'. The latter name is known from some of the manuscript copies of Syncellus and is used in various other sources including the *Historia Augusta*. 'Ballista' is the name for a Roman catapult, so it may have been a nickname for this intrepid individual, although it is also conceivable that it was his actual name. Little is known of Ballista the man. The *Historia Augusta* claims he had been a well-respected provincial governor much admired by Valerian, but that could be fabrication.[6]

Historians have doubted the story of the harem, seemingly on the cautious grounds that any interesting detail is inherently suspicious. However it is worth noting that Pompeiopolis does not appear on Shapur's list of fallen cities despite the fact that it is surrounded by places that do. Shapur himself is not mentioned as being present when Ballista attacked, hence he was probably commanding one of the columns attacking cities in the rugged interior. Under these circumstances, and in the knowledge that Shapur took other non-combatants like priests with him on campaign, it seems possible that he would have temporarily parked his harem on the breezy coastline south of Tarsus under the care of a subordinate, along with much of the accumulating treasure, intending to return in that direction and believing them to be safe from attack.

The easiest way to make sense of Syncellus's account is that Ballista had gathered remnants of the defeated force at or near Antioch. He may have been the commander of the Roman fleet at Seleucia Pieria (the *classis syriaca*) whose base, as we have seen, may have been destroyed for the second time that year. The fleet could easily have evacuated beforehand, however, and sailed down the coast to Tyre or even Egypt to join forces with the *classis alexandriae*. Reorganized, re-armed and intent on vengeance, they sailed around the coast to hunt down dispersed Persian army groups and to relieve the suffering of the coastal cities. The motivation may have been partly piratical because, as with Gallienus and Macrianus, such an operation could be highly profitable for the men involved.

Ballista's first victory was his surprise attack on the besieging army at Pompeiopolis which was defeated in the field and driven off. How tactical surprise was achieved – whether by landing at night or in a neighbouring cove – is not known. He then sailed on and re-occupied the naval base that

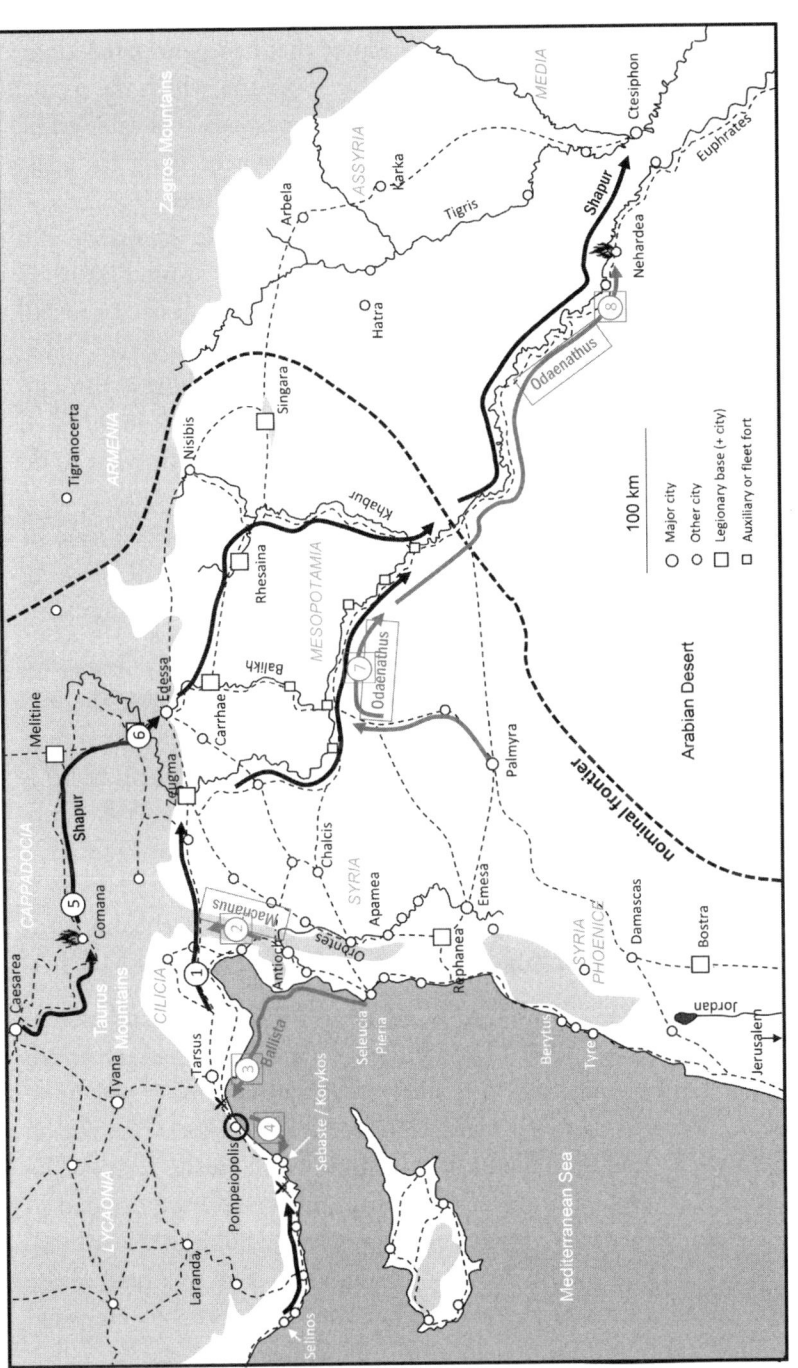

Map 26. The long Persian retreat, probably 260 CE. Persian army groups in Cilicia probably withdrew via the Amanus Mountains (1), harried by forces under Macrianus (2). Ballista's naval squadron relieved the siege of Pompeiopolis (3) and destroyed a Persian force beyond Sebaste (4). Shapur and the main force probably withdrew via Comana (5) and passed Edessa (6). Odaenathus attacked retreating Persian forces along the Euphrates (7) and deep into Persian territory, destroying the Jewish academy at Nehardea (8) and threatening Ctesiphon.

encompasses the twin coastal settlements of Sebaste and Korykos, and in doing so cut off the line of retreat of the Persian splinter that had penetrated along the coast as far as Selinos. He annihilated this force in turn, which the source says was 3,000 strong (a not excessive number, and so perhaps believable). The account seems to imply that an ambush was laid somewhere along the coast road. Ballista had thereby gained control of the entire coastline.

Shapur must have realized that he was facing a capable adversary and possibly appreciated that if more forces started to congregate around Ballista's banner they might threaten his retreat altogether. The very last city to fall may have been Comana, which suggests that rather than returning via Cilicia, as may have been the original plan, Shapur's main force withdrew through Cappadocia. Meanwhile, Ballista and Macrianus regrouped back in Antioch where they consulted on their next moves, including presumably, what to do with all the concubines.

Shapur's problems were not over because a few weeks later, by the time he reached Edessa, it was clear that a substantial force there was still blocking his line of retreat. This is the context of another of the surviving fragments of Petrus Patricius:

> He [Shapur] sent word to the soldiers of Edessa, promising to give them all the Syrian money he had with him, so that they would allow him to pass unhindered and not choose a venture which would lead them to be subject to attack on both sides and bring him loss of speed. He said that he did not offer them these things out of fear but because he was eager to celebrate the festival in his own home and did not want there to be any delay or any hold-up on his journey. The soldiers chose to take the money without risk and permit him to pass. [Petrus Patricius, Fragment 11.]

It may have been that Shapur hoped to be home in time for the Zoroastrian winter solstice feast of Maidyarem. Given the large area that he had traversed, and the multiple sieges conducted, it is likely that by this time it was quite late in the year. The existence of a significant force at Edessa is one reason to believe that the city had not fallen after the great battle in the spring. The troops in that important city, many of them local, may well have decided to wait out events behind the walls, protecting its people and holding the ground. The Syrian money offered by the Persians presumably refers to a haul of the much-debased tetradrachms of Antioch. They may have been of marginal value to Shapur who himself minted coins to a far higher silver standard.

But even when Edessa had been by-passed, the King of Kings was still a long way from home and encumbered by wagons full of booty as well as herds of miserable, thirsty and starving captives. An old foe still stood between him and the festivities at Ctesiphon, a man whose overtures he had previously snubbed, but who had spent the last few years steadily growing the military might of Palmyra: Odaenathus, Lord of Tadmor.

The Gates of Ctesiphon

The retreating Persian column was a juicy target, not just because it was carrying much of the portable wealth of Roman Cilicia and Cappadocia, but because the various army groups would inevitably have become strung out during their disorganized, harassed and fragmented withdrawal. More disinterested motives may also have been involved in attacking the Persians, including a chance to release many of the captives, avenge the Roman defeat, and possibly even bargain for the freedom of Valerian and his senior staff officers. Zonaras tells us that Odaenathus, 'allying himself with the Romans, destroyed many of the Persians, attacking them while they were returning from the Euphrates territory'. The only other detail he gives is that the Persian dead were found to include women equipped in the fashion of men and that some female warriors were also taken prisoner. Indeed it was not unusual for the Persians to enroll women in the military, including in combat roles.[7]

The Euphrates was the traditional sphere of operations of Palmyrene forces which included highly mobile camel corps. According to one Roman source, Odaenathus 'not only defended our border but even as the avenger of the Roman Empire, marvellous to say, forced his way to Ctesiphon'.[8] This might seem unlikely under the circumstances, but some possible corroboration can be found in the Babylonian Talmud which records the destruction of the rabbinical academy at Nehardea by someone called 'Papa ben Nasor'. This place had been set up by a learned rabbi called Samuel, apparently a friend and admirer of Shapur who was kindly towards the Jews in his dominions. Samuel is the man who had conspicuously *not* rent his clothes (mourned) at news of the death of 12,000 Jews at the hands of the Persians in Roman Caesarea. The academy was about 125km west of Ctesiphon on the banks of the Euphrates near modern Ramadi, and reputedly attracted thousands of students. A small window into academic life there tells us that if a scholar visited from the Land of Israel, the entire student body and the dean would turn out to hear him, and after class he would be deluged with academic questions. Unfortunately, this place was destroyed. 'Papa ben Nasor' has been identified as Odaenathus who is independently attested as the son of Nasor (ben Nasor) in Palmyrene inscriptions.[9]

The dubious *Historia Augusta* goes even further and claims that Odaenathus 'restored Roman power almost to its pristine condition', and captured even more of Shapur's hapless concubines whom, it informs us, 'Parthian monarchs hold dearer than treasure'. Despite this setback, Shapur was able to hold Ctesiphon with most of his booty. Some captives were freed in the Palmyrene raids, but the emperor Valerian was still held securely while Shapur and his advisers began to calculate what a king's ransom was worth in those days.[10]

As well as holding the emperor, Shapur had captured tens of thousands of Roman soldiers and civilians who were put to work on various building projects around his empire. Four new cities were founded to house this captive workforce, all named after the King of Kings: Gundishapur in the Province of Susiana, Buzurg Shapur on the banks of the Tigris, Bishapur in Fars, and Sod Shapur in Mesene. The people were employed building dams, bridges, roads, temples and palaces. Some of the bridges survive today, the high-quality design and build pointing to the work of captured Roman military engineers. Intriguingly, the architectural style of the new construction was typically Roman, and the cities were laid out in Roman fashion with a rectangular plan with main street (*cardo*) and cross-street (*decumanus*). At Bishapur, the most important of the new cities, a Corinthian column stood at the intersection with a dedication to Shapur dated to three years after the invasion, by which time, presumably, the work had been completed. Archaeological excavations of the palace there, where Valerian was supposedly held captive, revealed Roman style mosaics that are recognizably of the Antioch school as well as niches for free-standing statues which are otherwise very rare in Sassanian architecture. The original name of the city seems to have been 'Vehi Antiouk Shapur' or 'Better than Antioch Shapur' although whether the enslaved citizens appreciated the name we do not know.[11]

The Augsburg Victory Altar

In August 1992 a group of workers was excavating gravel from a silted-up arm of the Lech River at Augsburg in Bavaria, southern Germany, at a location which would have been just a few hundred metres outside the city limits of Roman Augusta Vindelicorum, the capital of Roman Raetia. A mysterious square stone slab was discovered, followed a few weeks later by an elaborately sculpted and inscribed altar stone. Because the base slab and altar stone were found together, it confirms that the monument had been set up exactly where it was found, beside the river at an old crossing point not used since antiquity, the main channel having long since changed its course. At some point the altar had foundered in the gravel, become overgrown and was covered by silt and gravel and remained there until the twentieth century. It is now on display at the Augsburg Romisches Museum.

The altar is dedicated to the personification of Victory and may well have originally supported a bronze statue of that goddess. One side shows Mars, God of War, in his traditional muscle armour with shield and spear, and on the opposing face is Victory herself, standing over a bound captive who sports the shaggy hair and beard that denotes a barbarian. In translation (with the abbreviations completed and chiseled out parts restored), the inscription reads:

> To the holy goddess Victory, on account of barbarians of the race of the Semnones or Iuthungi killed on the eighth and seventh days before the Kalends of May and put to flight by soldiers of the province of Raetia as well as Germani and locals, freeing many thousands of Italian captives; in fulfillment of his vow, Marcus Simplicinius Genialis, *vir perfectissimus* acting for the *praeses* with his army happily and deservedly erected this altar, dedicated three days before the Ides of September when the Emperor, our Lord Postumus Augustus, and Honoratianus were consuls.[12]

The discovery of the monument was greeted with considerable enthusiasm by historians as a rare relic from a period of chaos that can actually be fixed in time and place and because of its fascinating and information-packed content. It may be relevant that the Ides of September was a feast day sacred to Jupiter Optimus Maximus, so we can imagine a ceremony with the traditional sacrifices taking place at the very findspot, followed by a celebration and a feast. There can be little doubt that Marcus Simplicinius Genialis, the commanding officer, who is otherwise unknown, would have officiated. He had made his solemn promise to the gods before battle was joined to erect such a monument should he prove victorious, as was the Roman way.

The stone evidently commemorates a running battle fought six months earlier, over two days in late March of the year 260, against enemies identified as Semnones (a Germanic tribe who originated between the Elbe and Oder according to Tacitus writing a century earlier) and Iuthungi ('the Young Ones'), another Germanic grouping which had been mentioned by Dexippus and also appears in a fourth century work by Ammianus Marcellinus. Genialis is described as *vir perfectissimus* denoting a high equestrian rank, but was acting under the authority of a regional governor (*praeses*) who is not named.[13]

The composition of Genialis's army is interesting to contemplate. No specific unit is mentioned (whether regular legion or auxiliary cohort) but simply the 'soldiers of the Province of Raetia'. Many of the frontier forts of the province had been over-run during the invasion, so perhaps this was an army reconstituted from the survivors of various units, bent on revenge. This force was supplemented by 'Germani' and local people. The Germani were evidently Roman allies, possibly *foederati*, that is 'barbarians' enlisted by treaty under their own leadership to fight alongside the Romans. It seems very likely, then, that this was the group previously settled in neighbouring Pannonia by Gallienus in the 'Pipa treaty' with King Attalus of the Marcomanni. The 'local people' were presumably anyone able and willing to take up arms to avenge the devastation. The fact that Germani and local people get a mention

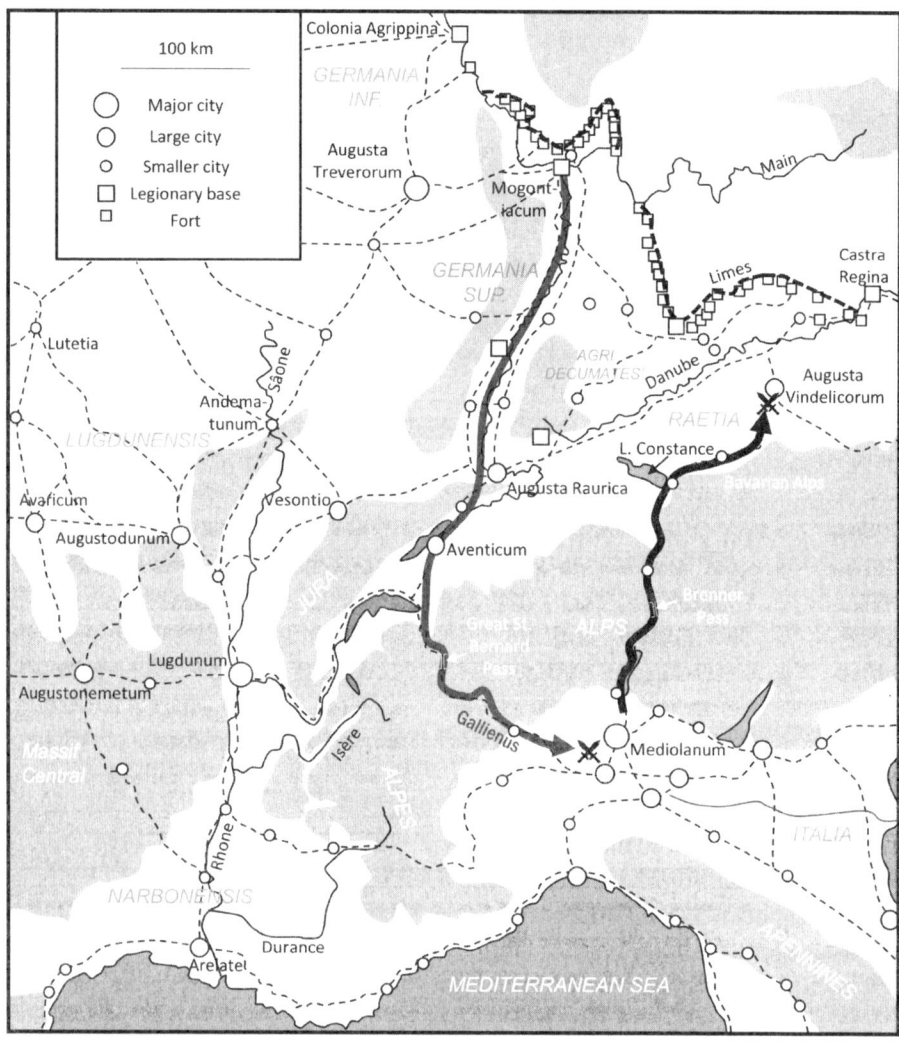

Map 27. The Battles of Mediolanum and Augusta Vindelicorum, probably 260 CE. Gallienus arrived in Italy by the Great St. Bernard Pass and defeated a large concentration of 'barbarians' near Mediolanum. One substantial group of raiders had already exited by the Brenner Pass only to be intercepted by a scratch force commanded by Simplicinius Genialis outside Augusta Vindelicorum.

strongly suggests that they were a significant factor in the winning the battle and were very likely present at the victory feast in large numbers.

The strategic setting for the engagement is clear enough (Map 27). Augusta Vindelicorum lies in undulating land north of the Bavarian Alps. The Semnones / Iuthungi had evidently been rampaging in Italy in 259/260 during which time they had captured thousands of citizens who had been herded across the Alps in late winter via the Brenner Pass, probably just as soon as it could be traversed – a most miserable slog. It is difficult to imagine any mercy being shown to those who could not keep the pace. No doubt there was much portable wealth as well. This group, and quite possibly others like them, had evaded Gallienus by exiting Italy in good order just as he was arriving by a different route. The Lech flows northward from the Alpine passes toward the Danube, beyond which (just 40km away) was safety as far as the raiders were concerned. However the scratch force under Genialis managed to intercept them, probably at the site of the monument: a river crossing was always a good ambush point. The fact that the battle was fought over two days suggests an initial engagement at which the 'barbarians' were defeated and dispersed, followed by a rout and running fight as Roman cavalry mopped up as many fleeing tribesmen as possible.

The 'many thousands' of freed captives from the estates and towns of Italy owed their lives to Genialis and his army, although their property was forfeit by ancient custom. They must have cursed the Emperor Gallienus, who had so conspicuously failed to protect them.

The Hercules from Deuso

The most striking aspect of the Augsburg inscription, as the reader may have spotted, is the name of the 'Emperor' Postumus. He was not an official emperor and Honoratianus was not an official consul. The altar stone therefore establishes the date for yet another rebellion, this time by the much admired general of the Rhine army, which at that time was the most powerful independent command in the empire.

By far the best account that we have of the rebellion is a passage by the late Byzantine writer Zonaras who must have had access to sources now lost to us:

> Postumus, who had been left to guard the Rhine frontier so as to impede the crossing into Roman territory for the barbarians dwelling beyond, attacked some, who, after they had crossed unnoticed, were taking much plunder as they were returning, and he killed many, recovered all the plunder, and immediately apportioned it to his soldiers. Albanus [the

Imperial representative and guardian of Saloninus], when he had learned this, sent messengers and demanded that the plunder be brought to him and to the young Gallienus [i.e., Saloninus]. Postumus called his soldiers together and exacted from them their shares of the plunder, scheming to incite them to rebellion. And that is exactly what happened. With them he attacked the city of Agrippina [Cologne], and the inhabitants of that city surrendered to him both the son of the sovereign and Albanus, and he executed them both. [Zonaras, *Extracts of History* XII.24.]

The Rhine army consisted of four legions and many other auxiliary units, although it was no doubt under-strength due to the ongoing warfare and because detachments had been included in the imperial armies of both Valerian and Gallienus. The legions were *legio* XXX *ulpia victrix* based at Vetera (Xanten), *legio* I *minervia* at Bonna (Bonn), *legio* VIII *augusta* at Argentoratum (Strasbourg), and *legio* XXII *primigenia* at Mogontiacum (Mainz). All these seem to have rebelled simultaneously and served as the motive power behind the insurrection. Postumus immediately took over the imperial mint at Augusta Treverorum (Trier) which started issuing coins in his name. The very first portraits look very like Gallienus, suggesting that the engravers did not initially know what the new man looked like, but soon enough they settled down to depicting a big, powerful-looking, rather full-faced man with luxuriant curly hair and beard. Another peculiarity of the very first issues – in gold as well as silver – is that they invariably spell his name 'Postimus', and it has even been suggested that it may have been misheard by an official amidst the clanging of the mint. It was soon to be corrected.[14]

Postumus seems to have taken more than the usual level of interest in the coinage as a means of conveying his propaganda. The gold in particular is exceptionally pure and well-made and includes some wonderfully innovative facing portraits that are admired as being among the glories of the Roman imperial series (Plate 8). The main reverse type of the first silver and bronze issues was *salus pronvinciarum* which can be translated as the safety, health, or well-being of the provinces (plural), a most appropriate message of course, with barbarians and plague both rampaging in their own separate ways.[15] Unlike other usurpers, Eternal Rome does not appear, nor is there any other theme associated with the Imperial City in the regular issues. Instead the main message seems to have been that Postumus would provide safety and security for the areas under his control, and Rome could solve its own problems.

Although Zosimus says that Postumus made himself 'sovereign of the Celts', this was not some sort of Gallic national revolt, throwing off the shackles of empire (or at least, not on the surface): everything about it, from the stately and religious symbolism (Postumus was *caesar augustus* and *pontifex maximus*) to the administrative structure and military organization, was entirely Roman. Postumus even set up a parallel senate, presumably housed at Trier, which elected consuls (as we have seen on the Augsburg inscription) and governed as if its counterpart in Rome simply didn't exist.[16]

An especially curious coin produced almost immediately in large numbers features *herculi deusoniensi* – 'of the Hercules from Deuso' – showing the demigod with his beefcake physique leaning on his trademark club and brandishing the bow with which he had supposedly killed various fantastic beasts and monsters. This unprecedented design was produced so quickly that it must have been ordered by Postumus himself. The location of Deuso (or Deusone) is not known for certain, but it may have been an insignificant place on the lower Rhine now called Duisburg (like several other places in Germany). From this arose the suggestion that it could have been Postumus's home town, making him Batavian by origin and giving his revolt some additional local character. 'Hercules of Deuso' might have been his military nickname and we can imagine him being acclaimed as such in full throated roar by the assembled soldiery.[17]

There is no indication in the historical accounts that news of Valerian's capture had reached the Rhine by the time of Postumus's rebellion. That must have occurred after Gallienus had left the sector, making the spring of 260 the most likely time for the rebellion. News of it may have been the reason for the aforementioned 'Cecrops' conspiracy formed by Gallienus's generals as they marched south. They all knew Postumus well and may have thought he would make a better emperor. That conspiracy failed, as we have seen, but Postumus quickly gained ground elsewhere as local army commanders began to receive delegations from the Rhine. News of the great defeat in the east, spreading at the same time, likely added fire to the rebellion. All of Gaul and Raetia declared for Postumus (the latter being evidenced by the Augsburg dedication), as did the administrations in Spain and Britain. There is no indication, however, that Postumus made preparations for a march on the imperial capital. Everything about the regime suggests that it was focused on internal security and government. In effect, an enormous chunk of the empire peeled away under the command of the Hercules from Deuso who well knew that the imperial administration could do very little about it.[18]

Insurrection on the Danube

The legions on the upper Danube had also had more than enough of Gallienus. Brutal suppression of the Ingenuus revolt had left deep scars. With Valerian in chains and Shapur rampant in Asia Minor, Gallienus widely lampooned, and with the area suffering from new-variant plague and possibly threatened by new inroads of Sarmatians, it was time for yet another revolt. This time it was centred on the city of Carnutum (east of modern Vienna), capital of Pannonia Superior and base of *legio* XIV *gemina*. Their new self-styled emperor was, according to his coins, P.C. Regalianus. The *Historia Augusta* says he was a Dacian nobleman and a descendant of the great Decebalus himself, the last King of Dacia who had fought against Trajan. More sober modern historians think he was a descendant of a former suffect consul, Caius Cassius Regallianus (with two 'l's), who is attested on a military diploma from earlier in the century, by which argument the rebel's name may have been Publius Cassius Regalianus. Of course, for the romantics out there, he could have been descended from both men.[19]

The little that the historical records say about Regalianus is that he had commanded the remnants of the Moesian legions who had survived the disaster at Mursa and subsequently 'performed many brave deeds against the Sarmatians', whether inside or outside the empire is not stated. The coins indicate that his wife, Sulpicia Dryantilla, was immediately declared *augusta* and the local mint issued in both of their names, apparently in roughly equal numbers, but always of very crude style and mostly simply overstruck on coins of earlier emperors. One type is 'Liberality of the Emperors' which indicates that the rebellion must have been lubricated with a generous handout of these poorly manufactured objects.[20]

An interesting aspect of these coins that has received little attention is that the reverse types almost always refer to two emperors (e.g., *virtus augg*, the two 'G's indicating two *augusti*), hence it seems likely that Regalianus and Dryantilla had a son who was also invested with imperial honours. If so, one can assume that there was an attempt to establish a dynasty.[21]

A silly story in the *Historia Augusta* claims that Regalianus had been chosen to rule because of his 'regal' name. The senior staff officers at Carnutum were discussing him, whereupon a schoolteacher who, conveniently, happened to be present, said the word *rex*, meaning king, declined grammatically thus: '*Rex, regis, regi, Regalianus*'. That, apparently, was good enough to claim the throne in those rebellious days! The actual declension is *rex, regis, regi, regem, rege, rex*; it would have made a better joke to stick the final, vocative, *rex* on the end, so on these limited grounds the author proposes that the anecdote was second hand to Trebellius Pollio, the supposed author of the tale, who was evidently no raconteur.[22]

The unsolved mystery of Sponsian

Before moving on, it is worth recording the existence of yet another possible rebel 'emperor' from around this time whose story – if genuine – is the most intriguing of all. The only evidence we have for him is a handful of gold coins which emerged in Transylvania (part of modern Romania) in 1713. At least five of these, possibly six or seven, appear to have been dug up from a single deposit along with a number of 'barbarous' copies of gold coins of Gordian III and Philip the Arab and older Republican-era coins. The first descriptions come from the 1770s, by which time there were five known specimens dispersed among four major European collections. The best image previously available of any Sponsian coin was a rather grainy black and white photograph of a specimen in Glasgow's Hunterian Museum. It is therefore a pleasure to show high quality colour photographs of the same coin, taken for this work following a request to the museum (Plate 8).[23]

All specialists agree that the Sponsian coins are of 'barbarous' manufacture quite unlike regular Roman imperial issues. However we have seen that other usurpers sometimes produced poor quality coins if they did not have access to a functioning mint and yet urgently needed currency to pay their men. So either they are forgeries, albeit made several hundred years ago, or they could be genuine evidence for a very obscure phase of history. Either way it makes a fine puzzle, so let us take a look at the evidence.

The first thing to notice is that Sponsian wears a radiate crown which, by convention, would indicate that they were intended as double-aurei (the denomination that numismatists sometimes call the 'binio'). The average weight of four known specimens is 10.02g which is more than twice that of Philip's aurei which weigh in at about 4.30g. The obverse legend *imp sponsiani* is very curious for a coin of this period. For one thing, it runs down one side of the head only whereas the universal practice was to wrap the text around the bust. It is in the genitive case (meaning 'of Sponsianus') which is unheard of for names on imperial coins and also rather minimalistic, as one would normally expect something like *imp(erator) c(aesar) sponsianus p(ius) f(elix) aug(ustus)* and perhaps some of his forenames as well. One way to explain this is if the engraver (whether Roman or eighteenth-century forger) was not very skilled or perhaps barely literate. Certainly the portrait is rather featureless with a curious blank eye and rather lacking in artistic merit.

Stranger still is the reverse design which features two toga-wearing figures with priestly implements standing either side of a column surmounted by a statue of a man with a beaded staff and with corn ears each side of it. The legend C AVG is written above. What is so odd is that this design is copied from Republican era coins minted by the moneyer Caius Minucius Augurinus in 135 BCE – that is, nearly 400 years before our period! The C AVG represents C[AIVS] AVG[VRINVS]. The design, for what it's worth, depicts a monument that once stood in Rome dedicated to Caius's distinguished ancestor, Lucius Minucius Augurinus. Back in 439 BCE, another three hundred years earlier, the city state had been afflicted by famine and the people were starving. This man had been put in charge of the corn supply and successfully ended the crisis, which explains why there are corn ears in the design. For this he had been elected consul by a grateful people. No satisfactory explanation has ever been proposed as to why this antique design was used, whether the coins are real or fake.[24]

Roman imperial coins were almost always struck by placing a heated blank between two hardened dies featuring designs in negative relief. The Hunterian Museum specimen has all the appearances of being cast, however. This form of manufacture begins with the production of solid 'hubs' in positive relief which are then impressed into clay and assembled front and back to make a mould. The mould is then fired and molten metal is poured in and allowed to cool. Finally, the mould is broken open revealing the end product. Evidence for this is the generally bland surface and – something that has apparently not been noticed before – the design on the reverse side seems to have slipped twice while being impressed into wet clay, as is best seen on the new photograph by following the beaded outline, which is discontinuous and oval rather than round. Some of the detail is repeated and the lettering is partly obscured. Casting may explain why the legend is short because it may have been difficult to produce sufficient detail for a more complete set of titles.[25]

Possibly the oddest feature of the Sponsian coins is that while four of them appear to have been cast from moulds made with the same set of hubs, a fifth (unless the illustration is very inaccurate indeed) may have been made from different obverse and reverse hubs. Because a hub can be used any number of times, this hints at the possibility that the coins we know of are part of a larger series originally manufactured – or perhaps that was all part of the deception.[26]

Even the name Sponsian is very peculiar, wrapping another enigma inside the mystery. It is a genuine Roman name, but is apparently only attested once, in an obscure inscription from first century Rome. The original was Nicodemus Sponsian, a *cubicularius* (bedchamber attendant) to the empress

Livia. But a forger in 1713 could not have known this because the inscription from Rome was not dug up until the 1720s.[27]

Nevertheless, most numismatists are of the opinion that the Sponsian series and the other coins found with them are part of an elaborate forgery that succeeded in convincing the specialists of the time. The standard catalogue *Roman Imperial Coins* lists Sponsian as an 'unsolved mystery'. While the forgery theory has to be considered the most likely solution at the time of writing, it is worth remarking that the new photographs appear to show superficial wear patterns consistent with the coins having been in circulation, and also solid earthen deposits in recesses of the type that are formed during prolonged burial. Those features can be faked too, but surely warrant further study. So, for the sake of argument, if we assume our man was a real usurper: what would the coins tell us about him?[28]

The find-spot is in Roman Dacia, the most exposed of all the provinces and a place that had been under attack for many years. There was no imperial mint there. There had in fact been a regional mint making bronze coins in operation until about 254, probably at the *civitas* and legionary base of Apulum. After its closure the province must have relied exclusively on money sent in from outside. What Dacia did have in abundance was gold from the Western Carpathians. The mining operation was enormous. Normally that gold would head to Rome as ingots, by boat, and money to pay for the mines would come back in the other direction. But if the garrisons became cut off, the only way of financing their very exposed military operation would have been to seize control of the mines. In such circumstances, a hypothetical commander called Sponsian may well have turned to crudely manufactured cast productions, which although 'barbarous' in appearance, would still have been literally worth their weight in gold.[29]

Those earlier historians who supposed this man really existed have generally suggested he had a brief flirtation with power around the time of the Emperor Philip, and he was often inserted in lists following the rebels Pacatian and Jotapian. The main reason for this seems to be that his coins were found with others of Philip and Gordian (albeit also 'barbarous' productions) and so he likely fits in around that time. It also seems to have been convenient for the early numismatists to insert him after those other transient rebels in their catalogues. But there is a problem: double aurei with radiate crowns were only introduced by Trebonianus Gallus after the crisis in the gold supply following the Battle of Abritus (and were continued by all subsequent emperors of the period). Therefore if Sponsian was a genuine usurper it would seem to indicate he belongs somewhere after the year 251. For this reason, this author favours the chaos of 260 as a more likely time for a hypothetical Sponsian regime to have appeared, possibly persisting for some years afterwards. The Roman province of Dacia was entirely cut off from the imperial centre by the rebellions of Postumus and Regalianus. Roman Dacia was sorely threatened once again and the legions there (*legio* V *macedonica* and *legio* XIII *gemina*) may have been forced to rely entirely on their own resources.[30]

Eastern rebels

We are on a surer footing when we turn to events in the eastern empire. The power vacuum in the Roman east magnified the importance of three individuals: the former finance minister, Macrianus; the admiral of the Syrian fleet (if that had indeed been his station), Ballista; and the Lord of Tadmor, Odaenathus. All three had done well by harrying the Persians during their long withdrawal and their men had accumulated significant riches, so their reputations were riding high. Macrianus and Ballista seem to have met up in Antioch. With Valerian captive and Gallienus hopelessly distant and possibly despised by all, they decided to set up a new administration. Macrianus was lame in one leg and so, apparently, passed over imperial glory, but he had two vigorous sons who were raised to the purple: Fulvius Junius Macrianus and Fulvius Junius Quietus. Ballista became master of horse and chief military strategist in the new regime, tasked with countering the Persians. Odaenathus, far distant in Palmyra or possibly still harrying Persian forces near Ctesiphon, was not party to these negotiations.[31]

The *Historia Augusta* contains an almost certainly fictitious account of the conference between Ballista and Macrianus, which claims to be derived from an eyewitness named as Maeonius Astyanax, but who was probably made up. The men lamented the capture of Valerian but agreed that his son, Gallienus, was unfit to rule. Ballista proposed the merits of the sons of Macrianus and offered to be their prefect. The elder Macrianus was also raised to the imperial purple, although there is no other evidence of this having happened. But, on this very dubious basis, the father is sometimes referred to as Macrianus I and his elder son Macrianus II.

It is not clear exactly how far the rebellion spread because of the widespread civil and military chaos pertaining at the time, but we do know that Macrianus (the younger) and Quietus were quickly recognized in Egypt. The first evidence is a papyrus from the Oxyrhynchus stash which is dated to the twentieth day of Thoth (17 September 260). The minting of coins in their names in Alexandria began around that time also.[32]

Of the younger Macrianus and Quietus we know rather little except the *Historia Augusta* claims that their mother was of noble birth, unlike their father who had risen through the ranks. That may well be baseless padding. Turning to the evidence of the coins, the first thing to notice is that they are of poor quality, not only in silver content but also in artistic style. The lettering is spidery and the portraiture has a cartoon-like quality, even in the gold issues, and the two emperors are indistinguishable. There is a complete discontinuity in style between the last issues of Valerian and the first issue of the brothers, which is more evidence that Antioch the Great really had been sacked in 260 at which time the die-engravers presumably joined the Antiochene mosaicists and other master craftsmen in captivity.

Modern numismatists think that the coins were minted at Samosata, which seems likely. It has been argued from this that perhaps that city had not in fact been sacked after the Battle of Edessa, despite Shapur's inscription and the evident direction of the Persian thrust. Perhaps, however, the new regime decided to move their operation to the ruins of Samosata because the area was protected from further Persian attention by the buffer of unconquered Edessa, and to ensure that Edessa remained within the Roman orbit. Another mint somewhere else in the east seems to have joined in after a while. Here the manufacture is even worse, and Harold Mattingly's official description of the portraiture of these coins is characteristically eloquent: 'the heads are usually long, on long scraggy necks, and the expression, with large, haggard eye, is gaunt and strange'. As for the reverse designs, they are run-of-the-mill Roman, including types such as Victory and Virtue, and they also feature Eternal Rome. Unlike Postumus, this eastern administration had set its sights on unseating Gallienus and taking over the entire empire.[33]

The Egyptian provincial coinage continued to maintain its quality but there was evidently turmoil in the banking sector. Direct evidence of this comes from an official decree which survives among the Oxyrhynchus papyri. Issued by the district governor and dated to the 28th of Hathyr (25 November) it reads:

> Since the public officials have assembled and accused the bankers of the banks of exchange of having closed them on account of their unwillingness to accept the divine coins of the emperors, it has become necessary that an injunction should be issued to all the owners of the banks to open them, and to accept and exchange all coin except the absolutely spurious and counterfeit, and not only to them, but to all who engage in business transactions of any kind whatever, knowing that if they disobey this injunction they will experience the penalties ordained for them previously by his highness the Prefect. [*Poxy* 1411, AD 260, cited by Burnett 1987, p. 104.]

People were shifting their wealth, a difficult thing for any government to control no matter how punitive they are prepared to be. One can imagine people turning up with sacks full of highly debased and poor quality coins from Syria to change for Egyptian. We do not know if the order had the desired effect, but the very fact that it had to be made shows how serious the economic situation had become.

And at this point, with the year 260 coming to a close, we will end our narrative also. The final chapter will attempt to review the chaos, and assess the long-term impact of the troubled years 248–260 on the Roman Empire and the subsequent course of human history.

Epilogue

Rome Abandons the Gods

The situation as the year 260 drew to a close, as far as can be determined, is illustrated in Map 28, although in reality there were no neat borders anywhere. The long distance imperial communication network had been disrupted and, for all parties, news must have been hard to come by. Postumus was firmly established in Gaul and Raetia, but how quickly the provinces of Britain and Spain declared for him is unclear – it may have taken many months or up to a year. Britain was hopelessly cut off from Rome, and with the island's economy heavily dependent on trade with the continent it was an obvious decision for the administration there to back the breakaway regime. Most of Spain seems to have joined the empire of Postumus for similar reasons except for the south (Baetica) which was more closely tied in to Mediterranean trade and seems to have remained loyal to Gallienus.

Map 28. Approximate situation at the end of 260 according to this narrative. In reality there was much chaos and the stance of many of the provincial administrations is unknown.

Postumus seems to have been content with his dominions, for now at least, and concentrated on internal security. The next few years were to demonstrate that his fragment of the empire was perfectly viable as an independent state, and of course it was far larger and more powerful than any of the Dark Age and Medieval kingdoms that eventually emerged across Europe in the post-Roman period.

There is sufficient doubt about the chronology to be highly uncertain that Regalianus was in power at the end of 260. How far his writ carried is also unknown. The answer is probably not very far as his coins are known only from the region around Carnutum. The recently settled followers of King Attalus of the Marcomanni may have been a significant force in the area but we do not know where their loyalties lay. As for Sponsian, who probably never even existed according to modern coin specialists, his dubious realm is shown on the map to emphasize that whatever the truth of the matter, Roman Dacia had certainly descended into chaos by this time.

As for Macrianus and Quietus, they were in control of Syria and Egypt and possibly much of Asia Minor but a potential thorn in their side was Odaenathus, the Lord of Tadmor, who refused to pay homage. For years, Palmyra had been acting more and more like an independent power, able to defy both Persia and Rome if it chose. By ostensibly remaining loyal to Gallienus, Odaenathus effectively became king of his own dominions.

Gallienus, for his part, still controlled much territory centred on Rome. Paradoxically, it might be argued that he was in a stronger position than before as he was now insulated from the Persians, Goths and the other Germanic tribes by the various rebel regimes. The political situation was obviously highly unstable, however, and his personal prestige was at rock bottom. War against the rebels would go on, and to emphasize that fact he issued a large series of new coins naming the seventeen legions who remained loyal to him. Unfortunately these were made of base metal and poorly manufactured, material witness to the financial crisis that was being experienced by the central administration.[1]

Trade across the Mediterranean continued despite the political collapse. A relic of this is a large hoard of about 40,000 coins that was unearthed in the 1930s near the tip of southern Spain. It includes coins of Gallienus and various of his official predecessors, mixing promiscuously in the pot with those of Postumus, Macrianus and Quietus. All are ostensibly the same denomination – the radiate crowned double-denarius, but the silver content ranges from a respectable fifty per cent to virtually nil and the production quality is equally variable. Perhaps this means that the face value of these coins was still holding up for now, whatever the quality, and irrespective of whether an official or rebel emperor was minting them. Two of the oldest and shiniest coins in the pot feature a goat with the legend SAECVLARES AVGG, as issued on the occasion of the millennium games of 248, a reminder of the old optimism before the chaos began.[2]

The reader will not be surprised to learn that all the principal characters alive in 260 were to meet violent ends. Valerian seems to have lived on in ignominious captivity at Shapur's court for some time, apparently being executed when it became obvious that no ransom was to be forthcoming. Macrianus and his father died in battle while attempting to march on Rome, whereupon Quietus was disposed of by Odaenathus. The Lord of Tadmor himself was later assassinated, but the independent policy he pursued was continued by his famously beautiful widow, the warrior Queen Zenobia. For a time she controlled most of the Roman East, including Syria, Mesopotamia, Egypt, and much of Asia Minor. Postumus and Gallienus lived on in their respective dominions, fighting an inconclusive war, until 268, in which year both were assassinated by regime insiders. Their respective empires continued under new leadership, however. Of the Gothic leader Cniva, victor of Abritus, nothing more is known, unless, as some historians think, he can be identified with an etymologically similar chieftain called 'Cannabas or Cannabaudes' who, according to the *Historia Augusta*, died fighting the Romans in 271. Cniva seems not to have established a dynasty and future kings were allegedly descended from the line of King Ostrogotha via his son, Hunuil.[3]

By the early 270s it must have seemed that the Roman Empire had split irrevocably into three parts, but against the odds it was to be re-united in a string of military campaigns masterminded by the Emperor Aurelian (none other than 'sword-in-hand' Aurelian who supposedly first came to prominence as one of Valerian's generals). By that time, however, Dacia had been deemed indefensible, and what remained of the Roman administration was withdrawn by him to the south side of the Danube. The reconstituted empire increasingly turned to the strategy of 'elastic defence', stationing mobile field armies in reserve, further developing the military reforms pioneered by Decius and Valerian.[4] Mindful of the 'barbarian' threat to Rome in 259–260, Aurelian ordered the construction of a gargantuan defensive perimeter around the metropolis, something that had not been thought necessary for over 500 years. His towering walls and gateways are still hugely impressive today and visible testament to the third century crisis that had rocked the empire and stand as undermined so many of the old certainties.

Looking back from about a hundred years after the peak of the crisis, Aurelius Victor summarized it in the following terms:

Throughout the whole world the mightiest things were mixed with the small, the lowest with the highest, as if by winds violently gusting from all directions. And at the same time the plague was ravaging Rome, which often occurs in times of unbearable anxieties and spiritual despair. [Aurelius Victor, *De Caesaribus* 33.2–4.]

The people had been promised a new Golden Age based on the approval of the gods. What happened instead was a ghastly pandemic and an unprecedented series of military disasters. The plague did eventually recede, but only after many waves of infection and fifteen years of devastation, according to the later chroniclers. That, presumably, was how long it took the empire to achieve herd immunity.[5]

It is telling that Victor's commentary highlights anxiety and spiritual despair because the most enduring consequence of the crisis was to be its effect on the religious life of the empire. In the Roman way of thinking, state and religion were inseparable, so it was inevitable that the virtual collapse of one would be mirrored by the other. The gods were supposed to protect the empire. Decius had ordered every single citizen to sacrifice in a universal show of piety for the good of all. How, then, had he lost his life and most of his army on the field of Abritus? Why had the gods not protected Valerian, who had promised to restore the human race but instead had ended up in miserable captivity? Where was Apollo Salutaris and the other healing deities when the plague spread all across the empire and ripped through provincial farmlands and the tenement blocks of the big cities alike?

The gods had not even protected themselves. 'Barbarian' invaders across the western empire had targeted temples which, for them, were a fabulous source of plunder. Glorious buildings in the civic centres of many cities had gone up in flames– the shrine at Clermont-Ferrand lamented by Gregory of Tours being just one example among many. The images of countless deities had been torn apart for scrap metal. Marble statues had been toppled and broken up. These cult objects harboured the power of the gods themselves and so, in a very real way, the gods themselves had been expunged.

In this context, it is, perhaps, appropriate to mention the jacket design, which features details from a work called *Destruction*, painted in oils by the Anglo-American artist Thomas Cole in 1836, now in the New-York Gallery of Fine Arts. It is part of a cycle of five works called *The Course of Empire* which features the rise and fall of a mythic imperial power (albeit with a strong Roman flavour) from its foundation to ultimate ruin and desolation. It has been argued that the paintings were a veiled critique of American expansionist policy under Andrew Jackson, and a warning of inevitable collapse that is inherent in all imperial pretensions. Such views have, of course, long haunted the western imagination. For our purposes it is worth noting that the plunder and destruction of the temples and religious statues feature prominently in *Destruction*, as does the misery of the people at the hands of invading barbarians.[6]

There was, of course, one group who could explain all this as the wrath of the one true God. Cyprian of Carthage had made this point forcefully during his own lifetime and later writers weighed in heavily along the same lines. Orosius specifically attributed the disasters of the period to the persecutions enacted by Decius and Valerian. 'The blood of the just cried out for vengeance' he said, and it was the Christian God himself who had unleashed the barbarian hordes from all sides. He claimed, possibly with an element of truth, that Gallienus had been so terrified of this judgment of God that after Valerian's capture he lifted the persecution.[7]

Another writer, Lactantius, wrote a wonderfully gory treatise on the fates of the persecutors themselves. Decius, as we have seen, had died at the hands of savage barbarians on the battlefield of Abritus, where 'stripped and naked he lay to be devoured by wild beasts and birds, a fit end for the enemy of God'. And as for Valerian, whom Eusebius had identified with 'The Beast' of the book of Revelation,

> God punished him in a new and extraordinary manner, that it might be a lesson to future ages that the adversaries of heaven always receive the just recompense for their iniquities…He squandered the remainder of his days in the abject form of slavery: for whenever Shapur, the king of the Persians, who had made him prisoner, chose to get in to the carriage or mount on horseback, he commanded the Roman to stoop and present his back… Afterward, when he had finished this shameful life under so great dishonor, he was flayed, and his skin, stripped from the flesh, was died with vermillion, and placed in the temple of the gods of the barbarians. [Lactantius, *De Mortibus Persecutorum* V.][8]

If the persecution edicts were intended to destroy Christianity or drive it underground, then evidently they failed. The religion emerged all the stronger for its ordeal, attracting ever growing numbers of converts. Crowds of people had witnessed harmless and charitable holy men and women pay the ultimate price for their unshakable beliefs. The absolute certainty of these people in times of mounting chaos must have drawn many to re-examine their own beliefs. The authorities had worked tirelessly to paint the Christians as a danger to the state, but people are attracted to dangerous ideas.

Given all this, it was not entirely impossible for a great and powerful emperor at the dawn of the fourth century, Constantine, to simultaneously honour Jesus Christ and the traditional gods of Rome. Signs and portents had led him, also, to fear the power of the Christian God, or so we are told. He ordered Christ's monogram, the chi-rho symbol, to crown his personal military standard and to be embossed upon his battle helmet. His mother Helena, who had been born about the year of Rome's millennium, had at some point in her life been converted to Christianity, and she may have been an influence on Constantine. Perhaps it was Helena who persuaded him to build a great church in Rome for the worship of Jesus Christ – San Giovanni in Laterano, still the official seat of the popes. Christians had hitherto worshipped in private homes, not formal temples, and perhaps because of this Constantine did not adopt the traditional temple style with its external columns and pediments, signalling a major break with the classical past. This new construction was in the style of a magnificent apsidal hall or basilica of the type normally used for civic architecture, and served as a forerunner of the medieval cathedrals.

Constantine issued a formal edict of toleration in 313 CE which established Christianity as an approved religion and it is said he was baptized into the faith on his deathbed in 337. His dynasty thrived for another quarter century, during which time the religion grew massively in strength, wealth and prestige. Of course, the traditional forms of worship did not disappear all at once. The old ways remained strong among the conservative upper classes, but they became unfashionable in the eyes of the imperial court so that ambitious individuals often converted. Eventually, towards the end of the fourth century, the old religions were systematically suppressed by the state.

Without worshippers, a god is nothing. Jupiter Optimus Maximus and all the other traditional gods, once revered by so many for so long and over so huge an area, eventually became totally extinct. They had paid the ultimate price for abandoning Rome in its hour of need.[9]

Literature Cited

Ancient sources

Agathangelos, *History of the Armenians*. Translated by R.W. Thomson, 1976. Extracts republished by Dodgeon and Lieu (1991).

Agathias, *Excursus on Sassanian History*. Translated by A. Cameron in Cameron (1969/1970).

Alexander Lycopolitanus, *contra Manichaei opiniones disputatio*. Translated by van der Horst and Mansfield and reproduced in Dodgeon and Lieu (1991, p. 65).

Ammianus Marcellinus, *History*. Translated by C.D. Yonge. Available online at http://www.tertullian.org/fathers/index.htm#Ammianus_Marcellinus

Anonymous Continuator of Cassius Dio. Translated by N.C. Lieu in Dodgeon and Lieu (1991).

Aurelius Victor, *De Caesaribus*. Translated by H. W. Bird (Liverpool University Press, 1984).

Cassius Dio, *Roman History*. Translated by E. Cary. *Volumes I-IX. Loeb Classical Libraries*. (Harvard University Press, Cambridge Mass., 1914).

Cedrenus, *Georgii Cedreni Historiarum Compendium*. Translated by T.M. Banchich and E.N. Lane; Banchich and Lane (2009).

Chronicon Paschale 284–628 AD. Translated by M. Whitby and M. Whitby (Liverpool University Press, 1989).

Chronography of 354. Available online at http://www.tertullian.org/fathers/index.htm#Chronography_of_354.

Codex Iustinianus. Available online at http://www.leges.uni-koeln.de/en/lex/codex-iustinianus/.

Corpus Inscriptionum Latinarum. Available online at http://cil.bbaw.de/cil_en/index_en.html.

Cyprian, *Epistles*. Translated by A. Roberts, J. Donaldson and A.C. Coxe (1885). Available online at https://www.andrews.edu/~toews/classes/sources/early/Cyprian%20Epistles.htm.

Cyprian, *Treatises*. Translated by R. Wallis (1886). Available online at https://www.newadvent.org/fathers/0507.htm

Dionysius of Alexandria, *Letters and Treatises*. Translated by C.L. Feltoe (1918). Available online at https://www.gutenberg.org/files/36539/36539-h/36539-h.htm.

Epitome De Caesaribus. Translated by T. M. Banchich. Available online at: http://www.roman-emperors.org/epitome.htm

Eunapius, *Vitae Sophistarum*, translated by W. Wright. Available online at http://www.tertullian.org/fathers/eunapius_02_text.htm.

Eusebios of Thessalonica, *Fragments of History*. Reproduced in Dodgeon and Lieu (1991).

Eusebius (Caesariensis), *Historia Ecclesiastica*, volume 2, translated by J.E.L. Outon, Loeb Classical Library (Harvard University Press, 1932). Available online at https://www.newadvent.org/fathers/2501.htm

Eutropius, *Breviarum*. Translated with an introduction and commentary by H. W. Bird. (Liverpool University Press, 1993).

Eutychius, *Annales* (Sa'id ibn Batriq, *Nazm al-Jauhar*). Translated in Dodgeon and Lieu (1991) from the Arabic text in Cheikho et al. (1906–1909). English translation partially available at https://www.roger-pearse.com/weblog/2014/10/31/what-does-eutychius-annals-contain/.

Festus, *Breviarum*. Translated by M.H. Dodgeon in Dodgeon and Lieu (1991, p. 71–72).
Firdawsi, *Shahnameh*. Translated by R. Levy in Levy (1967); reproduced in Dodgeon and Lieu (1991, p, 297–298).
Fredegar, *Chronicle*. Relevant passages cited and discussed by Frei (1969).
George the Monk, *Chronicle*. Translated by T.M. Banchich and E.N. Lane. In Banchich, T.M. and Lane, E.N., *The History of Zonaras* (London / New York, 2009).
Gregory of Neocaesarea ('the Wonderworker'), *Letters*. Translated by Heather and Matthews (1991).
Gregory of Nyssa, *Life of Gregory the Wonderworker*. Translated by M. Slusser in Slusser (1998).
Gregory of Tours, *History of the Franks*. Translated by E. Brehaut. Available online at https://sourcebooks.fordham.edu/basis/gregory-hist.asp#book1.
Herodian, *History of the Empire*. Translated by C. R. Whittaker. Loeb Classical Library. 2 volumes (Harvard, 1967–1969).
Itinerarium Burdigalense. Translated by A. Stewart and C. Wilson. Available online at http://www.christusrex.org/www1/ofm/pilgr/bord/10Bord01Bordeaux.html
Jerome, *Chronicle*. Collaborative translation. Available online at http://www.tertullian.org/fathers/jerome_chronicle_00_eintro.htm
John Chrysostom, *On St Bablas*. Available online at https://www.newadvent.org/fathers/1906.htm
John of Antioch, in Muller, C. *Fragmenta Historicorum Graecorum* (Paris, 1883).
John Lydus, *De Mensibus*. Translated by M. Hooker. Available online at http://penelope.uchicago.edu/Thayer/E/Roman/Texts/Lydus/de_Mensibus/home.html.
Jordanes, *Getica*. Translated by Charles C. Mierow, 1915. Available online with typographical corrections at http://people.ucalgary.ca/~vandersp/Courses/texts/jordgeti.html#gthird. An updated and amended translation by Þeedrich Yeat (undated) is at http://www.harbornet.com/folks/theedrich/Goths/Goths1.htm
Kirder, Inscription at Naqsh-e Rustam. Translated by Boyce (1984) and reproduced in Dodgeon and Lieu (1991).
Lactantius, *De Mortibus Persecutorum*. Translated by W. Fletcher (Fletcher, 1871). Alternative translation vailable online at https://people.ucalgary.ca/~vandersp/Courses/texts/lactant/lactperf.html
Libanius, *Orations*. Translated by A.F. Norman in Norman (1969–1977). Reproduced in Dodgeon and Lieu (1991).
Liber Pontificalis. Translated by L.R. Loomis (Loomis 1916). Available online at https://archive.org/details/bookofpopesliber00loom.
Livius, *Ab Urbe Condita Libri*. The Latin Library. Available online at http://www.thelatinlibrary.com/liv.html.
Lucian of Samosata, *The Syrian Goddess*. Translated by J. Garstang in Garstang (1913).
Malalas, *Chronographia*. Translated by E. Jeffreys, M. Jeffreys and R. Scott. Available online at https://en.calameo.com/books/000675905f2f4bf509d49. Selected texts also translated by N.C. Lieu in Dodgeon and Lieu (1991) and in Janiszewski (2006, p. 97–98).
Maurice, *Strategikon*. Translated by George T. Dennis. (University of Pennsylvania Press, Philadelphia, 1984).
Oracula Sibyllina XIII. Translated by D.S. Potter in Potter (1990).
Orosius, *History Against the Pagans*. Available online at http://attalus.org/info/orosius.html.
Panegyric of Constantius. Translated in Nixon and Rodgers (1994).
Passio SS Mariani et Iacobi. Translated by H.I. Musurillo in Musurillo (1972), 176–193.
Paul, *I Corinthians*. Translation available online at https://biblescripture.net/1Corinthians.html
Peter Patricius, Fragments. Reproduced in Dodgeon and Lieu (1991).

Philostratos of Athens, *Fragments of History*. Translated by E. Jeffreys, M. Jeffreys and R. Scott. Reproduced in Janiszewski (2006, p. 97–98).

Photius, *Bibliotheca*. Available online at http://www.tertullian.org/fathers/photius_03bibliotheca.htm

Polemius Silvius, *Laterculus*. Available online at https://archive.org/details/CalendarOfPhilocalusAndPolemiusSilviusFromIla/page/n9/mode/2up

Pontius, *Life of Cyprian*. Translated by E. Wallis. *The Life and Passion of Cyprian, Bishop and Martyr*. Available online at https://www.ccel.org/ccel/schaff/anf05.iv.iii.html.

Procopius, *De Aedificii*. Translated by H.B. Dewing (1940). Available online at http://penelope.uchicago.edu/Thayer/E/Roman/Texts/Procopius/Buildings/home.html.

Res Gestae Divi Saporis. Greek version translated by N.C. Lieu in Dodgeon and Lieu (1991). Persian version translated by J. Nabel and available online at http://parthiansources.com/texts/skz/skz-translation/.

Scriptores Historiae Augustae (Aelius Lampridius), *Alexander Severus*. Translated by D. Magie in Magie (1924), 179–313.

Scriptores Historiae Augustae (Julius Capitolinus), *Gordiani Tres*. Translated by D. Magie in Magie (1924), 380–447.

Scriptores Historiae Augustae (Julius Capitolinus), *Maximus et Balbinus*. Translated by D. Magie in Magie (1924), 448–485.

Scriptores Historiae Augustae (Trebellius Pollio), *Valeriani Duo*. Translated by D. Magie in Magie (1932), 2–15.

Scriptores Historiae Augustae (Trebellius Pollio), *Gallieni Duo*. Translated by D. Magie in Magie (1932), 17–63.

Scriptores Historiae Augustae (Trebellius Pollio), *Tyranni Triginta*. Translated by D. Magie in Magie (1932), 64–151.

Scriptores Historiae Augustae (Flavius Vopiscus of Syracuse), *Divus Aurelianus*. Translated by D. Magie in Magie (1932), 193–293.

Scriptores Historiae Augustae (Flavius Vopiscus of Syracuse), *Probus*. Translated by D. Magie in Magie (1932), 334–385.

Scriptores Historiae Augustae (Trebellius Pollio), *Divus Claudius*. Translated by D. Magie in Magie (1932), 152–191.

Strabo, *Geography*. Translated by H.C. Hamilton and W. Falconer (London, 1903). Available online at http://www.perseus.tufts.edu/hopper/text?doc=Perseus:text:1999.01.0198.

Suetonius, *The Twelve Caesars*. Translated by R. Graves (Penguin Classics, 2007).

Symeon Logothete, *Chronicle*. Translated by S. Wahlgren (Wahlgren, 2019).

Syncellus, *Chronography*. Translated by W. Adler and P. Tuffin (Oxford, 2002). Other extracts translated by S.N.C. Lieu in Dodgeon and Lieu (1991).

Tacitus, *The Annals of Imperial Rome*. Translated by Michael Grant (Penguin, 2003).

Tacitus, *Germania*. Translated by Lamberto Bozzi. Available online at http://www.crtpesaro.it/Materiali/Latino/De%20Origine%20Et%20Situ%20Germanorum.php.

Vegetius, *Epitome Rei Militaris*. Edited by M.D. Reece (Oxford, 2004).

Vergil, *Georgics*. Available online at http://classics.mit.edu/Virgil/georgics.html.

Widsith, Available online with English translation online at https://www.phil-fak.uni-duesseldorf.de/fileadmin/Redaktion/Institute/Anglistik/Anglistik_I/Downloads/Archiv/SS_06/VL06_Widsith.pdf

Zonaras, *Extracts of History*. In Banchich, T.M. and Lane, E.N., *The History of Zonaras* (London / New York, 2009). Also available online at https://openlibrary.org/books/OL7040945M/Ioannou_tou_Zonara_Epitome_historio.

Zosimus, *New History*. Translated by J. Davis. (Green and Chaplin, London, 1814). Available online at http://www.tertullian.org/fathers/zosimus01_book1.htm.

Modern literature

Adams, C., *Land Transport in Roman Egypt* (Oxford, 2007).
Adkins, L. and Adkins, R.A., *Dictionary of Roman Religion* (Oxford, 1996).
Adler, W. and Tuffin, P., *The Chronography of George Synkellos: a Byzantine Chronicle of Universal History from the Creation* (Oxford, 2002).
Alföldi, A., 'Some notes on late Roman mints' in *The Numismatic Chronicle and Journal of the Royal Numismatic Society Fifth Series*, 4 (1924), 69–75.
Alföldi, A., 'The numbering of the victories of the Emperor Gallienus and the loyalty of his legions' in *The Numismatic Chronicle and Journal of the Royal Numismatic Society*, 9 (1929), 218–279.
Alföldi, A., 'Die Hauptereignisse der Jahre 253–261 n. Chr. im Orient im Spiegel der Münzprägung' in *Berytus*, 4 (1937), 11–68.
Alföldi, A. *Studien zur Geschichte der Weltkrise des dritten Jahrhunderts n. Chr.* (Darmstadt, 1967).
Akerman, J.Y., *A Descriptive Catalogue of Rare and Unedited Roman Coins I* (London, 1834).
Amory, P., *People and Identity in Ostrogothic Italy, 498–554* (Cambridge, 1997).
Ando, C., *Imperial Rome AD 193 to 284* (Edinburgh, 2012).
Andreae, B., 'Zur Komposition des großen Ludovisischen Schlachtsarkophages' in *Festschrift Gottfried von Lücken, Wissenschaftliche Zeitschrift der Universität Rostock 17, 1968*, (Gesellschafts- und Sprachwissenschaftliche Reihe, Heft 7/8) (1968), 633–640.
Andrein, (2015) https://commons.wikimedia.org/wiki/File:Danube_Delta_evolution.gif.
Aparaschivei, D., 'Physicians and medicine in the Roman army of Moesia Inferior' in *Dacis* N.S., 61 (2012), 99–118.
Aylward, W. (ed.), *Excavations at Zeugma, Conducted by Oxford Archaeology*. 3 volumes (Los Altos, 2013).
Babcock, C.L., 'An Inscription of Trajan Decius from Cosa' in *The American Journal of Philology*, 83 (1962), 147–158.
Babelon, E., 'Sapor et Valérien, camée sassanide de la Bibliothèque Nationale' in *Monuments et mémoires de la Fondation Eugène Piot*, 1 (1894), 85.
Baird, J.A., *Dura-Europos* (London, 2018).
Bakker, L., 'Raetien unter Postumus. Das Siegesdenkmal einer Juthungenschlacht im Jahre 260 n. Chr. aus Augsburg' in *Germania*, 71 (1993), 369–386.
Baldus, H.R., 'Uranius Antoninus of Emesa: a Roman Emperor from Palmyra's Neighbouring-city and his coinage' in Gawlikowski, M (ed.), Palmyra and the Silk Road. *Les annales archéologiques arabes syriennes. Revue d'archéologie et d'histoire*, 42 (Damascus, 1997), 371–377.
Baldwin, B., 'Eusebius and the siege of Thessalonica' in *Rheinisches Museum fur Philologie*, 124 (1981), 291–296.
Ball, W., *Rome in the East: the Transformation of an Empire* (London / New York, 2000).
Baltzly, D., 'Stoicism' in *The Stanford Encyclopedia of Philosophy* (2019 Edition), https://plato.stanford.edu/archives/spr2019/entries/stoicism/
Banchich, T.M., 'Mareades/Mariades/Mariadnes/Cyriades (252 or 253 or 256 or 259 A.D.)' in *De Imperatoribus Romanis*. Available online at https://www.roman-emperors.org/mareades.htm (2002a).
Banchich, T.M., 'Marcus Aemilius Aemilianus' in *De Imperatoribus Romanis*. Available online at http://www.roman-emperors.org/aemaem.htm (2002b).
Banchich, T.M. and Lane, E.N., *The History of Zonaras* (London / New York, 2009).
Barnes, T.D., 'The Persian sack of Antioch in 253' in *Zeitschrift für Papyrologie und Epigraphik*, 169 (2009), pp. 294–296.
Bellamare, P.M., 'Meteorite sparks a cult' in *Journal of the Royal Astronomical Society of Canada*, 90 (1996), 287–291.

Bellinger, A.R., 'The numismatic evidence from Dura' in *Berytus*, 8 (1943–4), 64–71.
Beskow, P. 'Branding in the mysteries of Mithras?' in Bianchi, U. (ed.) *Mysteria Mithrae* (Leiden, 1978), 487–501.
Besly, E., 'The gold coinage of the Gallic Empire' in *The Numismatic Chronicle*, 144 (1984), 228–233.
Besly, E. and Bland, R., *The Cunetio Treasure. Roman Coinage in the Third Century AD* (London, 1983).
Bird, H.W., *Eutropius: Breviarium. Translated with an introduction and commentary by H. W. Bird* (Liverpool University Press, 1992).
Bird, H.W., *Aurelius Victor: De Caesaribus. Translated with an introduction and commentary by H. W. Bird* (Liverpool University Press, 1994).
Birley, A.R., 'The Roman governors of Britain' in *Epigraphische Studien*, 4 (1967), 63–102.
Birley, A.R., 'Mapping a Minefield – Michael Peachin: Roman Imperial Titulature and Chronology, A.D. 235–284. (Studia Amstelodamensia ad Epigraphicam, Ius Antiquum et Papyrologicam Pertinentia, 29.) Pp. xxviii + 515. Amsterdam: J. C. Gieben, 1990. fl. 260.' in *The Classical Review* 41 (1991a), 410–411.
Birley, A.R., 'A persecuting praeses of Numidia under Valerian' in *The Journal of Theological Studies*, 42 (1991b), 598–610.
Bland, R., 'The coinage of Jotapian' in M. Price, A. Burnett, R. Bland (eds.), *Essays in Honour of Robert Carson and Kenneth Jenkins* (London, 1993).
Bland, R. F., 'The development of gold and silver coin denominations, A.D. 193–253' in C. E. King and D. G. Wigg (eds.), *Coin Finds and Coin Use in the Roman World* (Gebr Mann, 1996), 63–100.
Bland, R., 'From Gordian III to the Gallic Empire (AD 238–274)' in W. E. Metcalf (ed.), *The Oxford Handbook of Greek and Roman Coinage* (Oxford, 2012), 514–537.
Bland, R., 'What happened to gold coinage in the 3rd c. A.D.?' in *Journal of Roman Archaeology*, 26 (2013), 263–280.
Bland, R., 'The gold coinage of Philip I and family' in *Revue Numismatique*, 171 (2014), 93–149.
Bland, R., and Burnett, A., *The Normanby Hoard and Other Roman Coin Hoards* (Trustees of the British Museum, 1988), 43–73.
Blockley, R.C., 'Was the first book of Zosimus' New History based on more than two sources?' in *Byzantion*, 50 (1980), 393–402.
Boschi, E., et al., 'Resonance of subsurface sediments: an unforeseen complication for designers of Roman columns' in *Bulletin of the Seismological Society of America*, 85 (1995), 320–324.
Boteva, D., 'On the chronology of the Gothic invasions under Philippus and Decius (A.D. 248–251)' in *Archaeologica Bulgarica*, 5 (2001), 37–44.
Boteva, D., 'Some considerations related to the *Scythica Vindobonensia*' in Mitthof, F., Martin, G. and Grusková, J., *Empire in Crisis: Gothic Invasions and Roman Historiography*, Tyche Supplement 12 (Vienna, 2020), p. 195–212.
Boyce, M., *Zoroastrianism: Textual Sources for the Study of Religion* (Manchester, 1984).
Bradley, H., *The Goths From the Earliest Times to the End of the Gothic Dominion in Spain* (London, 1888).
Bray, J., *Gallienus: A Study in Reformist and Sexual Politics* (Kent Town, 1997).
Breeze, D., 'Plague on Hadrian's Wall? Interpreting evidence for pandemics in Roman Britain' in *Current Archaeology* 365 (2020), 28–35.
Brent, A., *Cyprian and Roman Carthage* (Cambridge, 2010).
Brodersen, K., '*in modum fulminis*: Cniva und Ostrogotha bei Jordanes und in den *Scythica Vindobonensis*' in Mitthof, F., Martin, G. and Grusková, J., *Empire in Crisis: Gothic Invasions and Roman Historiography*, Tyche Supplement 12 (Vienna, 2020), p. 147–157.

Burns, J.P., *Cyprian the Bishop* (London / New York, 2002).
Bursche, A., *Złote medaliony rzymskie w Barbaricum* Światowit Supplement Series A: Antiquity, II (Warsaw, 1998).
Bursche, A., 'The battle of Abritus, the Imperial treasury and aurei in Barbaricum' in *Numismatic Chronicle*, 173 (2013), 151–171.
Bursche, A. And Myzkin, K., 'The Gothic invasions of the mid-3rd c A.D. and the Battle of Abritus: coins and archaeology in east-central Barbaricum' in *Journal of Roman Archaeology*, 33 (2020), 195–229.
Butcher, K., 'Coins and Hoards' in Aylward, W. (ed.) *Excavations at Zeugma, Conducted by Oxford Archaeology* (Los Altos, 2013), 1–92.
Cameron, A., 'Agathias on the Sassanians' in *Dumbarton Oaks Papers*, 23/24 (1969/1970), 67–183.
Campbell, I., 'A Sponsian re-discovered' in *The Numismatic Chronicle*, 157 (1997), p. 194–196.
Carrié, J.-P. And Moreau, D., 'The archaeology of the Roman town of Abritus: the *status quaestionis* in 2012' in Limes XII, *Proceedings of the 22nd International Congress of Roman Frontier Studies, Ruse, Bulgaria, September, 2012* (2012), 601–610.
Carson, R.A.G., 'The Hama hoard and the eastern mints of Valerian and Gallienus' in *Berytus*, 17 (1967–8), 123–142.
Casey, P.J., *Understanding Ancient Coins* (London, 1986).
Castritius, H., 'Ostrogotha' in *Reallexikon der Germanischen Altertumskunde*, 22 (2003), 349–350.
Chaumont, M.L., *Recherches sur L'histoire d'Armenie* (Paris, 1969).
Cheikho, L., Carra de Vaux, B., and Zayyat, H., *Eutychii Patriarchae Alexandrini Annales*, Corpus Scriptorum Christianorum Orientalium 50–51 (Scriptores Arabici ser. 3 nos. 6–7), 2 vols (Paris, 1906–9).
Christensen, A.S., Cassiodorus, Jordanes and the History of the Goths: Studies in Migration Myth (Copenhagen, 2002).
Christol, M., *L'Empire Romain du IIIs Siècle: Histoire Politique 192–325 aprés J.-C.* (Paris, 1997).
Christol, M., 'L'eclogue de l'empereur Gallien, défenseur et protecteur de l'empire' in Quet, M.-H. (ed.) *La "crise" de l'Empire Romain de Marc Aurèle à Constantin: Mutations, Continuetès, Ruptures* (Paris, 2006), 107–131.
Christol, M., 'Autour des travaux d'Hercule : Postume et Gallien' in *Revue Numismatique, 6e série, 171* (2014), 179–193.
Claes, L., 'Coins with power? Imperial and local messages on the coinage of the usurpers of the second half of the third century (AD 253–285)' in *Jaarboek voor Munt- en Penningkunde*, 102 (2015), 15–60.
Claytor, W.G., 'A Decian *Libellus* at Luther College (Iowa)' in *Tyche*, 30 (2015), 13–18.
Cohen, H. *Description Historique des Medailles Impériales* (Paris, 1860).
Cohen, H., *Description Historique des Medailles Impériales*. Second edition (Paris, 1893).
Crawford, M., 'Finance, coinage and money from Severus to Constantine' in *Aufstieg und Niedergang der Romischen Welt*, 2 (1975), 560–593.
Croke, B., 'Cassiodorus and the Getica of Jordanes' in *Classical Philology*, 82 (1987), 117–134.
Czysz, W., 'Brunnensturz und Bildersturm. Ikonoklastische Zerstörungen des 3. nachchristlichen Jahrhunderts im raetischen Limeshinterland' in E. Walde (Ed.), *Bildmagie und Brunnensturz. Visuelle Kommunikation von der klassischen Antike bis zur aktuellen medialen Kriegsberichterstattung* (Innsbruck / Wien / Bozen, 2009), 580–614.
Dando-Collins, S., *The Legions of Rome: The Definitive History of Every Imperial Roman Legion* (London, 2010).
Darley, R., and Canepa, M., 'Coinage, Persian' in Nicholson, O. (Ed.) *The Oxford Dictionary of Late Antiquity* (Oxford, 2018).

Davenport, C. and Mallan, C., 'Dexippus' "Letter of Decius": context and interpretation' in *Museum Helveticum*, 70 (2013), 57–73.

Davenport, C., 'Carausius and His Brothers: the construction and deconstruction of an imperial image in the late Third Century AD' in *Antichthon*, 53 (2019), 108–133.

Davies, R.W., 'M. Aurelius Atho Marcellus' in *The Journal of Roman Studies*, 57 (1967), 20–22.

De Blois, L., 'Odaenathus and the Roman-Persian war of 252–264 A.D.' in *Talanta*, 6 (1975), 7–23.

De Blois, L., *The Policy of the Emperor Gallienus* (Leiden, 1976).

De Blois, L., 'The reign of the emperor Philip the Arabian' in *Talanta*, 10–11 (1978–1979), 11–43.

De Blois, L., 'The Εἰς Βασιλέα of Ps.-Aelius Aristides' in *Greek, Roman and Byzantine Studies*, (1986), 279–288.

De Blois, L., *Image and Reality of Roman Imperial Power in the Third Century AD* (London / New York, 2019).

De Gregorio, G., Gamillscheg, E., Gruskova, J., Kresten, O., Martin, G., Mondrain, B., and Wilson, N., 'Paleographical and codicological remarks on the Vienna Dexippus palimpsest' in Mitthof, F., Martin, G. and Grusková, J., *Empire in Crisis: Gothic Invasions and Roman Historiography*, *Tyche* Supplement 12 (Vienna, 2020), p. 5–16.

De la Bédoyère, G., *Defying Rome: The Rebels of Roman Britain* (Stroud, 2003).

Demougeot, E., 'Les martyrs imputés à Chrocus et les invasions alamanniques en Gaule méridionale' in *Annales du Midi: Revue Archéologique, Historique et Philologique de la France Méridionale* 74, (1962), pp. 5–28.

Dennis, G.T., *Maurice, Strategikon* (Philadelphia, 1984).

Depeyrot, G., *La Propagande Monétaire (64–235) et le trésor de Marcianopolis (251)* (Wetteren, 2004).

Detschew, D., *Die Thrakischen Sprachreste*, 2 (Wien, 1976).

Dietz, K., *Senatus contra principem: Untersuchungen zur senatorischen Opposition gegen Kaiser Maximinus Thrax* (C. H. Beck'sche Verlagbuchhandlung, 1980).

Dijkstra, J.H.F., 'Blemmyes, Noubades and the Eastern Desert in late antiquity: Reassessing the written sources' in Barnard, H. and Duistermaat, K. (eds.) *The History of the Peoples of the Eastern Desert* (Los Angeles, 2012), 239–247.

Dikov, I., 'Archaeologists discover Roman era ritual pit inventories in Bulgaria's largest Ancient Thracian burial mound 'Maltepe" archaeologyinbulgaria.com/2016/10/20 (2016a).

Dikov, I., 'Archaeologists identify battlefield of 251 AD Roman-Goth battle of Abritus near Bulgaria's Dryanovets' archaeologyinbulgaria.com/2016/09/15 (2016b).

Dikov, I., 'Latest finds from Nebet Tepe fortress in Bulgaria's Plovdiv' archaeologyinbulgaria.com/2018/03/26 (2018a).

Dikov, I., 'Archaeologists discover "monumental" Roman era tomb of Thracian aristocrat in Bulgaria's largest burial mound', archaeologyinbulgaria.com/2018/07/26 (2018b).

Dikov, I., 'Bulgaria's largest Thracian mound proves to be tower tomb like in Petra, Palmyra, likely of Roman emperor Philip I the Arab', archaeologyinbulgaria.com/2019/01/16 (2019).

Dmitriev, S., '"Good emperors" and emperors of the third century' in *Hermes*, (2004), 211–224.

Dodgeon, M.H., and Lieu, S.N.C., *The Roman Eastern Frontier and the Persian Wars AD 226–363* (London / New York, 1991).

Doležal, S., 'Who was Jordanes?' in *Byzantion*, 84 (2014), 145–164.

Dordea, N.S., 'Head of wolf – standard of the Dacian warriors on the Roman coins' in *Istorie si Numismatica* online, https://istoriesinumismatica.wordpress.com/tag/the-sign-of-dacia/ (2016; accessed 06.06.2017).

D'Ossat, M.D.A., '"E Opera Stupenda": Notizie intorno al ritrovamento del Sarcofago Grande Ludovisi' in *Jahrbuch des Römisch-Germanischen Zentralmuseums*, 55 (2008), 577–592.

Drinkwater, J.F., *The Gallic Empire: Separatism and Continuity in the North-Western Provinces of the Roman Empire, A.D. 260–274* (Stuttgart, 1987).

Drinkwater, J.F., 'The Goths without the Getica' (Review of Heather, P., *Goths and Romans 332–349*; Oxford, 1991) in *The Classical Review*, 43 (1993), p. 118–120.

Du Mesnil du Boisson, R., 'Un guerre de mines en 256 apres J.-C.: Le siège de Doura-Europos d'après les fouilles récentes' in *Revue de Genie Militaire*, 76 (1937), 5–27.

Duch, M., *Economic role of the Roman army in the province of Lower Moesia (Moesia Inferior)* (Gneizo, 2017).

Dufraigne, P., *Aurelius Victor: Livre des Cesars* (Paris, 1975).

Dussubieux, L., and Van Zelst., L., 'LA-ICP-MS analysis of platinum-group elements and other elements of interest in ancient gold' in *Applied Physics A: Materials Science and Engineering*, 79 (2004), 353–356.

Eck, W., 'Prosopographische Bemerkungen zum Militärdiplom vom 20. 12. 202 n. Chr. Der Flottenpräfekt Aemilius Sullectinus und das Gentilnomen des Usurpators Regalianus' in *Zeitschrift für Papyrologie und Epigraphik*, 139 (2002), 208–210.

Eckardt, H., *Writing and Power in the Roman World: Literacies and Material Culture* (Cambridge, 2018).

Eckhel, J., *Catalogus Musei Caesarei Vindoboniensis Numorum Veterum* (1797, Vienna).

Eddy, S.K., 'The minting of anotoniniani A.D. 238–249 and the Smyrna Hoard' in *Numismatic Notes and Monographs*, 156 (1967), 1–133.

Edwell, P.M. *Between Rome and Persia: The Middle Euphrates, Mesopotamia and Palmyra under Roman Control* (Abingdon, 2008).

Ehrman, B.D., *Lost Christianities: The Battles for Scripture and the Faiths We Never Knew* (Oxford, 2003).

Ehrman, B.D., *How Jesus Became God* (San Francisco, 2014).

Elks, K.J.J., 'The eastern mints of Valerian and Gallienus: the evidence of two hoards from Western Turkey' in *The Numismatic Chronicle, Seventh Series*, 15 (1975), 91–109.

Elton, H., 'Zeugma's Military History in Light of the Rescue Excavations' in Aylward, W. (ed.) *Excavations at Zeugma, Conducted by Oxford Archaeology* (Los Altos, 2013), 375–380.

Ensslin, W., *Zu den Kriegen der Sassaniden Schapur I* (Munich, 1949).

Erich, A., *Gulichische Chronic* (Leipzig, 1611).

Estiot, S., 'L'empereur Silbannacus, un second antoninien' in *Revue Numismatique*, 151 (1996), 105–117.

Fah, D., et al. [9 authors], 'The earthquake of 250 A.D. in Augusta Raurica, a real event with a 3-D site effect?' in *Journal of Seismology* (2006) 10, 459–477.

Farrokh, K., *Shadows in the Desert: Ancient Persia at War* (Oxford, 2007).

Farrokh, K., *The Armies of Ancient Persia: The Sassanians* (Barnsley, 2017).

Faust, S., 'War in art, Roman' in Bagnall, S., Brodersen, K., and Champion, C.B. (eds.) *The Encyclopedia of Ancient History* (2017), 5 pp.

Felletti Maj, B. M., *Iconografia Romana Imperiale da Severo Alessandro a M. Aurelio Carino (222–285 d.C)* (Rome, 1958).

Feltoe, C.L., St. Dionysius of Alexandria: Letters and Treatises (London / New York, 1918).

Fitz, J., *Ingenuus et Régalien* (Brussels, 1966).

Fletcher, W., *The Works of Lactantius. Translated by William Fletcher, D.D., Vol II.* (Edinburgh, 1871).

Forsythe, G., *A Critical History of Early Rome: from Prehistory to the First Punic War* (University of California Press, 2005).

Frakes, J.C., Untitled review of *The Myth of Nations: The Medieval Origins of Europe* by P.J. Geary (Princeton, 2002) in *Journal of English and Germanic Philology*, 102 (2003), 592–596.

Franke, T., 'Hostilianus' in Cancik, H. and Schneider, H. (eds) *Brill's New Pauly*, English Edition by: Christine F. Salazar (2006). Consulted online on 27 April 2020 <http://dx.doi.org/10.1163/1574-9347_bnp_e518100>

Freeman, C., *A New History of Early Christianity* (New Haven, 2009).

Frei, P., 'Das romische Aventicum bei Fredegar' in *Museum Helveticum*, 26 (1969), 101–112.

Frier, B.W., 'More is worse: some observations on the population of the Roman Empire' in Schiedel, W. (ed.) *Debating Roman Demography* (Leiden, 2001), 139–59.

Fulminante, F., *The Urbanisation of Rome and Latium Vetus: from the Bronze Age to the Archaic era* (Cambridge, 2014).

Gallwey, H.D., 'A hoard of third-century antoniniani from southern Spain' in *The Numismatic Chronicle and Journal of the Royal Numismatic Society, Seventh Series*, 2 (1962), 335–406.

Garstang, J., *The Syrian Goddess; Being a Translation of Lucian's De Dea Syria, with a life of Lucian by Herbert A. Strong* (London, 1913).

Găzdac, C, and Alföldy- Găzdac, A., 'When the province takes care of its coin supply. The case of the town of Drobeta in Roman Dacia', in *Journal of Ancient History and Archeology*, 2 (2015), 26–28.

Găzdac, C., and Melchart, W. 'News on Regalianus and Dryantilla coins. A new coin of Dryantilla and correcting information on two more known coins' in *Journal of Ancient History and Archaeology*, 5 (2018), 37–40.

Geiger, M., *Gallienus* (Frankfurt-am-Main, 2015).

Genèvrier, M.-L., 'Le culte d'Hercule *Magusanus* en Germanie Inférieure' in *Annales littéraires de l'Université de Besançon*, 329 (1986), 371–378.

Gengler, O., 'Eine neue Datierung des Goteneinfalls gegen Griechenland unter Valerianus und Gallienus' in Mitthof, F., Martin, G. and Grusková, J., *Empire in Crisis: Gothic Invasions and Roman Historiography*, Tyche Supplement 12 (Vienna, 2020), p. 219–234.

Gensini, G.F., Yacoub, M.H., and Conti, A.A., 'The concept of quarantine in history: from plague to SARS' in *Journal of Infection*, 49 (2004), 257–261.

Gerov, B., 'Die gotische Invasion in Mösien und Thrakien unter Decius im Lichte der Hortfunde' in *Acta Antiqua Philippopolitana* II (1963), 127–146 .

Gerov, B., 'Die Einfälle der Nordvölker in den Ostbalkanraum im Lichte der Münzschatzfunde, I: Das II. und III. Jahrhundert (101–284)' in *Aufstieg und Niedergang der römischen Welt*, 6 (1977), 110–181.

Gibbon, E., *The Decline and Fall of the Roman Empire* (6 volumes; first published 1776–1784; reprinted by Everyman's Library, 1993).

Gilliam, J. F., 'The *Dux Ripae* at Dura' in *Transactions and Proceedings of the American Philological Association*, 72 (1941), 157–175.

Gilliam, J.F., 'Trebonianus Gallus and the Decii: III ET I COS,' in *Studi in Onore Di Aristide Calderini E Roberto Paribeni* (Milan, 1956), 305–311.

Gnoli, T., 'From *Praepositus praetenturae* to *Dux Ripae*. The Roman "Grand Strategy" on the Middle Euphrates (2nd-3rd Cent. AD)', in *The Late Roman Army in the Near East from Diocletian to the Arab Conquest. Proceedings of a Colloquium held at Potenza, Acerenza and Matera, Italy (May 2005), Lewin, A.S. (ed.)* (Pellegrini, 2007), 49–55.

Gobl, R., *Die Munzpragung des Kaiser Valerianus I, Gallienus, Saloninus (253–368), Regalianus (260), und Macrianus, Quietus (260–262)* (Vienna, 2000)

Goldsworthy, A., *How Rome Fell* (New Haven / London, 2009).

Goodman, M., *Rome and Jerusalem: the Clash of Ancient Civilizations* (New York, 2007).

Goosen, D., *A New Model for Level Areas* (Delft, 1974).

Grandazzi, A., *The Foundation of Rome: Myth and History* (Cornell, 1997).

Grierson, P., 'Election and inheritance in early Germanic kingship' in *The Cambridge Historical Journal*, 7 (1941), 1–22.

Grillone, A., *Iordanes, Getica. Edizione, traduzione e commento, a cura di A. Grillone* (Paris, 2017).
Grozdanova, L., 'Emperor Trajan Decius and his sons on the lower-Danubian Limes (AD 249–251)' in *Limes XII, Proceedings of the 22nd International Congress of Roman Frontier Studies, Ruse, Bulgaria, September, 2012* (2012).
Grozdanova, L., 'What about Herennius Etruscus?' in Mitthof, F., Martin, G. and Grusková, J., *Empire in Crisis: Gothic Invasions and Roman Historiography*, Tyche Supplement 12 (Vienna, 2020), p. 234–243.
Grusková, J., *Untersuchungen zu den griechischen Palimpsesten der Österreichischen Nationalbibliothek. Codices historici, Codices philosophici et philologici, Codices iuridici* (Wien, 2010).
Grusková, J., 2012. 'Further steps in revealing, editing and analyzing important ancient Greek and Byzantine texts hidden in palimpsests.' Zborník Filozofickej Fakulty University Komenskéko Ročník XXXIII-XXXIV Graecolatina et Orientalia. (Bratislava, 2012), 69–82.
Grusková, J. and Martin, G., 'Zum Angriff der Goten unter Kniva auf eine thrakische Stadt (Scythica Vindobonensia, f. 195v)' in *Tyche*, 30, 35–54 (2015).
Grysa, B., 'The legend of the seven sleepers of Ephesus in Syriac and Arab sources – a comparative study' in *Orientalia Christiana Cracoviensia*, 2 (2010), 45–59.
Gudea, N., 'The defensive system of Roman Dacia' in *Britannia*, 10 (1979), 63–87.
Gullini, G., *Maestri e botteghe in Roma da Gallieno alla Tetrarchia* (Torino, 1960).
Gustafson, M., 'Condemnation to the mines in the later Roman Empire' in *The Harvard Theological Review*, 87 (1994), 421–433.
Haegemans, K., *Imperial Authority and Dissent: The Roman Empire in AD 235–238*. Studia Hellenistica, No. 47 (Petters, 2010).
Haldon, J., and others, 'Plagues, climate change, and the end of an empire: A response to Kyle Harper's *The Fate of Rome* (1): Climate' in *History Compass* (2018a), doi: doi.org/10.1111/hic3.12508.
Haldon, J., and others, 'Plagues, climate change, and the end of an empire: A response to Kyle Harper's *The Fate of Rome* (2): Plagues and a crisis of empire' in *History Compass* (2018b), doi: doi.org/10.1111/hic3.12506.
Halsall, G., *Barbarian Migrations and the Roman West (376–569)* (Cambridge, 2007).
Halsberghe, G.H., *The Cult of Sol Invictus* (Leiden, 1972).
Harper, K., 'Pandemics and passages to late antiquity: rethinking the plague of c.249–270 described by Cyprian' in *Journal of Roman Archaeology*, 28 (2015), 223–260.
Harper, K., 'Another Eye-witness to the Plague Described by Cyprian and Notes on the "Persecution of Decius"' in *Journal of Roman Archaeology*, 29 (2016), 473–476.
Harper, K., *The Fate of Rome: Climate, Disease, & the End of the Empire* (Princeton, 2017).
Hartmann, F., *Herrscherwechsel und Reichskrise. Untersuchungen zu den Ursachen und Konsequenzen der Herrscherwechsel im Impérium Romanum der Soldatenkaiserzeit (3. Jahrhundert II. Chr.)* (Frankfurt / Berne, 1982).
Hasluck, F.W., 'A Roman Bridge on the Aesepus' in *The Annual of the British School at Athens*, 12 (1905/1906), 184–189.
Heather, P., 'Cassiodorus and the Rise of the Amals: Genealogy and the Goths under Hun Domination' in *The Journal of Roman Studies*, 79 (1989), 103–128.
Heather, P., *Goths and Romans 332–489* (Oxford, 1991).
Heather, P., *The Goths* (Oxford, 1996).
Heather, P., *The Fall of the Roman Empire: A New History* (London, 2006).
Heather, P., and Matthews, J., *The Goths in the Fourth Century* (Liverpool, 1991).
Heeren, S., 'The Theory of "Limesfall" and the material culture of the Late 3rd century' in *Germania*, 94 (2016), 185–209.

von Heintze, H., 'Studien zu den Porträts des 3. Jahrhunderts n. Chr. 4. Der Feldherr des grossen ludovisischen Schlachtsarkophages' in *Römische Mitteilungen*, 64 (1957).
Hekster, O., *Rome and its Empire 193–284* (Edinburgh, 2008).
Hellings, B., and Spoerri Butcher, M., 'Quantifying relative coin production during the reigns of Nerva and Trajan (AD 96–117): Reka Devnia reconsidered in the light of regional coin finds from Romania and the Northwest' in *Revue Belge de Numismatique*, 68 (2016), 53–86.
Hill, P.V., 'The temples and statues of Apollo in Rome' in *The Numismatic Chronicle and Journal of the Royal Numismatic Society Seventh Series*, 2 (1962), 125–142.
Hinchliff, P., *Cyprian of Carthage and the Unity of the Christian Church* (London, 1974).
Hirt, A.M., *Imperial Mines and Quarries in the Roman World* (Oxford, 2010).
Hodges, R., ' Zeugma's Last Secret' in *World Archaeology* 100 (2020), 42–49.
Holloway, R.R., *Constantine and Rome* (New Haven / London, 2004).
Hose, M., 'Historiographie in der Krise: Herausforderungen und Lösungen der Geschichtsschreibung im dritten Jahrhundert n. Chr.' in Mitthof, F., Martin, G. and Grusková, J., *Empire in Crisis: Gothic Invasions and Roman Historiography*, *Tyche* Supplement 12 (Vienna, 2020), p. 35–29.
Hostein, A., 'Note sur les dariques de Cniva (Dexippus Vindobonensis) et autre curiosites "barbare" ' in *Revue Numismatique*, 174 (2017), 37–64.
Hunger, H., *Katalog der griechischen Handschriften der Österreichischen Nationalbibliothek*, Band I: *Codices historici, Codices philosophici et philologici* (Museion N. F. IV/1, 1) (Wien, 1961).
Intagliata, E.E., Barker, S.J., and Courault, C., *City Walls in Late Antiquity: an Empire-Wide Perspective* (Oxford, 2020).
Ionita, M., Badulata, C.-A., Scholz, P., and Chelcea, S., 'Vanishing river ice cover in the lower part of the Danube basin – signs of a changing climate' in *Scientific Reports*, 8 (2018), 7498.
Jacoby, F., *Die Fragmente der griechischen Historiker (1958)*; available with English translation online via *Brill's New Jacoby* at https://referenceworks.brillonline.com/browse/brill-s-new-jacoby
James, S., 'Stratagems, combat, and "chemical warfare" in the siege mines of Dura-Europos' in *American Journal of Archaeology*, 115 (2011), 69–101.
James, S., *The Roman Military Base at Dura-Europos, Syria: an Archaeological Visualization* (Oxford, 2019).
Janiszewski, P., *The Missing Link: Greek Historiography in the Second Half of the Third Century and in the Fourth Century AD* (Warsaw, 2006).
Jarus, O., 'Remains of 'End of the World' Epidemic Found in Ancient Egypt' https://www.livescience.com/46335-remains-of-ancient-egypt-epidemic-found.html (2014).
Jehne, M., 'Überlegungen zur Chronologie der Jahre 259 bis 261 n. Chr. im Lichte der neuen Postumus-Inschrift aus Augsburg' in *Bayerische Vorgeschichtsblätter*, 61 (1996), 185–206.
Johnson, M.J., 'The "Sepulchrum Gordiani" at Zaitha and its significance' in *Latomus*, 54 (1995), 141–144.
Jones, C.P., 'Aelius Aristides, ΕΙΣ ΒΑΣΙΛΕΑ' in *Journal of Roman Studies*, 62 (2014), 134–152.
Jones, C.P., 'The New Dexippos'. Unpublished posting, *academia.edu* (2014).
Jones, C.P., 'Further Fragments of Dexippus'. Unpublished posting, *academia.edu* (04/12/2015) (2015).
Jones, C.P., 'Further Fragments of Dexippus (2)'. Unpublished posting, *academia.edu* (date uncertain).
Jones, C.P., 'Dexippus and the third-century plague' in Mitthof, F., Martin, G. and Grusková, J., *Empire in Crisis: Gothic Invasions and Roman Historiography*, *Tyche* Supplement 12 (Vienna, 2020), p. 159–164.
Jovanova, L., Veljanovska, F., Graorkovska, M., and Stankov, A., *A Glance into the Dark Side of the Roman History: Scupi – a Mass Grave* (Museum of the City of Skopje Exhibition Catalogue; Skopje, 2017).

Kacharava, D.D., 'Archaeological investigations on the Eastern Black Sea littoral, 1970–1980' in *Archaeological Reports* 30 (1983–1984), 98–101.
Kalmin, R., *Jewish Babylonia Between Persia and Roman Palestine* (Oxford, 2006).
Kebric, R.B., 'The Portonaccio Sarcophagus' Roman cavalry charge: new insights (and a postscript of the film Gladiator's clash with the Germans)' in *Athens Journal of History*, 1, (2015) 175–194
Kennedy, D.L., 'Ana on the Euphrates in the Roman Period' in *Iraq*, 48 (1986), 103–104.
Keresztes, P., 'Two edicts of the Emperor Valerian' in *Vigiliae Christianae*, 29 (1975), 81–95.
Kettenhofen, E., *Die römisch-persischen Kriege des 3. Jahhunderts n.Chr. nach der Inschrift Sāhpuhrs I. an der Ka'be-ye Zartost (SKZ)* (Wiesbaden, 1982).
Knapp, R., *The Dawn of Christianity: People and Gods in a Time of Magic and Miracles* (London, 2017).
Knipfing, J.R., 'The Libelli of the Decian persecution' in *Harvard Theological Review*, 16 (1923), 345–390.
König, I., 'Die Postumus-Inschrift aus Augsburg' in *Historia: Zeitschrift für Alte Geschichte*, 46 (1997), 341–354.
Körner, C., 'Rebellions During the reign of Phillip the Arab (244–249 A.D.): Iotapianus, Pacatianus, Silbannacus, and Sponsianus' in *De Imperatoribus Romanis*, http://roman-emperors.sites.luc.edu/philarab.htm (1999).
Körner, C., *Philippus Arabs, ein Soldatenkaiser in der Tradition des antoninisch-severischen Prinzipats* (Berlin / New York, 2002).
Kovács, P., 'Einige Bemerkungen zum Todesdatum von Decius (Aép 2003, 1415)' in *Acta Archaeologica Academiae Scientiarum Hungaricae*, 66 (2015) 305–314.
Kuelzer, A., 'The Byzantine Road system in Eastern Thrace: Some Remarks' in Bakirtzis, C., Zekos, N., and Moniaros, X. (eds) 4th International Symposium on Thracian Studies: Byzantine Thrace, Evidence and Remains, Komotini, 18–22 April 2007 Proceedings (Amsterdam, 2011), 179–801.
Kulikowski, M., *Rome's Gothic Wars* (New York, 2007).
Kulikowski, M., *Imperial Triumph: The Roman World from Hadrian to Constantine* (London, 2016).
Kuttner, A.L., *Dynasty and Empire in the Age of Augustus* (Los Angeles / Oxford, 1995).
La Follette, L., 'A contribution of Andrea Palladio to the study of Roman Thermae' in *Journal of the Society of Architectural Historians*, 52, 189–198 (1993).
Lancaster, L., 'Building Trajan's column' in *American Journal of Archaeology*, 103 (1999), 419–439.
Lanciani, R., *Pagan and Christian Rome* (Boston / New York, 1896).
Lavan, M., 'The manpower of the Roman fleets' in *Journal of Roman Archaeology*, 32 (2019), 183–200.
Le Bohec, Y., The Roman Imperial Army (London, 1994).
Legutko, P.A., 'The Revolt of Macrianus and Quietus and its effect on Alexandrian Coinage, AD 260–263' in *The Numismatic Chronicle*, 162 (2002), 135–168.
Lett, C., *St. Dionysius of Alexandria* (London, 1918).
Levy, R., *Firdausi. Shah-nama (Epic of the Kings)* (London, 1967).
Lieberman, S., 'Palestine in the Third and Fourth Centuries' in *The Jewish Quarterly Review*, New Series, 36 (1946a), 329–370.
Lieberman, S., 'Palestine in the Third and Fourth Centuries: III. Rabbinic Parallels to the Thirteenth Sibylline Book (Continued)' in *The Jewish Quarterly Review*, New Series, 37 (1946b), 31–54.
Liebeschuetz, J.H.W.G., 'Making a Gothic History: Does the Getica of Jordanes preserve genuine Gothic traditions? ' in *Journal of Late Antiquity*, 4 (2011), 185–216.

Lieu, S.N.C., 'Captives, refugees and exiles: a study of cross-frontier civilian movements and contacts between Rome and Persia from Valerian to Jovian' in P. Freeman and D. Kennedy (eds.) *The Defence of the Roman and Byzantine East* (Oxford, 1986), 475–505.

Loomis, L.R., *The Book of the Popes (Liber Pontificalis) I: To the Pontificate of Gregory I*. Translated with an Introduction by Louise Ropes Loomis, PhD. (New York, 1916).

Luttwak, E. N., *The Grand Strategy of the Roman Empire from the First Century to the Third* (Baltimore, 1976).

Lyne, M., 'Some New Coin Types of Carausius and Allectus and the History of the British Provinces AD 286–296' in *The Numismatic Chronicle*, 163 (2003), 147–168.

MacDonald, D., 'Dating the fall of Dura-Europos' in *Historia: Zeitschrift für Alte Geschichte* 35 (1986), 45–68.

MacDowall, S., *The Goths: Conquerors of the Roman Empire* (Barnsley, 2017).

MacMullen, R., *Paganism in the Roman Empire* (New Haven / London, 1981).

MacMullen, R., 'The Epigraphical Habit in the Roman Empire' in *American Journal of Philology*, 103 (1982), 233–246.

Madden, F.W., 'Account of a collection of gold coins, presented by Edward Wigan, Esq., to the trustees of the British Museum (continued)' in *The Numismatic Chronicle and Journal of the Numismatic Society*, 5 (1865), 81–125.

Madzharov, M., *Roman Roads in Bulgaria: Contribution to the Development of Roman Road system in the Provinces of Moesia and Thrace* (Veliko Tŭrnovo, 2009).

Magie, D., *Historia Augusta*, Vol. III. Translated with Introduction and Notes by D. Magie (Cambridge Mass. / London, 1932).

Maksymiuk, K., *Geography of Roman-Iranian Wars. Military Operations of Rome and Sasanian Iran* (Siedlce, 2015).

Mallan, C., 'In Praise of Gallienus? Reconsidering a Gallienic Date for the Εἰς βασιλέα of Pseudo-Aristides ([Aristid.] Or. 35 K)', in Mitthof, F., Martin, G. and Grusková, J., *Empire in Crisis: Gothic Invasions and Roman Historiography*, Tyche Supplement 12 (Vienna, 2020), p. 245–262.

Mallan, C., and Davenport, C., 'Dexippus and the Gothic Invasions: interpreting the New Vienna Fragment (*Codex Vindobonensis Hist. gr.* 73, ff. 192v–193r)' in *Journal of Roman Studies*, 105 (2015), 203–226.

Manders, E., 'Communicating messages through coins: a new approach to the emperor Decius' in *Jaarboek voor Munt-en Penningkunde*, 96 (2009), 17–38.

Manders, E., *Coining Images of Power: Patterns in the Representation of Roman Emperors on Imperial Coinage: A.D. 193–284* (Leiden, 2012).

Mango, C., 'The triumphal way of Constantinople and the Golden Gate' in *Dumbarton Oaks Papers*, 54 (2000), 173–188.

Marelli, U., 'L'epigrafe di Decio a Cosa e l'epiteto di "restitutor sacrorum"' in *Aevum*, 58 (1984), 52–56.

Martin, G., 'Fernbeziehungen in Dexipps *Skythika*' in Mitthof, F., Martin, G. and Grusková, J., *Empire in Crisis: Gothic Invasions and Roman Historiography*, Tyche Supplement 12 (Vienna, 2020), p. 95–110.

Martin, G., and Grusková, J., '"Dexippus Vindobonensis"? Ein neues Handschriftenfragment zum sog. Herulereinfall der Jahre 267/8' in *Wiener Studien* 127 (2014a), 101–20.

Martin, G., and Grusková, J., '"Scythica Vindobonensia" by Dexippus(?): new fragments on Decius' Gothic wars', in *Greek, Roman and Byzantine Studies* 54.4 (2014b), 728–54 .

Martin, G., and Grusková, J., 'Anhang I: *Scythica Vindobonensia alias Dexippus Vindobonensis* Vorläufige Transkription', in Mitthof, F., Martin, G. and Grusková, J., *Empire in Crisis: Gothic Invasions and Roman Historiography*, Tyche Supplement 12 (Vienna, 2020), p. 543–548.

Mateev, T., Древният Филипопол [Drevnijat filipopolol] (Plovdiv, 2012).

Matei-Popescu, F., *The Roman Army in Moesia Inferior* (Bucharest, 2010).
Mattingly, H., 'The reign of Aemilian. A chronological note' in *The Journal of Roman Studies*, 25 (1935), 55–58.
Mattingly, H., 'The great Dorchester hoard of 1936' in *The Numismatic Chronicle and Journal of the Royal Numismatic Society, Fifth Series*, 19 (1939), 21–61.
Mattingly, H., 'A New Roman Coin' in *British Museum Quarterly*, 14 (1940), 97.
Mattingly, H., 'The reigns of Trebonianus Gallus and Volusian and of Aemilian' in *The Numismatic Chronicle and Journal of the Royal Numismatic Society, Sixth Series*, 6 (1946), 36–46.
Mattingly, H. and Salisbury, F.S., 1924. 'A find of Roman coins from Plevna in Bulgaria' in *The Numismatic Chronicle and Journal of the Numismatic Society Fifth Series*, 4 (1924), 210–238.
Mattingly, H., Sydenham, E., Sutherland, C., and Humphrey, V., *Roman Imperial Coinage, Vol IV* (London, 1949).
McCormick, M., et al. (12 authors), 'Climate change during and after the Roman Empire: Reconstructing the past from scientific and historical evidence' in *Journal of Interdisciplinary History*, 43 (2012), 169–220.
McGuckin, J.A., *The Westminster Handbook to Origen* (Louisville, 2004).
McInerney, J., 'Dexippos (100)' in *Brill's New Jacoby* (2007). Available online at https://referenceworks.brillonline.com/browse/brill-s-new-jacoby.
McLanon, A., *The Empress Ariadne and the Politics of Transition* (New York, 2002).
McLaughlin, R., *The Roman Empire and the Indian Ocean* (Barnsley, 2014).
McMahon, R., 'Another view of Trajan Decius' in *De Imperatoribus Romanis*, https://www.roman-emperors.org/decius.htm#N_42_ (2002).
McSweeney, R., and Hausfather, Z., 'Mapped: How "proxy" data reveals the climate of the Earth's distant past'. https://interactive.carbonbrief.org/how-proxy-data-reveals-climate-of-earths-distant-past/ (2021).
Mecella, L., 'Kaiserliches Heer und Lokalmilizen in Aktion: die neuen Fragmente' in Mitthof, F., Martin, G. and Grusková, J., *Empire in Crisis: Gothic Invasions and Roman Historiography*, *Tyche* Supplement 12 (Vienna, 2020), p. 287–310.
Meckler, M.L., 'Philip the Arab (244–249 A.D.)' in *De Imperatoribus Romanis*, http://roman-emperors.sites.luc.edu/philarab.htm (1999).
Mennen, I., *Power and Status in the Roman Empire, AD 193–284* (Leiden, 2011).
Metcalf, W.E., 'The Reka Devnia hoard re-examined' in Gorini, G. (Ed.) *Ritrovamenti monetali nel mondo antico. Problemi e metodi. Atti del congresso internazionale, Padova 31 marzo – 2 aprile 2000* (Padova, 2002), 145–150.
Meyer, M., (ed.), *The Nag Hammadi Scriptures: the Revised and Updated Translation of Sacred Gnostic Texts* (New York, 2007).
Mierow, C.C., *The Gothic History of Jordanes in English Version with an Introduction and Commentary* (Princeton, 1915).
Millar, F., *The Roman Near East 31 BC–AD 337* (Cambridge, Mass., 1993).
Miller, A., 'Thomas Cole and Jacksonian America: The Course of Empire as political allegory' in *Prospects*, 14 (1989), 65–92.
Minchev, A., 'From Proconnessos to Odessos: unfinished Roman marble from Odessos and Marcianopolis (2nd-3rd c. AD)' in *Histria Antiqua*, 21 (2012), 49–60.
Mitthof, F., 'Bemerkungen zu Kaiser Decius und seinem Gotenkrieg 250–251 n. Chr.' in Mitthof, F., Martin, G. and Grusková, J., *Empire in Crisis: Gothic Invasions and Roman Historiography*, *Tyche* Supplement 12 (Vienna, 2020), p. 311–336.
Mitthof, F., Martin, G., and Grusková, J., *Empire in Crisis: Gothic Invasions and Roman Historiography* (Vienna, 2020).

Mommsen, T., *Monumenta Germaniae Historica, Auctores Antiquissimi 5* (Berlin, 1882).
Moorhead, S., Booth, A., and Bland, R., *The Frome Hoard* (British Museum Press, 2010).
Mouchmov, N.A., 'Une trouvaille de monnaies antiques près du village de Reka-Devnia (Marcianopolis)' in *Aréthuse*, 27 (1930), 49–52.
Mouchmov, N.A., *Le Trésor Numismatique de Réka-Devnia (Marcianopolis)* (Sofia, 1934).
Muller, C., *Fragmenta Historicum Graecorum IV* (Paris, 1839).
Münsterberg, R., 'Ein Siebenbürgischer gold münzen fund aus dem jähre 1713' in *Blätter für Münzfreund* (September, 1823) (1923), 425–428.
Musurillo, H.I., *The Acts of the Christian Martyrs* (Oxford, 1972).
Myzgin, K., 'Finds of Roman provincial coins from the territory of eastern Europe: Balkan cities mintage' in Ivanišević V. et al. (eds), *Proceedings of the International Numismatic Symposium Circulation of Antique Coins in southeastern Europe Viminacium, Serbia, September 15th-17th* (2017), 87–104.
Nathan, G. and McMahon, R. 'Trajan Decius (249–251 A.D.) and Usurpers During His Reign' in *De Imperatoribus Romanis* http://www.roman-emperors.org/decius.htm#Note%20B (2002).
Nefedkin, A.K., 'Goths on campaign from the mid-third to the mid-sixth centuries' in *Fasciculi Archaeologiae Historicae*, 15 (2002), 9–15.
Németh, A., 'Layers of restoration: Vaticanus gr. 73 transformed in the tenth-, fourteenth-, and nineteenth centuries' in Miscellanea *Bibliothecae Apostolicae Vaticanae*, 21 (2015) 281–330.
Németh, A., 'Dexippus in the *Excerpta Constantiniana* revisited: the preface to Dexippus' *Scythica*' in Mitthof, F., Martin, G. and Grusková, J., *Empire in Crisis: Gothic Invasions and Roman Historiography*, *Tyche* Supplement 12 (Vienna, 2020), p. 111–134.
Neumann, F., *Populorum et Regem Numi Veteres Inediti* (Vienna, 1799)
Nixon, C.E.V. and Rodgers, B.S., *In Praise of the Later Roman Emperors* (Berkeley, 1994).
Norman, A.F., *Libanius: Selected Works*, 2 vols (Massachussetts 1969–1977).
Oborn, G.T., 'Why did Decius and Valerian proscribe Christianity?' in *Church History*, 2 (1933), 67–77.
Oliver, J.H., and Dow, S., 'The American excavations in the Athenian agora: sixth report (1935)' in *Hesperia*, 4 (1935), 5–90.
Olmstead, A.T., 'The mid-Third Century of the Christian Era' in *Classical Philology*, 37 (1942), 241–262 and 398–420.
O'Reilly, D.F., 'The Theban legion of St. Maurice' in *Vigiliae Christianae*, 32 (1978), 195–207.
O'Reilly, D.F., *Lost Legion Rediscovered: The Mystery of the Theban Legion* (Barnsley, 2011).
Overlaet, B., 'A Roman Emperor at Bishapur and Darabgird: Uranius Antoninus and the Black Stone of Emesa' in *Iranica Antiqua*, 44 (2009), doi: 10.2143/IA.44.0.2034386.
Özsoy, E., Latif, M.A., and Beşiktepe, Ş., 'The current system of the Bosphorus Strait based on recent measurements' in *The 2nd Meeting on the Physical Oceanography of Sea Straits*, April 15–19 2002, Villefranche (2002), 177–180.
Panaite, A., 'Roman Roads in *Moesia Inferior*. Archaeological and Epigraphic Evidence' in *Limes XII, Proceedings of the 22nd International Congress of Roman Frontier Studies, Ruse, Bulgaria, September, 2012* (2012), 593–600.
Papathomas, A., 'Dexippos und Thukydides' in Mitthof, F., Martin, G. and Grusková, J., *Empire in Crisis: Gothic Invasions and Roman Historiography*, *Tyche* Supplement 12 (Vienna, 2020), p. 135–144.
Parker, P., *The Empire Stops Here: A Journey Along the Frontiers of the Roman World* (Pimlico, 2009).
Parkin, T.G., *Demography and Roman Society* (Baltimore, 1992).
Paunov, E.I., and Prokopov, I.S., *An Inventory of Roman Republican Coin Hoards and Coins from Bulgaria* (Milan, 2002).

Peachin, M., 'Gallienus Caesar?' in *Zeitschrift für Papyrologie und Epigraphik*, 74 (1988), 219–224.
Peachin, M., *Roman Imperial Titulature and Chronology*, A.D. 235–284 (Amsterdam, 1990).
Pearson, P.N., *Maximinus Thrax: From Common Soldier to Emperor of Rome* (Barnsley, 2016).
Pearson, P.N., 'Provenance and identity of a large bronze statue currently in the Metropolitan Museum of Art, New York' in *Journal of the History of Collections*, 30 (2018), 35–48.
Pelikan, O., 'Der Grosse Ludovisische Schlachtsarkophag' in *Mnema Vladimir Groh* (1964), 117–135.
Peterson, A.T., Bauer, J.T., and Mills, J.N., 'Ecologic and geographic distribution of filovirus disease' in *Emerging Infectious Diseases*, 10 (2004), 40–47.
Petrova, S., 'The application of the Roman Ionic order in Augusta Traiana' in *Studia Academica Šumenensia*, 4 (2017), 115–153.
Pflaumm, H.-G., 'P. Licinius Gallienus, nobilissimus Caesar et Imp. M. Aurelius Numerianus à la lumière de deux nouveaux milliaires d'Oum-el-Bouaghi' in *Bulletin d'Archéologie Algérienne*, 2 (1968), 175–1.
Pick, B., *Die antiken Münzen Nordgriechenlands. Dacien und Moesien I* (Berlin, 1898).
Piso, I., 'Das verhängnisvolle Jahr 262 und die amissio Daciae' in: Vagalinski, L., Raycheva, M., Boteva, D. and Sharankov, N. (eds.), *Proceedings of the First International Roman and Late Antique Thrace Conference "Cities, Territories and Identities"* (Plovdiv, 3rd – 7th October 2016) (Sofia, 2018), 427–440.
Piso, I., 'Bemerkungen zu Dexippos Vindobonensis (II)' in Mitthof, F., Martin, G. and Grusková, J., *Empire in Crisis: Gothic Invasions and Roman Historiography*, *Tyche* Supplement 12 (Vienna, 2020), p. 135–144.
Pitassi, M., *Roman Warships* (Woodbridge, 2012).
Pitassi, M., *The Roman Navy: Ships, Men and Warfare 350 BC–AD 475* (Barnsley, 2012).
Platner, S.B., *A Topographical Dictionary of Ancient Rome* (London, 1929).
Pohlsander, H.A., 'Did Decius Kill the Philippi?' in *Historia: Zeitschrift für Alte Geschichte*, 31 (1982), 214–222.
Pollard, N., and Berry, J., *The Complete Roman Legions* (London, 2012).
Porter, R.K., *Travels in Georgia, Persia, Armenia, Ancient Babylonia, &c., &c., during the years 1817, 1818, 1819, and 1820*. 2 volumes (London, 1821).
Potter, D.A., *Prophecy and History in the Crisis of the Roman Empire: A Historical Commentary on the Thirteenth Sybilline Oracle* (Oxford, 1990).
Potter, D.A., *The Roman Empire at Bay AD 180–395* (Abingdon, 2004).
Potter, D., 'War as Theater, from Tacitus to Dexippus' in W. Riess and G.G. Fagan (eds.) *The Topography of Violence in the Greco-Roman World*. (Ann Arbor, 2016), 325–348.
Potter, D., 'Dexippus' Gothic anthropology' in Mitthof, F., Martin, G. and Grusková, J., *Empire in Crisis: Gothic Invasions and Roman Historiography*, *Tyche* Supplement 12 (Vienna, 2020), p. 357–368.
Poulter, A., 'Why Did Most Cities in Moesia and Thrace Survive during the 3rd-Century 'Crisis'?' in Mitthof, F., Martin, G. and Grusková, J., *Empire in Crisis: Gothic Invasions and Roman Historiography*, *Tyche* Supplement 12 (Vienna, 2020), p. 369–387.
Prickartz, C., 'Philippe L'Arabe (244–249), civilis princeps' in *L'Antiquité Classique*, 64 (1995), 129–153.
Prieur, M., and Scmitt, L., *Le Monnayage de Trébonien Galle et de sa Famille* (Paris, 2001).
Radoslavova, G., Dzanev, G., and Nikolov, N., 'The Battle of Abritus in AD 251: written sources, archaeological and numismatic data' in *Archaeologia Bulgarica*, 15 (2011), 23–49.
Rathbone, D.W., 'The dates of recognition in Egypt of the Emperors from Caracalla to Diocletian' in *Zeitschrift für Papyrologie und Epigraphik*, 62 (1986), 101–131.
Rawlinson, G., *The Seven Great Monarchies of the Ancient Eastern World* Vol III (Boston, 1884).

Retsö, J., *The Arabs in Antiquity. Their History from the Assyrians to the Umayyads* (Abingdon, 2003).
Reuter, M., 'Das Ende des raetischen Limes im Jahr 254 n. Chr.' in *Bayerische Vorgeschichtsblätter*, 72 (2007), 77–149.
Rives, J.B., 'The decree of Decius' in *The Journal of Roman Studies*, 89 (1999), 135–154.
Rossignol, B., and Durost, S., 'Volcanisme global et variations climatiques de courte durée dans l'histoire romaine (Ier s. av. J.-C.- IVème s. ap. J.-C.): leçons d'une archive glaciaire (GISP2)' in *Jahrbuch des römisch-germanischen Zentralmuseums Mainz*, 54 (2007), 395–438.
Rostovtzeff, M.I., Bellinger, A.R., Hopkins, C., and Welles, C.B. (eds.), *The Excavations at Dura-Europos conducted by Yale University and the French Academy of Inscriptions and Letters. Preliminary Report of Sixth Season of Work, October 1932–March 1933.* (New Haven, 1936).
Rostovtzeff, M.I., '*Res Gestae Divi Saporis* and Dura' in *Berytus*, 8 (1943–4), 17–60.
Roueche, C., *Aphrodisias in Late Antiquity* (London, 1989).
Salisbury, F.S. and Mattingly, H., 'The reign of Trajan Decius' in *The Journal of Roman Studies*, 14 (1924), 1–23.
Saliou, C., and Dandrau, A., 1997. 'Données nouvelles sur les quartiers sud-est de Doura-Europos' in Leriche, P. and Gelin, M., (eds), *Doura-Euro-pos: Études IV, 1991–1993*, (Beirut, 1997), 95–106.
Sanders, C.S., 'Jupiter Dolichenus' in *Journal of the American Oriental Society*, 23 (1902), 84–92.
Sarfaraz, A.A., and Teimoury, M., 'Describing the spatial organization of Bishapur City based on archaeological findings' in *Journal of Art and Civilization of the Orient*, 1 (2013), 11–20.
Schindel, N., 'Sasanian Coinage' in Encyclopedia Iranica (2005). Available online at https://iranicaonline.org/articles/sasanian-coinage
Schlumbaum, M., Turgay, M., and Schibler, J., 'Near east mtDNA haplotype variants in Roman cattle from Augusta Raurica, Switzerland, and the Swiss Evoline breed' in *Animal Genetics* (2006) 37, 373–375.
Schulte, B., *Die Goldprägung der gallischen Kaiser von Postumus bis Tetricus* (Aarau, 1983)
Schwarcz, A., 'Die gotischen Seezüge des 3. Jahrhunderts' in Pillinger, R. et al. (eds.) *Die Schwarzmeerküste in der Spätantike und im frühen Mittelalter* (Vienna 1992), 47–57.
Seaby, H.A., *Roman Silver Coins. Revised by David R. Sear and Robert Loosley. Volume I. The Republic to Augustus. Third (Revised) Edition* (London, 1978).
Sear, D., *Roman Coins and Their Values.* Second edition (London, 1974).
Segal, A., 'Roman cities in the Province of Arabia' in *The Journal of the Society of Architectural Historians*, 40 (1981), 108–121.
Sellars, I.J., *The Monetary System of the Romans: a Description of the Roman Coinage from Early Times to the Reform of Anastasius.* E-book: https://books.google.co.uk/books?id=m_Y-CgAAQBAJ&sitesec=reviews&redir_esc=y
Seure, G., 'Trésors de monnaies antiques en Bulgarie III. Le trésor de Nicolaévo' in *Revue Numismatique* 26 (1923), 111–153.
Shahîd, I., *Rome and the Arabs: a Prolegomenon to the Study of Byzantium and the Arabs* (Washington, 1984).
Sharankov, N. and Hristov, I., 'A milestone of Emperor Philip the Arab from the road *Oescus – Philippopolis* found at the eastern wall of the *castellum* of Sostra' in *Archaeologia Bulgarica*, 23 (2019), 57–70.
Sidnell, P., Warhorse: *Cavalry in Ancient Warfare* (London / New York, 2004).
Sigl, M., et al. (20 authors), 'Timing and climate forcing of volcanic eruptions for the past 2,500 years' in *Nature* (2017), 523, 543–549.
Slusser, M., *St. Gregory Thaumaturgus: Life and Works* (Washington, D.C., 1998).
Smyth, H.W., *Descriptive Catalogue of a Cabinet of Roman Imperial Large-Brass Medals* (Bedford, 1834).

Sommer, M., *Die Soldatenkaiser* (Darmstad, 2004).
Soproni, S., *Der spätrömische Limes zwischen Esztergom und Szentendre* (Budapest, 1978).
Southern, P., *The Roman Empire from Severus to Constantine* (London, 2001).
Spoerri Butcher, M., 'Reka Devnia (Bulgaria): the challenges of creating a digital dataset of 80,000 coins' in Callegher, B. (ed.), *Too Big to Study? Troppo grandi da studiare?* (Trieste, 2019), 161–171.
Staccioli, R.A., *Rome, Past and Present* (Rome, 2001).
Stein, F.J., *Dexippus et Herodianus rerum scriptores quatenus Thucydidem secuti sint* (Bonn, 1957).
Steinacher, R., 'Hintergründe und Herkommen der Barbaren am Schwarzen Meer im 3. Jahrhundert n. Chr. und die Meistererzählung von der Wanderung" in Mitthof, F., Martin, G. and Grusková, J., *Empire in Crisis: Gothic Invasions and Roman Historiography*, *Tyche* Supplement 12 (Vienna, 2020), p. 403–421.
Stevenson, S.W., *Dictionary of Roman Coins* (London, 1889).
Suski, R., 'Dexippus and the repelling of the Gothic invasion in the years 267–268' in *Eos* 104 (2017), 303–316.
Sutherland, C. H. V., *Roman Coins* (Barrie and Jenkins, London, 1974).
Swift, L.J., 'The anonymous encomium of Philip the Arab' in *Greek, Roman, and Byzantine Studies*, 7 (1966), 267–289.
Syme, R., *Emperors and Biography: Studies in the* Historia Augusta (Clarendon Press, 1971).
Syvänne, I., *Military History of Late Rome 284–361* (Barnsley, 2014).
Syvänne, I., *The Reign of Emperor Gallienus: The Apogee of Roman Cavalry* (Barnsley, 2019).
Talbert, R.J.A. (ed), *Barrington Atlas of the Greek and Roman World* (Princeton, 2000).
Theocharaki, A. M., 'The ancient circuit wall of Athens: its changing course and the phases of construction', in *Hesperia* 81 (2011), 71–156.
Tiradritti, F., 'Of kilns and corpses: Theban plague victims' in *Egyptian Archaeology*, 44 (2014), 15–18.
Tobin, J., 'The Houses: Domestic Architecture, Dated Deposits, and Finds in Context' in Aylward, W. (ed.) *Excavations at Zeugma, Conducted by Oxford Archaeology* (Los Altos, 2013), 72–118.
Todd, M., *The Early Germans* (Oxford, 1992).
Torbatov, S., 'Roman roads in Thrace and Moesia' in Ivanov, R. (ed.) *Archaeology of the Bulgarian Lands* (Sofia, 2004), 76–95.
Torbatov, S., 'The garrison of Sexaginta Prista in the 1st-3rd centuries AD' in *Proceedings of the Rousse Regional Museum of History*, 15 (2012), 111–161.
Touratsoglou, I., *Greece and the Balkans Before the End of Antiquity* (Athens, 2006).
Toynbee, J.M.C., 'The shrine of St. Peter and its setting' in *The Journal of Roman Studies*, 43 (1953), 1–26.
Trankova, D., 'Maltepe Mound near Plovdiv is archaeological discovery of decade' in *Vagabond* 23/12/2019 (2019). Available online at https://vagabond.bg/raiders-treasure-mound-224.
Treggiari, S., 'Jobs in the Household of Livia' in *Papers of the British School at Rome*, 43 (1975), 48–77.
Trininova, P., Solakjov, D., Simeonova, S., Metodiev, M., and Stavrev, P., 'Regional pattern of the earth's crust dislocations on the territory of Bulgaria inferred from gravity data and its recognition in the spatial distribution of seismicity' in *Pattern Recognition in Physics*, 1 (2013), 25–36.
Tudor, D., 'În legătură cu Războiul lui Filip Arabul împotriva Carpilor' in *Pontica*, 9 (1976), 89–97.
Updegraff, R.T., 'The Blemmyes I: The rise of the Blemmyes and the Roman withdrawal from Nubia under Diocletian' in Haase, W. and Temporini, H. (eds.), *Aufstieg und Niedergang der Römischen Welt* (Berlin, 1988), 44–106.

Uggeri, G., 'L'urbanistica di Antiochia sull'Oronte' in *Journal of Ancient Topography*, 8 (1998), 179–222.
Vagalinski, L., 'The problem of destruction by warfare in Late Antiquity: archaeological evidence from the Danube limes' in Vagalinski, L., Sharankov, N., and Torbatov, S. (eds.), *The Lower Danube Roman Limes (1st-6th c. AD)* (Sofia, 2012), p. 311–326.
Varbanov, V., 'Barbarian invasions in the Roman provinces of Lower Moesia and Thrace in the mid- Third Century and the coin hoards from that period' in Vagalinski, L., Torbatov, S., and Sharankov, N. (eds) *The Lower Danube Roman Limes (1st-6th c. AD)* (Sofia, 2012), 287–308.
Varbanov, V., 'Small coin hoards like evidence for unrest. The case of Philippopolis, Roman Province of Thrace' in *Journal of Ancient History and Archaeology*, 7 (2020), 513–518.
Vincenti, A., di Cesare, V., Galassi, C., and Testini, P., *Basilicas and Catacombs of Rome* (Rome, 1986).
Vitiello, M., '"Antologizing their successes": Visions of the past in Gothic Italy' in Wiemer, H. (ed.) *Theoderich der Große und das gotische Königreich in Italien* (Berlin, 2020), p. 341–368.
Wahlgren, S., *The Chronicle of the Logothete. Translated with Introduction, Commentary and Indices by Staffan Wahlgren* (Liverpool, 2019).
Warmington, B.H., 'The municipal patrons of Roman North Africa' in *Papers of the British School at Rome*, 22 (1954), 39–55.
Watson, A., *Aurelian and the Third Century* (London / New York, 1999).
Welles, C.B., Fink, R.O., and Gilliam, J.F. (eds.), *Excavations at Dura-Europos, Final Report. Vol. 5, Pt. 1, The Parchments and Papyri* (New Haven, 1959).
Wieshofer, J., *Ancient Persia from 550 BC to 650 AD* (London, 1996).
Wilson, R.M., *The Lost Literature of Medieval England* (London, 2019).
Witschel, C., *Krise – Rezession – Stagnation? Der Westen des römischen Reiches im 3. Jahrhundert n. Chr.* (Frankfurt am Main, 1999).
Witschel, C., 'Germanische Einfälle in die Provinzen an Rhein und oberer Donau im 3. Jh. n. Chr.: Die Problematik der epigraphischen, numismatischen und archäologischen Zeugnisse' in Mitthof, F., Martin, G. and Grusková, J., *Empire in Crisis: Gothic Invasions and Roman Historiography*, Tyche Supplement 12 (Vienna, 2020), p. 423–530.
Wolfram, H., *History of the Goths*. Translated by Thomas J. Dunlap (Berkeley, 1990).
Wolfram, H., 'Kniva' in *Reallexikon der Germanischen Altertumskunde^2*, 17 (2006), 34–37.
Wolfram, H., 'Ostrogotha – ansicher Amaler oder glückloser Feigling' in Mitthof, F., Martin, G. and Grusková, J., *Empire in Crisis: Gothic Invasions and Roman Historiography*, Tyche Supplement 12 (Vienna, 2020), p. 17–34.
Wolfram, H., 'How to stay Gothic without a Gothic king' in Pachá, P. (ed.), *The Visigothic Kingdom* (Amsterdam, 2021), p. 139–156.
Yartzev, S.V., Zubarev, V.G., and Smekalov, S.L., 'The invasion of the Borans into the Bosporus in the 3rd Century A.D.' in *Humanities and Social Science Reviews*, 7 (2019), 852–857.
Yeat, Ƥ., Jordanes Getica sive De Origine Actibusque Gothorum with classicized grammar, normalized spelling and some emendations by Ƥeedrich Yeat. Available online at http://www.harbornet.com/folks/theedrich/Goths/Goths1.htm#X11 (undated).
Young, G.K., 'Emesa in Roman Syria: resistance, rebellion and regionalism in the Third Century AD' in *Prudentia*, 36 (2004), 31–48.
Zakrzewski, P., 'Reconstructing the phases of the fortifications of the legionary fortress at Novae (*Moesia Inferior*)' in *Journal of Roman Archaeology*, 33 (2020), 432–447.
Zecchini, G., 'Il problema poliorcetico nella storia militare e nella storiografia del III secolo d.C.' in Mitthof, F., Martin, G. and Grusková, J., *Empire in Crisis: Gothic Invasions and Roman Historiography*, Tyche Supplement 12 (Vienna, 2020), p. 531–539.
Żmudziński, M., 'An overall approach on the Roman economy of the Province of Upper Dacia' in *Journal of Ancient History and Archeology*, 2 (2015), 24–36.

Notes

Introduction
1. Mitthof, F., Martin, G., and Grusková, J., *Empire in Crisis: Gothic Invasions and Roman Historiography* (Vienna, 2020). The title of this book was arrived at independently.

Prologue
1. The year of the millennium games has been questioned but 248 CE fits the numismatic evidence and is supported firstly by the fact it was a century after the games of Antoninus Pius, and secondly that the late Roman author Aurelius Victor (Aurelius Victor, *De Caesaribus* 28) laments the fact that there was no repetition in 348 (see also Southern, 2001, p. 307, note 92). For Pales and the Parilia see Adkins and Adkins (1996, p. 82).
2. Livius, *Ab Urbe Condita Libri 1*.
3. Occupation in what is now central Rome undoubtedly predates even that remote period, stretching back at least another 500 years on the neighbouring Capitoline Hill where a fortified village once dominated a ford over the Tiber. For early Rome see Fulminante (2014); also Grandazzi (1997) and Forsythe (2005).
4. Suetonius, *Divus Cladius* 21.2. On that occasion the claim was received with some amusement because Augustus had celebrated secular games just a few decades before, based on an alternative counting scheme for the ages.
5. Cassius Dio, *Roman History* LXXII.36.4.
6. This aspect of ancient religion has been called 'apotropaism' from the Greek word for 'turning away' evil. It remains central to witchcraft. For a discussion of its importance at the time of the millennium see Brent (2010).
7. This and other quotations from this section are from Ammianus Marcellinus, *History* 16.10.
8. Note that the fifth century theologian Orosius claimed in relation to the millennium that "no author mentions any procession up to the Capitol nor any sacrifice of victims according to the usual custom" but he was using this argument to reinforce his contention that Philip was a Christian (Orosius, *History Against the Pagans* VII.20). The coinage is positive evidence that the traditional religion was in fact at the centre of the celebrations.
9. For the Temple of Rome and Venus see Ammianus Marcellinus, *History* 16.10 and Staccioli (2001, p. 15) for a reconstruction. The architect Apollodorus was banished and executed soon after making this remark according to Cassius Dio, *Roman History*, 69.4.
10. For the Circus Maximus see Staccioli (2001, p. 67); Ammianus Marcellinus, *History* 14.6.
11. Aurelius Victor, *De Caesaribus* 28.2.
12. *Scriptores Historiae Augustae* (Julius Capitolinus), *Gordiani Tres* XXXIII.1–2.
13. Bland (2012).
14. For Asinius Quadratus, the millennium and a discussion of the literature see Janiszewski (2006, p. 32–35). For Dexippus and the millennium see Janiszewski (2006, p. 44–45). Some might baulk at describing Dexippus as 'great'. Like other historians of the third

century, he has had a rough ride from some modern academics, but his corpus of works, including new fragments of the *Scythica* that have recently come to light, reveal his prodigious industry and narrative power and place him as the most distinguished historian of his generation. In this context it is worth remembering the assessment of the Byzantine patriarch and scholar Photius, who was not always complimentary in his literary criticism: 'I read the *History* of the events that happened after the death of Alexander the Great, by Dexippus, in four books; also his *Historical Epitome*, a chronicle going down to the time of Claudius. I also read his *Scythica*, describing the wars between the Scythians and Romans and other things of note. His style is free from redundancies, massive, and dignified; he might be called a second Thucydides, although he writes more clearly. His characteristics are chiefly shown in his last-mentioned work.' (Photius, *Bibliotheca* 82).
15. For instance a peculiar book called the *Thirteenth Sibylline Oracle* that purported to see the city's future, was actively playing down the idea (Potter 1990, p. 240).
16. Aurelius Victor, *De Caesaribus* 28.2.

Chapter 1

1. Wiesehofer (1996, p. 191).
2. Frier (2001).
3. Le Bohec (1994). For individual legions see Dando-Collins (2010) and Pollard and Berry (2012).
4. Crawford (1975).
5. La Rocca et al. (2015); Eckardt (2018).
6. For the diversity of religious belief see MacMullen (1981).
7. Baltzly (2019).
8. Goodman (2007). For an absence of persecution against the Jews in the Third Century see Lieberman (1946).
9. For an overview of early Christianity see Freeman (2009). For diversity of belief see Ehrman (2003). For the relationship of Christianity to other religions see Knapp (2017). For apocryphal and Gnostic texts see Meyer (2007). For the Infancy Gospel of Thomas see http://www.earlychristianwritings.com/infancythomas.html. For the Acts of Peter see Meyer (2007).
10. *Scriptores Historiae Augustae* (Aelius Lampridius), *Alexander Severus* XXIX.2.
11. For church organization see Eusebius, *Historia Ecclesiastica* 43.11 and Burns (2002). For evolving concepts of Jesus from preacher to god, see Ehrman (2014). The exclusivity of Christian salvation is based on Mark, 16.15–16 and elaborated, for instance, by Cyprian, *Letters* LXXII.
12. Tacitus, *Annals* 15.44.
13. Dionysius of Alexandria to Fabian in Eusebius, *Historia Ecclesiastica*, VI. 41. See also commentary in Potter (1990, p. 252–253).
14. Dionysius of Alexandria to Fabian in Eusebius, *Historia Ecclesiastica* VI.41; see also Eusebius, *Historia Ecclesiastica* VI.34; Jerome, *Chronicle*, p. 299. John Chrysostom, *On St Babylas* 1. Jordanes, *Getica* XVI.89 states that both Philip and his son were Christians. For a detailed discussion and an argument in favour of Philip's Christianity see Shahid (1984, p. 65–95). Syvänne (2019, p. 29) has gone so far as to suggest that Philip may have been baptised and thereafter refused military command although the historical sources say that he later commanded an army at the decisive battle with Decius. For the more prevalent view that Philip was not a practising Christian, see Korner (2002).
15. For Shahba see Segal (1981) and Körner (2002). For accounts of Philip's reign see De Blois (1978–1979), Prickartz (1995) and Körner (2002).
16. A translation is provided by Swift (1966). For articles suggesting Philip see Swift (1966), De Blois (1986) and the literature cited therein. Jones (1972) suggested that it is actually

by Aristides and relates to Antoninus Pius. Mallan (2020) makes a case for Gallienus following some earlier suggestions.
17. For the various conflicting accounts of the death of Gordian III see Swift (1966) and Potter (1990, p. 204–205). For the mausoleum of Gordian see Ammianus Marcellinus, *History* XXIII 5, 7, 17 and Johnson (1995).
18. For the gold coins see Bland (2014, p. 18). For peace with Persia see Roman Imperial Coinage (RIC) 69, 72; Mattingly et al., 1949, p. 76. The emperor Galerius later issued coins with the legend VICTORIA PERSICA.
19. Zosimus, *New History* 1.19–20. Historians who have entertained this theory have suggested that the brothers may have been working in league with a senior administrator called Atho Marcellus who was in charge of the corn barges on the Euphrates and who prospered in the coming years (see Davies, 1967, and De Blois, 1978–1979, p. 13).
20. Zosimus, *New History* 1.19–20. For *rector orientis* see Millar (1993, p. 156); see also Potter (1990, p. 37).
21. Jordanes, *Getica* XVI.89.
22. A brief account of the campaign against the Carpi is given by Zosimus, *New History* 1.20. Philip minted a special issue of coins celebrating VICTORIA CARPICA in 247 (RIC VI.66; Mattingly et al., 1949, p. 75). For inscriptional and archaeological evidence relating to the campaign see Tudor (1976) who records fortification work at Romula and Sucidava on the road north of the strategic crossing point at Oescus. That Philip campaigned in person is supposedly evidenced by imperial rescripts. It seems odd that the panegyric of pseudo-Aristides fails to mention this campaign, which might be considered evidence against the prevailing view and that it was not in fact about Philip.
23. Jordanes, *Getica* XVI.89 implies that the subsidy was withheld in the millennium year. See also Wolfram (1990).
24. Harper (2015, 2016, 2017). For possible reservoir species and the geographic origin of filoviruses see Peterson et al. (2004). Some Byzantine authors recorded that the plague began in Ethiopia (e.g., John of Antioch, *Excerpta Salmasiana* II.66).

Chapter 2

1. For coin hoards see Vagalinski (2012) and Varbanov (2012). The road network (dashed lines) has been reconstructed from a number of sources (Talbert 2000; Madzharov 2009; Panaite 2012). The nominal frontier is the Hadrianic line according to Gudea (1979). The Danube delta is reconstructed according to Andrein (2015).
2. For the Roman navy see Pitassi (2011, 2012).
3. For the strength of *classis moesica* see Lavan (2019, p. 194). For Sexaginta Prista see Torbatov (2012). Matei-Popesu (2010, p. 168–244) provides a detailed list with full references and discussion of all the auxiliary units that may have been in Moesia Inferior at this time, which are as follows: *ala* I *vespasiana dardanorum* at Arrubium (Mačin) on the delta, *ala* I *flavia gaetulorum*. possibly at Carsium in the Dobrudja, *ala* II *hispanorum et aravacorum*, possibly also at Carsium, *cohors* I *bracarorum civium Romanorum*, possibly at Trimammium (near Mechka) on the Danube, *cohors* II *bracaraugustanorum equitata*, location unknown, *cohors* II *flavia brittonum equitata* at Sexaginta Prista, *cohors* II *chalcidenorum sagittariorum*, possibly at Sucidava on the north bank of the Danube opposite Oescus, *cohors* I *cilicium milliaria equitata sagittariorum* also possibly at Sucidava, *cohors* I *cisipadensium* at Sostra on the *via traiana*, *cohors* III *collecta civium Romanorum* at Montana in the foothills of the Haemus Mountains in western Moesia Inferior, *cohors gemina decorum milliaria*, location unknown, *cohors* I *germanorum civium Romanorum* at Capidava in the Dobrudja, *cohors* II *reducum* at Sostra, and *cohors* I *claudia sugambrorum veteran equitata*, location uncertain. For more on the garrisons of Lower Moesia see Duch (2017).

4. Zosimus, *New History* 1.19 names Severianus as a son-in-law but this seems to be a mistake. See also Potter (2004, p. 238–239).
5. For 'unit commander' see Zonaras, *Extracts of History*, XII.19. The Danubian legions seem to have been in a semi-mutinous state for a decade, ever since the assassination of their champion Maximinus Thrax in the civil war of 238. At that time, they had just invaded Italy but had then been posted back to their home bases under the command of one of Maximinus's principal opponents, Tullius Menophilus. For a while, Menophilus was one of the great men of the empire, and he is named (although not depicted) on local coins, a significant honour that was not accorded to every provincial governor. But after a few years he himself was expunged from official records, possibly after some sort of revolt against the ensuing government of the young emperor Gordian. Gordian then came to the area himself in an attempt to restore order and it may be notable that his local coinage vigorously pumped out the message of *legio* VII *claudia* and *legio* IIII *flavia felix* as protectors of Moesia against the barbarians from across the frontier, making clear the role that the central government wanted them to perform. On these propaganda pieces the personification of Moesia is shown gesturing to a bull and a lion representing the two legions, sometimes with their standards and legionary numbers above them to be absolutely clear.
6. The well-informed commentary by 'Semper Victor' on the Paradox Forum gaming site has interpreted events in the same way (https://forum.paradoxplaza.com/forum/threads/the-rise-of-the-sasanians.1058552/page-9).
7. Antoniniani listed on cngcoins.com are given as 4.55g, 3.83 g, 3.13 g, 4.76 g, 4.20 g, 4.23 g, 4.53 g, 4.39 g, 4.71 g, 4.41 g, 4.38 g, 3.51 g, 4.22 g (mean 4.22g, standard deviation 0.47 g). Alföldy (1924, p. 75) was able to identify the distinctive handiwork of an engraver who cut dies for Philip at Viminacium and also engraved for Pacatian. Mattingly et al. (1949, p. 65–66) pointed out that the mint at Viminacium stopped issuing the local bronze coinage at this time because the mint was repurposed.
8. For Iotape see Syme (1971, p. 202) and Potter (1990, p. 248). For Jotapian's revolt see Polemius Silvius and Aurelius Victor, *De Caesaribus* 29. Dufraigne (1975) suggested that the Alexander mentioned by Aurelius Victor was the emperor Severus Alexander (ruled 222–235) and the idea has been frequently repeated in the literature (e.g. Young 2004, p. 36) but this seems unlikely given that the latter only married in 225, at the age of about 15, and no mention of a child exists. Jotapian may of course have been illegitimate but is unlikely to have been born any earlier than 225 which even then would make him just 23 years old in 248. The image on the coins seems to show a middle-aged man. Moreover, Victor has Jotapian 'boasting of his descent from Alexander', not that he was a son. Alexander the Great had one legitimate son, Alexander IV of Macedon, who did not survive to maturity, but he may have had other children also. Bird (1994, p. 129) also prefers to construe Victor's meaning as descent from Alexander the Great but does not give his reasoning. Potter (1990, p. 39) claims that Victor had suggested that Jotapian was related to the Samsigeramid house of Emesa: this inference follows from the assumed identification of 'Alexander' with the emperor Severus Alexander which is here considered unlikely. Also for this reason, Young (2004, p. 36–37) places Jotapian's revolt in Emesa rather than Cappadocia / Commagene which seems even more unlikely if Jotapian's mint was Nicopolis in Seleucia as numismatists have suggested.
9. For local rivalries see Potter (1990, p. 252). For Satala see Cassius Dio, *Roman History* 55.23; Pollard and Berry (2012, p. 50). For numismatics see Bland (1993); Sellars (2013, p. 275).
10. For an overview of Jotapian's coinage known up to that date see Bland (1993).
11. Antoniniani of Jotapian on www.cngcoins.com weigh 3.02 g, 4.21 g, 4.13 g, 4.10 g, 3.88 g, 3.01 g, and 3.67 g (mean 3.65 g, standard deviation 0.53 g). The one odd coin of

Jotapian has a wreathed head, rather than a radiate crown, which on the face of it would seem to indicate a single denarius, not a double. This is unusual, considering that the denarius had largely gone out of circulation, and that the weight is similar to the doubles. It has been suggested, quite reasonably, that this coin was a test strike for a gold *aureus*, a prestigious and valuable coin. The mint may well have started issuing gold pieces on this model, although none has survived.

12. Mattingly et al. (1949) suggested the FORTVNA REDVX message was a wish that Fortuna would bring Pacatian safely to Rome, but this seems a rather contrived explanation. For ROMAE AETER AN MIL ET PRIMO see https://www.cngcoins.com/Coin.aspx?CoinID=43827. Note that it was earlier asserted that the coins of this type were fakes (M. Loriot personal communication reported by Birley, 1991a).
13. Zonaras, *Extracts of History*, XII.19; Zosimus, *New History* 1, 21, 1. See also De Blois (1978–1979, p. 21).
14. Zonaras, *Extracts of History*, XII.19.
15. The quote is from *Epitome de Caesaribus* 29.2. For Decius's full name and background see Syme (1971, p. 194–196), Rives (1999, p. 138–9) and Dietz (1980, p. 190). Consul was the highest rank in the Roman government since the days of the republic, but there were only two 'ordinary consuls' per year, far too few to satisfy ambitious and talented men; hence the convention that men distinguished in this way quickly stepped down, to make way for a series of replacements – suffect consuls – who could take a slightly lesser share in this great honour.
16. For governor in Spain see Syme (1971, p. 196). The wartime titles recorded on Spanish milestones are a sixth and seventh imperial acclamation for Maximinus, and a fifth tribunician power (Haegemans 2010, p. 223). Crispinus is known to have been given the title *legatus augusti pro praetore provinciae Hispaniae Citerioris et Gallaeciae* (Haegemans, 2010, p. 223).
17. John of Antioch states that Decius was Urban Prefect in 249 although this is considered doubtful by Mennen (2011, p. 260); see also Syme (1971, p 196–198). The various sources that relate to these events, including alternative scenarios, were reviewed and discussed by Pohlsander (1982). The main alternative is the history of John of Antioch which has Philip killed by assassins in Thrace. Some modern authors favour aspects of this version (e.g. Ando 2012, p. 120). For the actions of Decius and Philip see Zonaras, *Extracts of History* XII.19. For *dux moesiae et pannoniae* see Bird (1994, p. 127, n. 7). For the money see Salisbury and Mattingly (1924, p.3).
18. Examples from prior history include Germanicus and the mutiny on the Rhine as described by Tacitus *The Annals of Imperial Rome*, 31–39 and Pupienus at Aquilea as described by *Scriptores Historiae Augustae* (Julius Capitolinus), *Maximus et Balbinus* XII, 7–8.
19. Jovanova (2017); Boteva (2020).
20. Jordanes's account makes no mention of Pacatian's revolt and implies that Decius was sent against Ostrogotha by Philip but he 'could do nothing against the Getae' (Jordanes *Getica*, XVI). Similarly it has been suggested that Decius may have campaigned in Dacia before he was proclaimed emperor as a way of explaining an obscure verse from the Thirteenth Sibylline Oracle in which Decius 'emerged from the Dacians' (Mitthof 2020, p. 314). However the chronology allows very little time for substantial military campaigns. The suggestion that Cniva's attack on Philippopolis could have occurred at this time (Boteva, 2020) is also considered unlikely by this author for this reason.
21. For Decius's reluctance see Zonaras, *Extracts of History*, XII.19. Evidence that he did not mint coins comes from the fact that a large hoard of about 4,000 coins from his later reign was found in Bulgaria, but every piece was apparently minted in Rome and not locally (Salisbury and Mattingly, 1924, p. 2). For FIDES EXERCITVS coinage see Mattingly et al. (1949, p. 63–64).

22. Mitthof (2020) suggests June 249 as the most likely month.
23. Zosimus 1.22.1. An alternative tradition based on John of Antioch puts the clash in a completely different place, far away at Beroea in Moesia (see discussion and references in Boteva, 2020, p. 205–6), but that is likely a confusion with a later battle.
24. The decapitation story is from *Epitome De Caesaribus* 28.2. Aurelius Victor, *De Caesaribus*, 28 says, of the Battle of Verona, 'When news of this had reached Rome his son was killed in the praetorian camp.' Jerome, *Chronicle* p.300 also says the younger Philip was slain in Rome. See Pohlsander (1982) for a discussion of these and all the other sources, including an alternative tradition that says Philip II also dies in battle.
25. Tiradritti (2014); Jarus (2014); Harper (2015, 2017). Note that these interpretations have been questioned by Haldon et al. (2018b) as part of a general argument playing down all the other evidence for the impact of the Cyprianic plague.
26. Letter of Dionysius to the Brethren of Alexandria quoted in Eusebius, *Historia Ecclesiastica* VII.22.1–10. This account follows the chronology of Harper (2015) but that has been questioned by Haldon et al. (2018b) who criticize Harper for being selective and rhetorical and argue that the letter of Dionysius may be from a later date, claiming that scholarship 'unanimously' dates it, and another related one (see the following footnote), to the 260s (despite also citing scholars who agree with Harper). The basic problem is that Eusebius, the church historian of the fourth century who had access to the letters of Dionysius, clearly attempted to organize his material chronologically. After recounting Dionysius's description of the plague he then goes on to say that 'After this epistle, when peace had been restored to the city...' Several more letters are then discussed, after which he 'wrote again' about events in the 250s and 260s (Eusebius, *Historia Ecclesiastica* VII.22.11, 12) but these passages come after descriptions of events of the 250s and 260s, so the chronology is evidently confused and perhaps not recoverable. On the balance of evidence this author considers it reasonable, with Harper (2015), to link the pestilence described by Dionysius with that described by Cyprian for which the dating is more secure. It is worth noting that Jerome, following an earlier chronicle of Eusebius, links the accounts of Dionysius and Cyprian together and groups them in 253, the year that the pestilence seems to have peaked rather than when it originated (Jerome, *Chronicle* p. 301).
27. Eusebius, *Historia Ecclesiastica* VII.21, dated to 249 CE according to Harper (2015); see also Parkin (1992, p. 63–64).

Chapter 3
1. It is possible that Decius allocated the Balkan command to his son Herennius Etruscus (Syvänne 2019, p. 30) or even the Dacian command as discussed in Chapter 6.
2. For the *damnatio memoriae* of Philip see McMahon (2002) and references therein.
3. Aurelius Victor; whether before or after the Battle of Verona is not known.
4. For coinage minted locally see Grozdanova (2012). The staff is usually said to carry the head of an ass, as has been described many times, including for instance by Mattingly et al. (1949) and Besly and Bland (1983, p. 75) and in the summary of Decius's coinage by Manders (2012, p. 253–267). However, Dordea (2016) has written a detailed blog post suggesting it must have been a wolf or *draco* (dragon consisting of wolf's head on a serpentine body, although the latter part is not shown on the coins). Dordea credits the initial 'error' to Stevenson (1889), and the ass, in this case, is presumably whichever person perpetuates the error. However the debate goes further back even than that, and in this context we can do no better than repeat the elegant prose of Smyth (1834, p. 277), the learned hydrographer, astronomer and numismatist, who describes the Dacia reverse thus: '*A stolated female, with her hair richly attired, and holding a staff surmounted with the head of an animal which, from its shape, and ears, most men would pronounce to be that of an ass. But this is a point much disputed among antiquaries, apparently because so*

ignoble an animal seems unworthy of a national standard. Engelius, whose coin was probably in an indifferent condition, says that it is part of a dragon, of which the body and tail have been omitted by the artist; Padre Blasi calls it the head of a horse, for a reason equally applicable to five hundred other countries, "that of the people being great riders"; and Mons. le Bon, who makes out a beard, will have it to be the true "tête d'une chevre," on account of Dacia's being mountainous. It is, however, clearly an ass's head, and I think the medal before me would have convinced the doubters. The origin of this symbol is now unknown: some think it was assumed as a warlike ensign, because the bray of an ass resembled the Paphlagonian trumpet: others suppose it was derived from the Scythian custom of sacrificing the long-eared beast to Apollo; and a third set consider it to be the emblem of valour…'.

5. That adopting the name Trajan may have signified an aggressive frontier policy has been suggested by Southern (2001) and Christol (1997). The propaganda purposes of Decius's coinage has been reviewed by Manders (2009).
6. Salisbury and Mattingly (1924, p. 4–5).
7. Her full name is Herennia Cupressinia Estruscilla, which according to Syme (1971, p. 197) is patently Etruscan. Manders (2012, p. 260) is in error by stating that 'no indications that *pudicitia* applied to imperial women are found on Decius's coins' because it is a common type for Herrennia Etruscilla.
8. Gensini et al. (2004).
9. The *censor* story is from Trebellius Pollio, the most unreliable of the writers of the *Historia Augusta*, and is regarded as spurious by Magie (1932) and most subsequent commentators; *Scriptores Historiae Augustae* (Trebellius Pollio), *Valeriani Duo* V.4–8. For *restitutor sacrorum* see Babcock (1962). Note that the name of Decius has been obliterated in *damnatio memoriae*, probably by later Christians (Marelli, 1984).
10. Libellus Number 3 in Knipfing (1923).
11. Oborn (1933) suggests that the motive was primarily financial because the number of banishments was large and much property was seized. The Jews seem to have earned a special exemption from such necessities as of olden times. While there is no positive evidence of a Jewish exemption to Decius's decree, it seems likely, and we do know they were excused from a later edict along similar lines.
12. Ando (2012, p. 139). Manders (2009, p. 35) claims that the edict 'seems to have been issued in order to legitimize power and not as part of any comprehensive religious policy' although no other emperor took a similar course at the beginning of their reign.
13. Bishop Dionysius of Alexandria to Bishop Fabian of Antioch: Eusebius *Ecclesiastical History* 41.11–12.
14. Eusebius *Ecclesiastical History* 41.15–20.
15. Cyprian, *De Lapsis* VIII; Brent (2010).
16. Philippians 3.10–11.
17. Feltoe (1914); Lett (1918).
18. Cedrenus 453, 6–23 (Banchich and Lane 2009, p. 95). *Qu'ran*, Surah 18, Verses 9–26; see Grysa (2010) for Syriac, Arab and Islamic sources.
19. For the hoard see Demougeot (1962, p. 6). See also Bird (1994, p. 137). Eutropius, *Breviaram* LX.4.
20. For hoarding see Vagalinski (2012, p. 312). For Decius in Dacia see Southern (2001, p. 75). For Restorer of Dacia see *Corpus Inscriptionum Latinarum* iii, 1176; discussed by Salisbury and Mattingly (1924, p. 17). For milestones see *Corpus Inscriptionum Latinarum* II 4949 discussed by Ando (2012. P. 154). Southern (2001, p. 75) infers that Decius actively fought in Dacia; see also Grozdanova (2012) who discusses the inscriptional evidence. One inscription proclaiming him as DACICVS MAXIMVS from *Hispania Tarroconensis* can be dated to the latter half of 250 by the imperial titles.

21. Mattingly and Salibury (1924); Franke (2006). Note that there is confusion in the literature with many secondary sources saying that Hostilian was made *caesar* in the following year. It is possible that Hostilian was made Caesar at Viminacium on the Danube because a medallion was minted there in his name, something that is usually taken to indicate that he was there in person (Pick 1898; Grozdanova 2012). Evidence for the timing of this particular event comes from inscriptions and dated papyri in Egypt.
22. For Blemmyes see Strabo, *Geography* 17.1.53; quoted by Dijkstra (2012). For trade see McLaughlin (2014).
23. Dijkstra (2014, p. 281); Updegraff (1988, p. 69).

Chapter 4

1. The palimpsest had originally been noticed by Hunger (1961) but at that time it was not possible to decipher the text. Only modern spectral imaging and image analysis techniques made that possible. (Grusková 2010, 2012). Two pages (192v and 193r) are illegible but are reportedly under analysis at the time of writing (Gengler, 2020; Jana Grusková pers. comm. 2021). An account of the decipherment is in Martin and Grusková (2020).
2. This is not so desperate a hope as it may seem. Part of the introduction to the *Scythica* has also recently been discovered in a Vatican Library palimpsest (Németh 2015, 2020). It is valuable as a statement of the author's intentions.
3. Mitthof et al. (2020).
4. For full details of Cassiodorus and Jordanes see Croke (1987) and Christensen (2002). For Jordanes's background and sources see Liebecheuetz (2011), Doležal (2014), Vitiello (2020).
5. Jordanes, *Getica* IV.28; V.43. Heather (1991, p. 35–36) has pointed out instances where oral tradition seems to have been used. Jordanes tells us that in addition to Cassiodorus, an earlier scribe called Ablabius had apparently helped turn this tradition into written history. See also Jordanes, *Getica* VI.47; IX.60.
6. Jordanes, *Getica* XIV.82. For 'spurinym' see Heather (1989, p. 108). For other critical accounts of the *Getica* see Heather (1991, p. 34–67; 1996, p. 116); also see Drinkwater (1993) who likens Heather's deconstruction of the *Getica* with the nineteenth century historians who undermined the *Historia Augusta* (that view too now needs to be changed); Vitiello (2020) cites other authors who considered Ostrogotha to be mythical; see also Wolfram (2006); MacDowall (2017).
7. Widsith, 113–114; see Wilson (2019) and references therein.
8. This issue was discussed long ago by Grierson (1941, p. 5). To these arguments we can add that Theodoric himself seems to have believed in the reality of Ostrogotha because he gave the female version 'Ostrogotho' to one of his daughters. Of course, it may still be that the King Ostrogotha in Jordanes might ultimately derive from Roman history such as Dexippus himself, whom Jordanes cites in another context (*Getica* XXII.113), or others lost to us, rather than Gothic oral tradition. Cassiodorus could have picked up his name by reading the *Scythica* and then decided to insert it into a mythical royal lineage, so as to glorify Theodoric (as argued by Wolfram 2021, p. 142). But there are various reasons this scenario stretches credibility. One is that Ostrogotha is described as engaging in a war against a rival Gothic (Gepid) king, something no Roman historian recorded and which is probably Gothic tradition (Liebecheuetz 2011). Another is that Ostrogotha does not come across in an especially positive light in the new Dexippus, at least in the fragments that we have of it. Various other heroic kings are praised in Jordanes (including Cniva) but were not inserted into the Amal pedigree, which would have been an obvious thing to do if the genealogy was simply concocted. Finally, the scholarly argument that the Ostrogotha in the *Scythica Vindobonensia* was 'not a king, certainly no Amal', and not

superior to Cniva (as Jordanes had it) (e.g. Wolfram, 2021, p. 142), may place rather too much emphasis on the exactitude of Dexippus's Greek terms *archon* and *basileus*, used in passing with respect to Ostrogotha and Cniva in a very fragmentary text in relation to people he called the Scyths, and how those terms may relate to the Gothic hierarchy and indeed be rendered in modern English. Vitiello (2020) provides an extended discussion of the similarities and differences of the Ostrogotha of the *Scythica Vindobonensia* and in Jordanes.

9. For Dexippus on Scyths and Goths see Potter (2020) and citations therein.
10. Wolfram (1990); Heather and Matthews (1991); Heather (2006); Syvänne (2014, p. 79); Steinacher (2020).
11. See, for instance, Todd (1992, p. 139) who describes the migration as 'almost certainly merely the foundation myth of the Goths'. For ethno-fabrication see Frakes (2003). For a recent discussion of migration stories as foundation myths see Steinacher (2020). On the other hand the evidence of Bursche and Myzgin (2020), as discussed in a later chapter, supports a close association between the kingdom of the Goths and the Wielbark and Černjachov cultures.
12. Halsall (2007); Steinacher (2020). On a specific issue, Boteva (2020) has pointed out that various ancient sources (most notably Lactantius, who was writing early in the fourth century, and was therefore relatively close to events) refer to the invasions at the time of Decius as being led by the Carpi, and that this should be preferred over the account of Jordanes. This argument seems undermined by the fact that the new fragments of *Scythica* reinforce the leading roles of Ostrogotha and Cniva, both of which are Gothic names. As Jordanes states, the Carpi were involved as allies of the Goths, and it is reasonable to conclude that Lactantius was referring to them in this capacity.
13. Here I follow the chronology developed by Boteva (2001) and Davenport and Mallan (2013) and, partly, Zecchini (2020), which makes the most coherent and internally consistent narrative. For an alternative chronology see Wolfram (1990). Like this author, Zecchini (2020) has noticed the problem of reconciling the two Dexippan passages relating to siege(s) of Philippopolis which he resolves by switching the second fragment to 267/268, also a viable solution. The main problem with that, however, is that it requires Cniva's presence in a second, later invasion and a second concerted siege of a city that had already been sacked.
14. Wolfram (2021, p. 142) considers the number incredible. Grillone (2017) prefers the reading 30,000 (see discussion in Mitthof, 2020). MacDowall (2017) states that the Goths were 'a number of individual bands numbering in the low thousands at best' that 'operated independently rather than under a single command'.
15. Syvänne (2014, p. 86).
16. See Martin and Gruskova (2014a). For coin hoards see Varbanov (2012).
17. For the meaning of Argaithus and Guntheric see notes by Þeedrich Yeat at http://www.harbornet.com/folks/theedrich/Goths/Goths1.htm (accessed 11.12.2020). In contrast, Boteva (2020, p. 198), citing Detschew (1976) has argued that Argaith is a Thracian name. For 'Argunt' see Scriptores Historiae Augustae (Julius Capitolinus), *Gordiani Tres* 31.1. Another possibility is that 'Argunt' is a playful contraction of both names.
18. For coin hoards see Gerov (1963) and Varbanov (2012). For Trajan's invasion see Parker (2009).
19. For the city fortifications see Poulter (2020). The timing of the sieges of Marcianopolis and Philippopolis are fundamentally uncertain because they occur in three undated fragments of *Scythica*. This author prefers to follow the account of Jordanes (and elaborated by Boteva, 2001) by placing the siege of Marcianopolis in the raid that was led by Argaithus and Guntheric (see also Poulter, 2020) and by providing separate objectives for the two leaders. In contrast, Martin (2020), Mitthof (2020) and Piso (2020) have

all recently suggested that the besieger could have been Ostrogotha in a subsequent invasion, on the grounds that Ostrogotha was to be criticized for his lack of success in stark contrast to Cniva. This does not seem to be a convincing argument to this author because Ostrogotha's lack of success could just as easily have happened elsewhere, such as in Dacia the following year. Moreover the reconstruction preferred here assumes that the two fragments of Dexippus that record Philippopolis being besieged were in different years rather than two phases of the same siege as has generally been assumed (e.g. Martin, 2020). The reason for preferring this interpretation is that the two accounts do not seem to belong to the same stream of narrative, especially as there is no mention of a large body of Thracian auxiliary troops in the first fragment which become a major feature in the second. Similarly, Cniva is only mentioned in the second fragment. The first fragment goes to some lengths to describe the heroic resistance of the people, which contrasts with the second which criticises the lack of care taken by the defending garrison and their drunken neglect. Syvänne (2019, p. 193) also concluded that the two fragments relate to different sieges but that the first relates to a later event in the reign of Gallienus.

20. Minchev (2012).
21. Konstantinos VII Porphyrogennetos, *Excerpts on Stratagems*, 5 in Jacoby (1958; Brill's New Jacoby BNJ 100 F 27).
22. Stein (1957) suggested that Dexippus transplanted material relating to the siege of Philippopolis straight from Thucydides, however that was criticized by Blockley (1971). There is no doubt that Dexippus wrote in the style of Thucydides (e.g., Martin 2020; Papathomas 2020), but as we shall see, details of the second siege of Philippopolis can be confirmed on the ground.
23. Konstantinos VII Porphyrogennetos, *Excerpts on Stratagems*, 5 in Jacoby (1958; Brill's New Jacoby BNJ 100 F 27).
24. Jordanes, *Getica* XVI, 92; XVII, 94.
25. For the suggested identification of Galtis as 'Galt', see Mommsen (1882). For the identification of German Galt with Romanian Ungra see https://en.wikipedia.org/wiki/Ungra. It should be noted for the record that some historians have linked Jordanes's account with a statement in a Latin panegyric to Maximian (reigned 286–305 CE) that in his reign (and to his great implied credit) various 'barbarian' groups were busy massacring each other. The list includes the remark that 'another group of Goths, with the help of a band of Teifali join battle with the Vandals and Gepids' (*Panegyrici Latini* XI, 17). This led to the view, still commonly articulated, that Jordanes must have got the timing of his Battle of Galtis out by about 40 years (e.g. Schwarcz, 1992; Wolfram, 2001, 2021; Castritius, 2003; Brodersen, 2020) and even to the placement of a historical Ostrogotha about the year 290; or to the idea that there were two Ostrogothas whom Jordanes got confused (which is of course possible). However it is to be noted that Jordanes specifically links the invasions of Thrace and Moesia around 250 as one of the causes of the Gepid war. The panegyric does not mention any names. Occam's razor leads this author to prefer the fairly detailed account in Jordanes and to conclude that the panegyric of Maximian refers to another battle or, given the context, simply endemic and ongoing conflict between Goths and Gepids, and that the Ostrogotha of the newly discovered *Scythica* is the same real historical character as the Ostrogotha of Jordanes.
26. For Palladio see La Follette (1993). For the Colosseum and *porticus decii* see Platner (1929). Jerome, *Chronicle* p. 300 claims that the amphitheatre in Rome was burned down.
27. Bland (1996, p. 72). The standard work on the coinage (Mattingly et al., 1949, p. xxii-xxiii) made another suggestion for the tariff of the new coin. Basing their observation that Decius took old denarii and overstruck them as doubles, they suggested that if the double-denarius was worth one old denarius then the double sestertius might have been tariffed at two to the double-denarius. This argument does not seem very convincing to

this author because the radiate crown had signified a double since the reign of Nero two hundred years before.
28. Mattingly et al. (1949, p. 111).
29. The series is discussed by Mattingly et al. (1949, p. 113). The list of emperors is interesting to contemplate, both for who is included in the roll-call and who is not: the featured emperors are Augustus (27 BCE–14 CE), Vespasian (69–79), Titus (79–81), Nerva (96–98), Trajan of course (98–117), Hadrian (117–138), Antoninus Pius (138–161), Marcus Aurelius (161–180), Commodus (177–192), Septimius Severus (193–211), and Severus Alexander (222–235). However, some other deified emperors like Claudius (41–54) and Pertinax (193) were not included. Also omitted is the young emperor Gordian III (238–244) whom Philip may have betrayed but who had, nevertheless, been deified by him. Gordian may have been left out because he was from the family who had rebelled against Maximinus. Philip (244–249), of course, was not to be considered a god by the man who had defeated him in battle. Of the famous Julio-Claudian emperors it is not surprising that Tiberius (14–37), Caligula (37–41) and Nero (54–68) were left out, as they had decidedly mixed reputations, but the deified Claudius (41–54) might have merited inclusion. Severus Alexander is especially interesting because he was the man killed in the coup that had brought Maximinus to power, and Decius was known to have been a supporter of Maximinus. Perhaps it was a sop to those who supported the other side in the civil war of 238. The most surprising inclusion is Commodus, who despite being the son of the revered Marcus Aurelius, was a psychotically deranged individual who committed a series of appalling crimes before eventually being assassinated, to general relief at the time; nevertheless he had been deified by a successor perhaps to underline the fact that whatever his deeds, his right to rule was absolute.

Chapter 5

1. In this reconstruction of events I follow Salisbury and Mattingly (1924) in contradiction to the majority of recent writers who suggest that Cniva over-wintered in hostile (Roman) territory. None of the historical sources indicate this happened, and it would have created considerable logistical difficulties for Cniva if his army had been anything like as large as Jordanes and Dexippus indicate (see also 'Semper Victor' at https://forum.paradoxplaza.com/forum/threads/the-rise-of-the-sasanians.1058552/page-9).
2. For the suggestion that the Goths attacked when the river was frozen see Salisbury and Mattingly (1924). The lower Danube used to freeze over every year until the mid-twentieth century (Ionita et al., 2018). The reconstruction preferred here is based largely on the evidence of Jordanes which implies that the attack led by Argaithus and Guntheric occurred before (and presumably in a different year from) the campaign that included the loss of Philippopolis and the battles of Beroe and Abritus. In this respect the scenario preferred here follows Gerov (1963, 1977) and Boteva (2001) and differs from the chronology preferred by Mitthof (2020) and others who place Beroe in 250 and speculate that Cniva overwintered in Philippopolis. For auxiliaries at Sucidava see Matei-Popescu (2010).
3. This author found Oescus much as previously described by Parker (2009) in his evocative travelogue round the borders of the empire.
4. Wolfram (1990, p. 45) based on the account of Jordanes, *Getica* XVI, 90 which may refer to the previous year, but even so the conjecture is likely.
5. For the name Cniva see Þeedrich Yeat at http://www.harbornet.com/folks/theedrich/Goths/Goths1.htm. Jordanes describes Ostrogotha as a king but does not use the same term for Cniva. In the previous invasion Ostrogotha had put two nobles, Argaithus and Gutheric in command so it would seem that Cniva may have had a similar role on this occasion. Jordanes never described Cniva as a king although historians have

long assumed that he succeeded Ostrogotha. It is possible that Jordanes did not regard Cniva as legitimate because he was not of the Amal lineage. It is interesting that the new fragment of the *Scythica* has Cniva as '*basileus*' (= king or emperor) but Ostrogotha merely as a leader (ἄρχων). From this it has been suggested that Ostrogotha was in some way junior to Cniva (e.g., Potter, 2020). This author prefers to regard Dexippus's testimony as consistent with the idea that Ostrogotha was a king and senior to Cniva because one can be both a king and a leader. The division of Cniva's force into two in this reconstruction, making a third division, follows Jordanes, *Getica* XVIII.101. It also follows the inferred strategy of the Goths which was to overwhelm the border forces by force of numbers allowing others to roam freely in search of loot.
6. Mattingly and Salisbury (1924). Note that these authors suggest late 250 as the earliest possible date for burial but that depends on the argument (from the Oxyrhynchus Papyrus x.1284) that Hostilian was appointed Caesar in late 250 which is now thought to be incorrect.
7. One ingenious theory is that the name Valens derives from part of the name of the *Caesar* Hostilian. Some of his coins have the obverse legend C VALENS HOS MES QVINTVS. Hence an over-enthusiastic historian of the fourth century could have inferred that this 'Valens' must have been a usurper. This idea was proposed by Mattingly (1946, p. 45) as '*almost* obvious' (my italics!). What is not so obvious is where the names Julius and Lucinianus came from.
8. Aurelius Victor, *De Caesaribus* 31; *Epitome de Caesaribus* 29.5; Scriptores Historiae Augustae (Trebellius Pollio), *Tyranni Triginta* XX. See discussions in Bird (1994, p. 129–130, n. 7) and Nathan and McMahon (2002). Grozdanova (2012) has suggested that Hostilian may have been absent from Rome, prompting the revolt, but the timing is speculative. It has been suggested that an obscure passage in Cyprian *Epistles* 55 may also relate to this revolt (e.g. Southern 2001, p. 75) but this is not convincing to this author.
9. Brent (2010).
10. Cyprian, *Epistles* 20.2.
11. Brent (2010).
12. Brent (2010, p. 12–13).
13. Paul, *1 Corinthians* 11.4–6.
14. Banchich and Lane (2009, p. 95).
15. Aparaschivei (2012).
16. For the battle between Gallus and Cniva see Jordanes, *Getica* XVIII.101. For destruction outside Novae see Poulter (2020) and references therein. For the head of Claudius see http://archaeologyinbulgaria.com/2016/03/18/condemned-bronze-head-of-roman-emperor-gordian-iii-from-nicopolis-ad-istrum-to-be-showcased-by-bulgarias-veliko-tarnovo/. For the curtain wall see Zakrzewski (2020, p. 446).
17. Jordanes, *Getica* XVIII.101.
18. For the *thermoperipatos* see Petrova (2017). It has been suggested that Nicopolis fell to the Goths and was plundered (Wolfram, 1990, p. 46) but this author has found no evidence to support that assertion and it contradicts Jordanes, *Getica* XVIII.101 who would have mentioned it as a Gothic victory if he had known about it.
19. Destruction of a milestone at Sostra attributed to this time is described by Sharankov and Hristov (2019).
20. The source that mentions the Gothic loss of 30,000 men is Syncellus, *Chronography* AM 5746 which fits with the account of Jordanes, Getica XVIII.102, 'When the Emperor Decius drew near, Cniva at last withdrew to the Haemus, which were not far distant.' The whole historical basis for the Battle of Nicopolis has been questioned by Mitthof (2020) who argued that Syncellus badly confused the sequence of events and there may have been no battle there at all. However, that seems to ignore the testimony of the 'Letter

to Philippopolis' discussed in the next section in which Decius begins by referring to a recent victory that scattered the barbarians, and later goes on to specifically mention a victory at Nicopolis (Fragment from Konstantinos VII Porphyrogennetos, *Excerpts on Proverbs*; in McInerney, 2007).

21. For IMP II see Peachin (1990). Syncellus, *Chronography* AM 5746 implies that the Goths sacked Nicopolis before Decius reached them (Wolfram, 1990, p. 45; Syvänne, 2019, p. 31–32) but there is no other evidence for this, including in the new fragments of *Scythica* or the Letter to Philippopolis which seems to rule out the possibility; moreover, Jordanes, who provides a much more informed account than Syncellus, would surely have recorded the sacking of Trajan's 'City of Victory' had he known about it.
22. There is no historical evidence for a defensive screen but it is a highly defensible spot. A small force holding the Shipka Pass was a decisive feature of the so-called 'Liberation of Bulgaria' campaign during the Russo-Turkish War of 1877–1878.
23. This man's name and position are known from surviving inscriptions AE1932, 28 and SEG 55, 761. See Grozdanova (2012). Some earlier writers confused this Priscus with Philip's brother (e.g., Bradley, 1888, p. 27). For a detailed discussion of Priscus and his likely rank and station see Piso (2020).
24. Fragment from Konstantinos VII Porphyrogenetos, *Excerpts on Proverbs*. Translated by J. McInerney (2007).
25. Discussed by Poulter (2020).
26. As discussed by Vegetius, *Epitome rei militaris*, Book 3.
27. Jordanes, *Getica* XVIII.102.
28. A similar situation occurs with the Battle of Abritus discussed below. The same location for the battle as suggested here has also been independently proposed by 'Semper Victor' at https://forum.paradoxplaza.com/forum/threads/the-rise-of-the-sasanians.1058552/page-9
29. For the elevation of Herennius see Grozdanova (2020, p. 238) and references therein. Mattingly and Salisbury (1924, p. 220) suggested that the VICTORIA GERMANICA issue refers to the Goths.
30. Martin and Grusková (2014b). A slightly different interpretation and translation of the texts is provided by Jones (2015).
31. Dexippus would have known very well what Roman gold coins were like as they would have been his means of personal payment for official duties. For his archaic style see for example Hostein (2017). Bursche and Myzgin (2020) think there is 'no doubt' that Dexippus must have been referring to gold Roman aurei. However, it is not clear that Cniva would have had a ready source of these prior to the Battle of Abritus, discussed in a later chapter. Potter (2020, p. 363) has suggested 'barbarian' coinage – that is, imitation Roman pieces. Such pieces were produced prior to 250 but not in great quantities (more were produced in later years) and it is doubtful if Cniva's treasury could have contained thousands of them. The Sassanians called their new gold coin (minted since the reign of Ardashir in the 220s) the 'denar' after the Roman 'denarius aureus', but Dexippus can be excused from knowing that. It has been suggested that these coins, which were considerably heavier than their Roman equivalents, were minted for prestige, for gifts and ceremonial purposes and to compete with Roman gold, rather than for general circulation in the Persian Empire (Schindel, 2005; Darley and Canepa, 2018).
32. Dexippus, *Scythica Vindobonensia* f195r-v; translation of Jones (2015). It should be recorded that while most historians date the action in this new fragment of Dexippus to the reign of Decius and 251 in particular, a minority including Zecchini (2020) prefers a later date in 267/268.
33. Martin (2020) has suggested that the reference to the stadium in Decius's letter to the Philippopolitans is a literary device on the part of Dexippus to introduce the location

to his readers. That may be true, but it was also the largest communal gathering place within the walls.
34. Evidence for this is a statement in Aurelius Victor, *De Caesaribus* 29 that 'the supreme power was offered to Lucius Priscus, who was ruling Macedonia as governor, as a result of an incursion of the Goths, after they had plundered most of Thrace'. Jordanes, *Getica* XVIII.103 simply reports that Cniva 'allied himself to Priscus, the commander of the city'.
35. Ammianus Marcellinus, *Roman History* XXXI.5.15.
36. For coins see Varbanov (2012, p. 9). For the Nebet Tepe tower see Dikov (2018). For more recent remains see Varbanov (2020). Poulter (2020, p. 377–378) cites additional archaeological evidence for destruction but argues that there is no good evidence that the city as a whole was destroyed.

Chapter 6

1. Dexippus, *Scythica Vindobonensia* 194r-194v (for 194r see Martin and Grusková, 2014b; for 194v see Grusková and Martin, 2015). Jones (2015) provides and alternative translation of both. Martin (2020) has suggested that the significance of Thermopylae in this passage is a literary device on the part of Dexippus to introduce the location to his readers.
2. Wolfram (2021, p. 142) considers the number 50,000 as 'incredible', for reasons not given.
3. Dexippus, *Scythica Vindobonensia* 194v; translation of Martin and Grusková (2014).
4. Historians generally do not accept ancient writers' numerical estimates of army sizes because of the logistical problems they would generate, so for instance Piso (2016, 2020) estimates a figure of about 15,000 for Decius's army instead. However, Mitthof (2020, p. 315–321) has reviewed the troops potentially available to Decius at this time and suggests that the number is actually plausible. To this can be added two other arguments. First, by giving Decius a larger army than Ostrogotha at this stage, Dexippus cannot be suspected of exaggerating the Scythian (Gothic) army for effect. Second, in the newly discovered introduction to the *Scythica* found in the Vatican palimpsest, Dexippus states his intention of recounting details of battles so that lessons can be learned from them. If that was indeed his intention and not just a stylistic trope then as a man accustomed to military command, it is reasonable to infer he would have tried to get his facts right. The issue of numbers is discussed again in the account of the Battle of Abritus, below.
5. The text can be interpreted in radically different ways and the reconstruction of events depends on whether there is any attempt to harmonize it with Jordanes, which is this author's strategy. According to Martin and Gruskova's (2014) translation it reads: *'And for the moment, having built a trench at Hamisos [?], a place of Beroina [?], he stayed inside the encampment together with his army, watching for when the enemy were to cross.'* The places are considered unknown. However the reading of the text is difficult at this point, hence the query marks. An alternative reading by Jones (2015) renders the names 'Asmios' and 'Beroea', the latter being identified with the city of Beroe. If so, it indicates that Decius had re-crossed the mountains into Thrace by the Shipka Pass and may have built a palisade and camp at the site of the previous defeat to prevent Cniva's re-crossing. (Note that intriguing crop marks at 42°42'44.82"N; 25°19'20.30"E might conceivably be the ditch and outer – western – palisade at this point.) But that interpretation is problematic, not least because it would not protect the main route across the mountains along the *via traiana* and the Beklemeto Pass. That could have been protected by Gallus, of course, but it then begs the question of how Cniva could possibly have made it across the Haemus Range as far as Abritus without fighting a major battle with one or other force. Hence this author prefers to infer that Decius set up a field camp somewhere strategic north of the mountains in Moesia or even in Dacia where he could potentially react to moves

by both Cniva and Ostrogotha. Finally, others have inferred that the mention of Beroe implies that the action in the fragment predates the battle of that name as mentioned by Jordanes (although it was a surprise attack in that account and there is no mention of a ditch and palisade). In the interpretation preferred here, the action comes after Beroe because it explains the 'mishap in that plain' mentioned in the fragment.
6. Dexippus, *Scythica Vindobonensia* 194v; translation of Martin and Grusková (2014).
7. Jordanes, *Getica* XVII.100. In that account Ostrogotha dies before Cniva leads his army across the Danube but the new fragment of *Scythica* shows that the two armies were operating simultaneously but in different sectors. This is the main difference between Jordanes and Dexippus and it is best explained by Jordanes, or more probably his source Cassiodorus, covering up for the fact that Ostrogotha, an Amal king and ancestor of Theodoric, was defeated in battle and possibly captured or killed in the campaign.
8. Maurice, *Strategikon* in Dennis (2001, p. 53–54). Syvänne (2019) has made a significant contribution by highlighting the importance of this work in understanding the campaign of Decius. He has argued that the strategy of feigned retreat is appropriate to a cavalry 'tagmata' (a Byzantine word) and therefore it implies the army of Decius was largely of cavalry, similar, in his view, to Cniva's Goths. It is not necessary to make such an inference, however. The 'Letter to Philippopolis' specifically refers to the Goths fielding 'considerable cavalry and a large army of both heavy and light infantry' (McInerney, 2007) and both are shown on the Great Ludovisi sarcophagus. See also the comment of 'Semper Victor' at https://forum.paradoxplaza.com/forum/threads/the-rise-of-the-sasanians.1058552/page-9
9. Jordanes, *Getica* XVIII.103. It is worth emphasizing that the plain sense of Jordanes's account places this significant battle, and the death of Herennius Etruscus, in a different place and earlier in the narrative than the Battle of Abritus, which we will come to in due course. The *Epitome de Caesaribus* 29.3–4 simply says that Herennius died in the same war, and similarly Ammianus Marcellinus, *History* 31.5.16; Eutropius, Breviarum IX.4 says (incorrectly) that both died in enemy territory; but other Roman/Greek historical sources reflect a different tradition and specifically state that Herennius died at Abritus (Aurelius Victor, *De Caesaribus* 29; Malalas, *Chronographia* XII, p. 227; *Chronicon Paschale* p. 505.4–6; Zonaras, *Extracts of History*, XII.20). This has become the usual interpretation among historians (e.g., Potter, 2004; Banchich and Lane, 2009; Grozdanova, 2020; also the museum displays at Abritus as of 2019). However, it is easier to see how the two events of Jordanes could be combined rather than separated, so the idea that Herennius died in a separate battle is preferred herein (see also Seure, 1923, cited by Salisbury and Mattingly, 1924, p. 18).
10. For details of the discovery see D'Ossat (2008).
11. A clear fore-runner is the Portonaccio sarcophagus which has the facial features of the main character unfinished (Kebric 2015).
12. The 'submission' scene on the lid represent a survival of a tableau familiar since the time of Augustus (Kuttner 1995) which underlines the highly traditional nature of the sarcophagus. The features of the woman are very similar to a marble bust of a diademed lady in the British Museum that is thought to be the likeness of Herennia Etruscilla (British Museum 1873, 0820.734; see https://www.britishmuseum.org/collection/object/G_1873-0820-734). The lady on the sarcophagus lacks a diadem, possibly because she too is depicted on campaign. There is an inscription from central Italy that describes her as *mater castrorum* (mother of the camps) (CIL IX, 4056 from Carsioli, discussed by Salisbury and Mattingly, 1924, p. 15).
13. The identification as Hostilian was by Von Heintze (1957). For branding and Mithras see Bianchi (1979, p. 488-489). Scholars who generally accepted the identification include Felleti Maj (1958) and Beskow (1978).

14. The identification as Herennius was previously suggested by Gullini (1960) and discussed by Pelikan (1964). Although there has been surprisingly little further discussion about this far more obvious attribution, the museum information panel does raise it as a possible alternative to Hostilian. For the deification of Herennius Etruscus see Eutropius, *Breviarium* 9.4.
15. Cassius Dio, *Roman History* 68.9.1.
16. Faust (2017) has suggested that the sarcophagus shows a battle against Gothic *and* Persian enemies, the Phrygian cap indicating Persians, but this is not necessary. Later Gothic rulers such as Theodoric's daughter, the regent Queen Amalsuintha of the sixth century were associated with this headgear or something very similar, which by that time might have been associated with the nobility of eastern (Ostro-) Goths in particular (McClanan, 2002; see also discussion in Amory, 1997, p. 341-2).
17. This interpretation is somewhat complicated by the left-hand panel, which is part of the composition although not finished in deep relief, and shows two other individuals with the Phrygian cap attacking from the left. The first is in full charge with cavalry lance ready to strike, the second (directly below) apparently dismounting with drawn sword. Either or both of these could be interpreted as the same individual or other 'pileati' involved in the battle. The hypothetical barbarian commander on the main panel is virtually identical with a top quality sculpture in finest variegated marble known as the 'Farnese barbarian', dug up long ago on the Palatine hill in Rome. He also has shaggy hair and wears a Phrygian cap. That sculpture is in fact a pedestal, but what statue it supported is not now known. It is currently attributed to the first or second centuries for reasons that are not clear to this author. It may be a depiction of Decebalus himself, or a generic 'barbarian' nobleman, but it could also hail from the third century and represent the same individual as depicted on the Ludovisi Sarcophagus, in which case it is tempting to think he supported a statue of the deified Herennius Etruscus.
18. This legionary symbolism was widely current at the time. For instance the standard bronze coinage of Dacia from the period typically shows the personification of the province holding legionary standards inscribed V and XIII, beneath which are an eagle and a lion respectively. She also wears the Phrygian cap to emphasize her nobility and carries the curved *falx*. The symbolism is not certain however because at least one individual has both an eagle and lion on a helmet, and of course eagles were associated with every legion.
19. In considering the new evidence from the Vienna palimpsest, Mitthof (2020) has suggested that Ostrogotha may have been killed in battle at this time. Piso (2020), sensitive of the tradition that Germanic groups had a democratic aspect, has suggested he may have been de-selected as leader and replaced by Cniva, although that would require communication and agreement between two army groups on active campaign. If Ostrogotha had been captured and executed, many of the later Christian epitomators were extremely hostile to Decius because of the persecution and so might easily have omitted the detail. The puzzle, however, is the late fifth century pagan historian Zosimus who was well-disposed toward Decius and would surely have mentioned the fact if he knew of it. But while Zosimus seems to have used Dexippus's summary *Chronicle* for the third century part of his history, he evidently was not aware of the *Scythica* and relates few firm details of the campaigns. He claims that Dexippus was 'victorious in every battle', which is clearly not the case, and does not mention the names of the Gothic commanders. For a discussion of Zosimus's sources see Blockley (1980).
20. Harper (2015, 2016, 2017). For a response to some of Harper's ideas see Haldon et al. (2018). Details of ebola and its symptoms see https://www.who.int/news-room/fact-sheets/detail/ebola-virus-disease

21. Note that there is no reference in this passage to the massive military defeat and death of the emperor that might also have been referred to if that news was current at the time of writing.
22. Zonaras, *Extracts of History* XII.20. Zosimus, *New History* 1.23.1. Examples of this from the third century include the Gallic Emperor Postumus who was killed by his own troops when he forbade them from sacking the city of Mogontiacum (Mainz); and that of Carausius, the naval commander, who was accused of allowing Saxon raiders to plunder cities before attacking them and taking the booty for himself.
23. Zonaras, *Extracts of History* XII.10.
24. Inscriptions indicate that the Roman fortress at Razgrad is indeed Abritus (or Abrittus). Syncellus, *Chronography* p. 459.5–19 gives an alternative name as Forum Thembronium, which probably derives from Dexippus's *Chronicle*. It has also been rendered Forum Terebronii (see Carrie and Moreau, 2012). Also see the discussion in the following chapter on a possible linkage between the name and the name Trebonianus Gallus. For the battlefield see Dikov (2016b).
25. Scriptores Historiae Augustae (Trebellius Pollio), *Gallieni Duo* XIII.9 tells us that at a later battle in 268 CE the Goths made 'a barricade of wagons' (*facta carrigine*). Ammianus Marcellinus, *History* XXXI.7.7 tells us that the word 'carrago' was Gothic. See also Nefedkin (2002).
26. According to an online article, archaeologist Georgi Dzanev is quoted as saying '[Based on] the available archaeological and numismatic finds, we have concluded that the last camp of Emperor Trajan Decius was located in this area, and the battle itself took place along the valley of the Beli Lom River, at the foot of a hill' (Dikov, 2016b). It is worth recording that elsewhere Dzanev is quoted as having said that the battlefield was selected by the Romans who were blocking the route to the Danube and would have benefitted from the flat ground (https://brewminate.com/roman-goth-battle-of-abritus-251-ce-battlefield-identified-near-bulgarias-dryanovets/). However the historical sources suggest that Cniva chose the field (e.g. Zonaras, *Extracts of History* XII.20), which also seems to make sense considering the overall course of the campaign and likely movement of the armies as described herein.
27. News spread slowly around the empire making the timing of the battle a subject for discussion, but the combined evidence from dated altar stones and papyri points to the middle of May (Kovács, 2015).
28. Mitthoff (2020) has reviewed the historical sources that provide numerical estimates of the size of 'barbarian' armies and also the many modern writers who have been sceptical of such figures and suggest between a maximum of about 20,000 and perhaps just a few thousand. To these can be added MacDowall (2017) who has estimated Cniva's army at Abritus at about ten thousand. A force that small would have found it impossible to hold ground against cavalry on a battlefield a kilometre across and could easily have been outflanked. In contrast, Mitthof's (2020) view is that the numbers reported by Dexippus are possible.
29. This reconstruction assumes that both Goths and Romans fielded a traditional mixed force of infantry, cavalry, archers and artillery. Syvänne (2019) has argued that both armies could have been mainly cavalry. His reconstruction of Abritus (Syvänne 2019, p. 35) does not take into account the restricted size and constricted flanks of the battlefield. Also the discovery of a gladius indicates that Roman infantry likely took part in the battle.
30. Radoslava et al. (2011).
31. The tactic was described thus by Maurice: 'The troops are lined up in front of the swamp and, when the action begins, they feign flight, heading over the passageways, and lead the army to fall right into the swamp. Then the troops in ambush on the flanks suddenly

charge upon them, and the men feigning retreat overpower and destroy the enemy. The Scythians used this against the Roman emperor Decius when they crossed the Danube and invaded Thrace and waged open war against him round Moesia. Up to that time Decius had been successfully employing the same strategy, simulated retreat, in intensive warfare which enabled him to destroy many of them'. *Strategikon* p.53. See also Zosimus I.15.

32. Lactantius, *De mortibus persecutorum* IV, 2–3; See Boteva (2010) for commentary.
33. Mouchmov (1930, 1934). The *terminus post quem* of Reka Devnia is a vital piece of information, but suggestions in the literature vary. Depeyrot (2004) and Spoerri Butcher (2019) give it as 251, but elsewhere it is given as 250 (e.g. http://archaeologyinbulgaria.com/marcianopolis-marcianople-devina-devnya-bulgaria/). The former seems correct because the issue of Decius featuring the two Pannoniae in the hoard is thought to have been from one of his later issues (Salisbury and Mattingly, 1924; RIC 21b). An alternative suggestion from Metcalf (2002) is 241 – ten years earlier – because issues after that date are rare and may be intrusive (i.e., not belong to the hoard proper). Metcalf pointed out that coins of Philip the Arab are absent, but Paunov and Prokopov (2002, p. 49) indicate c. 4–5 of his coins were originally present 'according to Professor B. Gerov' but do not exist in the current inventory. Spoerri Butcher (2019) describes it as one of the largest silver hoards ever found. As a result there is quite a large body of numismatic literature that refers to the hoard. As recently as 2019 a convenient digital database was made available http://chre.ashmus.ox.ac.uk/hoard/3406?fbclid=IwAR3VF1xU3YkB-rt3JqDikISizD0vPgqTEN5dJUpvh46Y9x3JwFmJ61CLDoE.
34. Casey (1986); see also Hellings and Spoerri Butcher (2016, p. 54–55).
35. For the provincial coins of Marcianopolis see http://www.wildwinds.com/coins/greece/moesia/markianopolis/i.html. Many towns of the second and third centuries had cult religious centres, and Marcianopolis was no exception. One of them features the 'Three Graces', goddesses of feminine beauty, joy and dance. The most prominent, however, was dedicated to the rather foreboding Egyptian god Serapis. This deity started off as a kind of fusion of the very ancient Egyptian cults of Osiris and the Apis bull. He was regarded as the husband of Isis, and there is evidence that he was strongly promoted as a Zeus-like figure in the Ptolemaic period to help fuse Egyptian and Greek cultures. Serapis became increasingly popular throughout the Roman Empire during the imperial period as Egyptians travelled far and wide, eventually being honoured in Rome itself and by the emperors. In some minds he was regarded as the supreme deity, similar or perhaps the same as the Roman Jupiter, or of the sun god Sol. Even some of the Jews and Christians seem to have thought of Serapis as a manifestation of their own deity, not least because the revered Greek translation of the Hebrew scripture (the so-called Septuagint) was housed in the precinct of Serapis in Alexandria. Serapis often appears on the obverse side of the provincial bronzes minted in Marcianopolis alongside the emperor himself, with the reverse showing him seated in his tetrastyle temple (that is, a temple with four pillars at the front). It is not known whether the possible temple discovered by Mouchmov is the lost Serapeum of Marcianopolis (certainly he never claimed that it was) but it does at least seem possible.
36. Zosimus, *New History* 1.42.1; 4.10.3; Jordanes, *Getica* XVI.93.
37. If so they managed to somehow avoid having it confiscated in 235 CE when the then Emperor Maximinus ordered the seizure of temple funds across the empire to fund his wars.
38. Poulter (2020, p. 376) specifically cautioned against linking the hoard to the destruction of the city but does not mention that the hoard was sealed by a destruction layer.
39. Bursche (2013); Bursche and Myzgin (2020).

40. At least one (2014, p. 6) has apparently turned up in a Polish auction since Bursche's compilation – see Bland (2012). There is also a large influx of regular provincial bronze coinage which has been related to the Gothic raids (Myzgin, 2017).
41. Bursche (2013); Bursche amd Myzgin (2020). See also Bland (2014) and Myzgin (2017).
42. Bursche and Myzkin (2020, p. 196). The distribution of bronze Roman bronze artefacts and provincial bronze coins is similar.
43. Jordanes, *Getica* XVIII.103.

Chapter 7
1. Potter (2018, p. 18); Kulikowski (2016, p. 154).
2. The main reason for thinking that Gallus was proclaimed in Arbritus is that it was later called Forum Thembronium which may be a recollection of the name Trebonianus as suggested by Carrié and Moreau (2012, p. 604). The sources that allege treachery are Zonaras, *Extracts of History* XII.20 and Zosimus, *New History* 1.23.3. Zosimus goes on to say that Gallus 'published an open declaration that Decius and his army had perished by his contrivance' (Zosimus, New History 1.24.1) which is extremely unlikely, especially given that Gallus would have had nothing to gain by admitting to such an infamous act. The best interpretation is that Zosimus was the victim of fake news.
3. Jordanes, *Getica* XIX, 106; Zosimus, *New History* 1.23; Zonaras, *Extracts of History* XII.21.
4. An inscription from Rome on 9 June 251 (CIL VI 31129) assumes he is still alive but one from 24 June (CIL VI 36760) has him consecrated and a god (Potter 1990, p. 278; Kovács 2015). For the deification of Decius see Eutropius, *Breviarium* 9.4.
5. Evidence for this is that he seems to have appropriated the record of tribunician power from his adopted father (Mattingly 1946, p. 46, Appendix C).
6. An inscription from central Italy that describes Herennia Etruscilla as wife of an *augustus* and mother of two *augusti* presumably dates to this time (CIL IX, 4056 from Carsioli, as discussed by Salisbury and Mattingly, 1924, p. 15; see also Mattingly, 1946).
7. Sear (1974, p. 240); Bursch and Myzgin (2020). The double aureus is sometimes called a 'binio'. For production rate see Bland (2013). The co-*augustus*, Hostilian, was not awarded the honour of gold coinage which is one indication, perhaps, of tension between the imperial families.
8. Besly and Bland (1983, p. 40).
9. As this author has previously argued, a magnificent oversize nude bronze statue in the Metropolitan Museum of Art that was previously supposed to be of Gallus, and is his usual image on internet pages, is more likely to be a representation of the Emperor Maximinus Thrax (reigned 235–238) (Pearson, 2018).
10. Quotations are from Symeon the Logothete, *Chronicle* 77; Zosimus, *New History* 1.26; Zonaras, *Extracts of History* XII.21; Orosius, *History Against the Pagans* 7.27.10. These are all discussed by Harper (2015) who suggests that Orosius was making a learned allusion to the plague described in Vergil, *Georgics* III. Harper (2015) argues that the original source was Philostratus, who is cited by some, but it is also possible that some of the information came from lost portions of the *Scythica* of Dexippus (Jones 2020) which, if true, would add to the credibility of these accounts.
11. Banchich and Lane (2009, p. 106–107). Note that George the Monk and Cedrenus attribute the plague to the time of Valerian but their chronology is obviously confused at this point (discussed by Banchich and Lane 2009, p. 107–108).
12. Gregory of Nyssa, *Life of Gregory the Wonderworker* 956–957, cited by Harper (2015). According to modern World Health Authority guidelines, re-hydration is a vital part of treating patients, although a disaster such as the Cyprian's plague would clearly have

overwhelmed whatever rudimentary public health system existed in Roman times as well as extracting a severe mortality from those who ministered to the sick.
13. Scriptores Historiae Augustae (Trebellius Pollio), *Gallieni Duo* V.5 where it is placed in the year 262 so it may refer to a later resurgence.
14. For Volusian as *augustus* see Ando (2012, p. 155); also ILS 525. Hostilian is last attested as alive in early July 251 (Mattingly 1946; Ando 2012, p. 155). Evidence for the timing of his death comes from the distributions for the new regime from the imperial mint, and especially their relative frequencies in the great Dorchester hoard, as discussed by Mattingly et al. (1946). The estimate of late July for Hostilian's death is made according to this author's re-calculation of the duration of the coinage issues.
15. Mattingly (1946) initially considered this explanation and other possibilities following an initial suggestion by C.H.V. Sutherland (one of which, mourning for Decius, clearly does not work because the star is not present in the first issue). For astronomical events see Pagnotta et al. (2018). Note that, in contrast to the inference from the coins of the deification of Hostilian, it has been suggested by McMahon (2002) that Decius and his family were subjected to *damnatio memoriae* by Gallus at the time of Hostilian's death, or even earlier (see also Syvänne 2019, p. 36). This is based on their names having been erased from inscriptions and even a military diploma from Dura Europos. The *damnatio* of Decius would seem an unnecessary and provocative step for Gallus, hence an older interpretation (Gilliam, 1956), that the *damnatio* was a later Christian act (whether official or unofficial) is preferred here.
16. Aurelius Victor, *De Caesaribus* 30.
17. Cyprian, *Treatises* V (*Ad Demetriam*).
18. A detailed post on this coin type was made by 'Jochen1' on cointalk.com who concludes that Juno Martialis was related to combating the plague. She allegedly holds small shears or scissors for the cutting of hair. A similar explanation was made long ago by Smyth (1834, p. 286) who says 'she was now invoked, with all the Gods of Olympus, to stay the plague which afflicted the empire'. For the article by Jochen1 see: https://www.cointalk.com/threads/juno-martialis.329837/. The most spectacular propaganda piece of the time is a bronze medallion of high artistic merit with confronted busts of Gallus and Volusian, and on the reverse the temple festooned with garlands. It seems likely that the new emperors restored this building and perhaps commemorated the dedication of the temple on Nones (7th) of March 252, which was the goddess's feast day, the Junonalia (see the calendar of Philocalus).
19. For Apollo Salutaris see Harper (2015, p. 225). For Apollo see Livius, *Ab Urbe Condita Libri* IV, 25. 3 and Hill (1962). For Hadrian's Wall see Breeze (2020).
20. Agathangelos, *History of the Armenians* I, 26. Subsequent quotations follow from this.
21. Eutychius, *Annales* X.7. An alternative translation is available at https://www.roger-pearse.com/weblog/2015/01/21/the-annals-of-eutychius-of-alexandria-10th-c-ad-chapter-10-part-2/. The tenth century Islamic scholar and historian Al-Tabari, using an unknown source, dated the Persian capture of Nisibis to the eleventh year of Shapur's reign which probably dates to 251 (depending on whether one counts his joint reign with his father Ardashir). Olmstead (1942b, p. 401) suggested 251. Potter preferred 252, but as Edwell (2008, p. 185) pointed out, that does not seem to fit with Shapur's invasion strategy as discussed in further detail elsewhere in this book. It is also the case that Eutychius seems to date the great Persian invasion as having occurred 'afterwards' which might refer to a subsequent year (Dodgeon and Lieu, p. 296).
22. Agathangelos, *History of the Armenians* I.36. One who escaped was Trdat (=Tiridates), the infant son of King Khusrow, who much later became an Armenian national hero.
23. The empire-wide call is necessary to explain the troop concentration in Raetia the following year (Aurelius Victor, *De Caesaribus* 32).

24. Zosimus, *New History* 1.27.
25. Syvänne (2016, p. 57) has suggested that Valerian may have withdrawn the Black Sea fleet to the Mediterranean.
26. Zosimus, *New History* 1.28.1.
27. Translation from Heather and Matthews (1991, p. 3) with restoration included and punctuation amended.
28. Zosimus, *New History* 1.28.1–2; Zonaras, *Extracts of History* XII.21.
29. *Liber Pontificalis*, p.26.
30. For the theft of Silanus by the Novatianists see the *Deposito Martirum* in the Chronography of 354 for VI Idvs Ivlio: '*hunc Silanum martirem Novati furati sunt*'. For the relocation of the saints see *Liber Pontificalis*, p. 26. It is fair to say that some scholars reject the story of the moving of the graves as either invented or confused (e.g., Chadwick, 1957). A building interpreted as the shrine of St. Peter and dating to no later than 170 CE was excavated directly beneath the central point of the cathedral in 1950, generating a large literature as to whether the tomb of St. Peter had been discovered. What was discovered was not demonstrably a tomb (despite claims that it was) but it is quite possible that both Peter and Paul were originally interred on the Appian Way and later moved to their shrines (e.g., Toynbee, 1953).
31. *Liber Pontificalis*, p. 27–28. Note that the emperor in this account is named as Decius who was of course dead, so if the story has any truth in it, it would have been Gallus. There are differing accounts of the death of Cornelius and the year is also uncertain (possibly 252 or 253).
32. The story of De Rossi's discovery is related by Lanciani (1892, p. 215–217). De Rossi's restored slab remains on display in the tomb.
33. Cyprian, *Epistles* LXI.

Chapter 8

1. Dionysius, *Letters and Treatises. Letter to Hermammon*, p. 65.
2. This is the spelling of the name in Malalas, *Chronographia* XII. Alternatives are Myriades, Mareades (Ammianus Marcellinus, *History* 23.5.3), and Mariadnes (Anonymous Continuator of Cassius Dio, *Excerpta de Sententis* 157, p. 264). The name is thought to be from the Aramaic Maryad'a, 'My Lord Knows' (Dodgeon and Lieu 1991, p. 363 and references therein). In Scriptores Historiae Augustae (Trebellius Pollio), *Tyranni Triginta* 2.1–4, it is rendered Cyriades or Kyriades, which is probably a Greek version of the same name, which interestingly implies the use of an unknown Greek source (Dodgeon and Lieu 1991, p. 363; Banchich, 2002). Note that the historical sources are confused and contradictory on the timing of Mariades's treachery. This account follows the most likely timing as established by Dodgeon and Lieu (1991).
3. For robbing his father see Scriptores Historiae Augustae (Trebellius Pollio), *Tyranni Triginta* 2.1–4. For the Thirteenth Sibylline Oracle see Potter (1990, p. 268–273).
4. Eunapius, *Vitae Sophistarum* VI, 5, 1–10. See also Malalas, *Chronographia* XII (Dodgeon and Lieu, 1991, p. 52–53); Libanius, *Orations* XXIV, 38 (Dodgeon and Lieu 1991, p. 53).
5. Malalas, *Chronographia* XII, 295–296; Ammianus Marcellinus, *History* XXIII.5.3. For the story being 'inconceivable' see Potter (1990, p. 306–307). For a map of the ancient city showing the theatre see Uggeri (1998). For the re-fortification see Procopius, *De Aedificii* II.10.3. Edwell (2008, p. 190–192) also considered the accounts plausible and provided some photographs of Mount Silpios from the site of the ancient city.
6. Libanius, *Orations* XV.16. Another account of the capture of Antioch (the Anonymous Continuator of Cassius Dio) records that Shapur and Mariades camped two and a half miles from the city: some fled and some, including friends of Mariades, remained (Olmstead 1942, p. 402).

7. Malalas, *Chronographia* XII, 296; Ammianus Marcellinus, *History* XXIII.5.3. Note that in a very doubtful passage, the *Historia Augusta* claims that 'Cyriades' was made *caesar* then *augustus* – Scriptores Historiae Augustae (Trebellius Pollio), *Tyranni Triginta* II.3. The 'Thirty Tyrants' is full of dubious fable and padding and reads very much like the author knew a few facts and embellished the rest. Nevertheless, a rabbinical text also lists Cyriades as a Roman usurper (see discussion in Potter, 1990). Gibbon (1776) was inclined to accept the story and was followed by Porter (1821) and Rawlinson (1884, p. 47) who interpreted one of the Sassanian relief carvings at Naqsh-i-Rustam as showing Shapur exhibiting Cyriades to captured Roman troops as their emperor (see also Syvänne 2019, p. 37). Most modern authors do not follow this interpretation although see Barnes (2009).
8. Note that Birtha Arupan appears only in the Persian version of the text.
9. Farrokh (2007, 2017). In particular, Farrokh (2017) is a mine of information on everything related to the *spah*.
10. The reconstruction made here is heavily indebted to Olmstead (1942), Kettenhofen (1982), Dodgeon and Lieu (1991), Edwell (2008) and Maksymiuk (2015), but differs from all of them in some respects. I have preferred to see the attack on Antioch as having been launched from Chalcis, in accordance with the late source of John Malalas (probably relying on the lost chronicle of Domninos), rather than it being done by an army advancing north after capturing Apamea (that army, I think, would have been busy in the vicinity of Emesa, which held out). I also think the first Seleucia on the list is most likely Seleucia Pieria, captured after Antioch and listed out of order in the great inscription, thereby obviating the reservation expressed by Dodgeon and Lieu (1991, p. 361).
11. For Birtha Arupan see https://www.dainst.org/en/projekt/-/project-display/52456 [accessed September 2019]. For Ana see Kennedy (1986).
12. Gilliam (1941); Gnoli (2007).
13. Lucian of Samosata, *The Syrian Goddess* 29.
14. Alexander Lycopolitanus, *contra Manichaei opiniones disputatio* 2. Sanders (1902).
15. Malalas, *Chronographia* XII, p. 64–65; see Dodgeon and Lieu (1991, p. 52).
16. Ensslin (1949, p. 104); Chamont (1969, p. 63).
17. Malalas, *Chronographia* XII.26; Janiszewski (2006, p. 97–98).
18. Some of the details recorded by Malalas / Philostratos and Kirder to relate to Shapur's campaign of 260, but on that occasion he did not exit through Cappadocia or get as far as the Black Sea coast (Pontus), so if the details are correct, this most likely happened in 253.
19. Butcher (2013). It is fair to say that the *termiunus post quem* of 252/3 does not preclude a later date as was pointed out by MacDonald (1986, p. 54) in his discussion of the coin evidence from Dura-Europos. The Antioch mint stopped making tetradrachms in 253 which may have had nothing to do with the Persian invasion, producing a series of *terminus post quem* dates. However, the ending of the mint is also explained by the sacking of Antioch and the additional evidence of the dating of the rebellion of Uranius Antoninus fits well. By extension, the data seem to support the contention of Rostovtzeff (1943–4) that Dura-Europos fell twice to the Sassanians, once around 253 (although possibly only the city's hinterland) and then around 256.
20. Tobin (2013).
21. Elton (2013).
22. Hodges (2020). For the excavation reports see https://zeugma.packhum.org/toc.
23. For the religion of Emesa see Ball (2000, p. 37–47).
24. Olmstead (1942, Part 2). Although this interpretation seems to have been widely accepted, it is fair to say that it is rather speculative.

25. For the temple complex of Baalbek and the dynasty of the Samsigeramids see Ball (2000, p. 35–47). The various coins featuring the baetyl are reviewed by Overlaet (2009) and Bellamare (1996). The nobility of Emesa had long been inducted into the priesthood of Elah Gabal but the cult's high point came in 218 when one of their number, a young man with a dubious claim to be the natural son of the Emperor Caracalla, was made emperor of Rome on the battlefield. Known to history as Elagabalus (or Heliogabalus), he was one of the more extraordinary emperors, making himself unpopular by (among many other offences) attempting to install his religion in the sacred heart of Rome and bringing the meteorite to the capital. He met a violent end after just a few years of ostentatious rule and the sacred stone was discreetly returned to its temple near Emesa.
26. The dating of the coins of Uranius has been much discussed over the years and an alternative theory is that Uranius began to assert his independence as early as the end of Philip's reign (e.g., De Blois, 1978–1979). This author considers it unlikely that Decius would have permitted this for so long (also Olmstead, 1942; Young, 2004, p. 37–38). It is noted in passing that a radically alternative theory has been suggested by Overlaet (2009) in which Uranius Antoninus was forced to pay homage to Shapur and surrendered the famous black stone of Emesa to him which, in this interpretation, accounts for a mystery object on the so-called Bishapur III relief.
27. For the coins of Uranius see Mattingly et al. (1949, p. 217) and Baldus (1997). It is possible that we are reading too much into these pieces because another one, which is thought to be genuine, has the bizarre legend P.M.TR.P.XVIIII.COS.III.P.P., a full panoply of imperial titles, ostensibly indicating that Uranius is highest priest, tribune of the people for the eighteenth time, consul for the third time, and father of the fatherland. The only previous emperors to hold this particular combination of titles simultaneously had been Hadrian in 134/135, Marcus Aurelius in 163/164, and Septimius Severus with his son Caracalla in the year 211. Perhaps, for some unknown reason, the die cutter selected a random reverse design from a former year and replicated it without understanding what it signified.
28. Bland (1996, p. 72–73).
29. Jordanes, *Getica* XIX.105.
30. The Balkan mint coinage is very rare so evidently was not produced for very long (Mattingly et al., 1949, p. 190).
31. Aurelius Victor, *De Caesaribus* 32. Zosimus, *New History* I.28.3 says Valerian had been dispatched from Rome, but this seems unlikely (Banchich and Lane, 2009, p. 104).
32. Aurelius Victor, *De Caesaribus* 31; Zonaras, *New History* XII.21; Jerome, *Chronicle* p. 301. The Balkan mint coinage uniquely gives the emperor's full name as M. Aemilius Aemilianus (Mattingley et al., 1949, p. 190).
33. Eutropius, *Breviarum* IX.5.
34. Zonaras, *New History* 12.22. Some historians question that he ever entered Rome (e.g., Banchich, 2002b) because the sources clearly refer to him writing to the Senate. However it is difficult to imagine him camping out in the Apennines for months waiting for subsequent events to unfold and not allowing his victorious troops into the capital. It seems more likely that this letter, which may have existed in the archives, was a formality enacted immediately following the non-battle at Interamna, paving the way for his *adventus*.
35. An inscription from Algeria names her not only as *augusta* (empress) but specifically as wife of Aemilian (ILS 9498).
36. Mattingly (1935). Note that this date seems to preclude the possibility that the Gothic raid of Thrace and Asia Minor, Aemilian's victory over them and his expedition to free the captives all took place earlier in the same year, which is why this author places those events in 252, which in turn suggests that Aemilian may not immediately have declared

himself emperor after these victories. A gap in time also allows him scope for reaching an agreement with the legions of Pannonia.
37. Mattingly et al. (1949, p. 108).
38. Note that Aurelius Victor, *De Caesaribus* 31.3 has Aemilian die of disease, but the more detailed account of Zonaras is preferred here. It may be a case of confusion with Hostilian.
39. Mattingly (1940). For Mercury in Gaul see MacMullen (1981).
40. Hartmann (1982, p. 94; p. 161).
41. RIC6, Cunetio 428 (Besly and Bland, 1983).
42. 'Our Hatch knows his mythology: What does it mean? Mercury. Messenger of the gods.' (Yabo Yablonsky's screenplay for *Escape to Victory*, Paramount Pictures, 1981).
43. RIC 142b; Cunetio 333 (Besly and Bland, 1983).
44. Estiot (1996). For Julius Germanicus see https://www.cointalk.com/threads/silbannacus-coin.308455/.
45. Zonaras, *New History* XII.22; Anonymous Continuator of Cassius Dio cited by Dodgeon and Lieu (1991, p. 104). Syvänne (2019, p. 42) has independently suggested this possibility although he did not link it to the accounts of Aemilian's letter to the senate recorded by Zonaras and the Anonymous Continuator.
46. Rumours on the internet of a third Silbannacus coin from around 2005 seem to relate to a piece that was determined to be a fake on closer inspection.
47. These include Gholaia (Bu Ngem) and Cidamus (Ghadames) – Parker (2009, p. 433).
48. This account is based on a fragment of Dexippus's *Scythica* described by Martin and Grusková (2014a) and translated into English by Mallan and Davenport (2015) who provided much additional context and discussion. The year in which this particular Gothic invasion took place is a matter of considerable dispute. Martin and Grusková (2014a) and Suski (2017) suggested 267/268 CE, the year of the so-called 'Herulian invasion', in which Thessalonica was besieged, but that seems unlikely because on that occasion Athens was attacked first and there is no mention in the sources of a defence of Thermopylae (see Mallan and Davenport, 2015, p. 215–220). Instead, authors such as Jones (2014, 2015), Mallan and Davenport (2015) and Gengler (2020) have pointed out the close correspondence of the events to a much-abbreviated passage in a later work by Syncellus which places very similar events in the joint reign of Valerian and Gallienus, specifically near the beginning of that reign (Syncellus, *Chronicle* 466.1–7). Thus it seems likely that the events took place soon after the governor of Moesia, Aemilian, had stripped the frontier troops and marched on Rome, defeating the emperor Gallus and briefly took the imperial throne himself before being defeated in turn by Valerian. That all happened in 253. Most writers therefore think this particular invasion occurred in 253 or 254 (see also Wolfram, 1990, Potter, 2016 and Janiszewski, 2006). That also fits with several known coin hoards buried around this time (M. Spoerri Butcher, 2012, *fide* Jones, date uncertain). It is worth noting however that Mallan and Davenport (2015) and Piso (2018) prefer the year 262 based on the evidence of imperial acclamations given to the Emperor Gallienus at that time and a marked increase in activity of the mint which they suggest may have been to pay for the construction of the Athenian wall, combined with the suggestion of Theocharaki (2011) from archaeological evidence that the wall was strengthened during the sole reign of Gallienus. Despite those arguments, this author prefers what Mallan and Davenport (2015, p. 218) describe as the 'canonical' contention of 253/254. Although we may never know for sure, this solution has the advantage of not dismissing the clear date given in the account of Syncellus (see also Jones, 2014, 2015) and it does not preclude the possibility of later work on the Athenian walls (Gengler, 2020). It explains why there was no response from Valerian who was busy marching on Italy and stabilizing the situation there. It also fits with the numismatic evidence from Thessalonica (Touratsoglou, 2006; Boteva, 2020).

49. For Greek nationalism and the Panhellenion see Mecella (2020).
50. See Oliver and Dow (1935, p. 51–52). Jones (date uncertain) suggests that he may have been a member of the family of the historian. Janiszewksi, (2006, p. 109) says that 'epigraphic sources… associate Philostratus with the historian Dexippus and his family'. Martin and Grusková (2014) were of the opinion that the named Dexippus was the historian himself but Jones (2014, 2015), Mallan and Davenport (2015) and Suski (2017) identified the named man with Cnaeus Curtius Dexippus, an official of Boeotia.
51. Jacoby, F., 1 reproduced in Janiszewksi (2006, p. 65). For a discussion of this fragment see Baldwin (1981) who condems the history of Eusebios as a 'flosculus' (flowery little piece) largely derivative from Herodotus and Thucydides with questionable historical content. See Janiszewski (2006 p. 65–69) for placing the fragment to the years 253/4.
52. Jacoby, F., 2, 5 reproduced in Janiszewksi (2006, p. 66).
53. Zonaras says that the Scythians 'once more enslaved the Thracian territory and besieged the illustrious city of Thessalonica, but nevertheless did not take it'. (Zonaras, *New History* XII. 23). See also Dexippus, *Scythica Vindobonensia* 192^v.
54. The Greek government had already capitulated by that time and the Greek army played no role in defending the pass. For many Greek anti-Nazis this failure was seen as a national disgrace, especially given the history, and one can see their point.
55. Scriptores Historiae Augustae (Trebellius Pollio), *Divus Claudius* XVI, 1–3. Trebellius Pollio (if he existed) is the least reliable of the authors of the *Historia Augusta* and these details come from an almost certainly fictitious letter in which the future Emperor Claudius II is placed in command of the redeployment to Thermopylae and lavishly praised in the process. The letter purports to be from Decius, who was of course dead by this time, to Messala, the Governor of Achaea, who is probably fictitious. Most historians are wont to dismiss it altogether, but Pollio, or whoever wrote the life of Claudius, may have been aware of a heroic defence at the pass by the Peloponnesians around this time – the event would have had an impact, not least because of the historical precedents – and he could even have known some genuine details about it to add verisimilitude to his piece of fiction.
56. English translation from Mallan and Davenport (2015); see Jones (2014) for an alternative English translation and detailed commentary.
57. Zonaras, *New History* XII.23.

Chapter 9

1. Genetic evidence from cow bones indicates sophisticated cattle breeding in the area including the introduction of varieties from the Roman near east (Schlumbaum, et al., 2006).
2. Fah et al. (2006).
3. De Blois (2019, p. 211–212). Reuter (2007) has posited a major invasion of Raetia in 254, destroying the border forts, but this has been questioned by Wetschel (2020, p. 486).
4. For border forts see Demougeot (1961, p. 7). For the archaeological record of raiding see Witschel (2020). The Neupotz hoard is on display at the NeuesMuseum in Berlin. Hagenbach is in the Historiches Museum at Pfalz Speyer.
5. Besly and Bland (1983, p. 25).
6. MacMullen (1982).
7. For a debate on the 'crisis' see Witschel (1999). For town walls being anything other than for protection against barbarian raids see various papers in Intagliata et al. (2020).
8. For an introduction to climate proxies see McSweeney and Hausfather (2021). The best review of climate proxy evidence for our period is McCormick et al. (2012). There is also an enlightening discussion in Rossignol and Durost (2007) and a general summary in Harper (2017). For volcanic eruptions see Sigl et al. (2015).

9. Harper's (2017) book focused on the negative consequences of environmental change but provoked a response by Haldon et al. (2018a, b) who argued that his analysis is selective and biased. They cited contrary evidence, also selectively (it is impossible not to be selective). Interested readers are encouraged to read both sides of the debate. However, I would like to take this opportunity of dismissing the idea that there were two 'world-quakes' in 242 and 262 CE that were especially significant in history, as articulated by De Blois (1976) and resuscitated by Syvänne (2019, p. 43). De Blois (1976, p. 10) based this astonishing claim on two passages in the *Historia Augusta* and a paper by Goosen (1974) that has never been cited in any other context. In some sense, every significant earthquake is a 'world-quake' in that it can be detected globally. Globally destructive seismicity is entirely possible in extreme circumstances, such as a large meteorite impact, but there is no reason whatsoever to back up this apocalyptic idea for the third century. The episodes documented in the *Historia Augusta* relate to local, albeit potentially devastating happenings. For 242: 'There was a severe earthquake in Gordian's reign – so severe that whole cities with all their inhabitants disappeared in the opening of the ground' (Scriptores Historiae Augustae, Julius Capitolinus, *Gordiani Tres* XXVI.1). For 264, 'In the consulship of Gallienus and Fausianus, amid so many calamities of war, there was also a terrible earthquake (*terrae motus*) and a darkness for many days. There was heard, besides, the sound of thunder, not like Jupiter thundering, but as though the earth were roaring. And by the earthquake many structures were swallowed up together with their inhabitants, and many men died of fright. This disaster, indeed, was worst in the cities of Asia: but Rome too was shaken and Libya also was shaken. In many places the earth yawned open, and salt water appeared in the fissures. Many cities were even overwhelmed by the sea.' (Scriptores Historiae Augustae, Trebellius Pollio, *Gallieni Duo* V.2–6). These accounts are eloquent testimony for local but devastating occurrences such as frequently occur in Asia Minor, Italy and elsewhere.
10. Aurellius Victor, *De Caesaribus* 32.2. Valerian appears in the history books during the civil war of 238. Although the historical accounts of his role are somewhat confused it seems that he was serving in Africa in some capacity alongside the provincial governor Gordian who was proclaimed *augustus* in a rebellion against the harsh rule of the Emperor Maximinus Thrax. Valerian was sent to Rome as an envoy to the senate to argue Gordian's case, but before that he was tasked with the job of assassinating the Praetorian Prefect Vitalianus (essentially, Maximinus's prime minister) in the palace. He secured the Senate's backing partly by spreading the fake news that Maximiunus was himself also dead. His daring role in the overthrow of Maximinus would have made him especially favoured in the subsequent administration of Gordian's nephew, Gordian III (reigned 238–244) and, as we have seen, he had been a close associate of Decius.
11. Mattingly (1946, p. 37); see also Syvänne (2019, p. 40). However, if the surviving historical accounts are a guide to the true character of the man, he may not even have wanted the throne of the Caesars. He was just the man who had happened to be in command of a large body of imperial troops in Raetia which were diverted against a dangerous rebel (Aemilian) on behalf of a legitimate emperor (Gallus). Valerian was the man who had supposedly been proposed as *censor* by Decius and the senate to uphold the public morality. Being a model of rectitude himself, he may have had no intention of allowing his troops to proclaim him emperor on the field at Narnia. It is easy to envisage him writing to the Senate saying he had fulfilled his duty and insisting that they must choose the next emperor. He may even have pleaded his age: the role was extraordinarily burdensome and the level of personal risk involved must have been clear to all. The Senate in return may have begged him to take on the onerous task for the sake of the state, supported by the expressed will of people of Rome in the streets and the army high command. This alternative bit of power-play might account for the passage

in the *Historia Augusta*, that 'he was chosen emperor, not, as often happens, in a riotous assembly of the people or by the shouting of the soldiers, but solely by the right of his services, and, as it were, by the single voice of the entire world.' (Scriptores Historiae Augustae (Trebellius Pollio), *Valeriani Duo* III.V. Trebellius Pollio is the most unreliable of the *scriptores* and not beyond using extensive fabrication to flesh out his account. By his own admission he also dictated his accounts in a rush. The first half of the vita is lost (claims by modern historians that it never existed are utterly unconvincing to this author) but it must have contained an account of the accession of Valerian, something along the lines here suggested, otherwise the quotation above would make no sense.

12. For biographies of Gallienus see Bray (1997), Geiger (2015) and Syvänne (2019). The ages of the princes is uncertain.
13. It has been suggested (Sommer, 2004, p. 48; Syvänne, 2019, p. 51) that Gallienus could have accompanied the Rhine army back to its bases, fought a campaign, and then returned to Rome at the end of the year, but the evidence is thin.
14. For the consecration see Ando (2012, p. 156). For the Christians see Eusebius, *Historia Ecclesiastica* VII.10.2–3. For the death of Origen see McGuckin (2004, p. 22–23). Zonaras, *New History* XII; see Banchich and Lieu (1991, p. 49). Origen died shortly after his release, but because he had been freed at the last moment he was not to be counted among the martyrs, a fact that may have affected his posthumous reputation down the ages. He had been one of the first to wrestle with the idea that although there was only one God, he had three manifestations as God the Father (who had created the world), the Son (Jesus Christ, who had died to redeem the sins of mankind) and the Word (the spirit that had descended on the apostles and through which the Christian sacraments operated). Although this characterization was a close fore-runner of eventual church orthodoxy, it was not close enough, because Origen arranged them in a distinct hierarchy. Even more of a problem for later Christians is that he could not countenance an Almighty God that would include everlasting suffering for a large proportion of his creation as part of the plan. Instead Origen taught that hell was not eternal and that after a period of purification, all souls – including those of unbelievers and apostates – would be restored to unity with God. Writing in the twelfth century, Zonaras opined that God had not judged Origen worthy of martyrdom: 'He vomited forth from the evil treasure of his heart blasphemies both toward the holy trinity and toward the divine incarnation, and he became the founder of virtually every heresy.'
15. Many current history texts say that Gallienus was made *augustus* immediately on Valerian's accession but a short period as *caesar* was argued by Pflaumm (1966); see also Peachin (1988). A rare coin from the Cunetio hoard (Besly and Bland, 1983, no. 434) from the first issue of Valerian at the Rome mint has the legend ADVENTVS AVGG (arrival of the two *augusti*) which suggests that Gallienus may have been raised to *augustus* at the time of arrival in Rome or that inscriptions that give him the rank of *caesar* may have been early errors on the part of the provincial administrators. Ando (2012, p. 157) notes that Gallienus was *augustus* by 22 October (see also Witschel, 2020, p. 462. For Salonina see Bray (1997) and references therein.
16. It should be admitted at this point that it is increasingly a challenge to put events in the right order, and even in the right year. Because much of the contemporaneous history is lost, we must rely very heavily on the accuracy of the later historical summaries of the Byzantine authors which themselves are sometimes contradictory. A vital alternative source of information comes from large coin hoards that span the period of interest, including four from the province of Britannia. The first, consisting of over 20,000 coins, was found in the city of Dorchester (Roman Durnovaria) in 1936. The remaining three were all discovered by metal detectorists. The largest, with 55,000 coins, was dug up in 1978 near Marlborough in Wiltshire on the site of a Roman town called Cunetio which

gives the hoard its name. The next, from Normanby in Lincolnshire, was found in 1985 and consists of nearly 48,000 pieces. The fourth, from Frome in Somerset in 2010, has over 52,000 coins. Careful cataloguing of the contents of these hoards combined with stylistic and die-linkage analysis has allowed numismatists to establish a tight chronology for the output of the various mints from all over the empire. The coins track the imperial propaganda messages very effectively and help provide a backbone for the historical narrative. For Dorchester see Mattingly (1939) and Mattingly et al. (1949). For Cunetio see Besly and Bland (1983). For Normanby see Bland and Burnett (1988). For Frome see Moorhead et al. (2010).
17. For *germanicus maximus* see Cunetio 472 in Besly and Bland (1983).
18. The mound is known as 'Maltepe' (treasure hill). Official publications of the excavations have yet to appear at time of writing. This account is based on Dikov (2016a, 2018b, 2019) and Trankova (2019) plus the author's own visit in 2019. See the online reports for stunning pictures of the structure.
19. The possibility of Philip the Arab was widely touted because he was of roughly the right date and came from the east, although that explanation never seemed very convincing to this author given that Philip had been damned to memory after losing the Battle of Verona.
20. European Victory statues adorn the Brandenburg Gate in Berlin, the Altare della Patria in Rome, Hyde Park Corner in London, and the Grand Palais des Champs-Elysées in Paris. For earthquakes see Trininova et al. (2013) and Boschi et al. (1995).
21. Trajan's column in Rome has a foundation that is about 5m square which is slightly smaller than the Manole foundation and smaller than the marble plinth directly above, which is about 9m square. Unlike Manole, the foundation is made of poured concrete, not bricks and rubble. Its depth is not known. Trajan's column was built on flattish land in the centre of Rome atop earlier occupation layers, hence the engineering challenge was considerably different from the alluvial soils at Manole. Nelson's column in London may be a better comparison: it is built on gravels and clay of the lower Thames terrace and was supported by a broad concrete foundation sunk 12 feet below the ground surface and by a brickwork pyramid above ground (covered in steps) that helps spread the load outward.
22. We know the name of Sernota because it appears in a meticulous list of roadside stops, and the distances between them, that was made by an anonymous Christian who, in 333 CE, made a great pilgrimage from his home town of Bordeaux (Roman Burdigalia) to the Church of the Holy Sepulchre in Jerusalem (the so-called *itinerarium burdigalense* or 'Burdigal Guide'). Not only did this worthy pilgrim record all his overnight stops, but even the places where he changed horses (*mutatio*) and presumably had a bite to eat. The relevant day's journey of 30 Roman miles is as follows: *City of Philippopolis / Change at Sernota – miles x / Change at Paramvole – miles viii / Halt at Cilium – miles xii* (*Itinerarium Burdigalense* 568). Determining who commissioned the structure and why will depend critically on establishing exactly when it was built. The heyday of column building was the second century, with major victory columns in Rome commissioned by Trajan, Antoninus Pius and Marcus Aurelius. There are, however, later examples including the fourth century Column of Constantine (reigned 306–337) in Istanbul which, at about 40m high, was taller even than Rome's monuments. Even more pertinent, perhaps, is the 18.5m 'column of the Goths' which also still stands in Istanbul and commemorates a victory over the Goths and may have been commissioned by Claudius II (268–270). The column originally had a statue of Tyche (Victory) at the top (John Lydus, *De Mensibus* 4.132). It bears the inscription *fortunae reduce ob devictos gothos* (To Fortuna Redux [on return from] Victory over the Goths). This replaced an earlier Latin inscription of unknown content. The column is generally attributed to Constantine I or Claudius II because both are known to have claimed Victory over the Goths. It is unlikely to have

been commissioned by Valerian because the enemy tended to be called Germani at that time, as indicated by the coins. On the other hand, if there was an earlier inscription it may conceivably have been dedicated by Valerian whose words were later obscured (see discussion in Mango, 2000).
23. Another eastern mint, possibly Samosata or Cyzicus (both in modern Turkey) also minted coins, but although the die engraving and manufacture was of good quality there was so little silver in some of them they are effectively base metal.
24. Some coins from the second issue at Antioch refer to the emperor in his first consulship and thus were minted in 254 (RIC 207, Cunetio 805; Besly and Bland, 1983). For *restitutor gener humani* see RIC 220, Cunetio 820 (Besly and Bland, 1983).
25. The document is P.Dura 32; see http://papyri.info/ddbdp/p.dura;;32#.
26. One surviving monument to the rebuilding is a pleasant inscription found at Batnae in Osrhoene, one of the cities that had fallen to Shapur: '*Aurelius Dasius, the most distinguished prefect of Osrhoene rebuilt the city wall at Batnae and refurbished in that place a public hostel and a shady shelter so that those who take refuge in it because of the heat might rest and find some relief*'; Dodgeon and Lieu (1991, p. 56). Coins from the Third Issue at Antioch bear the legend *fortuna redux* celebrating the safe return of the emperor to that city from one of his eastern forays. A glimpse at the restoration programme in the east comes from one of the Oxyrhynchus papyri which records the requisition of plough-oxen from Egypt and orders for their transport to wherever they may be needed in Syria. Presumably this was to replace animals killed or taken by the Persians. At least it indicates that there were still people left to till the soil, even if they didn't have the animals to do it (the Oxyrhynchus Papyri P.Oxy XLIII 3109); see Adams (2007, p. 152). The papyrus document dated to 254 concerns the division of property after the divorce of one Julius Antiochus of *legio* IIII *scythica* and a local woman Aurelia Amimma) – Papyrus P.Dura 32 http://papyri.info/ddbdp/p.dura;;32; see Welles et al. (1959) and Baird (2018). For fortification of the desert wall see Rostovtzeff (1943–4) and James (2011, fig. 3).
27. Aurelian is in Scriptores Historiae Augustae (Flavius Vopiscus of Syracuse), *Divus Aurelianus* X.3. The reference to Saracens is interesting although it seems not to have attracted much previous scholarly attention. The words *sex cohortibus saracenis* are very clearly legible on pages 201–202 of the tenth century Palatine codex which is the oldest surviving copy of the *Historia Augusta* and can be viewed online at the excellent Vatican Library website (https://digi.vatlib.it/view/MSS_Pal.lat.899). The term Saracen is also used in the life of Pescennus Niger (allegedly by a different author, Aelius Spartianus) where his army was attacked in Egypt. With regard to the reference in the life of Pescennius, it has been argued by Retsö (2003) that the term 'Saracens' might be an anachronism from the time the *Historia Augusta* was written and may have simply replaced the term 'Arabs' in the lost original, but two occurrences by supposedly different authors perhaps makes that less likely, and in any case the term 'Arab' is used frequently in the *Historia Augusta* without being changed to 'Saracen'. The term Saracens or similar is also used by various other Roman-era writers from Ptolemy onward for a tribe inhabiting the area bordering Sinai and the north-west Arabian peninsula (Retsö 2003, p. 505–506). It has been suggested that Artabassis the Syrian may have been a mutated form of Artavasdes the Armenian which might begin to make sense of the passage (Magie 1932, p. 342).
28. AE 1965, no. 304; the inscription is a rescript addressed to the city of Philadelphia in Lydia confirming their rights (see Potter 1990, p. 30 and references therein).
29. Dietz (1980).
30. The 'Roman' bridge, now known as the Misis Bridge, still stands today although it has been rebuilt many times and it is unlikely much of the original superstructure remains: https://kantaratlas.blogspot.com/2017/06/misis-bridge.html

31. As recently as 250, during the second consulship of Decius, a centurion called Marcus Ratinus Saturninus from *legio* I *italica* had left a dedication there having restored a military leisure facility and bath-house: it has been suggested he may have been posted to this faraway place to gather intelligence on the movements of the Goths (Potter, 2004, 244, n. 121). There is no evidence that Ratinus was engaged in intelligence gathering, however plausible it may seem. *Legio* I *italica* had been supplying vexillations to the Chersonesus for over a century; see Matei-Popescu (2010, p. 87–88).
32. Kacharava (1983–4). For *legio* III *apollinaris* see Schwarcz (2020).
33. The year 255 for the first raid of the Borani is favoured by Alföldi (1937) and most other authors although some prefer 254. The main written source is Zosimus, *New History* 1.27 which is thought to have been based on a lost part of Dexippus's *Scythica*. For the make-up of the Borani see Yartsev et al. (2019).
34. Zosimus, *New History* 1.31.1.
35. The *Historia Augusta* says that the future emperor Aurelian distinguished himself as tribune of *legio* VI *gallicana* at Mogontiacum at this time. No such legion is known, but Demougeot (1962, p. 6) has suggested that *legio* VI *victrix* could have been re-named *legio* VI *gallicana* on being transferred from Britain. A more likely explanation is that the detail was invented to help create a back story for Aurelian; for *legio* XX *valeria victrix* see also Witschel (2020, p. 442).
36. Eutropius, *Breviarum* IX.8. RIC 141; Cunetio 565 (Besly and Bland 1983).
37. Scriptores Historiae Augustae (Trebellius Pollio), *Gallieni Duo* 21.3; Scriptores Historiae Augustae (Trebellius Pollio), *Tyranni Triginta* 3.4; Aurelius Victor, *De Caesaribus* 33; *Epitome De Caesaribus* 33.1. Note that most authors have placed the 'marriage' of Pipa/Pipara a few years later in 258 or 259 (e.g. Syvänne, 2019, and references therein).
38. It should be noted, however, that Syvänne (2019, p. 63) has argued that all these details might be true. See Scriptores Historiae Augustae (Flavius Vopiscus of Syracuse), *Divus Aurelianus* XII.4–6; Scriptores Historiae Augustae (Flavius Vopiscus of Syracuse), *Probus* V.6. The chieftains are almost certainly fictional and were rendered in German as Hildegast, Hartmund and Hildemund by Erich (1611) and various others.
39. For M. Acilius Glabrio see Mennen (2011, p. 84).
40. For the capture of Nisibis see Christol (2006); Syvänne (2019, p. 57).
41. The letter is translated and discussed by Heather and Matthews (1991).
42. Other evidence for the two emperors in Cologne is a damaged inscription of a letter or rescript discovered in Aphrodisias that is dated 23 August from Cologne in the name of them both (Roueche 1989). It is good evidence that Valerian himself was physically in Cologne, and not just in name, because Aphrodisias (in modern Turkey) was probably part of his jurisdiction. Unfortunately the year is not given. Most authors have preferred 256, but Christol (1997) argued for 257 based on the assumption that Valerian would have needed more time in the east (see also Millar, 1993, p. 164, n. 22; Witschel, 2020). An updated account of the inscription and a detailed discussion of it can be found at http://insaph.kcl.ac.uk/iaph2007/iAph090043.html. See also Potter (2004, p. 254). Note that Southern (2001, p. 78) appears to be in error by stating that the inscription is also in the name of Valerian II. The restored gateway is CIL XIII.8261 in which the city has the title '[?Valerian]a Galliena'. Another coin of the second series in Rome that dates to around this time has the legend VICTORIA AVGG IT GERM (RIC 130; Cunetio 500). 'IT' may be short for 'ITER' which would mean 'Repeated Victory of the two Emperors in Germany'; see Alföldi (1929). The victory tax was known as *aurum coronarium*.
43. The rescript is dated six days before the ides of October 256 (*Codex Iustinianus* 6.42.15). The rescript is in the joint names of both emperors so it is equally logical that it could record the presence of Gallienus or both men together. However it seems more likely that

Gallienus would have remained with the army of the Rhine for the marching season after Valerian had shown himself present. One argument that has been proposed for Gallienus joining Valerian in Rome for the New Year was that they were both slated to take the consulship once more (see discussion in Potter, 2004; Ando, 2012, p. 158). It should be noted, however, that the argument is not very strong because as we have noted, in 255 it seems they must have taken the consulship *in absentia*.

Chapter 10

1. For the dispute between Cyprian and Stephen and its theological consequences see Hinchliff (1974, p. 92–114) and Brent (2010, p. 290–327).
2. Eusebius, *Historia Ecclesiastica* VII.10.5–10.
3. It has been suggested that a new persecution of the Christians may have begun in 255 on the basis of a story dating from the sixth to ninth century called the *Acts of the Greek Martyrs*. In this account, a group of Greek immigrants to the city are hunted down by the City Prefect, named Maximus, on the orders of the emperor Valerian. This brings to mind the old patrician Lucis Valerius Maximus who, as we have seen, was Prefect in 255. The story stretches credulity, however, when Maximus dresses as a beggar to trap the charitable Christians who, seeing through the disguise, nevertheless invite him to their crypt where he is possessed by demons who are cast out. Seeing the light, the City Prefect is baptized by Pope Stephen but, when Valerian finds out, he is killed and tossed into the Tiber. All things considered this legend seems a thin reason for dating the onset of the persecution to 255. For the alleged martyrdom of Stephen see 'The Golden Legend' of the thirteenth century. For a discussion of the edicts see Keresztes (1975).
4. For *damnatio ad metalla* see Gustafson (1994) and Hirt (2010). Cyprian's letter is in Cyprian, *Epistles* 76. For the replies see Cyprian, *Epistles* 77, 78, and 79. For the mines at Sigua see Miller (2004, p. 141).
5. Eusebius Caesariensis, *Historia Ecclesiastica* VII.11.
6. The full account is in Zosimus, *New History* 1.34.1–1.36. Jordanes, *Getica* XX.107–109 describes a similar raid under the leadership of Respa, Widuco and Thurwar involving the crossing of the Bosporus and an attack on Chalcedon but that is specifically dated by events to be somewhat later and the accounts of Zosimus and Jordanes cannot be reconciled in detail. It remains possible that the events recorded by Jordanes are a composite or summary of two or three incursions in the area in which case one of the named individuals could have been the leader on this occasion. Widuco transliterates and translates into Gothic as Widuka 'Warrior of the Wooden Spear' and Thurwar as Þurwar 'Bold-wary' according to Yeat (undated).
7. De Blois (2019, p 31, note 39).
8. Constantine later built a bridge over the Rhyndacus (Hasluck 1905/6, p. 189) but it is unclear if any earlier bridge existed at the same crossing point. The bridge is now known as the Macestus Bridge (https://en.wikipedia.org/wiki/Macestus_Bridge). Zosimus, *New History* 1.36.
9. Dating the final fall of Dura depends heavily on numismatic evidence, in that one of the bodies of the victims was buried with two radiate coins of Valerian struck in either 256 or 257. This has led to a technical debate about which year is most likely for the siege. The coins belong to the penultimate issue of Valerian from the Antioch mint (so-called Issue IV of Besly and Bland, 1983, p. 108); see also discussion by MacDonald (1986, p. 64). Bellinger (1943–4) originally suggested a *terminus post quem* of 256 based on the numismatic scheme of Alföldi (1937) but as MacDonald (1986, p. 63) pointed out that date moves to 257 according to the more recent scheme of Carson (1967–8). Besly and Bland (1983, p. 40) date Issue III to 255 and Issue V to 257, suggesting by implication that Issue IV may date to 256 although there was a little more than one issue per year

from the mint. However the critical point remains that the Issue IV coins must have reached Dura before the siege, which was likely early in the year, hence 257 is preferable. There were just three regular pay days [*stipendia*] in a year for the soldiers, on 1 January, 1 May and 1 September, and there is actually a papyrus from the reign of Decius from Dura that confirms these dates; Bellinger (1943–4). Despite that, James (2011) and James (2019) retains 'circa 256'. For occupation after the fall see Saliou and Dandrau (1997).

10. Du Mesnil du Boisson (1937); James (2011).
11. Although the Holy Grail of archaeology is the Holy Grail.
12. For a compilation of inscriptions and texts relating to Odaenathus used in this and the following paragraphs see Dodgeon and Lieu (1991, p. 68).
13. Translated by N.C. Lieu in Dodgeon and Lieu (1991, p. 68–69). The most plausible time for this exchange would be the period when Shapur was besieging Dura. For dating the exchange to the fall of Dura see Watson (1999, p. 30). If so, it seems probable that Dura had not been garrisoned by *cohors* XX *palmyrenorum* during its final occupation as it had often been before, otherwise Odaenathus would not have been able to claim that he had done nothing against the Persians. The make-up of the final garrison has so far eluded scholars.
14. For the coinage see Besly and Bland (1991).
15. For *restitutor galliae* see RIC 27, 29 (Besly and Bland, 1983). For Gallienus at Cologne see Witschel (2020).
16. Historians are split on whether the rebellion took place in 258, as the *Historia Augusta* states, or in 260, as is implied by Aurelius Victor and some of the other sources (e.g., Demougeot, 1962; De Blois, 2019). A detailed case for 258 was made by Fitz (1966). To this can be added the observation made by Potter (1990, p. 345), although not in this context, that when the *Historia Augusta* dates events by consulships in this period it is likely following Dexippus and so may be considered more reliable than normal. Placing the revolt in 258 also allows time for Gallienus to be involved in other events as argued by Syvänne (2019, p. 71).
17. Anonymous Continuator of Cassius Dio, Fragment 5.1; see Banchich and Lane (2009, p. 111).
18. Scriptores Historiae Augustae (Trebellius Pollio), *Tyranni Triginta* IX.1–3; Aurelius Victor, *De Caesaribus* 33. The 'Gallienus with his Army' legend (RIC V.7) was discussed by Alföldi (1929). A similar but much more common type from the Lugdunum mint around the same time features a plinth inscribed 'IMP C E S' which must mean 'Emperor with his Army'. The creation of a cavalry core by Gallienus has been discussed by Syvänne (2019).
19. Zonaras, *Extracts of History* XII.24. Syvänne (2019, p. 70–73) provided a map of the region and discussed the possible locations of the battle and the composition of the respective armies.
20. 'The Letter of Peter to Philip' is from the Nag Hammadi cache of early Christian writings, date uncertain but probably third century, translated by M. Meyer (Meyer 2007).
21. For Valerian as The Beast see Eusebius, *Historia Ecclesiastica* VII.10.2. Most accounts suggest that Valerian was in Rome in the summer but Cyprian's text referring to the swirling and contradictory rumours, and the fact that he dispatched people to Rome to find out what was happening, all suggests a passage of time as does the technical term 'rescript' which was a written reply to the Senate; if he had been in Rome he could have addressed them personally. Hence Potter (2004) is probably right that the origins of the order may have been in January and it was only in the summer that the letter of the edict was made clear. Southern (2001, p. 79) says that Valerian travelled to the east by way of Illyricum in 258, arriving at Antioch in May, but the reason for that inference is not clear to this author.

288   The Roman Empire in Crisis, 248–260

22. For *Liber Pontificalis* see Loomis (1916, p. 29–30). The same source provides the details in the following paragraph. The tombs of Felicissimus and Agapitus still exist in the Catacombs of Praetextatus on the Appian Way.
23. The martyrdom of Cyprian is in Pontius, *Life of Cyprian* 4–6. A church (Basilica Mappalia) was later built on the site of his grave only to be destroyed by Vandals. The modern Basilique de Saint Cyprien is believed to be on the same spot. The *Martyrologium Romanum* claims that on 24 August the governor at Carthage constructed a blazing lime kiln and offered three hundred Christians the choice of sacrificing to Jupiter or jumping in to the inferno. Naturally they chose the latter, and it was noted that their remains congealed into an amorphous white mass (*massa candida*). However this story is very doubtful, like much later Christian martyrology.
24. Eusebius, *Historia Ecclesiastica* VI.11.20; *Passio SS Mariani et Iacobi* in Musurillo (1972), 176–193. See also Birley (1991b).
25. Eusebius, *Historia Ecclesiastica* VII.11; Feltoe (1918).
26. Warmington (1954, p. 42).
27. CJ 5.3.5, 9.9.18; Potter (2004).

Chapter 11

1. The years 259 and 260 are the hardest of all for which to establish a reliable chronology, resulting in considerable and ongoing disagreement among scholars about what happened when, and in what order. Part of the problem may be that the Byzantine summarisers themselves were unclear or simply ignorant of what happened. The strategy here, as before, is to develop a narrative that is as plausible as possible using a total evidence approach (history, archaeology, reasonable timings and likely cause and effect) while documenting major alternatives and ongoing debates in the footnotes. There is an anomaly regarding the consulship because coins indicate that Gallienus apparently took his fourth term this year concurrent with his seventh tribunician power (Cunetio 719/720; Besly and Bland, 1983, p. 105). It may be a mistake at the mint or could be explained if, for instance, the ordinary consul Aemilianus had died early in the year and Gallienus replaced him as suffect consul.
2. No Roman Emperor had ever abdicated up to now. Tiberius had effectively retired from public life, at least for a time. The vast majority of emperors never ruled long enough for it to be a consideration. Diocletian and Maximinan were to be the first to formally abdicate in 305. For the coins of Gallienus and Valerian in this period see Besly and Bland (1983, p. 105–109).
3. Destruction at Wiesbaden (Roman *Aquae Mattiacorum*) on the east bank opposite Mainz has been dated to around 259 (Witschel 2020).
4. Soproni (1978); Vagalinski (2012, p. 312).
5. *Panegyric of Constantius* 10.2; see Nixon and Rodgers (1994, p. 123). Another Chrocus, King of the Vandals, is recorded from the early fifth century in the Chronicle of Fredegar.
6. Demougeot (1962), see especially her map on his page 11. The locations of Demougeot's hoards are re-plotted here according to Google Earth coordinates based on named villages, resulting in many alterations from her map, but the over-all picture is little affected.
7. For a discussion of Fredegar and Avenches see Demougeot (1962), Frei (1969) and Witschel (2020, p. 466). Fredegar places the event in Valerian's eighth year, which must be a miscalculation, so 259 or 260 is reasonable. The fact that Fredegar blames the indolence and debauchery of Gallienus fits with the general situation and also the criticism in the *Panegyric of Constantius* which was written a few decades later and therefore may reflect the prevalent view at the time.
8. The evidence touted in favour of the action is an undated inscription of third century style from Saint-Maurice D'Aguane (Demougeot 1962, p. 11; Witschel 2020, p. 466–467).

This strategic location was later (in 286 CE) to be defended by the so-called 'Theban legion' raised in Egypt and composed of Christians. According to the legend, which may have some basis of truth, this legion under its commander Maurice refused to punish the local Christian population when ordered to do so and were executed to the last man. For the possible historicity of this, with interesting remarks on coinage issues featuring *vexillae*, see O'Reilly (1978, 2011).
9. The more prominent later Chrocus was a Roman ally instrumental in proclaiming Constantine I as emperor in York in 306 (Aurelius Victor, *De Caesaribus* 41.3). It is possible that this Chrocus was a descendant of Gregory's, or even the same man 46 years later (Demougeot 1961, p. 24). For the Place de Jaude temple see Demougeot (1962) and references therein and also http://www.augustonemetum.fr/News/Info-430/Le-Vasso-Galate.html.
10. Zosimus, *New History* 1.36.1. For Moorish troops see Petrus Patricius, Fragment 9, FHG IV, p. 187; Dodgeon and Lieu (1991, p. 62). For sources that discuss the duration of the plague see footnotes to Chapter VI.
11. For Nummius Albinus see Mennen (2011, p. 260).
12. Eutropius, *Breviarum* IX.8.
13. There is no other attestation of this cohort from Roman Britain but a cavalry unit, *ala* I *asturum* is known from an inscription at the fort of Condercum at Benwell near Newcastle (Birley 1967, p. 90). The inscription is *Corpus Inscriptionum Latinarum* VIII, 9047. We cannot be certain that these works were written by the man commemorated at Azuria, but historians agree that it is probable. In the *Historia Augusta* there are two mentions. In Scriptores Historiae Augustae (Aelius Lampridius), *Alexander Severus* 37.9, a Gargilius is mentioned as a contemporary historian who had written a great deal about the food enjoyed by Severus Alexander. In Scriptores Historiae Augustae (Flavius Vopiscus of Syracuse), *Probus* 2.7, Gargilius Martialis is cited in a list of previous historians noted for truth rather than eloquence (a list which also includes Aelius Lampridius).
14. The tribes were to cause trouble for decades to come (Birley 1991b, p. 598–599).
15. Most recently by Septimius Severus (twice), Caracalla (through vile treachery) and Severus Alexander.
16. Petrus Patricius, Fragment 9, FHG IV, p. 187; Dodgeon and Lieu (1991, p. 62). Zosimus, *New History* XI.36.
17. Many commentators (e.g., Potter 1985:336; Dodgeon and Lieu p. 367) have suggested the battle took place between Edessa and Carrhae, which might make more sense if Valerian had reached Edessa first, but the inscription states that the battle took place beyond both.
18. Levy (1967) and Dodgeon and Lieu (1991) identify Bazanush with Valerian, presumably on the grounds that he is captured in battle, but the sense of the words paints him as a champion warrior and not Caesar himself.
19. Syncellus, p. 466, 8–15; Dodgeon and Lieu (1991, p. 63).
20. Babelon (1894). Note that historians have differed widely on the likely date of Valerian's capture, with some placing it in 259 or 258, or even 257 (Elks 1975). Those who argue for an earlier date base it partly on the statement of Aurelius Victor, *De Caesaribus* 33.2, that it preceded the revolt of Ingenuus. However arranging events around that statement creates multiple problems with other aspects of the chronology and numismatics, and for once this author prefers to interpret Aurelius Victor as having been mistaken and confusing the revolt of Ingenuus for another, similar episode centred on Regalianus as discussed in the next chapter.
21. Anonymous Continuator of Cassius Dio, Fragment 3. Translated by S.N.C. Lieu (Dodgeon and Lieu 1991, p. 65–66).
22. Syncellus, p. 466, 8–15 (Dodgeon and Lieu 1991, p. 63). Edessa is not among the list of conquered territories in the *Res Gestae* of Shapur, so it seems the siege was lifted after Valerian's capture.

23. For provincial issues by mint see https://www.wildwinds.com/coins/greece/i.html.
24. For crossing of the Amanus see Potter (1990, p. 338).
25. For the second sack of Antioch on the Orontes see Zonaras, *Extracts of History* XII.23 and Syncellus, p. 466, 8–15 (Dodgeon and Lieu 1991, p. 63). For the suggestion that the capture of Antioch was more in the line of a historical trope see Potter (1990, p. 339). The evidence is discussed at length by Barnes (2009) who favours a single sack in 253.
26. For the Talmud see https://www.jewishvirtuallibrary.org/caesarea-in-cappadocia. There are different versions of the text and varying translations. An alternative is that the walls of Laodicea were 'split' (Lieberman 1946b, p. 35), or 'collapsed' (Kalmin 2006, p. 142). The sense seems to be this happened because of the noise of the arrows in Caesarea, but it is evidently confused.
27. Potter (1990, p. 339–340) suggested that after Tarsus a group moved westward along the Mediterranean coast. However, Syncellus is clear that Pompeiopolis was besieged by a Persian army after having laid waste to Lycaonia.
28. Lieberman (1946b, p. 34–35); see also https://www.jewishvirtuallibrary.org/caesarea-in-cappadocia. Zonaras, *Extracts of History* 23; Agathias, *Excursus on Sassanian History* IV.24.3.

Chapter 12

1. Cecrops may or may not be the same man as a later 'Cecropius' who commanded a unit of Dalmatian cavalry, for whom see Bray (1997, p. 302) and Syvänne (2019, p. 151–154).
2. Zonaras, *Extracts of History* XII.24.
3. It has been argued that Valerian's coinage may have ceased on his death and not on his capture (Elks 1975) but that depends on an alternative chronological scheme that this author thinks is unlikely, as discussed previously.
4. The *Historia Augusta* (Scriptores Historiae Augustae, Trebellius Pollio, *Valeriani Duo* I-IV) contains a curious series of fake letters supposedly written by various eastern potentates to Shapur advising that he relinquish the captive Valerian or be prepared to face retribution from the might of Rome. There is little doubt that these letters do no more than exhibit the imagination of Trebellius Pollio, the named author of this particular biography, or even of the master forger of the *Historia Augusta* that most modern historians think (not this one, however) masqueraded as six authors and faked the whole work. For the plague see Zosimus, New History 1.37.
5. *Thirteenth Sibylline Oracle*, 164. For Macrianus as the stag see Lieberman (1946b, p. 47) and Potter (1990, p. 341). For the deformed leg see Zonaras, *Extracts of History* XII.24.
6. In Zonaras's late account the hero of the hour is also called Callistus. A man named Ballista is mentioned in several places in the *Historia Augusta*, although not in reference to this event – it merely states that Valerian withdrew out of fear of Ballista. The Thirteenth Sibylline Oracle appears to include a play on the name Ballista in one of its obscure verses (Potter 1990, p. 343 and references therein) which, because it is a roughly contemporaneous source, indicates it was the original form of the name. It has been debated whether a scribe at some point confused the name of Ballista and Callistus or whether Ballista may have been a nickname. With no known inscriptions referring to Callistus or Ballista the issue seems impossible to resolve. Mentions of Ballista in the *Historia Augusta* are all in *vitae* attributed to Trebellius Pollio, at Scriptores Historiae Augustae (Trebellius Pollio), *Valeriani Duo* 4.4; Scriptores Historiae Augustae (Trebellius Pollio), *Gallieni Duo* 1.2, 3.1; and Scriptores Historiae Augustae (Trebellius Pollio), *Tyranni Triginta* 12.1, 14.1, 18.13. See discussion in Potter (1990, p. 343). A fictional Ballista is the main protagonist in Harry Sidebottom's acclaimed *Warrior of Rome* series of novels.
7. Zonaras, *Extracts of History* XII.23. Note that Zosimus, *New History* I.39.1–2 records that Odaenathus advanced 'not merely once, but a second time as far as Ctesiphon' but the

occasions are not dated. The interpretation preferred here is that the first time was in 260 when harrying Shapur's forces returning from Cilicia, and the second time, with greater effect, during a later campaign. For women in the *spah* see Farrokh (2017).
8. Festus, *Breviarum* 23. Other accounts collected in Dodgeon and Lieu (1991) may relate to this or a later occasion.
9. De Blois (1975). For the academy see https://en.wikipedia.org/wiki/Nehardea_Academy. The Talmud dates the destruction to 259, not 260, but there are reasons to question the precise chronology.
10. Scriptores Historiae Augustae (Trebellius Pollio), *Valeriani Duo* IV.4. One Arabic source, called the *Chronicle of Se'ert*, tells us that Shapur built three new towns which he populated with the prisoners, providing them with homes and land to till. Chronicle of Se'ert D and L, p. 297. This source also adds, rather implausibly, that Valerian was imprisoned in 'the land of the Nabateans'.
11. Lieu (1986); Ball (2000, p. 115–123). For 'Vehi Antiouk Shapur' see Sarfaraz and Teimoury (2013).
12. Bakker (1993); König (1997).
13. Tacitus *Germania*, XXXIX.
14. For the gold issues see Schulte (1983) and Besly (1984).
15. For a chronology of the radiate issues of Postumus and mint of Trier see Besly and Bland (1983) and Bland and Burnett (1988).
16. Sutherland (1974); Drinkwater (1987); De la Bédoyère (2003). Note that some issues of Postumus do allude to 'Eternal Rome; and 'Hercules Romanorum' but these are prestige medallions (Madden, 1865). On 'SC' as evidence of a parallel senate see Madden (1865, p. 84) and, for instance, Roman Imperial Coinage RIC 135, 147, 169. De la Bédoyère, (2003, p. 136) is in error by stating that all the sestertii lack this mark.
17. Postumus appears to have been a big man, and if he had been born locally it would of course have played well among the Rhine army. That idea has been questioned, though, because there is nothing to indicate a Gallic origin in his full name which the coins tell us was Marcus Cassianius Latinius Postumus (see De La Bédoyère, 2003, p. 129). An overlooked piece of evidence that may clinch this debate is a unique gold aureus in the British Museum described in 1865. On the obverse is the emperor in an ornate military helmet with the legend *postumus aug(ustus)* but on the reverse, with the legend *herculi deusoniensi*, is an image of Hercules of Deuso wearing a laurel wreath but with the facial features of the emperor himself. The portrait coin of Postumus as Hercules of Deuso was apparently overlooked in previous discussions, e.g. Christol (2014) who refers only to the images of Hercules from classical mythology, although in fairness it might be argued that the reverse bust shows just Hercules rather than 'Postumus as Hercules'. Some of Postumus's later coins depict Hercules standing in a temple which seems to confirm that Deuso was a cult centre although it is also possible that Postumus founded one there as part of his 'imperial cult'. A final twist to the story is that *herc deusoniensi* was also issued early in the reign of Carausius (ruled 287–293) but it has been argued that was a copy of Postumus's design by engravers who were unaware of its allusions to Postumus personally (Lyne, 2003, p. 152). The main problem with this theory is that Postumus later issued coins (albeit exceedingly rarely) for 'Hercules of Magusanus', which, unlike Deuso, was a known cult centre to Hercules favoured by the soldiery that is well attested by an altar stone and a variety of other inscriptions and votive objects from throughout the second and third centuries. Postumus cannot have been born in two places, so the current consensus seems to be that Deuso housed an otherwise unknown temple dedicated to Hercules that had some special significance for Postumus or his rebellion; see discussion in Davenport (2019) and references therein. For the cult of Hercules Magusanus see Genèvrier (1986). For the 1865 description see Madden (1865, p. 82–86, Pl. 5, fig. 5).

18. It is not entirely clear how quickly the rebellion spread through the provinces, the chronology of the entire period being so murky. The discovery of the Augsburg dedication has led to the suggestion (Potter, 2004, p. 257) that Postumus was involved in that action as well as Genialis, and it was the spoils gained from the Iuthungi that lay at the heart of his revolt. That is not followed by this author, as Postumus is not mentioned on the inscription except in his capacity as emperor. Moreover the spoils of war referred to by Zonaras are firmly located in the Rhine sector near to Cologne where Albanus and Saloninus were based, not on the upper Danube near Augusta Vindelicorum. Zosimus, *New History* 1.38 is also clear about this point.
19. For Decebalus see Scriptores Historiae Augustae (Trebellius Pollio), *Tyranni Triginta* X.8–9. For the ancestral Regallianus see Eck (2002).
20. The year of usurpation of Regalianus is much debated, with some authors preferring 258, 259 (De Blois 1976), or even 261 (Claes 2015), although everyone is agreed it came after that of Ingenuus. This author agrees with the recent assessment of Witschel (2020) that places it early in 260. For Decebalus see Scriptores Historiae Augustae (Trebellius Pollio), *Tyranni Triginta* X.9. For the coins of Regalianus and Dryantilla see Găzdac and Melchart (2018) who refer to 133 known examples of which 61 are of Regalianus and 72 of Dryantilla.
21. Eutropius, *Breviarium* IX.8 refers to a 'Trebellianus' which could be a corrupted form of Regalianus. Note that Claes (2015) has suggested that the AVGG endings refer to his presumed wife the *augusta* Dryantilla. If that is the case it would be very unusual, if not unique, as other empresses were not associated with their husbands in this way, despite their honorary titles of *augusta*. In other words AVGG almost always refers to male co-emperors, usually father and son. To cite just one example, when Philip was sole emperor his coins have AVG endings despite his being married to the empress Otacilia Severa who was honoured on the coins as *augusta*. Only when the son was raised to *augustus* did the coins have AVGG endings (Mattingly et al. 1949, p. 57). It would also be strange if a female was associated with VICTORIA AVGG, implying she was a military commander, and even more so manly VIRTVS AVGG. As part of the argument, Claes (2015, p. 24) points to a 'marital scene' coin which appears to show Regalianus and Dryantilla clasping hands, with the legend CONCORDIA AVGG. However this was a normal convention for such coins only – for instance coins of Tranquillina (wife of Gordian III) have this legend, while all his regular coins were just AVG. On the other hand, an observation that may be in Claes's favour that is also unusual and probably unique is that coins of Dryantilla were produced in equal numbers to her husband (indeed more Dryantilla coins are known than for Regalianus; see previous footnote), so perhaps they were an exceptional happy couple who shared power, or maybe Dryantilla wore the toga in that relationship.
22. Scriptores Historiae Augustae (Trebellius Pollio), *Tyranni Triginta* X.5–8. This author believes on stylistic evidence that Trebellius Pollio actually existed, in defiance of the post-Symeian academic orthodoxy prevalent at the time of writing. Unfortunately, his output is little more than 'mythistoria' (a term that is known only from the *Historia Augusta*). This author cannot suppress the thought that he was, in fact, an enthusiastic *juvenile* author, but such an hypothesis must be left to future generations of stylometricians.
23. The new images were taken in collaboration with Jesper Ericsson, Curator of Numismatics at the Hunterian Museum and Art Gallery, Glasgow. The best previous photographs were by Campbell (1997). Münsterberg (1923) briefly discussed the circumstances in which two of the coins were acquired by the Vienna Cabinet and included photographs of three other specimens. Although supposedly discovered in 1713, the Sponsian coins seem to have been described first in the same year by Eckhel (1779) and Neumann (1779). The first line illustration seems to have been Neumann (1783) followed by

Akerman (1834), possibly a re-drawing of the same specimen, but if so the drawing is very inaccurate and there are reasons to doubt the accuracy of Neumann's drawing as well. Another specimen was illustrated by Cohen (1860, 1892) who also referred to the existence of a coin in silver. Other silver specimens that are almost certainly modern forgeries crop up on online trading websites from time to time: *caveat emptor*. Various details were discussed by 'Nefarius Purpus' (this author's avatar) on the coin talk web forum. Cohen (1892) regarded all the Sponsians as 'modern' forgeries and this was also the view of Münsterberg (1923) and Bursche (1998) but Eddy (1967), Hartmann (1982), Prickartz (1995) and Meckler (1999) seem to have accepted Sponsianus as real, whereas Campbell (1997) and Körner (1999) left the issue undecided. More recent overviews of the period simply omit to mention Sponsian, giving the impression he is slipping into total obscurity (Southern 2001; Potter 2004; Ando 2012; Manders 2012; Kulikowski 2016; Hebblewhite 2017). Despite Cohen's assessment, Sponsian is listed in the standard catalogue of *Roman Imperial Coinage* by Mattingly et al. (1949, p. 106) where they are described as an 'unsolved mystery' (on p. 47).

24. That the reverse design is a copy of this Republican coins was recognized immediately by Eckhel (1779) and Neumann (1779). See description 'Minucia 3' in Seaby (1978, p. 67). No satisfactory explanation has so far been proposed as to why the strange Augurinus reverse design should have been selected. The peculiar fact that more than one antique denarius seems to have been used in the manufacture suggests it was a conscious choice. Perhaps Sponsian was descended from the ancient clan of the Minucii, or thought he was, and counted those distinguished old consuls as ancestors and was keen to advertise his nobility. The trouble with this is that all the old Republican families are mostly thought to have been extinct long before this time. Alternatively, perhaps the 'C AVG' of the reverse was intended to be read as a kind of continuation from the obverse as in IMP[ERATOR] SPONSIANI C[AESAR] AVG[VSTVS] which would be more like a normal coin legend, albeit oddly distributed. It is even possible that for a general like Sponisan to claim *imperium* (supreme military command) in extremis when cut off from the emperor was not a capital crime (as we have already considered in the case of Uranius Antoninus), whereas claiming the titles *caesar augustus* was obvious treason. Perhaps, then, Sponsian may have been playing a clever game to give the impression of full imperial authority without actually stepping over the legal line. This explanation is admittedly as far-fetched as the first, but it is the best this author can do.
25. Casting was used in the manufacture of the very earliest Roman coins but was soon replaced by the far superior method of striking from dies. However, casts continued to be used by counterfeiters throughout ancient (and modern) history, using real coins as hubs. The level of detail attained by this method is usually far less and it is generally easy to spot a fake of this type.
26. The odd one out is the coin illustrated by Neumann (1783) from the collection of Baron Samuel von Bruckenthal, the Habsburg governor of Transylvania from 1774–1787. The obverse shows a radiate crown with all long rays and the reverse has a flatter land surface and no obvious column base, plus other minor differences. The coin illustrated by Akerman (1834) has other oddities, but may be a poor copy of Neumann's illustration. The coin illustrated by Cohen (1860, 1892) has further peculiarities (the beaded column edges for instance) and appears to be yet another specimen possibly using a different reverse hub.
27. For Sponsianus as a Roman name see Treggiari (1975, p. 71).
28. Campbell (1997) suggested that metallurgical analysis might help solve the question. Laser ablation ICP-MS seems the best approach (e.g., Dussubieux and Van Zelst 2004) which would ideally be done in conjunction with analysis of other regular and 'barbarous' issues of the period and gold coins of the 1700s where the influence of 'New World' gold

294 The Roman Empire in Crisis, 248--260

in the palladium and platinum content should be evident. Such a method could very well establish a high probability of forgery, but proving they are ancient is more problematic as ancient gold could have been recycled in the eighteenth century.

29. For the Apulum mint see Găzdac and Alföldy-Găzdac (2015) and https://www.wildwinds.com/coins/moushmov/dacia.html. For gold mining in Dacia see Żmudziński (2015). One hill alone has a mapped total of 70km of galleries which go down as far as 600m underground.
30. For Sponsianus following Pacatian and Jotapian see Akerman (1834), Boyne (1865), Cohen (1892) and Mattingly et al. (1949). For weights see Mattingly et al. (1949, p. xxi) and Campbell (1997). Caracalla had minted a few radiate double-aurei as part of his reform which included the introduction of the double-denarius (*antoninianus*). The double aureus made a re-appearance under Trebonianus Gallus, but at a reduced weight, and it was also issued by Valerian, Gallienus, Postumus and others (Bland 2012, p. 522).
31. Zonaras, *Extracts of History* XII.24, Scriptores Historiae Augustae (Trebellius Pollio), *Tyranni Triginta* XII. Elsewhere it states that Ballista had at some point assumed imperial power but that historians disagree on the point – Scriptores Historiae Augustae (Trebellius Pollio), *Tyranni Triginta* XVIII.
32. Rathbone (1986); Legutko (2002). The dating provided by the Oxyrhynchus papyri is very important for the chronology of the entire period. Both Valerian and Gallienus were recognized in Egypt as late as August. If the Macriani rebelled soon after Valerian's capture in early summer, then the date makes perfect sense. Those who prefer to date Valerian's capture to one, two or even three years previously have to greatly expand their chronology to accommodate this hard evidence.
33. For discussions of the Syrian coinage and the likely mints see Mattingly (1954), Alföldi (1967), Göbl (2000) and Claes (2015). The quote is from Mattingly (1954, p. 58). For the Alexandrian coins see Legutko (2002). For the relatively high proportion of 'Romanitas' imperial types see Claes (2015).

Epilogue
1. For the legionary series see Besly and Bland (1983, p. 33).
2. Gallwey (1962). There are a few later pieces but the majority is thought to have been assembled near the beginning of Gallienus's sole reign. For the SAECVLARES issues see Gallwey (1962, p. 364). For a detailed study of the coins of Macrianus and Quietus see Mattingly (1954).
3. For all the accounts of Valerian's slavery and death, including non-Christian sources, see Dodgeon and Lieu (1991, p. 61–65). For Canabas / Cannabaudes see Scriptores Historiae Augustae (Flavius Vopiscus of Syracuse), *Divus Aurelianus* XXII.2 and Wolfram (1990, p, 46).
4. Luttwak (1976, fig. 3.1).
5. Zonaras, *Extracts of History* 12.21.
6. For Thomas Cole see Miller (1989).
7. Orosius, *History Against the Pagans* VII.22.5.
8. Translated by Fletcher (1871) and updated by Dodgeon and Lieu (1991).
9. For Constantine see Holloway (2004). For the end of the traditional religion see MacMullen (1981). It should be noted that there is a revivalist movement who dedicated a temple to Jupiter in the year 2770 since the founding of Rome (equating to 2017 of the Common Era) which is to be followed by temples to the full Roman pantheon; but even they accept that nobody worshipped Jupiter for over a millennium; http://templvm.org/his_vision_goals.html.

Index

Abgar X (king of Osrhoene), 184–5
Ablabius (historian), 263 (n.5)
Abritus (city), 94, 97, 109
    Battle of, *see* Battles, Abritus
Achaea (province), 152–4, Map 20 (p.154)
Adana (city), 207–209, Map 25 (p.208)
Aeeta (king), 172
Aegean Sea, 121–2, Map 15 (p.122)
Aelius Aristides (historian), 12
Aemilian, Marcus Aemilius Aemilianus (commander and emperor), 115, 123, 141–7, 151, 160, 162, 164, 278 (n.31), 278 (n.32), 278–9 (n. 36), Map 19 (p.146), Plate 6
    background, 123
    coins, 142, 144–5, 278 (n.31), 278 (n.32), Plate 6
    commander, 115, 122–3, 127, 162, 164
    death, 147, 279 (n.38)
    Goths, defeat of, 122–3, 127, 162, 164
    Moor, 123
    Narnia, Battle of, *see* Battles, Narnia
    proclamation, 141–2
    Senate, letter to, 144, 149, 278 (n.34), 279 (n.45)
Aemilianus, Lucius Mussius (prefect), 178
Aemilianus (consul), 194
Aesculapius (deity), 114
Africa (province), 34, 64–5, 116, 123, 145, 150–1, 171, 191–2
Agapitus (Christian), 191, 288 (n.22)
Agathangelos (historian), 117–19
Agri decumates (region), 161, 196, Map 23 (p.196)
Agrippiada, *see* Anazarbus (city), Map 25 (p.208)
Ahura Mazda (deity), 119
Aigeae (city), 207–209
Alans (people), 47
    Gate of, 137
Albania (region), 137
Albanus (person), 189, 221

Albinus, Marcus Nummius (city prefect), 200
Alemanni (people), 174, 195
Alexander, Bishop of Jerusalem, 38
Alexander, the Great of Macedon, 13, 23, 259 (n.8)
Alexander (Christian, Numidia), 192
Alexander (Christian, Palestine), 192
Alexander Severus, *see* Severus Alexander (emperor)
Alexandria/Alexandretta (city, Syria), 130–1, 133, 136, 207–208, 210, 273 (n.35), Map 17 (p.133), Map 25 (p.208)
Alexandria, 8, 10, 32, 112, 191, 229
    millennium riots, 10
    mint, *see* mints, Alexandria
    persecution of Decius, 38–9
    plague, 32, 91, 112
Alps, 145, 159, 197–8, 212–13, 199, 201, 220–1, Map 23 (p.196), Map 27 (p.220)
Al-Tabari (historian), 275 (n.21)
Alutis (river), *see* Olt (river)
Amal (Gothic king and dynasty), 45, 85, 110
Amalsuintha (Gothic queen), 271 (n.16)
Amanian Gate, 208–209, Map 25 (p.208)
Amanus mountains, 208–209, 213, Map 25 (p.208), Map 26 (p.215)
Ammianus Marcellinus (historian), 81, 128–9, 219, 270 (n.9)
Amphiopolis (city), 153, Map 20 (p.154)
Anak (Parthian), 117–20
Anatha (city), 130, Map 16 (p.131)
Anatolia (region), 121, 209
Anazarbus (city), 207–209
Anchialus (city), 20, 179
Anemourium (city), 207–208, Map 25 (p.208)
Anonymous Continuator of Cassius Dio (historian), 149, 188, 189, 276 (n.6), 279 (n.45)
Antioch (city), 11, 14, 24, 112, 127–9, 131, 133, 135, 136, 137, 144, 161, 164–5,

166, 167, 169, 171, 181, 190, 193, 202, 206–207, 214, 228, 276 (n.6), 277 (n.10), Map 17 (p.133), Map 25 (p.208)
   mint, *see* Mints, Antioch
   sack of, first, 127–9, 131, 133, 135, 276 (n.6), 277 (n.10), Map 17 (p.133)
   sack of, second, 206–207, 229, 290 (n.25), Map 25 (p.208)
Antiochia-ad-Cragum, (city) 208–209, Map 25 (p.208)
Antiochus III (Greek king), 154–5
Antoninus (commander), 212
Antoninus Pius (emperor), xvi, 124
Anubis (deity), 7
Apamea (city, Syria), 130–1, 133, 136, 138, Map 17 (p.133)
Apamea (city, Bithynia et Pontus), 179–80, Map 22 (p.180)
Aphrodite (deity), 139
Apollo (deity), 116, 193, 234
   Apollo Salutaris, 116, 234
Apollonius of Tyana, 7, 9, 210
Apotropaism, 256 (n.6)
Apennine Mountains, 142, 278 (n. 34)
Apulum (military base), 41, 66–7, 227, 294 (n.29)
Arabia (province), 11, 204
Arabs (people), 171
Archaeology, 28, 49, 66, 67, 72, 74, 79–81, 94, 97, 101–103, 125–6, 137–8, 162–4, 182–4, 199, 218, 258 (n.19), 269 (n.36), 272 (n.26), 279 (n.48)
   Abritus, 272 (n.26)
   Athens, 152, 279 (n.48)
   Augsburg, 218
   Bishapur, 218
   Clermont-Ferrand, 199
   Dryanovets, 94, 97
   Dura-Europos, 182–4
   Luxor, 32
   Manole, 162–4, Plate 7
   Marcianpolis, 101–103
   Nicopolis, 67
   Novae, 66
   Plovdiv, 72, 74, 79–81, 269 (n.36)
   Rome, xv, 125–6
   Romula, 258 (n.19)
   Skopje, 28
   Zeugma, 137–8, Plate 6
Ardashir I (Sassanian king of kings), 12–13, 134

Argaithus (Gothic leader), 47–54, 59, Map 4 (p.51)
Argentoratum (city), 222
Argunt (Gothic king), 49, 264 (n.17)
Ariminum (city), 142, Map 18 (p. 143)
Ariste (city), 130–1, 133, Map 17 (p.133)
Armenia (kingdom), 14, 117–20, 127, 137, 142, 200
Arsacid dynasty, 12, 14
Arsinoe (city), 37
Artabassis the Syrian, 166, 284 (n.27)
Artangil (city), 130–1
Artaxerxes I (king), 13
Arupan, *see* Birtha Arupan (city)
Asia (province), 180, 204
Asia Minor (region), xxi, 8, 12, 36, 121, 144, 161, 167 181, 224, 232, 233, Map 15 (p.122)
Asinius Quadratus (historian), xx
Asporakos, *see* Birtha Asporakan (city)
Astringi (people), 48
Asurestan (Sassanian province), 13
Atagartis (deity), 134
   temple of, 134
Athena (deity), 7
Athens, xx, 152, 153–4, 279 (n.48)
Athenians, 82
Atho Marcellus (official), 258 (n.19)
Attalus (German king), 170, 194, 220, 232
Auganum (village), 198
Augousta (city), 207–209, Map 25 (p.208)
Augsburg, *see* Augusta Vindelicorum
Augsburg Victory Altar, 218–21, 292 (n.18), Plate 8
Augurinus (Christian), 192
Augurinus, Caius Minucius (consul), 226, 293 (n.24)
Augurinus, Lucius Minucius (consul), 226
Augusta (title), xx, 34, 111–12, 161, 224
Augusta Raurica (city), 156–8, 197, Map 23 (p.196)
Augusta Treverorum (city), 169, Map 23 (p.196)
   mint, *see* Mints, Augusta Treverorum
Augusta Vindelicorum, 197, 218
Augustenometum (city), see Clermont-Ferrand
Augustus (emperor), xvi, xviii, 55
Augustus (title), xvi, 24, 25, 79, 111–12, 115, 141, 161, 164, 222
Auha (river), 55

Aurelia Ammonous (priestess), 37
Aurelian (emperor), 166, 188, 233
    manu ad ferrum, 166
Aurelius Victor (historian), 61, 81, 115, 142, 170, 188, 201, 233–4, 256 (n.1), 269 (n.34), 270 (n.9), 279 (n.38), 287 (n.16), 289 (n.20)
Aureolus (general), 188–9, 212
Aureus (coin), 5–6, 79, 141, 150, 191
    denarius aureus, 13
    double aureus (binio), 112, 225, 274 (n.2), 294 (n.30)
    weight reduction, 112, 120
Autokrator (title), 141
Auxiliaries, Roman army, 20, 59, 67
    ala I *asturum*, 289 (n.13)
    ala I *thracum victrix*, 71
    cohors I *asturum*, 201
    cohors I *cilicium milliaria equitata sagittariorum*, 58–9
    cohors I *thracum sagittaria*, 71
    cohors I *thracum syriaca*, 71
    cohors II *flavia brittonum equitata*, 20
    cohors XX *palmyrenorum*, 185, 287 (n.13)
Auzia (city), 201, 289 (n.9)
Avenches, *see* Aventicum (city)
Aventicum (city), 196–7, Map 23 (p.196)
Ayrarat (Armenian province), 118

Baal (deity), 8
Baalbek, Temple, 140
Babylas, Bishop of Antioch, 11, 38
Babylonian Talmud, *see* Talmud, Babylonian
Baebiana, Afinia Gemina, 111–12, 144
Baetica (region), 231
Balasagan (region), 137
Balikh (river), 204
Balkan Mountains, *see* Haemus Mountains
Ballista (commander), 213–16, 228, 290 (n.6), 294 (n.31), Map 26 (p.215)
Baltic Sea, 14, 46–7, 104
Barbalissos, 203–204
    Battle of, *see* Battles, Barbalissos
Barbaricum, 15
Bassus, Mummius (consul), 187
Bassus, Pomponius (consul), 194
Bastarnae (people), 47, 59
Baths of Decius, *see* Decius, Baths of
Batna(e) (city), 130–1, 133, 284 (n.26), Map 17 (p.133)

Battles
    Abritus, 43, 93–101, 104, 111, 115, 141, 142, 164, 227, 234, 270 (n.9), 272 (n.29), Plate 5, Map 14 (p.98)
    Augusta Vindelicorum, 219–21, Map 27 (p.220)
    Barbalissos, 128–33, 171, 192, 204, Map 16 (p.131), Map 17 (p.133)
    Beroe, 74–7, 78, 83, 94, 269–70 (n.5), Plate 3, Map 8 (p.76)
    Edessa, 204–207, 289 (n.17), Map 24 (p.203), Map 25 (p.208)
    Emesa, 138–40 Map 17 (p.133)
    Galtis, 51, 265 (n.25), Map 4 (p.51)
    Interamna Nahars, 142–3, 149, Map 18 (p.143)
    Mediolanum, 212–13, Map 27 (p.220)
    Mishik, 13, 104
    Mursa, 188–9, 212, 224, 287 (n.19)
    Narnia, 145–7, 148, 151, Map 19 (p.146)
    Nicopolis, 67–70, 72–3, 78, Map 6 (p.68), Map 7 (p.70)
    Novae, 66–7, Map 6 (p.68)
    Rhesaina, 13
    Romula (hypothetical), 82–6, 90, 270 (n.9), Map 11 (p.84)
    Verona, 29–31, 33, 67, 261 (n.22), Map 3 (p.30)
Bavares (people), 202
Bazanush (soldier), 205, 289 (n.18)
Bede (historian), 11
Berbers (people), 202
Beklemeto Pass, 69–70, 269 (n.5), Map 6 (p.68), Map 7 (p.70)
Belarus (modern country), 103, 104
Beli Lom (river), 94–6, 99, Map 14 (p.98)
Beroe (Thracian city), Battle of, *see* Battles, Beroe
Beroea (Syrian city), 130–1, 133, 135, Map 17 (p.133)
Besas (soldier), 39
Binio, *see* Aureus (coin), double aureus
Birtha (city, Lycaonia), 207–208, Map 25 (p.208)
Birtha Arupan (city, Mesopotamia), 130–2, 277 (n.8), Map 16 (p.131)
Birtha Asporakan (city), 130–2, Map 16 (p.131)
Bishapur (city), 218
Bithynia et Pontus (province), 121–2, 178–81, 194, 204, Map 22 (p.180)

Black Sea, 14, 18, 34, 46, 47, 48–9, 114, 121–2, 156, 167–9, 172–4, 178–81, 194, Map 15 (p.122), Map 20 (p.154), Map 21 (p.168), Map 22 (p.180)
Blemmyes (people), 42, 46, 57
Boeotians (people), 72
Bonna (city), 222
Borani (people), 167–9, 172–4, 178, 285 (n.33), Map 21 (p.168)
Bosporan Kingdom, 168–9, Map 21 (p.168)
Bosporus, 120, 179–81, Map 15 (p.122), Map 22 (p.180)
Bostra (city), 185
Brenner Pass, 145, 220–1, Map 17 (p.133), Map 27 (p.220)
Brigetio (military base), 89
Britain/Britannia (province), xxi, 20, 34, 116, 145, 150, 157, 169, 223, 231
Budalia (village), 26
Buddhism, 7
Bug (river), 46
Bulgaria, 50, 52, 59, 162–4
Burdigal Guide, 283 (n.22–3)
Bursche, Aleksander (numismatist), 103–105
Buzurg Shapur (city), 218
Byzantium (city), 26, 120, 161, 166, 179–81, Map 22 (p.180)

Caesar (title), 36, 41, 111, 160, 172, 189, 223
Caesarea (Cappadocia), city, 137, 208–11, 217, Map 25 (p.208)
Caesarea (Palestine), city, 65
Callistus, *see* Ballista (commander)
Cannabaudes, *see* Cannabus (king)
Cannabus (king), *see* Ciniva, Cannabus
Capitoline Triad (deities), 6, 56, 59
Cappadocia (province), 23, 119, 121–2, 130, 136–7, 152, 161, 172, 181, 203–204, 215–16, 217, Map 24 (p.203)
Capricorn, 89, 138
Carnutum (city), 224–5, 232
Carpi (people), 15, 41, 47, 48, 59, 89, 264 (n.12)
Carpathians Mountains, 15, 55
Carrago, *see* Goths, Carrago
Carrhae (city), 136, 203, 204, Map 24 (p.203)
Carthage (city), xxi, 39–40, 64, 150, 177
  persecution of Decius, 39–40

Cassiodorus (statesman and historian), 44, 85
Cassius Dio (statesman and historian), xvi
Castor and Pollux (deities), xviii
  Temple of, xviii
Castra Regina (fortress), 142, 143, 195, Map 17 (p.133), Map 23 (p.196)
Caucasus Mountains, 137
Cavalry, Roman, 20, 185, 188–9, 270 (n.8)
Cecrops (commander), 212, 223, 290 (n.1)
Cedrenus, George (chronicler), 41, 65, 113–14, 274 (n.11)
Celts (people), 48
Centumcellae (city), 124
Cephro (city), 178
Černjachov culture, 46–7, 104, 263 (n.11)
Chalcedon (city), 179–81, Map 22 (p.180)
Chalcis (city), 130–1, 133, 135, 277 (n.10), Map 17 (p.133)
Chamath (city), 130–1, 133, Map 17 (p.133)
Chanar (city), 130–1, 133, Map 17 (p.133)
Charioviscus (German king), 171
Chemical warfare, 183–4
Chernyakhiv culture, *see* Černjachov culture
Chersonesus (city), 168, 285 (n.31), Map 21 (p.168)
Christianity, xxi, 8–11, 36–41, 62–5, 123–5, 150–1, 160, 173–4, 189–93, 235–6
  Acts of Peter, 9
  baptism, 177
  Christ (anointed one), 8
  confessors, 63–4
  Dura-Europos, church, 165
  edict of toleration, 236
  Gnosticism, 9
  God of, 9, 116, 282 (n.14)
  headscarves, 65–6
  Infancy Gospel of Thomas, 9
  Jesus, as Christ and God, *see* Jesus (of Nazereth)
  libellatici, 64
  martyrdom, 39–40, 63–4, 288 (n.23)
  organization, 9–10
  persecution prayer, 189, 287 (n.20)
  persecution under Decius, 36–41, 176
  persecution under Gallus, 116
  persecution under Valerian, 176–8, 189–93, 287 (n.21), 288 (n.23)
  sacrificati, 64
  San Giovanni in Laterano, 236

schisms, 176
Slavery, 174
Theban legion, 288–9 (n.8)
thurificati, 64
Chrocus (king), 198, 288 (n.5), 289 (n.9)
Chronicon Paschale, 42, 270 (n.9)
Chrysogonus (person), 179
Chrysotom, John (archbishop and preacher), 11
Cilicia (province), 137, 204, 208–11, 215–16, 217, Map 25 (p.208), Map 26 (p.215)
Cilician Gate, 208, 210
Circesium (city), 130, 131, 135, 136, Map 16 (p.131)
Circus Maximus, xviii
Cirta (city), 150
City Prefect, *see* Rome, City Prefect
Cius (city), 179–80, Map 22 (p.180)
Claudius (Christian), 191
Claudius (emperor), xvi
Cledonius (official), 206–207
Clermont-Ferrand (modern city), 198–9, 234
  Augustenometum, Map 23 (p.196)
Clibanarii, 185
Climate change, 158–9
Cniva (Gothic leader), 44–5, 59, 66–71, 74–7, 82, 110, 162, 164, 187, 194, 233
  Abritus, Battle of, *see* Battles, Abritus
  army, size of, 99
  Beroe, Battle of, *see* Battles, Novae
  Cannabus, identification with, 233
  king (?), 109, 266–7 (n.5)
  Marcianopolis, sack of, 103
  name, 59
  Novae, Battle of, *see* Battles, Novae
  Philippopolis, Siege of, *see* Sieges, Philippopolis
Cohorts, auxiliary, *see* Auxiliaries, Roman Army
Colchis (kingdom), 168–9, Map 21 (p.168)
Cole, Thomas (artist), 234–5
Colluthion (city), 178
Cologne (modern city), *see* Colonia Agrippina (city)
Colonia Agrippina (city), 169, 174–5, 187, 188, 189, 222, 285 (n.42)
  mint, *see* Mints, Colonia Agrippina
Colosseum, xvii, xix, 55, 265 (n.26)

Comana (city), 207–208, 215, Map 25 (p.208), Map 26 (p.215)
Commagene (region), 23, 185
Concord (Temple of), xvii
  Concord of the Army, 22
Constantine (I, the Great, emperor), 18, 236
Corinth, Isthmus of, 153–4, Map 20 (p.154)
Cornelia Supera, Gaia (empress), 144, 278 (n.35)
Cornelius (Bishop of Rome), 64–6, 124–6, 191, 276 (n.31)
Corycus, *see* Korykos (city)
Cosa (city), 36
Crescentius (Christian), 191
Cresces, Lucius Voluminis (officer), 151
Crete, 153–5
Crinitus, Ulpius (commander), 166
Crispinus, Rutilius Pudens (senator), 27, 260 (n.16)
Crocodile, 37
Crocodilopolis (city), 37
Ctesiphon, 13, 217–18, 228, Map 26 (p.215)
Cunetio hoard, *see* Hoards, Cunetio
Cursus honorum, 27
Curubis (city), 177, 178
Cybele (deity), 8
Cyprian, Bishop of Carthage, 39–40, 62–5, 91–3, 113, 116, 124–5, 150–1, 157, 159, 176–8, 190–3, 235
  death, 191
  Demetrian, against, 116
  De Mortalitate, 91–2
  lapsed, on the, 63–5, 124
  persecution of Decius, in hiding 39–40, 62
  persecution of Valerian, 190–3
  plague of, *see* plague of Cyprian
  ransoming captives, 150–1
Cyrrhus (city), 130–1, 133, Map 17 (p.133)
Cyzicus (city), 180–1, Map 122 (p.180)

Dacia (deity), 34
Dacia (province), xxi, 15, 20, 41, 46, 55, 59, 66–7, 144, 188, 195, 204, 224, 227–8, 233, 269 (n.5), Map 11 (p.84)
  Dacia Malvensis (region), 15, Map 11 (p.84)
Dacians (people), 89
Dalmatia (region), 21
Danube (river), 14, 18, 20, 21, 22, 25, 26, 28, 34, 35, 41, 47, 48, 50, 56, 57, 58,

60–1, 67, 83, 85, 89, 142, 161, 162, 175, 188, 192, 197, 224–5, 233, 266 (n.2), Plate 2, Map 2 (p.19), Map 5 (p.60), Map 6 (p.68)
freezing, 58, 266 (n.2), Map 5 (p.60)
Dardanelles, 121–2, Map 15 (p.122)
Dardania (region), 154–5
Darial Pass, *see* Alans, Gate of
Daric (coin), 78–9, 268 (n.31), Plate 3
Dativus (bishop), 177
Decebalus (Dacian king), 89, 224, 271 (n.17)
Decius, Caius Messius Quintus Decius Valerinus (emperor), 26–31, 34–5, 40–1, 42, 48, 61, 67–70, 83–4, 89–101, 124, 142, 147, 164, 165, 168, 171, 233, 234, 260 (n.20), 262 (n.20), Map 3 (p.30), Map 6 (p.68), Plate 2, Plate 5
  Abritus, Battle of, *see* Battles, Abritus
  accession, 29
  army, size of, 269 (n.4), 272 (n.28)
  background, 26–7
  Baths of, 55
  Beroe, Battle of, *see* Battles, Beroe
  building programme, 55
  censor, 36
  census, 36
  City Prefect, 27
  coins, 34, 56, 78, 101, 260 (n.20), 266 (n.29), Plate 5
  consul, 27, 36, 55
  Dacia, possible presence in, 41, 261 (n.3), 262 (n.20), Map 5 (p.60), Map 6 (p.68)
  dacicus maximus, 41, 262 (n.20)
  daughter, 111
  death, 101
  deification, 111, 274 (n.4)
  dux moesiae et pannoniae, 27
  imperator II, 69
  letter to Philippopolis, *see* Philippopolis, letter to
  monetary reform, 56
  name, 26
  Nicopolis, Battle of, *see* Battles, Nicopolis
  persecution of Christians, 36–41, 114, 176
  pontifex maximus, 33
  reputation, 109
  restitutor sacrorum, 35–6
  Romula, hypothetical Battle of, *see* Battles, Romula (hypothetical)
  speech, 83
  statue of, 56–7, Plate 2
  Trajan Decius, 33
  Verona, Battle of, *see* Battles, Verona
Demetoiupolis (city), 207–208
Demetrian (writer), 116
Demosthenes (commander), 210–11
Demougeot, Emilienne (historian), 195–9
Denarius, 5
  Double-denarius, 56, 112, 165, 232
De Rossi, Giovanni Battista (archaeologist), 125–6, 276 (n.30)
Destruction (painting), 234–5
Deuso (city), 223
Devnya (modern village), 50
Dexippus of Athens (historian, soldier and statesman), xx, 33–5, 46, 52, 59, 72–4, 78–81, 82–3, 110, 151–5, 219, 256 (n.14)
  Chronicle, xx, 123
  Millennium, xx
  reputation, 256 (n.1)
  Scythica, fragments, 53, 72–4
  scythica vindobonensia, 33–5, 52, 78–81, 82–3, 151–5, 263 (n.1), 279 (n.48), Plate 2
  Scyths, use of, 46
Dexippus, Cnaeus Curtius, of Boeotia, 152, 258 (n.19)
Diana (deity), 172
Dikhor (city), 130–1
Dio, Cassius, *see* Cassius Dio
Dionysius, Bishop of Alexandria, 10, 11, 32, 38–9, 40, 62, 112, 127, 176, 177, 178, 191–2
  persecution of Decius, 62
  persecution of Valerian, 178, 191–2
Dioscorus (Christian), 39
Dneiper (river), 104, 105
Doliche/Dolichene (city), 8, 130–1, 133, 135, Map 17 (p.133)
Domana (city), 130–1, 136
Dometioupolis (city), 207, Map 25 (p.208)
Donatus, Gaius Julius, 200
Dorchester hoard, *see* Hoards, Dorchester
Druidism, 10
Dryantilla, Sulpicia (wife of Regalianus) 224–5, 231, 292 (n.18), 292 (n.21), Map 28 (p.231), Plate 8
  augusta, 224, 292 (n.21)
  coins, 224, 292 (n.18), 292 (n.21), Plate 8
Dryanovets (modern village), 94, 99, 101

Du Mesnil, Robert du Mesnil du Boisson (archaeologist), 182–4
Dura/Dura-Europos (city), 130–2, 135, 136, 165, 181–4, 185, 187, 200, 275 (n.15), 277 (n.19), 284 (n.26), Map 16 (p.131)
  Siege of, *see* Sieges, Dura-Europos
Durostorum (military base), 20, 59, 94–5, 120, 160, Map 2 (p.19), Map 13 (p.96)
Dux, title, 27, 132, 181, 188, 192, 212
  dux moesiae et pannoniae, 27
  dux per africam et mauretaniam, 192
  dux ripae, 132, 181

Earthquakes, 156, 164, 281 (n.9)
Eastgota, *see* Ostrogotha (Gothic king)
Ebola, 17, 92, 113
Edessa (city), 135, 136, 184, 202–207, 215, Map 24 (p.203), Map 26 (p.215)
  Battle of, *see* Battles, Edessa
  Siege of, *see* Sieges, Edessa
Egypt, xxi, 33, 35, 36–7, 178, 229–30, 231, 232, 233
Elagabalus (emperor), 278 (n.25)
Elah Gabal (deity), 139–40, 278 (n.25)
Elbe (river), 187, 219
Emesa (city), 133, 136, 138–41, 164, 185, 202, 278 (n.25), Map 17 (p.133)
Ephesus (city), 40, 121–2, Map 15 (p.122)
  seven sleepers of, 40–1
Epitome de Caesaribus, 61, 145, 170, 270 (n.9)
Equites singulares augusti, *see* Horseguard, imperial
Ericsson, Jesper, 292 (n.23)
Estio, Sylviane (numismatist), 148
Ethno-fabrication, 47
Etruscilla, Herennia, *see* Herennia Etruscilla (empress), 34
Euboean Sea, 153–4, Map 20 (p.154)
Eulogius (Christian), 192
Euphrates (river), 23, 131–3, 165, 203–205, 216–17, Map 16 (p.131), Map 17 (p.133), Map 24 (p.203), Map 26 (p.215)
Europa (region), 120, Map 15 (p.122)
Eusebios of Thessalonica (historian), 152–3, 280 (n.51)
Eusebius of Caesarea, 11, 235
Eutropius (historian), 142–4, 147, 170, 201, 270 (n.7)
Eutychius of Alexandria (historian), 119, 275 (n.21)

Fabian (Bishop of Rome), 38, 63
falx, 89, 271 (n. 18)
Faraxen (rebel), 201–202
Farnese 'barbarian', 271 (n.17)
Fastida (king of Gepids), 51, 54–5, 110
Fecunditas (deity), 34, 141
Felicissimus (deacon, Carthage), 63–5
Felicissimus (Christian, Rome), 190, 288 (n.22)
Felicitas (deity), 56
Felix (bishop), 177, 178
Felix, Lucius Mummius Felix Cornelianus (?) (general), 181
Filovirus, 16–18
Firdawsi, 203
Flavian Amphitheatre, *see* Colosseum
Flavias (city), 207–208, Map 25 (p.208)
Fleets, Roman
  classis alexandriae, 214
  classis britannica, 150
  classis germanica, 157
  classis moesica, 18–20, 59, 258 (n.3)
  classis pontica, 121, 178, 276 (n.25)
  classis syriaca, 214
Fortuna (deity), 10, 22
  fortuna redux, 22, 284 (n.26)
Fortunatus (Bishop of Carthage), 65
Forum Flaminii (town), 142
Forum Thembronium, 272 (n.24), 274 (n.2)
Franks (people), 174, 195, 201, 212
Fraxinenses (people), 202
Fredegar (historian), 197, 199, 288 (n.5), 288 (n.7)
Frome hoard, *see* Hoards, Frome
Fructuosus (Christian), 192
Frumentarii, 21

Galatia (province), 34, 204
Galilee, Sea of, 11, 171
Gallienus, Publius Licinius Egnatius (emperor), 160, 161–2, 164, 166, 175, 186, 187, 192, 194, 195, 197, 200–201, 212–13, 214, 221, 222, 223, 229, 232, 235, 283 (n.17), Plate 6
  army, personal, 175, 188, 287 (n.18)
  augustus, 161, 282 (n.15)
  caesar, 160, 282 (n.15)
  coins, 161, 165, 170, 176, 194, 195, 232, Plate 6
  consul, 166, 288 (n.1)

germanicus maximus, 161–2, 170, 174, 195, 283 (n.17), Plate 6
Mediolanum, Battle of, *see* Battles, Mediolanum
Mursa, Battle of, *see* Battles, Mursa
Pipa/Pipara, 169–70
restitutor gener humani, 165
Rhine campaigns, 169–70, 187
Viminacium, 161, 166
Gallus, Gaius Vibius Afinus Trebonianus (commander and emperor), 48, 59–60, 67–71, 75, 94, 109–12, 120, 122, 127, 137, 141, 150, 160, 171, 227, Map 5 (p.60), Plate 6
 appearance, 112, Plate 6
 character, 187
 coins, 111, 112, 115, 137, 150, 188
 consul, 116
 death, 142
 deification, 160
 governor, 48
 Interamna Nahars, Battle of, *see* Battles, Interamna Nahars
 name, 48
 Novae, Battle of, *see* Battles, Novae
 peace treaty with Goths, 110
 plague, 115
 proclamation, 109, 274 (n.2)
 statue (alleged), 274 (n.9)
 treachery, alleged, 109–10, 141
 wife, *see* Baebiana, Afinia Gemina
Galt (modern town), *see* Ungra
Galtis (town), 55, 265 (n.25)
 Battle of, *see* Battles, Galtis
Gargilius, Quintus Gargilius Martialis (commander and historian), 201–202, 289 (n.13)
Garhasp the Lion (soldier), 205
Gaul (province), xxi, 35, 41, 145, 147, 148, 176, 194–9, 231
 invasion of 259/260 CE, 194–9, Map 23 (p.196)
 rebellion of Postumus, 221–3, 231
 unrest under Decius, 41, 147
Gazientep Museum, 138
Gdansk (modern city), 46
Gemellae (fort), 151
Genialis, Marcus Simplinius (commander), 219–21, 292 (n.18)
George the Monk (chronicler), 113–114, 274 (n.11)
Georgia (region), 137
Gepids (people), 51, 54–55, 110
Germani (people), 220–1
Germania (province), 13, 15, 195, 196, 204
Germanicia (city), 130–1, 133, 136, Map 17 (p.133)
Getica (Jordanes), *see* Jordanes, *Getica*
Gibbon, Edward, 59
Gigen (modern village), 59
Gindaros (city), 130–1, 133, Map 17 (p.133)
Girba (city), 123
Glabrio, Manius Acilius (consul), 154, 171
Glabrio, Marcus Acilius (consul), 171
Gladiators, xviii–xix
Gladius, 87, 97, 138, 272 (n.29)
Gnosticism, *see* Christianity, Gnosticism
Goat, xix
Golden Age, xvi, 6, 10, 16, 25, 141, 175, 234
Gordian III (emperor), 12–13, 14, 25, 66, 119, 225, 227
 death of, 12–13, 25
 mausoleum of, 12
Gothia (land), *see* Goths
Gothiscandzan (region), 46
Gothland (modern region), 46
Goths, 15, 16–17, 27–9, 47–54, 57–60, 72–81, 89–90, 120–3, 162, 164, 167–9, 172–4, 175, 194–5, 232
 Black Sea raids, 167–9, 172–4
 carrago (wagon circle), 272 (n.24)
 Gothia (land), 13, 14–15, 104–105
 invasion of 248 CE, 18–21, Map 2 (p.19)
 invasion of 250 CE, 47–54, Map 4 (p.51)
 invasion of 251 CE, 58–81, Map 5 (p.60), Map 6 (p.68), Map 7 (p.70), Map 8 (p.76), Map 9 (p.77), Map 10 (p.80), Map 11 (p.84), Map 12 (p.95), Map 13 (p.96), Map 14 (p.98)
 invasion of 252 CE, 120–123, Map 15 (p.122)
 invasion of 253 CE, 151–155, Map 20 (p.154)
 invasion of 257/8 CE, 178–81, Map 22 (p.180)
 Phrygian cap, 89
 subsidy from Rome, 15–16, 18, 29, 79
Gratus, Gaius Vettius (consul), 35–6
Great Ludovisi Battle Sarcophagus, *see* Ludovisi Battle Sarcophagus
Great Saint Bernard Pass, 197–8, 212, 220, Map 27 (p.220)

Index   303

Greece, xxi, 151
Gregory Thaumaturgus (the Wonderworker), Bishop of Neocaesarea, 114, 173–4
Gregory of Tours (historian), 198–9, 234
Gundishapur (city), 218
Guntheric (Gothic leader), 47–54, 59, Map 4 (p.51)

Hadrian (emperor), xviii
Hadrian's Wall, 116
Haemus (Balkan) mountains, 20, 50, 59, 68–71, 74, 93, Map 6 (p.68), Map 7 (p.70), Map 8 (p.76), Map 9 (p.77), Map 10 (p.80)
Hagenbach hoard, *see* Hoards, Hagenbach
Hairan (prince of Tadmor), 185
Haldagates (German king), 171
Hamisos (place), 83, 269 (n.5)
Harem, *see* Shapur, harem
Hariomundus (German king), 171
Hasdingian Vandals, *see* Astringi (people)
Heidelberg (modern city), 41
Helena (mother of Constantine), 236
Hercules (deity), 223, 291 (n.17)
  Hercules Deusoniensis, 223, 291 (n.17)
  Hercules Magusanus, 291 (n.17)
Hera (deity), 7
Herennia Etruscilla (empress), 34, 87, 90, 111–12, 115, 144, 270 (n.12), 274 (n.6), Plate 4
  coins, 115, 262 (n.7), Plate 4
  Ludovisi Battle Sarcophagus, 87, Plate 4
  mater castrorum, 87, 270 (n.9)
  name, 262 (n.7)
Herennius Etruscus, Quintus (emperor), 34–5, 88, 271 (n.14, 17)
  augustus, 79
  caesar, 36
  coins, 78, 101, 148, Plate 4
  consul, 55
  death, 85–6, 270 (n.9)
  deification, 271 (n.14)
  Ludovisi Battle Sarcophagus, 88, Plate 4
Herodian (historian), 140
Herodotus (historian), 46
Heruls/Heruli (people), 47, 195
Hierapolis (city), 130–1, 133–5
  Temple of Atargatis, *see* Atagartis (deity), Temple of
Hildomundus (German king), 171

Hippopotamus, xix–xx, Plate 1
Hispania (province), 27, 204
Historia Augusta, 49, 62, 114, 147, 154, 155, 160, 166, 170, 187, 188, 201, 202, 214, 217–18, 224–5, 233, 263 (n.5), 276 (n.2), 281 (n.9), 277 (n.10), 284 (n.27), 285 (n.35), 287 (n.16), 289 (n.13), 290 (n.4), 290 (n.6), 292 (n.22)
Hoards, 15, 18, 41, 49, 61, 100–101, 150, 195, 260 (n.21), 279 (n.48), Map 23 (p.196)
  Cunetio, 282 (n.15), 282–3 (n.16)
  Dorchester, 275 (n.14), 282–3 (n.16)
  Dryanovets, 100–101
  Frome, 282–3 (n.16)
  Hagenbach, 157, 280 (n.4)
  Neupotz, 157, 280 (n.4)
  Normanby, 282–3 (n.16)
  Pleven, 61
  Reka Devnia, 101–103, 273 (n.33)
  Spain, 232
Honoratianus (Gallic consul), 219
Hormizd (Sassanian prince), 120, 136
Horseguard, Imperial, 31, 33, 67, 199
Horus (deity), 7
Hostilian (emperor), 35, 41, 61–2, 88, 111
  augustus, 111
  caesar, 41, 263 (n.21)
  coins, 61, 88, 274 (n.7)
  death, 115, 275 (n.14)
  deification, 115
  Ludovisi Battle Sarcophagus, 88
  princeps iuventutis, 41
Hunterian Museum, Glasgow, 225
Hunuil (Gothic king), 45, 110, 233

Iconium (city), 207–208
Illyricum (region), 62, 170, 188, 192, 213
Imperator (title), 24, 141, 293 (n.24)
Imperium, 165, 293 (n.24)
India, 7, 42
Inflation, 5–6, 112, 157
Ingenuus (rebel), 187–9, 192, 195, 212, 224, 287 (n.16), 289 (n.20)
Interamna Nahars, Battle of, *see* Battles, Interamna Nahars
Isauria (region), 204
Isis (deity), 273 (n.35)
Istria (region), 204
Invictus (title), 25
Iotape (princesses of Commagene), 23

Iotapianus, *see* Jotapian (usurper)
Iran, 12–13, 204
Iraq, 12
Iuthungi (people), 195, 219, 221, 292 (n.18)

Jader (bishop), 177, 178
Januarius (Christian), 191
Janus (deity), xvii
    Temple of, xvii
Jerome (historian), 11
Jerusalem, 8, 139
Jesus (of Nazereth), xxi, 8–9, 178, 236
    Christ, 9, 236
    as God, 10
Jews, 8, 210, 211, 215, 217
    Caesarea, massacre, 211, 217
    Decian persecution, 262 (n.11)
    diaspora, 8
    Nehardea, academy, 215, 217
    revolt, 8
    Temple, destruction of, 8
'Jochen1', online commentator, 275 (n.18)
Jordanes (historian), 11, 14–15, 18, 20, 28, 44, 46, 48–54, 55, 74–5, 82–3, 85–6, 87, 115, 142, 270 (n.7), 286 (n.6)
    Getica, 18, 19, 44, 46, 48, 55, 74–5, 86, 87, 115, 270 (n.7), 286 (n.6)
Jotapian, Marcus Fulvius Rufus Jotapianus (usurper), 22–5, 34, 147, 185, 227, 259 (n.8, n.11), Plate 1
    coins, 23–4, 259 (n.8, n.11), Plate 1
Judaism, 8–9, 10, 165, 177, 273 (n.35)
Judea (province), 204
Julian (Christian), 38
Julian Alps, 31, 142, Map 3 (p.30), Map 17 (p.133)
Julianus, Julius (commander), 132
Julius Capitolinus (historian, disputed), 49
'Julius Germanicus', online commentator, 149
Julius Priscus, *see* Priscus, Gaius Julius (brother of Philip I)
Juno (deity), xvii, 6, 7, 34, 56, 59, 116
    Juno Martialis, 116, 275 (n.18)
Jupiter (deity) xvii, 6–8, 34, 56, 59, 193, 211, 219, 236, 294 (n.9)
    Jupiter Capitolinus (deity), 8
        Temple of (Palestine), 8
    Jupiter Dolichenus (deity), 8, 135

Jupiter Optimus Maximus (deity), xvii, 6, 7, 211, 219, 236
    Temple of (Rome), xvii
Justinian (emperor), 31, 129

Kastabala (city), 207–208, Map 25 (p.208)
Katabolon (city), 207–208
Kelenderis (city), 207–208, Map 25 (p.208)
Khalkhal (city), 117
Khusrov II (king of Armenia), 117–18
Kirder (priest), 135, 137, 277 (n.18)
Konya (city), Map 25 (p.208)
Korykos (city), 207–208, 214–16, Map 25 (p.208), Map 26 (p.215)
Kronos (deity), 140
Kybistra (city), 207–208, Map 25 (p.208)

Lactantius (Christian writer), 101, 235
Lambaesis (city), 150, 202
Lamian War, 153–5
Lampridius, Aelius (historian), 202, 289 (n.13)
Lanciani, Rudolfo (archaeologist), 126
Laodicea (city), 208, 210, 290 (n.26), Map 25 (p.208)
Laranda (city), 207–208
Larmenaz (city), 130–1, 133, Map 17 (p.133)
Laurentius (Christian), 191, 200
Lawrence, Saint, *see* Laurentius (Christian)
Lech (river), 218–20
Legions (Roman Army), 5
    legio I *adiutrix*, 89–90
    legio I *italica*, 20, 50, 59, 61, 94, 123, 145, 187, 285 (n.31)
    legio I *minervia*, 222
    legio I *parthica*, 132
    legio II *apollinaris*, 285 (n.32)
    legio II *parthica*, 31, 67, 199
    legio III *augusta*, 151, 192
    legio III *cyreneica*, 185
    legio III *gallica*, 132
    legio III *italica*, 142, 145, 195
    legio III *parthica*, 132
    legio IIII *flavia felix*, 21, 259 (n.4)
    legio IIII *scythica*, 132, 138
    legio V *macedonica*, 34, 67, 88–90, 228, 271 (n.18)
    legio VI *gallicana*, 285 (n.35)
    legio VI *victrix*, 169, 285 (n.35)

legio VII *claudia*, 21, 259 (n.5)
legio VIII *augusta*, 222
legio X *fretensis*, 139
legio XI *claudia*, 20, 50, 59, 94, 120, 123, 145, 187
legio XII *fulminata*, 23, 119, 132
legio XIII *gemina*, 34, 41, 66, 88–90, 228, 271 (n.13)
legio XIV *gemina*, 224
legio XV *apollinaris*, 23
legio XVI *flavia firma*, 132, 135, 204
legio XX *valeria victrix*, 169, 285 (n.35)
legio XXII *primigenia*, 222
legio XXX *ulpia victrix*, 222
Leonidas (king), 153
Letter to Philippopolis, *see* Philippopolis, letter to
Libellus, 36–37, Plate 2
Liber pontificalis, 124–125, 191
Litteus (bishop), 177
Livia (empress), 227
Londinium (city), 157
Lorica hamata, 87
Lorica squamata, 87, 97
Lucian of Samosata (writer), 134
Lucina (Christian), 124–5
Lucinianus, Valens, *see* Valens (usurper)
Lucius, Bishop of Rome, 126, 160, 176
Lucius, bishop, 177, 178
Ludi saeculares, xvi–xvii
Ludovisi Battle Sarcophagus, 86–90, 270 (n.7), Plate 4
Lugdunum (city), 198, Map 23 (p.196)
Lutetia (city), 198
Luxor (city), 32
Lycaonia (province), 204, 208, 210, 213–15
Lycia (province), 204
Lydia (province), 204, 284 (n.28)

Macedonia (region), 20, 72, 153
Macrianus (the Elder), Fulvius, 177, 205–207, 209, 213–14, 215, 216, 228–30, 233, Map 26 (p.215)
 death, 233
Macrianus, Fulvius Junius (usurper), 228–9, 231, 232, 233, 294 (n.32), Plate 8, Map 28 (p.231)
 coins, 229, Plate 8
 death, 223
Magie, David (historian), 166

Magnus (Christian), 191
Mainz, *see* Mogontiacum (city)
Malchus (Christian), 192
Malalas, John (historian), 127, 129, 139, 270 (n.9), 277 (n.10)
Mallos (city), 207–209
Maltepe mound, *see* Manole mound
Malvensis, *see* Dacia Malvensis (region)
Mani (prophet), 135
Manicheism, 135
Manole mound, 162–4, 283 (n.18), 283 (n.18), 283–4 (n.22), Plate 7
Marcianopolis (city), 20, 50, 273 (n.35)
 sack of, 102–103
 siege of, *see* Sieges, Marcianopolis
Marcomanni (people), 46–7, 170, 194
Marcomannic Wars, 47, 50
Marcus Aurelius (emperor), 47, 50
Mare nostrum, xxi
Mariades, 127–9, 135, 276 (n.1), 277 (n.7)
Marianus (general), 152, 154–5
Mariniana (wife of Valerian I), 160
 coins, 160
Marinianus, 160, Map 20 (p.154)
Marmara, Sea of, 121–2, 178–81
Mars (deity), xv, 7, 10, 112, 116, 124, 147–8, 219
 Mars Propugnator (the Champion), 147, 149
 Mars Ultor (the Avenger), Temple of, xviii
Matthew (Christian evangelist), 40
Mattingly, Harold (numismatist), 160, 229
Mauretania (province), 15, 201, 204, 212
 cavalry, 15, 199, 201
Maurice (emperor and strategist), 85–6, 270 (n.8), 272–3 (n.31)
Maximinus I Thrax (emperor), 22, 27, 174, 259 (n.5), 273 (n.37)
Maximus (priest), 38
Maximus (leader of Marcianopolis), 53–4, 102
Maximus, Galerius (proconsul), 191
Maximus, Lucius Valerius Claudius Priscillianus (consul), 166, 171, 286 (n.3)
Maximus, Lucius Valerius Poplicola Balbinus (consul), 127, 151
Maximus (Bishop of Carthage), 65
McInerny, J., 72

Mediolanum (city), 56, 145
  Battle of, *see* Battles, Mediolanum
  mint, *see* Mediolanum, mint
Megabaroi (people), 42
Meiakarire (city), *see* Caesarea in Cappadocia
Melitine (city), 23, 119, 132, 133, 203–204
Menophilus, Tullius (general), 259 (n.5)
Mercury (deity), 7, 147–8
Mesiche, *see* Mishik (city)
Mesopotamia (region), 12, 128–40, 161, 171, 200, 204, 233, Map 16 (p.131), Map 17 (p.123)
Meteorite, 140, 278 (n.25)
Metras, Christian, 10
Metropolitan Museum of Art, New York, 274 (n.9)
Millennium, *see* Rome, millennium
Mines, 5–6
Minerva (deity), xvii, 6, 56, 59
Mints
  Alexandria, 144, 228, 229
  Augusta Treverorum (Trier), 175, 222, 291 (n.15)
  Antioch, 14, 112, 137, 165, 193, 209–10, 277 (n.19), 284 (n.26), 286–7 (n.9)
  Colonia Agrippina (Cologne), 169, 175
  Mediolanum (Milan), 56, 145
  Nicopolis in Seleucia, 23
  Rome, xix–xx, 112, 148, 194, 285 (n.42), Plate 1
  Samosata, 193, 229, 284 (n.23)
  Viminacium, 165, 259 (n.7)
Misiche, *see* Mishik (city)
Mishik (city), 13
  Battle of, *see* Battles, Mishik
  Peroz–Shapur, 13
Mithras (deity), 8, 88
Moesia (region), 18, 20, 49, 54, 58, 66–71, 93–100, 110, 111, 122–3, 151, 169, 187, 192, 204
  Moesia Inferior (Lower Moesia, province), 20, 21, 22, 46, 48, 50, 59–61, 93–100, Map 2 (p.19), Map 4 (p.51), Map 5 (p.60), Map 6 (p.68), Map 7 (p.70), Map 12 (p.95)
  Moesia Superior (Upper Moesia, province), 21, 161
Mogontiacum (military base), 41, 169, 195, 201, 222, Map 23 (p.196), Map 27 (p.220)

Mopsuestia (city and bridge), 166, 181, 207–10, 284 (n.30), Map 25 (p.208)
Mosaics, 138, Plate 6
Mouchmov, N.A. (numismatist), 101–103, 273 (n.35)
Moyses (priest), 38
Mursa, Battle of, *see* Battles, Mursa
Myonpolis (city), 207–208
Myrlea (city), *see* Apamea (city, Bithynia et Pontus)
Mysian Mount Olympus, 180, Map 22 (p.180)
Mystery cults, 8–9
Mystus (person), 37
Myzgin, Kirill (numismatist), 101

Naissus (city), 21
Naqsh-i-Rustam, 13, 14, 104, 128, 129–30, 135, 277 (n.7)
Narnia, Battle of, *see* Battles, Narnia
Nasor, Papa ben, *see* Odaenathus, Papa ben Nasor
Nefarius Purpus, 293 (n.23)
Nehardea (city), 215, 217, Map 26 (p.215)
Nemesianus (bishop), 177, 178
Nemesis (deity), 139–40
Neocaesarea (city), 114
Neoplatonism, 7, 9
Neopythagoreans, 7
Nero (emperor), 124
Neronias (city), 207–208, Map 25 (p.208)
Neupotz hoard, *see* Hoards, Neupotz
Nicaea (city), 179–81, Map 22 (p.180)
Nicomedia (city), 179–81, Map 22 (p.180)
Nicopolis-ad-Istrum (city), 67–70, 72–3, 78, 93
  Battle of, *see* Battles, Nicopolis
Nicopolis in Cilicia (city), 23, 130–1, 133, 207–208, Map 17 (p.133), Map 25 (p.208)
Nicostratus (priest), 38
Nike (deity), 24
Nile (river), 16, 31–2, 159
Nisibis (city), 119, 171, 181, 275 (n.21)
Noricum (region), 204
Normanby hoard, *see* Hoards, Normanby
Noubai (people), 42
Novae (military base), 20, 59–60, 66–7, 123, 160
Novatian (Bishop of Rome/antipope), 64–5, 124

Index   307

Noviodunum (military base), 18, Map 2 (p.19)
Nubia (province), 42, 57
Numidia (province), 150

Octavian (emperor, *see* Augustus)
Octavianus, Marcus Cornelius (general), 192
Odaenathus, Septimius (ruler, Palmyra), 184–6, 193, 215, 217–18, 228, 231, 232, 233, Map 26 (p.215), Plate 7
    death, 233
    embassy to Shapur, 185–6, 287 (n.13)
    invasion of Sassanian Empire, 217–18, 290–1 (n.7)
    Papa ben Nasor, 217
    rš' dy tdmwr (Lord of Tadmor), 185
Oder (river), 105, 219
Odessus (city), 20
Odrysian Kingdom, 162
Oescus (city), 58–60, 69–70, 75, 82, 93–4, Map 5 (p.60), Map 8 (p.76), Plate 2
Oeta, Mount, 153–4, Map 20 (p.154)
Officinae (departments of the mint), xix–xx
    Mediolanum, 56
    Rome, xix–xx
Oge, Julius Aurelius (commander), 185
Olt (river), 55
Olympiad, xx
Origen, Bishop of Alexandria, 40, 65, 114, 160, 282 (n.14)
Orontes (river), 127, 129, 136, Map 17 (p.133)
Orosius (historian), 113, 235, 256 (n.8)
Orpheus (deity), 9
Osiris (deity), 7, 273 (n.35)
Osrhoene (province), 135, 136, 184, 200, 202–207
Ostia (city), 35, 124
Ostrogotha (king), 18, 28, 34, 44–5, 46, 49, 52, 54, 55, 58, 59–60, 66–9, 74, 82, 85, 90–1, 110, 195, 233, Map 2 (p.19), Map 5 (p.60), Map 6 (p.68)
    ancestry, 85, 263 (n.8)
    Dacia, possible campaigns in, 51, 54, 55, 59–60, 66–9, 82, 85, Map 5 (p.60), Map 6 (p.68)
    death, 85, 271 (n.19)
    Galtis, Battle of, *see* Battles, Galtis
    invasion of 248 CE, 18–21, Map 2 (p.19)
    Ludovisi Battle Sarcophagus, 90–1, Plate 4
    prisoner, 90–1, Plate 4
    Widsith, 45
Ostrogoths (people), 44
Otacilia Severa, Marcia (empress), xx, 31
    coins, xx
Otacilius Severianus, *see* Severianus, Otacilius
Ourima (city), 130–1, 133, Map 17 (p.133)
Oxyrhynchus papyri, 228, 229, 284 (n.26), 294 (n.32)

Pacatian (usurper), 20–2, 25–6, 27, 28, 46, 52, 147, 227, 259 (n.7), 260 (n.12), Plate 1
    coins, 22, 25, 259 (n.7), 260 (n.12), Plate 1
Pahlav (area), 117
Palatine Hill, xv
Pales (deity), xv
Palestine (region), 34, 192
Palimpsest, 43, Plate 2
Palladio, Andrea (architect), 55
Palmyra (city), 185–6, 200, 202, 228, 232, 233
Paluina (region, unknown), 205
Pamphylia (province), 36, 204
Panhellenion, 152
Pannonia (region), 21, 26, 34, 89, 142, 170, 187, 204, 220
    Pannonia Inferior (Lower Pannonia), 34
    Pannonia Superior (Upper Pannonia), 34, 89, 170, 224
Paris cameo, 206, Plate 7
Parthian dynasty, 12, 117, 119
Paul (apostle), 8, 39, 65, 124, 276 (n.30)
Pax (deity), 193, Plate 6
Pax romana, xxi, 156
Perez-Shapur (city), 13
Persepolis (city), 13
Persians (people), 3, 12, 110, 117–20, 166, 181–4, 202–18, 232
    Armenia, conquest, 117–20
    spah (army), 130–7, 181–4, 202–18, 277 (n.8)
    Dura-Europos, 181–4
    invasion of 253 CE, 128–41, 277 (n.18), Map 16 (p.131), Map 17 (p.133)
    invasion of 260 CE, 202–18, Map 24 (p.203), Map 25 (p.208), Map 26 (p.215)
    peace with Philip, 12
Persephone (deity), *see* Proserpine

Pessinus (city), 121–2, Map 15 (p.122)
Peter (apostle), 9, 124–5, 276 (n.30)
Peter Patricius (historian), 186, 216
Petesouchos (deity), 37
Peuce, island of, 48–9, Map 2 (p.19)
Peucini (people), 48, 49
Phasis (city), 168, 172
Pharzanes (Bosporan king), 168
Philocalus, calendar, 275 (n.18)
Phileatina, Lake of, 179–80, Map 122 (p.180)
Philip of Macedon (king), 52
Philip I, Marcus Julius Philippus (emperor), xvi–xvii, xxi, 10–11, 15, 25, 27, 52, 56, 104, 110, 147, 225, 227, Map 3 (p.30), Plate 1, Plate 7
  accession, 13, 14
  cancellation of Gothic subsidy, 15, 18, 21, 110
  Carpi, 15
  Christian (possible), 10–11, 16, 256 (n.8)
  coins, xix–xx, 14 Plate 1
  damned to the memory, 33
  death, 31, 260 (n.17)
  peace treaty with Persia, 12, 14, 104, Plate 7
  Philippeion, 12
  rebellions against, 20–6
  Verona, Battle of, *see* Battles, Verona
Philip II (emperor), 14
  coins, xv
  death, 31, 261 (n.24)
Philokalos of Stratonicea, 121
Philostratus, Lucius Flavius, of Athens (historian), 113, 152, 274 (n.10)
Philippopolis (Syrian city), *see* Shahba
Philippopolis (Thracian city), 50–4, 69, 72–4, 82, 92–3, 162, 164, Map 10 (p.80)
  letter to, 72–4, 100, 101, 270 (n.8)
  sack of, 80–1, 92–3, Map 10 (p.80), Map 11 (p.84), Plate 3
  Sieges of, *see* Sieges, Philippopolis
  Trimontium, name for, 52
Phoenicia (region), 204
Photius (historian), 256 (n.1)
Phreata (city), 130–1
Phrygia (province), 204
Phrygian cap, 88–9, 271 (n.16, n. 17)
Pileati, 89, 271 (n.17)
Pileus, *see* Phrygian cap

Pipa/Pipara (princess), 169–70, 194, 201, 220, 285 (n.37)
Pityus (city), 168–9, 172–4, Map 21 (p.168)
Pius IX (pope), 125–6
Plague, xv–xvi, 57, 112–17, 127, 175, 188, 199, 202–203, 206, 213
  of Cyprian, 16–17, 35, 57, 90–3, 112–17, 175, 188, 199, 202–203, 206, 213, 224, 234, 274–5 (n.12)
  animals, in, 113
  army of Valerian, 199, 202–203, 206
  Carthage, 90–3, 261 (n.26)
  Egypt, 32, 35, 57, 261 (n.26)
  epidemic phase, 32, 35, 37
  filovirus, 16–17
  herd immunity, 234
  Illyricum, 213, 224
  Neocaesarea, 114
  Numidia, 150
  origins, 16–17, 258 (n.24)
  pandemic phase, 112–16
  Rome, 113, 114
  symptoms, 92, 114
  of Justinian, 35
  of Publius Publicola, xv–xvi
Plato (philosopher), 7
Pliny the Elder (writer), 42
Plotinus (philosopher), 7
Plovdiv (modern city), 52, 72, 79–81, 162, 164, Plate 3
Pluto (deity), xvi, 7
Poland (modern country), 54, 103, 104
Polianus (bishop), 177, 178
Pollio, Trebellius (historian), 276 (n.30), 277 (n.7)
Pompeiopolis (city), 208–209, 213–15, Map 25 (p.208), Map 26 (p.215)
Pontius (deacon), 91
Pontus (province), 114, 121–2, 137
  Sea of, *see* Black Sea
Pontifex maximus (title), xvii, 10, 33, 222
Portnaccio sarcophagus, 270 (n.9)
Postumus, Marcus Cassinianus Latinius (Gallic emperor) 189, 201, 219, 228, 229, 231, 291 (n.17), Plate 8
  background, 291 (n.17)
  coins, 222–3, Plate 8
  Gallic Empire, 231, 232, Map 28 (p.231)
  Hercules Deusoniensis, 223, 291 (n.17)
  proclamation, 221–2, 291 (n.17)

Potaissa (legionary base), 67
Praetorian Guard, 31, 33, 67, 199
Princeps iuventutis (title), 41
Priscus, Gaius Julius (brother of Philip I), 14, 20, 22, 24, 31
  rector orientis, 14, 24
Priscus, Titus Julius (commander and usurper), 71–2, 75, 81, 268 (n.23), Plate 3
Priscus (Christian), 192
Pristis (warship), 18
Probus (emperor), 166, 171
Prosperpine (deity), xvi
Prusa (city), 179–81, Map 122 (p.180)
Ptolemaios (general), 82
Publius Valerius Publicola (consul), xv
Pudicitia (deity), 34
Pyramus (river), 166, 181
Pythagoras (philosopher), 7

Qitmir (dog), 40–1
Qreiye (fort), 130–2
Quadi (people), 46, 195
Quietus, Fulvius Junius (usurper), 228–9, 231, 232, Map 28 (p.231), Plate 8
  coins, 229, Plate 8
  death, 233
Quinquegentanei (people), 202
Quinta (Christian), 10
Qu'ran, 41

Radiate crown, 56
Raetia (province), 151, 204, 218–20, 231, 275 (n.23)
Ra's al'-Ayn (modern town, Syria), 13
Raurici (people), 156
Razgrad (modern city), 94, 272 (n.24)
Red Sea, 42
Regalianus (usurper), 224–5, 228, 231, 232, 289 (n.20), 292 (n.20), Plate 8
  coins, 224, 232, 292 (n.20), Map 28 (p.231), Plate 8
Regallianus, Caius Cassius (consul), 224
Reka Devnia (modern village), 101–102
  Hoard, *see* Hoards, Reka Devnia
Religio licita, 8, 37
Rephanea (city), 130–3, 135, 136, Map 17 (p.133)
Res Gestae Divi Saporis, 13, 128, 130, 204, 207
Rhakoundia (city), 207–208

Rhesaina (city), 13, 132
  Battle of, *see* Battles, Rhesaina
Rhescuporis V (Bosporan king), 168
Rhine (river), 15, 22, 35, 56, 57, 150, 156, 157, 161, 169, 187, 192, 195, 212, 221–2, 223
Rhinoceros, xix
Rhone (river), 196, 198–9
Rhyndacus (river), 180–1, 286 (n.8), Map 122 (p.180)
Roma (deity), xviii, xx, Plate 1
  Roma and Venus (Temple of), xviii, xx, Plate 1
Roman army, 5
  auxiliaries, *see* auxiliaries
  fleets, *see* fleets, Roman
  legions, *see* legions, Roman army
Roman Empire, 3–5, Map 1 (p.4)
  administration, 3, 35
  population, 3
Romania, 225
Romanus (Christian), 191
Rome (city), xv–xx, 26, 35, 41, 56, 61, 86, 111, 172, 175, 212
  Aventine Hill, 55
  Capitoline Hill, xvii, 35, 55, 256 (n.3)
  Capitoline Museum, 56–7
  City Prefect, 27
  Decius, building programme, 55
  Eternal City, xviii
  foundation myth, xv, xx
  millennium, xv–xx, 22, 56, 252, 256 (n.1), Plate 1
  Palatine Hill, xx, 271 (n.17)
  riots in Alexandria, 10
  romae aeternae, xx, Plate 1, Plate 6
  Vatican Museum, 112
Romula (city), 15
  hypothetical battle of, *see* Battles, Romula
Romulus (founder of Rome), xv
  and Remus, xv, xx

Sacramentum, 26, 29
Saecularis, Publius Cornelius (city prefect and consul), 191, 200
Saeculum novum, xx, 34, Plate 1
Sa'id ibn Batriq, *see* Eutychius of Alexandria (historian)
Salonina, Cornelia Salonina Chrysogone (empress), 161, 170, 172, 179, 188, 191, 201, Plate 6
  coins, 161, 170, 191, 201, Plate 6

Saloninus (emperor), 160, 189, 212, 222
   caesar, 189
   coins, 189
   death, 222
Salus (deity), 10, 114
Samian Ware, 157–8
Samosata (city), 132, 133, 135, 203, 206, 207, 229, Map 17 (p.133), Map 24 (p.203)
   mint, *see* Mints, Samosata
Sampsigeramos (priest), *see* Uranius Antoninus (usurper), Sampsigeramos
Samuel (rabbi), 217
Saracens (people), 166, 171, 284 (n.27)
Sarmatians (people), 47, 170, 188, 195, 224
Sassanians (people), *see* Persians
   Sassanian Empire, 3
Satala (city), 23, 130–1, 133, 135, 136, Map 17 (p.133)
Saturn (Temple of), xvii
Savus (river), 26
Sciri (people), 47
Scupi (city), 28, 154, 155, Map 20 (p.154)
Scythica, *see* Dexippus, *Scythica*
Scythians (people), 172
Sebaste (city), 207–209, 214–16, Map 25 (p.208), Map 26 (p.215)
Sebastia (city), 207–208
Seleucia (Cilicia, city), 206–208, Map 25 (p.208)
Seleucia (Syria, inland city), 130–1, 133, Map 17 (p.133)
Seleucia Pieria (Syria, coastal city), 130–1, 133, 136, 210, 277 (n.10), Map 17 (p.133), Map 25 (p.208), Map 26 (p.215)
Selinos (city), 207–208, 210, 215–16, Map 25 (p.208), Map 26 (p.215)
Semis, coin, 56
Semnones (people), 219, 221
'Semper Victor' (online commentator), 259 (n.6), 266 (n.2), 268 (n.28), 270 (n.7)
Senate (of Rome), xvi, 31, 109, 144, 149, 165, 171, 189–90, 200, 278 (n.34), 279 (n.45), 281–2 (n.11)
Senate House (of Rome), xvii
Senectus mundi, xvi
Septimius Severus (emperor), 26, 150
Serapis (deity), 8, 273 (n.35)
Serdica (city), 21
Sernota (town), 164, 283 (n.22)
Sestertius, 5, 56, 112
   double sestertius, 56, 265–6 (n.27)

Severianus, Otacilius, 20, 21, 31, 259 (n.4)
Severus (Christian), 191
Severus Alexander (emperor), 9, 27, 138, 202, 259 (n.8)
Sexaginta Prista, 20, 94, Map 2 (p.19), Map 13 (p.96)
Shahba (city), 11, 23
   renamed Philippopolis, 12
Shahnameh, 204–205
Shapur I, the Great (Sassanian king of kings), 13, 104, 128–41, 152, 175, 185, 202–16, Plate 7
   Armenia, conquest, 117–21
   harem, 213–14, 218
   invasion of 253 CE, 128–41, 185
   invasion of 260 CE, 202–18
Shipka Pass, 71, 74–5, 93, 269 (n.5), Map 7 (p.70), Map 8 (p.76), Map 9 (p.77), Plate 3
Sicily, xxi
Sieges, 50–4
   Dura-Europos, first siege, 132, 136, Map 16 (p.131)
   Dura-Europos, second siege 181–4, 277 (n.19), 286–7 (n.9)
   Edessa, 203–207, 289 (n.22), Map 24 (p.203)
   Marcianopolis, siege of, 50–4, 264 (n.19), Map 4 (p.51)
   Philippopolis, first siege of, 50–4, 264 (n.19), Map 4 (p.51)
   Philippopolis, second siege of, 72–4, 76–9, 264 (n.19), 265 (n.22), Map 7 (p.70), Map 8 (p.76), Map 9 (p.77), Plate 3
   Thessalonica, 152–4, 279 (n.48), 280 (n.53), 280 (n.55), Map 20 (p.154)
Sigua (city), 178
Silanus (saint), 124, 276 (n.30)
Silbannacus (emperor? usurper?), 147–50, Plate 6
Silk Road, 13, 138
Silpios, Mount, 129, 135, 276 (n.5)
Silvanus (person), 189
Simon Magus, 9
Singidunum (city), 21
Singara (city), 131–2, Map 16 (p.131)
Sinzara (city), 130–1, 133, Map 17 (p.133)
Sirmium (city), 26
Sixtus II, Bishop of Rome, 177, 190, 200
Skopje (modern city), 28
Sod Shapur (city), 218

Souid (city), 130–1
Souisa (city), 130–1, 136
Spain, xxi, 21, 145, 223, 231
Spah, *see* Sassasians, *spah*
Spartans, 72, 153
Sponsian (usurper?), 225–8, 231, 232, 293 (n.24), Map 28 (p.231), Plate 8
Sponsian, Nicodemus, 226–7
Spurinym, 45–6
Stara Zagora (modern city), 74
Stephen, Bishop of Rome, 176–7, 286 (n.3)
Stephen (Christian), 191
Stipendium militum, 5
Stoic philosophy, xvi, xxi, 7, 62, 165
Storgosia (posting station), 61
Strabo (geographer), 42
Stratonicea (city), 121–2
Successianus (commander and praetorian prefect), 169, 171, 206
Successus (bishop), 190, 191
Sucidava (military base), Map 5 (p.60), 58–9
Suebi (people), 195
Superstitio, 8
Sura (city), 130–2, 133, Map 16 (p.131)
Surah Al-Khaf, 41
Susiana (province), 218
Symeon the Logothete (historian), 274 (n.10)
Syncellus (historian), 151, 207, 209, 213–14, 267 (n.20), 279 (n.48), 290 (n.27)
Syncretism, 7–9
Syria (region), 11, 12, 13, 130–7, 144, 161, 162, 164, 208–11, 231, 232, 233, Map 17 (p.123)

Tacitus (historian), 10, 219
Taifali (people), 48
Talmud, Babylonian, 210, 211, 217, 291 (n.9)
Tarabostes, 89
Tarsus (city), 207–10, 214, Map 25 (p.208)
Taurus mountains, 208, 210, Map 25 (p.208)
Taxation, 5, 12
Tertullian (Christian), 40
Tervingi (people), 47
Theodorus (Christian), 192
Theodoric the Great (king), 44–5, 85
Theodosius II (emperor), 40
Thermopylae, 82, 151–5, 162, 171, 279 (n.48), Map 20 (p.154)

Thessalonica, 152
  Siege of, *see* Sieges, Thessalonica
Thessaly (region), 82
Thirteenth Sibylline Oracle, 127–8, 138–9, 213, 257 (n.15), 290 (n.6)
Thrace (province), xxi, 18, 20, 46, 49–54, 58, 110, 122, 144, 151, 162, 169, 179, 204, Map 8 (p.76), Map 9 (p.77), Map 10 (p.80), Map 15 (p.122)
Three Graces (deities), 273 (n.35)
Tiberius (emperor), xxi
Tigers, xix
Trimontium, *see* Philippopolis (Thracian city), Trimontium, name for
Tomis (city), 20, 179
Trajan (emperor), 15, 33–4, 49, 69, 102–103, 109, 224
  conquest of Dacia, 33–4
Trajan's column, 33, 89, 283 (n.21)
Trajan Decius, *see* Decius (emperor)
Transylvania, 225
Trapezus (city), 171–2, 178
Trebellius Pollio (historian), 147, 170, 187, 225, 280 (n.55), 290 (n.4), 292 (n.22)
Trebonianus Gallus, *see* Gallus (emperor)
Trier, *see* Augusta Treverorum (city)
Troglodytes (people), 42
Tuscus, Marcus Nummius (consul), 187
Turkey (modern country), 114, 120, 138
Tyana (city), 207–209, Map 25 (p.208)

Ukraine (modern country), 103, 104
Underworld, xvi
Ungra (modern town), 55
Unwen, *see* Hunuil (Gothic king)
Uranius Antoninus (usurper), 139–41, 164–5, 185, 278 (n.26)
  coins, 140–141, 278 (n.26), 278 (n.27), 293 (n.24)
  Sampsigeramos (priest), 139, 140

Valarshapat (city), 118
Valens, Julius (usurper), 61–2, 267 (n.7)
Valentinus (person), 188
Valentus, Marcus Flavius (officer), 151
Valerian I, Publius Licinius Valerianus (emperor), 142, 151, 164, 166, 169, 171, 175, 177, 180–1, 186, 189–93, 194, 199, 200, 202, 211, 213, 214, 222, 223, 233, 234, 235, Plate 6
  Antioch, 164, 166, 190, 209

army reform, 161, 233
background, 281 (n.10)
Beast of Revelation, 190, 235
Cappadocia expedition, 179–81
captive of Shapur, 206, 213, 218, 223, 224, 233, 235, 289 (n.20), 290 (n.3), 291 (n.10), 294 (n.32), 294 (n.3), Plate 7
censor, 36, 281 (n.11)
coins, 161, 165, 200, 209, 285 (n.42), 286–7 (n.9), 290 (n.3), Plate 6
Cologne, 174–5, 285 (n.42)
commander in Raetia, 142, 143
consul, 159, 166, 176
death, 235, 290 (n.3), 294 (n.3)
Dura-Europos, restoration, 164, 181
Edessa, Battle of, *see* Battles, Edessa
germanicus maximus, 161–2, 174
Narnia, Battle of, *see* Battles, Narnia
persecution of Christians, 176, 177–8, 189–93, 287 (n.21)
plague in army, 199, 202–203, 206
proclamation as emperor, 147, 281–2 (n.11)
restitutor gener humani, 165, Plate 6
senator, 159
Valerian II (emperor), 160, 172, 188, 194
caesar, 172
coins, 188
death, 188
Vandals (people), 46, 47, 195, 198
Vasso Galatae (temple), 198–9
Vatican, 124
Venus (deity), 81
Verona (city), 29–31
Battle of, *see* Battles, Verona
Vetera (city), 222
Vespasian (emperor), 26
Vesta, Temple of, xvii
Vexilla, 145
Via appia, 125
Via diagonalis, 21, 164
Via egnatia, 153, 154, Map 20 (p.154)
Via flaminia, 142, 145
Via postumia, 31
Via sacra, xvii, 35
Via traiana, 69, 82, 269 (n.5)
Victor, Aurelius, *see* Aurelius Victor (historian)
Victor (bishop), 177

Victoria (deity), *see* Victory (deity)
Victory (deity), xviii, xx, 24, 148, 151, 174, 218, 283 (n.20)
Vienna (modern city), 34, 43
National Library of, 43
Viminacium (city), 21, 22, 25, 27, 29, 31, 41, 161, 166
mint, *see* Mints, Viminacium
Vincentius (Christian), 191
Vindobona (city), 34
Virtus (deity), 193
Visigoths (people), 47
Vistula (river), 46, 54, 105
Volusian, Gaius Vibius Volusianus (emperor), 111–12, 150, 151
augustus, 115
caesar, 111
coins, 150, Plate 6
consul, 116, 127, 151
death, 142
Interamna Nahars, Battle of, *see* Battles, Interamna Nahars
marriage, 111
Vopiscus, Flavius, of Syracuse (historian), 166, 170

Wibilus (chieftain), 197
Widsith, 45, 110
Wielbark (culture), 46, 104, 264 (n.11)

Xerxes I (king), 13, 153

Zaitha (city), 12
Zeno (Christian), 192
Zenobia (queen), 233
Zephyrion (city), 207–208, Map 25 (p.208)
Zeugma (city), 130–3, 135, 136, 137–8, Map 16 (p.131), Map 17 (p.133)
Zeus (deity), 7, 121, 140, 273 (n.35)
Zeus Panêmêrios, 121
Zonaras (historian), 31, 93, 94, 120, 122–3, 142, 145–7, 149, 151, 188, 189, 205, 209, 210–11, 212, 217, 221–2, 270 (n.9), 274 (n.2), 279 (n.38), 280 (n.53), 282 (n.14)
Zoroastrianism, 8, 119, 135, 216
Zosimos of Samosata (mosaicist), 138
Zosimus (historian), 15, 29, 31, 93, 101, 120, 121–3, 1689, 169–70, 172–3, 178–81, 189, 200, 212, 222, 271 (n.19), 274 (n.2)